God Is Not a Republican

God Is Not a Republican

Please Stop Dragging Him into Your Party

DANIEL KORIE

RESOURCE *Publications* · Eugene, Oregon

GOD IS NOT A REPUBLICAN
Please Stop Dragging Him into Your Party

Copyright © 2024 Daniel Korie. All rights reserved. Except for brief quotations in critical publications or reviews, no part of this book may be reproduced in any manner without prior written permission from the publisher. Write: Permissions, Wipf and Stock Publishers, 199 W. 8th Ave., Suite 3, Eugene, OR 97401.

Resource Publications
An Imprint of Wipf and Stock Publishers
199 W. 8th Ave., Suite 3
Eugene, OR 97401

www.wipfandstock.com

PAPERBACK ISBN: 979-8-3852-1405-1
HARDCOVER ISBN: 979-8-3852-1406-8
EBOOK ISBN: 979-8-3852-1407-5

VERSION NUMBER 040924

Scripture quotations marked (NIV) are taken from the Holy Bible, New International Version®, NIV®. Copyright © 1973, 1978, 1984, 2011 by Biblica, Inc.™ Used by permission of Zondervan. All rights reserved worldwide. www.zondervan.com The "NIV" and "New International Version" are trademarks registered in the United States Patent and Trademark Office by Biblica, Inc.™

Scripture quotations marked (NKJV) are taken from the Holy Bible, New King James Version®. Copyright © 1982 by Thomas Nelson. Used by permission. All rights reserved.

Contents

Acknowledgment | vii
Introduction | ix

PART 1—POLARIZING SOCIAL AND POLITICAL ISSUES

Chapter 1
Socialism, Communism, and Capitalism | 3

Chapter 2
Social Programs and Biblical Values | 20

Chapter 3
Abortion—A Political Punch Bag | 38

Chapter 4
Social Justice | 53

Chapter 5
Gun Laws and Firearms-Related Violence | 81

Chapter 6
Immigration Laws and DACA | 100

PART 2—EVANGELICAL LEADERS AND TRUMPISM

Chapter 7
Evangelical Leaders and Trump's Chaotic Presidency | 115

Chapter 8
False Prophecies about the 2020 Presidential Election | 127

Chapter 9
Was the 2020 Presidential Election Stolen? | 153

Chapter 10
The Hidden Blessing of the Capitol Riot | 178

Chapter 11
The Danger of Falling into Mr. Trump's Corrupt Bidding | 198

Chapter 12
Remnants Beware | 221

Conclusion | 234

Bibliography | 239
Index | 263

Acknowledgment

With sincere thanks to Dr. Keith Whitworth for your support in writing this book. Your encouragement, reviews of the early stages of this book, supply of resources, and feedback significantly motivated me to successful completion of this book.

Introduction

The falsification of notions that God is a Republican or that he endorses the Republican Party agendas is not only hypocritical but delusional. The wide spread of such hypocrisy was amplified in the 2020 election in which some Christian Evangelical leaders advanced such misinformation to coerce their followers to vote for a divisive, dishonest, and unchristian president, and to vote only for the GOP candidates.

The Christian Evangelical leaders' affiliation with the Republican Party gives the impression that God is a Republican. Some leaders, such as Jerry Falwell Jr, Pat Robertson, and Franklin Graham, have publicly endorsed their support of Republican presidents, governors, and lawmakers while shunning the Democrats. They use their platforms to promote the Republican Party's political agendas as if the agendas are biblical or endorsed by God. Furthermore, Christian networks, such as Trinity Broadcasting Network (TBN), *Daystar*, and other Christian radio stations, give platforms to GOP career politicians and individuals who promote the Republican Party's political memos. These Christian networks highlight the deeds of Republican presidents while demonizing the accomplishments of Democratic presidents, even when such efforts were humanitarian.

Christian Evangelical leaders are quick to present GOP presidents or presidential candidates as people of high moral integrity and believers of the Lord Jesus even when there is no evidence to support their claims. In contrast, the Democratic presidents or candidates are characterized as immoral and unsaved people even when they confess Jesus as their Savior. In 1972, President Richard Nixon received 84 percent votes of white Evangelicals during his reelection because of their perceived "high moral integrity" of Mr. Nixon, as purported by Harold Ockenga, a Boston pastor, who was the founder and president of the National Association of Evangelicals and other Evangelical leaders.[1] However, the atrocities of the Watergate scandal

---

1. Swartz, "Ron Sider and Evangelicals," para. 7.

shattered the false claims of Nixon's high moral standards. Also, Mr. Trump has been portrayed as a believer in the Lord Jesus and a "saved" person by some Evangelical preachers when he has not even asked God for the forgiveness of his sins because according to him, "he has not done anything wrong" to ask God for forgiveness. But the Scripture says, "For all have sinned and fall short of the glory of God" (Rom 3:23 NKJV). If someone does not believe that he has sinned, it suggests that he does not believe in the sacred Scripture nor believe in his heart that Jesus died for his sins; therefore, he cannot accept Jesus as his Savior. Mr. Trump's series of lies, corruption, unforgiveness, self-exaltation as a god, prideful spirit, inciting speeches of hate and violence, and disregard of biblical teachings are proof that he is not a believer in the Lord Jesus. But pro-Trump Evangelical leaders introduce him as a saved person because of his partial opposition to abortion. However, Mr. Trump does not support restrictive abortion policy. All these deeds of Christian Evangelical leaders to support GOP presidential candidates give the impression to their followers and even, to some extent, outsiders that God must be a Republican or he approves of the Republican Party's political memoranda. Thus, the only righteous vote for a Christian is to vote Republican. However, nothing could be further from the truth, as compelling biblical truths presented in this book are juxtaposed with the misinformation of Christian Evangelical leaders.

Furthermore, on December 8, 2022, a *Raw Story* publication titled "Deal with the Devil: Evangelical Pastor Testifies about Bargain Christian Conservatives Made with GOP" revealed the testimony of Reverend Robert Schenck before the House Judiciary Committee, in which he described a secret meeting he and other Evangelical leaders had with the GOP to overturn Roe v. Wade.[2] To solidify the Faustian bargain, the GOP demanded that Evangelical leaders accept and promote the entire political agendas of the GOP, including policies considered objectionable. Pause for a moment and think about the demands of this Faustian bargain, that is, to promote policies considered objectionable, which may include unbiblical, immoral, and inhumane policies. As detailed in this book, some Evangelical leaders have indeed compromised the preaching of the gospel to promote Republican Party policies and agendas, including those inconsistent with biblical teachings. Evangelical leaders' unholy alliance with the Republican Party and promotion of their political schemas paints a false image of the God of the Christians. It presents the Christian God as if he supports hate, lies, marginalization, violence, and corruption, and all these are common characteristics of fierce supporters of the Donald Trump–led Republican

---

2. Reed, "Deal with the Devil," paras. 1–5.

Party. Throughout the Scripture, there was no single example where God supported or approved a man who displayed the same ungodly behavioral patterns as Mr. Trump but was condemned by God.

Three weeks prior to the midterm election of 2022, as it has always been in past elections, the focal points of some Christian Evangelical pastors' preaching, such as Pastor John Hagee, Dr. Jack Graham, and a host of them, centered on socialism, capitalism, and abortion, with collaborative efforts to induce subliminal messages to their followers that the GOP political outlines are biblical; therefore, voting for Republicans is the only godly vote for a Christian.

These Evangelical leaders have used abortion as a political punch bag to advance their political rhetoric. The fact of the matter is that because someone runs for an election under the Republican Party ticket and claims to be pro-life does not mean he or she is less murderous or sinful than a Democratic candidate who supports abortion. Let me keep the record straight, the support and practice of abortion are ungodly, and so are the many murderous and ungodly practices within the Republican Party. This book details several unspoken and inhumane practices within the Republican Party that sharply contradict God's commandments. However, Christian Evangelical leaders who are supporters of the Republican Party have primarily focused their efforts on demonizing the agendas of the Democratic Party while ignoring or excusing the ungodliness of the Republican Party. Their inability to see and acknowledge the unbiblical practices within their camp is very typical of common characteristics of hypocrites. A major aspect of the behavioral patterns of hypocrites is to magnify the sins of others while concealing theirs. So, Jesus says, "Hypocrite! First, remove the plank from your own eye, and then you will see clearly to remove the speck from your brother's eye" (Matt 7:5). Because these hypocrites have not removed the plank from their eyes, they could not see the sins within their own party. The practices of some of these Christian Evangelical leaders who passionately support the Republican Party strongly correlate with the practices of the Pharisees in the Bible. Thus, I consider their behaviors to be of "modern-day Pharisees." They are political preachers (poli-preachers) who have directed their efforts toward political passions rather than Christ's passions. To them, salvation is linked to one's political affiliation rather than a relationship with Christ. They cunningly twist their preaching and teachings to promote the Republican Party's memos. They focus their efforts on converting people to Republicans rather than to Christ-followers. So, Jesus rebuked the Pharisees saying, "Woe to you, scribes and Pharisees, hypocrites! For you travel land and sea to win one proselyte, and when he is won, you make him twice as much a son of hell as yourselves" (Matt 23:15). The same hypocritical behaviors during the biblical days have dominated some Christian churches today that are involved in partisan politics, and many are blindly partaking in the hypocrisy.

For pastors, the remnants, who have not compromised their calling with partisan politics, I encourage you to act for the sake of declaring the truth of God's word. This is not the time to be silent while those who have embraced the doctrine of Balaam continue to deceive many unwitting individuals with their perversion of God's word. The presentation of a man that several sources, including a research study, concluded as the most dishonest and lying president in the history of the United States, as a savior and God's anointed is a deception from Satan. Scripturally, Jesus is the Truth and Satan is the Liar; thus, an effort to promote a liar is directed to displacing Christ as the Messiah and Savior of our country and the world. The same individuals who are propagating Mr. Trump as God's anointed will soon be preaching that Mr. Trump is the messiah and savior, and not Jesus. The remnants cannot be silent any longer even though the preaching of the gospel should not be intertwined with partisan politics; however, as a pastor/leader, you can direct your congregation to resources that present the truth of God's position concerning critical social and political issues in our country. The inaction of the remnants empowers the adversaries and apostates in their desperate efforts to pervert God's truth.

While I have presented the contents of this book from the standpoint of value neutrality, by confronting dishonesty and misinformation that have saturated our political system, as well as sabotaged truth to normalize lies and deceptions, I do not expect that my objective approach in writing this book will shield me from being vilified by right-wing extremists and those who display the characteristics of modern-day Pharisees because the contents of this book were not presented to support and enhance their falsehoods and propaganda. Some will deliberately misinterpret my position on some critical issues, and some will purposefully accuse me of things not written in the book.

However, this book is to capture the attention of the Christian community and those who have compromised their Christian faith with partisan politics. Even though some of them may not agree with everything presented in this book, they will be challenged with the truths according to the word of God, assuming that they care about God's truths. In addition, their consciences will be awakened to examine their heart and to view cultural issues from a godly standpoint.

In addition, this book is to help Christians break away from groupthink that has blinded some and limited their ability to think outside the box, as well as to challenge them to think critically, and logically process information they receive from other group members and leaders who may have ulterior motives, and to reasonably evaluate every information with the truth of God's word. The Scripture says, "Beloved, do not believe every spirit, but test the spirits, whether they are of God; because many false prophets have gone out into the world" (1 John 4:1). The undeniable evidence of false teachers and prophets that have gone out into the world is all around us presently, and they are relentless in their effort to deceive many. Therefore, the necessity to debunk falsehoods, expose deliberate amplifications of misinformation, and present the truth from biblical perspectives have motivated me to write this book.

Thus, I invite you to join me in examining significant political and social issues that some preachers have used to persuade their followers to believe that the Republican Party is God's party or that the party's platform reflects God's standards. Although several structural and functional differences exist between the Republican Party and the Democratic Party, examining their policies will reveal which political party practices are most likely to coincide with biblical teachings. It is essential to know that "things are not always what they seem." It takes an honest, inquiring mind to search out the matter to ascertain the truth. After all, the truth will set us free (see John 8:32). Thus, embrace yourself for a paradigm shift as the content of this book takes you on an intellectual journey of exploring the truth using God's word and uncovering facts using observable, editorial, and empirical data. These approaches reflect valid means of discovering the truth and facts of life. Consequently, any other means is subjective and subject to biases and inaccurate interpretations.

PART 1

Polarizing Social and Political Issues

Chapter 1

Socialism, Communism, and Capitalism

Socialism is one of the most dominant social issues that Christian Evangelical leaders use to persuade their followers to believe God endorses the Republican Party agenda. Socialism has become a catchphrase of a doom and gloom economic system that does not represent God's perspective. To others, it embodies the assumption that socialism undermines the concept of the Protestant work ethic and espouses Marxist economic utopianism. Discourse about socialism will often elicit comments like, "The Scripture says, 'If a man does not work, he should not eat,'" and "To save our children's future." Given the tendency of some of the Republicans and Christian Evangelical leaders to misapply social programs for socialism either by ignorance or to deceive their followers prompted the initiative to differentiate the two. Furthermore, this chapter explores the social programs that have been disparaged as socialism and ungodly and their relations to biblical values. The first step in this endeavor is to define the three economic systems in existence today globally and discuss their similarities and differences.

WHAT IS SOCIALISM?

Socialism is an economic system in which its means of production, distribution, and exchange are cooperatively owned rather than individuals.[1] The government plays the role of managing the economy on behalf of the workers. Socialism is primarily more economic than a political system, unlike some people have purported. However, political movements have been the vehicle to ratify socialist ideas. It is one of the two leading economic

---

1. Schaefer, *Sociology*, 339.

systems that exist in modern societies. It was developed as a reaction to the working-class exploitation by the capitalists, especially during the Industrial Revolution. The concept of socialism is to combat massive economic disparity between the *bourgeoisie*, known as the business owners, and the *proletariat*, the working class. Just like what we see today in the business world, while business owners amass an exorbitant amount of wealth, they subject the working class to a cycle of perpetual poverty. Socialist countries tend to enhance the lives of their citizens,[2] and democratic socialist countries like Finland, Denmark, Iceland, Switzerland, The Netherlands, Norway, and Sweden are often ranked among the happiest countries in the world.[3] It is logical to assume that people will be happier and have a better life if they do not bear the immense burden of paying their medical bills and sending their children to college.

WHAT IS COMMUNISM?

Communism is an economic system in which the community owns all property, and an individual's skills and abilities are not recognized.[4] Communism is both an economic and political system that sharply opposes the core tenets of capitalism. It is an extreme form of socialism that seeks to eliminate social stratification by creating a classless society. *The Communist Manifesto*, written by Karl Marx and Friedrich Engels in 1848, features the history of class struggles and advocates for the working-class revolution to overthrow business owners who exploit them. It suggests a radical economic approach to counterbalance the type of greed that exists in capitalism. Communism is associated with an authoritarian, centralized type of government that exerts total control in every sphere of economic activity. Although no society has achieved the ideal social philosophies of communism, its desired goal is to create an equal class system and eliminate private ownership of property. Examination of communist countries like China and Cuba shows that these countries have implemented private property rights, which creates the pathway for their members to be stratified economically.

---

2. Akulich and Kazmierczyk, "Socio-Economic Approach," 246.
3. Bloom, "20 Happiest Countries," paras. 1–3.
4. Schaefer, *Sociology*, 340.

WHAT IS CAPITALISM?

Capitalism is a free economic enterprise that allows private ownership of means of production.[5] The incentive for capitalism is to make a profit with limited government involvement. It operates on the principles of supply and demand of goods and services in which owners compete against each other to maximize their profit. It is one of the two primary economic systems in contemporary societies. Just like socialism, capitalism is only an economic system but is mostly associated with democracy. The United States is one of the leading countries in capitalism, although capitalism did not originate in the US.

DIFFERENCES AMONG SOCIALISM, COMMUNISM, AND CAPITALISM

Although there are different types of socialism, the primary goal of socialism is to meet the basic needs of the people or organizations. In socialism, an individual's ability, innovation, and contribution to the economy are recognized and rewarded accordingly, unlike communism which does not make distinctions based on an individual's contribution to the economy. Socialism allows a varying degree of personal ownership of property, and by contrast, communism does not nurture individuals' property ownership. Socialism tends to be associated with a democratically elected government, while totalitarianism is usually the type of government associated with communism. As you may have noted, a number of common characteristics found in capitalism also exist in socialism, although not at the same scale. However, a significant factor differentiating socialism from capitalism is that in the former means of production, such as industries, corporations, tools, etc., are publicly owned, and the latter involves private ownership.[6] In socialism, the goal is not to make a profit but to meet the needs of the people. In contrast, the driving force of capitalism is profit maximization. In capitalism, the government does not control the distribution of goods, services, and pricing. Thus, it is misleading to label one of the leading capitalist countries, the United States of America, as a socialist country or tag its economy as socialism. Furthermore, all the means of production in the United States are owned individually or organizationally and not by the government, which is a crucial factor that differentiates capitalism from socialism. The question then is why Christian Evangelical pastors deviate from

---

5. Giddens et al., *Essentials of Sociology*, 415.
6. Akulich and Kazmierczyk, "Socio-Economic Approach," 249.

preaching the gospel to preaching the Republican Party's deceitful message and labeling the US economy as socialism. Thus, the US economic system is not socialist, and its economic practices are far from socialism.

DO SOCIAL PROGRAMS MAKE THE UNITED STATES A SOCIALIST COUNTRY?

Absolutely not! The interchangeable use of socialism and social programs can be misleading; however, both connote different meanings. Socialism, as described above, is the public ownership of means of production, while social programs are a subcategory or an aspect of socialism that involves governmental efforts to provide economic assistance to the needy. Additionally, the exclusivity of socialism as an economic system is non-existent. In other words, socialism does not function mutually exclusively as an independent economic system; rather, it functions in conjunction with other economic systems, including capitalism. Thus, the introduction of social programs in a capitalist society like the United States is not inconsistent with the typical economic operations of capitalism. Much of the social programs in the United States today are an outgrowth of socialist philosophy; however, they do not exclusively constitute socialism. Here are some examples of social programs that have been in existence in the US for decades: Social Security benefits, farm subsidies, business grants, unemployment benefits, Medicaid, Medicare, etc. These social programs have not and will not convert the US robust free-market capitalist system into socialism; as such, it would be disingenuous to make such an absurd assumption. Again, neither capitalism nor socialism exists independently; they both influence each other to a certain degree, including communism.

EXTENDED LIST OF EXAMPLES OF SOCIAL PROGRAMS IN THE UNITED STATES

Several economic activities sponsored by the federal government fall under the classification of social programs. Categorizing some of these programs as socialist programs depends on which lens one is using to view them. If you are using a conservative lens, some of these programs are deemed socialism, especially if they are directed to help the poor, and if the programs are for the rich, they are considered an entitlement.

Social security

Medicaid

Medicare

Unemployment benefits

Corporate/Business subsidies

Public defender (Court-appointed lawyer for a defendant)

Public schools

501(c)(3) (Tax-exemption for nonprofit organizations such as religious, charitable, or educational organizations)

Tax exemption on a pastor's house (parsonage)

Grant for churches and non-profit organizations

Tax break for corporations

Corporate bailout

Bankruptcy

Disability insurance (SSDI)

Food stamps

Free lunch program

Stimulus checks

COVID-19 vaccines

WIC

Mortgage deduction

Temporary Assistance for Needy Families (TANF)

FEMA

BIBLICAL EXAMPLES OF THE THREE ECONOMIC SYSTEMS

Biblical examples illustrate that the Jews practiced all three economic systems (socialism, communism, and capitalism). First, social programs, which are often associated with socialism, are presented in the Bible as God's ideal economic approach to helping the poor, widows, orphans, and needy. As revealed in his word, God's position is absolute regarding his commandment to help the poor. Thus, he says, "For the poor will never cease from the land; therefore, I command you, saying, 'You shall open your hand wide to your brother, to your poor and your needy, in your land'" (Deut 15:11). God's directives were not limited to the mere helping of the poor but to help them generously. Also, God instructed business entities to help the poor in their business practices. For example, God says, "And you shall not glean your vineyard, nor shall you gather every grape of your vineyard; you shall leave them for the poor and the stranger: I am the LORD your God" (Lev 19:10). The "stranger" from biblical perspective means an immigrant. God is a loving and compassionate helper of marginalized groups, so he commands those in better financial positions, business owners, organizations like churches, and the government to help the needy. The benefit of obeying God's instruction in helping the poor was revealed in Ruth 2:1–23, in which Boaz instructed his workers to allow some grains to fall on purpose for Ruth to glean to feed herself and her mother-in-law. Ruth was an immigrant from Moab and dwelled in the land of Israel with her mother-in-law, Naomi. Both Ruth and Naomi's husbands were dead, and by sovereign arrangement, Boaz married Ruth and they gave birth to Obed, and Obed was the father of Jesse, and Jesse was the father of David the great king of Israel. Thus the lineage of Jesus was connected to Boaz and Ruth.

Second, capitalism is an effective economic system that rewards hard work, creativity, and a disciplined lifestyle and is a better wealth-generating economic system than socialism or communism. The caveat about capitalism is that it tends to be associated with exploitation, corruption, inequality, and other forms of social injustice. However, God hates exploitation and social injustice, and he promised to judge those who engage in such behavior. In Mal 3:5, God says, "'And I will come near you for judgment; I will be a swift witness . . . against those who exploit wage earners and widows and orphans, and against those who turn away an alien—because they do not fear Me,' says the Lord of hosts."

Surprisingly, denying people job opportunities and exploiting them because of their minority statuses, such as race, national origin, and social class, indicates that the person does not have reverence for God, who created them; consequently, such behavior could lead to God's judgment upon the perpetrators.

In addition, capitalism opens the door to greediness and the love of money. So, the Scripture says, "For the love of money is a root of all kinds of evil, for which some have strayed from the faith in their greediness and pierced themselves through with many sorrows" (1 Tim 6:10). The problem is the love of money, not the money itself. In the same sense, the love of capitalism is the problem, not capitalism itself. Due to human flaws and the likelihood of displacing God's position in their life with money, the pursuit of wealth can inadvertently feed on the human tendency to covetousness, materialism, idolatry, and other forms of social injustice and ungodliness.

Nehemiah 5:1–19 reveals how the pursuit of profit, which is associated with capitalism, will lead to ungodly practices. It also reveals government intervention for the poor in the form of loan forgiveness, which is also a social program. On the other hand, Jesus used the parable of talents to illustrate the concept of capitalism (see Matt 25:14–30). While there are several ways to interpret the parable, some major aspects of the interpretation include the significance of stewardship, investment, and disciplined work ethic that produce success, which represents the notion of capitalism.

Third, as repugnant as communism may sound to some people, at least one biblical event embodied the concept of communism. The event that took place with the early church in the book of Acts chapter 4, where believers sold their lands or houses and brought the proceeds to the apostles, was not even a socialist program or socialism, but communism. The Scripture says:

> Now the multitude of those who believed were of one heart and one soul; neither did anyone say that any of the things he possessed was his own, but they had all things in common. And with great power the apostles gave witness to the resurrection of the Lord Jesus. And great grace was upon them all. Nor was there anyone among them who lacked; for all who were possessors of lands or houses sold them, and brought the proceeds of the things that were sold, and laid them at the apostles' feet; and they distributed to each as anyone had need. And Joses, who was also named Barnabas by the apostles (which is translated Son of Encouragement), a Levite of the country of Cyprus, having land, sold it, and brought the money and laid it at the apostles' feet. (Acts 4:32–37)

The above scriptural verses suggest that none of the believers in this historical event treated any property as a personal possession but rather owned in common. Communal ownership of property and the elimination of a stratification system that ranks people economically in a vertical order is the very essence of communism, which is an even more extreme economic system than socialism.

As indicated above, the three economic systems have been implemented at some point by God's people, and none of them was condemned by God. Furthermore, social programs have been associated with God's blessings throughout the Scripture. Therefore, the act of politicizing social programs for the poor is ungodly and detestable before God.

Some people claim that they heard from God or that God revealed to them the evil associated with socialism. My question to them is, Are you sure you truly heard from God, and not your biased thoughts or emotional resentment toward social programs eliciting such negative thoughts at an unconscious level, which you have wrongly interpreted to come from God? For God does not give a man revelation that contradicts his word nor a half-hearted truth so that he can use it to denigrate and condemn his political opponents; it was the Pharisees who practiced such behavior. God's revelation is to liberate, for the Scripture says, "Now the Lord is the Spirit; and where the Spirit of Lord is, there is liberty" (2 Cor 3:17).

CORPORATE WELFARES

The apocalyptic warnings about socialism and the evil it embodies have become a familiar playbook of GOP lawmakers and some Christian Evangelical leaders concerning welfare programs for needy families. However, they support or keep silent regarding welfare programs for the rich and corporations. Thus, corporate welfare often comes in the form of government tax breaks, monetary grants, subsidies, and other special treatments for corporations. Some may argue that such government assistance to corporations helps create jobs and sustain the economy. Still, the upshot of such aid is the increase in the CEOs' and other top management positions' income, which further widens the gap between the rich and the poor. The billions of dollars in the bailout to airlines and other corporations during the 2020–21 pandemic crisis in which a large portion of the fund was a grant is a social program. In 2020, fifty-five corporations paid zero federal taxes on their income, and each of the corporations received at least $500 million due to the Coronavirus Aid, Relief, and Economic Security (CARES) Act.[7] Additionally, multinational corporations escape paying an estimated federal income tax of $90 billion every year by taking advantage of loopholes in the tax code known as a tax haven.[8] The loopholes in the tax code allow corporations to offshore income generated in the US to foreign countries with little or zero tax burdens. The resultant effect of such tax behavior is increased tax burdens on the average American taxpayer.

In a nutshell, corporations and the rich are also beneficiaries of the federal government's social programs; thus, it is deeply cynical to portray welfare only from programs designed for those in poverty. Therefore, Republican Party members who often oppose welfare programs for the poor

---

7. Gardner and Wamhoff, "55 Corporation Paid $0 in Federal Taxes," paras. 5–13.
8. Phillips et al., "Offshore Shell Games," para. 5.

and decry socialism should also decry socialism for the programs that benefit corporations and the rich. They should also give up all the tax breaks and other benefits they and their family members receive from the federal government; otherwise, they are hypocrites.

Additionally, Christian Evangelical pastors and leaders who erroneously believe that they have a mandate from God to demonize social programs for the poor should first denounce the 501(c)(3) privileges, tax exemptions on parsonages, and other benefits they and their ministries receive from the government. Otherwise, they are hypocrites. Some contend that the government should not be involved in welfare programs. However, the same government that provides social programs for the poor also gives tax exemptions for your parsonages and churches. Thus, it is disingenuous to condemn government-sponsored programs to help the disadvantaged when you and your church also receive benefits from the government in different forms. Most of these pastors and their ministries save tens of thousands and hundreds of thousands of dollars each year from government-sponsored programs they deem socialism. If the poor had received such welfare benefits from the government, some of the preachers would have labeled them "socialism." No scriptural mandate says parsonages and ministries should be exempted from taxes. My position is not to suggest that taxes should be levied on parsonages and churches but to confront the hypocrisy and hardness of the hearts of preachers who disparage social programs for needy families as socialism.

CORPORATIONS' PROFITS AMID INFLATION

While Christian Evangelical preachers are busy fulfilling their portion of the Faustian deal with the Republicans by preaching socialism, they remain silent about unscrupulous business practices by some corporations at the expense of the working class. The economic downturn during the pandemic crisis had been perverted into an unprincipled opportunity for crafty corporations and companies to expand their profits, again, at the expense of the working class. For example, Exxon Mobile had its highest earnings ($56 billion) ever in 2022, during which we experienced one of the highest costs of gasoline in American history.[9] The 2022 profits supersede the 2008 record profits, and guess what the American economic status was like in 2008: it was also a year of high inflation. Recent reports from several sources suggest that companies are experiencing the highest profits since 1950 amid

---

9. Valle, "Exxon Smashes Western Oil," para. 1.

the US inflation.[10] It is obvious that inflation presents greater opportunities for corporations and companies to expand their profits while the average American consumer pays the cost. Therefore, why wouldn't these dishonest corporations and companies increase the price of their products since they are without government regulations to justify their reasons for price hikes? While respecting the concept of capitalism, a free economic enterprise, it is essential for government regulations in situations like inflation to discourage dishonest business practices that allow corporations that take advantage of adverse situations to increase their profits to the detriment of struggling American citizens. The poor are getting poorer in the US while the rich are getting richer, making it harder for some people to achieve the American dream. It is not because the poor are lazy but because of an unequal power structure that exists between the bourgeoisie and the proletariat, as well as structural problems within our institutions. In the past forty years, income inequality has increased, as well as the number of homeless people.[11] A significant number of homeless people are employed, but because of low pay, they cannot afford to pay their rent. The Evangelical preachers will not preach against such economic practices, but they are quick to condemn the working class who receive a small amount of financial aid from the government to support their families, which is hypocrisy.

Those who are sounding the false alarm about social programs bankrupting the US economy should start paying taxes on their ministries and parsonages to boost the economy. In the same manner, you preach about God's economy to your followers and challenge them to have faith in God and donate to your ministry; you should also have the same level of faith and believe that God will replenish and bless a government that takes care of the poor. According to Prov 19:17, "He who has pity on the poor lends to the Lord, and He will pay back what he has given." Thus, helping the poor is lending unto God, which is associated with God's blessing. The Scripture also says, "The righteous considers the cause of the poor, but the wicked does not understand such knowledge" (Prov 29:7). It takes someone with a sacred heart to understand the conditions of the poor and show compassion to them.

---

10. Reuter and Kiersz, "Companies Are Pocketing," paras. 1–2; Pickert, "U.S. Corporate Profits," para. 1.

11. Griggs, "Wealth Inequality," para. 7.

Vignette

The blatant disregard of God's word and unholy alliance with a secular entity like a political party leads to a compromising position of God's truth and diminishes one's moral authority as a godly person to condemn ungodly behaviors. As the Scripture says, "Friendship with the world is enmity with God" (see Jas 4:4).

REPUBLICANS' OPPOSITIONS TO SOCIAL WELFARE PROGRAMS TO THE POOR

Historically, the congressional Republicans have not been the group to promote or support social programs that will protect and help non-affluent Americans. According to an NPR National Security Correspondent interview with Rep. John Dingle, the Republicans hated social programs from Social Security to Medicare.[12] Although some Republicans supported the passing of these programs, their initial attempt to oppose Social Security was unsuccessful because congressional Democrats outnumbered them.

The Affordable Care Act (ACA), nicknamed Obamacare, was signed into law by President Barack Obama on March 23, 2010, and was designed to make health care affordable to millions of Americans who could not afford health coverage. However, GOP members spent a significant amount of time for over a decade repealing a healthcare program that would help the poor obtain medical coverage, including coverage for pre-existing conditions, without offering an alternative plan to make health coverage affordable to the poor. Their latest effort to strike down Obamacare was rejected by the Supreme Court in a seven to two vote on June 17, 2021, making it the third time the Supreme Court had rejected such an effort by the Republicans.[13] It is estimated that thirty-one million people receive health care from Obamacare. Ironically, many people who depend on Obamacare for health coverage voted for the Republicans who are working against them. For some of you, it is time to re-evaluate your relationship with a group that consistently works against programs that benefit you but would support programs that benefit the rich. Your continued support of them without holding them accountable for their reckless actions only empowers them to treat you as second-class citizens.

---

12. Welna, "GOP's History of Resistance," para. 6.
13. Cillizza, "Affordable Care Act," para. 1.

In 2019, while President Donald Trump was boasting about spending $16 billion to bail out farmers, he proposed restructuring eligibility requirements to eliminate over three million families with children from receiving food stamps.[14] The 2017 tax reform, known as the Tax Cuts and Job Act (TCJA), signed into law on December 22, 2017, by President Donald Trump, was a major victory for banks and corporations and provided a substantial financial gain for them. The tax reform permanently lowered the corporate tax rate to 21 percent from 35 percent, while the individual tax rates were lowered temporarily, between 1 percent and 4 percent.[15] The huge tax rate reduction for corporations, without a doubt, boosted the income of their executives and the income of their shareholders. The corporate tax receipts were lowered by more than $90 billion in 2018 due to the tax cut, while the national deficit increased to $984 billion by 2019 from $665 billion in 2017.[16] In addition, some wealthiest people in the US pay little or zero federal income taxes.[17] This is possible because of their ability to utilize tax strategies to minimize or eliminate their income tax obligations in a particular year or multiple years. The advantage for the wealthy to minimize or eliminate their federal income tax burdens is a welfare program, which is not available to an average taxpayer.

For the Christian Evangelicals who pledge their unwavering support to the congressional GOP members in their opposition to welfare programs for non-affluent Americans while supporting the programs that benefit the rich, it is important to pay attention to what the word of God says, "Whoever oppresses the poor to increase his own wealth or gives to the rich, will only come to poverty" (Prov 22:16). Throughout the Scripture, God's steadfast commitment to helping the poor is very clear to take a risk in an ungodly alliance with a political party that does not reflect God's values. The degree of secular humanism within the Republican Party is evident in their opposition to several social issues, like welfare programs for the poor, social justice, immigration, gun control, etc. There is no demonstrated evidence to suggest that the GOP's anti-abortion position (which the Christian Evangelicals have deceptively used to promote the Republican Party as God's party) is extended to lives outside their mothers' wombs, especially to those who belong to marginalized groups. Their anti-abortion rhetoric simply gives them a political platform to advance their selfish political aspirations and does not indicate care for human life.

14. Bump, "Selective Socialism," paras. 3–4.
15. Floyd, "Explaining the Trump Tax," para. 6.
16. Long and Stein, "U.S. Deficit," paras. 1–4.
17. Eisinger, et al., "Secret IRS Files," para. 1.

The danger of the Christian Evangelicals' ungodly partnership with the Republican Party is expressed in their double standards and higher levels of deception. The intensive efforts by some of the Christian Evangelical leaders who support the Republican Party by painting negative pictures about the Democratic Party's political agenda while at the same time keeping silent about the ungodly practices within the Republican Party are very duplicitous. Suppose you are one of those who are always demonizing programs initiated by the Democrats and pretend as if the evil within the Republican Party does not exist; in that case, you are engaging in hypocritical behavior. Do you think that God is in heaven applauding the Republican Party's political agendas and denigrating the ones by the Democrats? If you think so, you must be devoid of God's knowledge. The Scripture says, "For there is no partiality with God" (Rom 2:11). God uses the same standard to judge both the Democrats and the Republicans. It is not the group that confesses and pretends to know God when their actions are incongruent with God's word that will be justified, but the group whose actions are consistent with God's commandments. So, Paul declares, "For not the hearers of the law are just in the sight of God, but the doers of the law will be justified" (Rom 2:13).

Vignette

> The support of the Republican Party's opposition to welfare programs for the poor creates paradoxical effects on the significance of God's command that says, "You shall love your neighbor as yourself" (Matt 22:39).

My question to the Christian Evangelicals who promote the Republican Party as God's party: How do the Republican Party's political philosophies and positions concerning the poor correlate with biblical teaching? Alternatively, How does your support for the rich instead of the poor coincide with God's position? For believers in the Lord Jesus, God's passion should be our passion also, and his passion is to help the poor, and that should also be our passion.

UNFOUNDED CLAIMS FOR OPPOSITIONS TO SOCIAL PROGRAMS

The opponents of welfare programs for the poor often claim that people on welfare are lazy or that some people abuse the system. It is important to remind individuals who embrace such a view that poverty is more of a structural problem than laziness, given the history of disenfranchisement of marginalized groups in the United States. Furthermore, no system or living organism is perfect to expect perfection from the welfare system. Thus, it is not justified to rely on the insignificant number of people who may have abused the welfare programs to deny help to families who truly need the help or denigrate the welfare programs and the recipients. Our legal system or biblical teaching does not support the act of condemning people without concrete evidence. Additionally, using isolated incidences to build a dangerous doctrine or theory against the guiltless is ungodly and hypocritical.

MYTHS ABOUT WELFARE PROGRAMS AND FEDERAL DEFICIT

One of the myths that the Republicans have propagated to oppose welfare programs for the poor is their claim of the rising federal deficit or debt. Some people believe that the Republicans are better stewards of the national economy, including reducing the deficits, than the Democrats; however, nothing could be further from the truth with such belief. The Democrats are referred to as the party of fiscal responsibility because they have consistently reduced the deficit.[18] On the other hand, the Republicans have steadily increased the deficit through tax reforms that benefit corporations and the rich despite their empty promises of balancing the budget. An examination of deficit change in percentage points of gross domestic product (GDP) from 1977 to 2018 reveals an increase in deficit under every Republican president from 0.4 percent to 4.7 percent and a decrease in deficit under every Democratic president from .01 percent to 5.0 percent.[19] The House Committee on the Budget report suggests that GOP presidents (Ronald Regan, George H. W. Bush, and Donald Trump) in the last four decades passed tax reforms that tremendously benefited the wealthy and corporations and consequently increased the deficits. At the same time, the GOP justified its actions to cut spending on the necessary programs for American families like Social Security and Medicare.

A study at Princeton University found that economic growth is enhanced when the president is a Democrat than when the president is a Republican, and the average growth is 18.6 percent under a Democratic president and 10.6 under a Republican president.[20] Furthermore, if both houses of Congress are controlled by Democrats and the president is a

18. Leonhardt, "Democrats," para. 1.
19. Leonhardt, "Democrats," paras. 1–4.
20. Blinder and Watson, "Presidents and the U.S. Economy," para. 2.

Democrat, the same study shows that the economic growth is higher than with a Republican president or Congress. The growth in the US economy under a Democratic president is also reflected in the real GDP, higher job creation, lower unemployment rate, and higher corporate profits and investment. In January 2023, the US unemployment rate reached its lowest level at 3.4 percent since 1969, which was under a Democratic president, Joe Biden.[21] There was also a significant decline in the number of unemployed people, including weekly jobless claims. In addition, the total number of nonfarm-related employment increased above expectation by 517,000 in January 2023, from government employment, health care, and construction to manufacturing.[22] In 2021, the US economy experienced the highest rate of growth in almost forty years at 5.7 percent, the largest number of job creation in a single year, and the highest reduction in unemployment claims in a single year.[23] All these economic records took place just as the country was experiencing economic setbacks, including inflation, due to the pandemic. In summary, the baseless claims of the Republicans of being a better steward of the economy are untrue and hypocritical.

SUMMARY

The structural functions of the two political parties are juxtaposed in values, with one party more aligned with biblical teachings than the other. The social issues presented in this chapter have been explored through a biblical lens, observable and editorial data to enable one to decide which political party is more likely to reflect biblical values. The opponents of social programs for the poor will often overzealously portray welfare programs for the needy as evil. The irony is that some of them, either currently or in the past, have benefited from welfare programs. Biblical accounts demonstrate examples of institutional and personal social programs to serve as a standard of the significance of helping economically disadvantaged people. The tragic irony is that Christian Evangelical leaders, who are supposed to be the chief proponents of social programs for the poor and the needy, as instructed by God, have formed an ungodly partnership with a political party to oppose these biblical values. Since the Republican party's social welfare programs contradict biblical teachings; therefore, it cannot be a party endorsed by God.

21. U.S. Department of Commerce, "Unemployment Is at Its Lowest," para. 1.
22. Cox, "Job Report Shows," paras. 1–3.
23. U.S. Department of Commerce, "Unemployment Is at Its Lowest," para. 1.

Furthermore, taking a nuts-and-bolts approach to analyze the concept of socialism logically, I have endeavored to define socialism and differentiate it from social programs. The concept of social programs originated with God, as demonstrated in the Bible. Thus, it is absurd to label them socialism. Throughout the Scripture, from Genesis to Revelation, the idea of social programs is emphasized significantly. The practice of social programs to help the poor indicates one's love for God. Additionally, there is no scriptural verse that condemns people for helping the poor and needy; in fact, the reverse is the case. Only the Pharisees will twist the Scripture to condemn those who help the poor and needy. The Pharisees, on multiple occasions, condemned Jesus because he healed the maimed on the Sabbath. Mark 3:1–6 says:

> And He entered the synagogue again, and a man was there who had a withered hand. So they [Pharisees] watched Him closely, whether He would heal him on the Sabbath, so that they might accuse Him. And He said to the man who had the withered hand, "Step forward." Then He said to them [the Pharisees], "Is it lawful on the Sabbath to do good or to do evil, to save life or to kill?" But they kept silent. And when He had looked around at them with anger, being grieved by the hardness of their hearts, He said to the man, "Stretch out your hand." And he stretched it out, and his hand was restored as whole as the other. Then the Pharisees went out and immediately plotted with the Herodians against Him, how they might destroy Him.

There are three important lessons to glean from the above verses: First, it is lawful to do good and save life even on a Sabbath, which is a day you should not work. Applying Jesus' views to the issues of social programs in our contemporary society, it is lawful to help the poor and the needy even if you think they are lazy and do not deserve your help. Scripturally, there is no justification for not helping people. Second, as Jesus looked at the Pharisees with anger and was grieved because of the hardness of their hearts, he is also grieving today because of the hardness of the hearts of the modern-day Pharisees. Third, the Pharisees have no compassion for the needy; they are only concerned about fulfilling their legal and political agenda. The lack of compassion for the needy is ungodly behavior.

The Pharisees do not acknowledge their own sins; they always have magnifying glasses to scoop into other people's sins. In another episode, they accused Jesus of healing a disabled woman on the Sabbath, which they considered work. For the Scripture says:

> Now He was teaching in one of the synagogues on the Sabbath. And behold, there was a woman who had a spirit of infirmity eighteen years, and was bent over and could in no way raise herself up. But when Jesus saw her, He called her to Him and said to her, "Woman, you are loosed from your infirmity." And He laid His hands on her, and immediately she was made straight, and glorified God. But the ruler of the synagogue answered with indignation, because Jesus had healed on the Sabbath; and he said to the crowd, "There are six days on which men ought to work; therefore come and be healed on them, and not on the Sabbath day." The Lord then answered him and said, "Hypocrite! Does not each one of you on the Sabbath loose his ox or donkey from the stall, and lead it away to water it? So ought not this woman, being a daughter of Abraham, whom Satan has bound—think of it—for eighteen years, be loosed from this bond on the Sabbath?" And when He said these things, all His adversaries were put to shame; and all the multitude rejoiced for all the glorious things that were done by Him. (Luke 13:10–17)

In the above verses, the Pharisees did not acknowledge that taking their ox or donkey to water it on the Sabbath was sinful, but they were eager to condemn Jesus for doing good (healing) on the Sabbath. Translating this incident in today's society, these modern-day Pharisees, who preach against social programs and deceptively label the US economy as socialism, while their ministry, church, and parsonage receive welfare from the US government in the form of 501(c)(3), they on the other hand condemn the programs for the poor. That is hypocrisy!

Chapter 2

Social Programs and Biblical Values

The primary purpose of social programs is to help the underprivileged and meet the people's or organizations' basic needs. In a broader sense, I will describe social programs in the following manner: First, as programs in which the recipient is not paying for the goods or services received; second, the recipient receives a subsidy; third, the recipient is abdicated from the full or partial financial obligations during the time the goods or services were received or later; and fourth, the recipient receives other forms of assistance or benefits from the federal government, state government, local government, organizations, or even from another individual. In a nutshell, a social program involves receiving benefits or forgiveness of debts that could not have been possible if an entity had not acted kindly to extend such benefits or forgiveness to another.

ARE THERE BIBLICAL EXAMPLES OF SOCIAL PROGRAMS?

Examining the historical records of the Bible, both the Old and New Testaments, reveals an undeniable fact that the poor, widows, orphans, and other marginalized groups are at the center of God's heart. Several scriptures and biblical events alluded to God's desire and commandment for those in a better financial position to bless and help the poor unconditionally. These views were reinforced during Jesus' ministry. Helping the poor should not rest on their ability to repay the financial assistance they receive. Giving to the needy should be based on obedience to God's command and our compassion to help someone who is in need. Just like paying tithes or giving offerings to the church, ministry, or ministers of the gospel should be influenced by obedience to God's commandment. God commands his people to give generously to the poor and to supply all their needs sufficiently. Withholding help to the poor is a sin before God, especially if they cry out to God:

> If there is among you a poor man of your brethren, within any of the gates in your land which the Lord your God is giving you, you shall not harden your heart nor shut your hand from your poor brother, but you shall open your hand wide to him and willingly lend him sufficient for his need, whatever he needs. Beware lest there be a wicked thought in your heart, saying, "The seventh year, the year of release, is at hand," and your eye be evil against your poor brother and you give him nothing, and he cries out to the Lord against you, and it becomes sin among you. You shall surely give to him, and your heart should not be grieved when you give to him, because for this thing the Lord your God will bless you in all your works and in all to which you put your hand. For the poor will never cease from the land; therefore I command you, saying, "You shall open your hand wide to your brother, to your poor and your needy, in your land." (Deut 15:7–11)

The above scriptural verses reveal God's heart condition toward the poor and his uncompromising command to help them. Helping and giving to the needy is fundamental to biblical doctrine. Thus, preaching against government-sponsored programs to help the poor while keeping silent about government programs that enrich the wealthy is morally wrong and unbiblical. A political party that sponsors programs to benefit the affluent and laments socialism for programs to help the poor cannot be endorsed by God because such behavior contradicts God's standards. It is the obedience to helping the poor that pleases God and attracts his blessings, as stated above. Additionally, God requires that all debts be canceled at the end of every seven years. Therefore, harassing debtors for debts that are more than seven years old or debts that have been discharged through bankruptcy is an ungodly practice and invokes God's judgment on the perpetrators. God's position concerning seven or more years old debts is as follows:

> At the end of every seven years you shall grant a release of debts. And this is the form of the release: Every creditor who has lent anything to his neighbor shall release it; he shall not require it of his neighbor or his brother, because it is called the Lord's release. (Deut 15:1–2)

The Bible reveals an occasion where the love of money led to ungodly practices. In the book of Nehemiah 5:1–19, Nehemiah was confronted with economic crises due to famine in Judah. The severity of the famine forced people to mortgage their houses and farms and sell their children into slavery to buy food. Since the debtors could not afford to pay back their debts and the interest, their creditors took over their property and children. So, when Nehemiah heard the cry of the debtors against their kinsmen, the creditors, he said this:

> And I became very angry when I heard their outcry and these words. After serious thought, I rebuked the nobles and rulers, and said to them, "Each of you is exacting usury from his brother." So I called a great assembly against them. And I said to them, "According to our ability we have redeemed our Jewish brethren who were sold to the nations. Now indeed, will you even sell your brethren? Or should they be sold to us?" Then they were silenced and found nothing to say. Then I said, "What you are doing is not good. Should you not walk in the fear of our God because of the reproach of the nations, our enemies? I also, with my brethren and my servants, am lending them money and grain. Please, let us stop this usury! Restore now to them, even this day, their lands, their vineyards, their olive groves, and their houses, also a hundredth of the money and the grain, the new wine and the oil, that you have charged them." So they said, "We will restore it, and will require nothing from them; we will do as you say." Then I called the priests and required an oath from them that they would do according to this promise. Then I shook out the fold of my garment and said, "So may God shake out each man from his house, and from his property, who does not perform this promise. Even thus may he be shaken out and emptied." And all the assembly said, "Amen!" and praised the Lord. Then the people did according to this promise. (Neh 5:6–13)

Although taking pledges of property for loans is an accepted practice, allowing a poor man access to his pledge is considered a righteous act before God (see Deut 24:12–13). However, demanding interest on a loan is an ungodly practice (see Exod 22:25). The actions of Nehemiah as the governor of Judah reflect biblical standards of government approach to debt resolution, assistance to the poor, and restraint of greedy business practices often found in capitalism.

Apostle Paul, in his effort to emphasize the significance of helping the poor, reminded believers of the commandment of our Lord Jesus to render help to the weak, in which he says: "I have shown you in every way, by laboring like this, that you must support the weak [poor]. And remember the words of the Lord Jesus, that He said, 'It is more blessed to give than to receive'" (Acts 20:35). You noticed that Apostle Paul said, "You must support the weak," not that you should preach socialism to condemn them. Preachers who are driven by partisan politics will rather convolute the Scripture to support their political party's agenda than obey the word of God.

THE GREATEST COMMANDMENTS

A lawyer, a member of the Pharisees, asked Jesus this question: "Teacher, which is the greatest commandment in the law?" (Matt 22:36). Then Jesus responded to his question, saying:

> "You shall love the LORD your God with all your heart, with all your soul, and with all your mind." This is the first and great commandment. And the second is like it: "You shall love your neighbor as yourself." On these two commandments hang all the Law and Prophets. (Matt 22:37–40)

Jesus' response to the lawyer's question provides a comprehensive answer that encompasses both vertical and horizontal relationships and the totality of God's demands of the human relationship with him. True love (*agape* love) originates with God. Human beings lack the innate ability to love one another unconditionally unless they have first cultivated in their heart, soul, and mind love toward God unconditionally. Because humans' type of love is based on conditions, which I will describe as pseudo-love, the so-called love falls apart once the expected conditions are not met. This type of quasi-love is common in all human relationships, including marriages. Even with couples who are engaged to be married or married couples who may claim to love one another passionately, the basis of their love is the conditions that they meet each other's expectations. If the expectations fall short, so the love falls short. That is why there are high divorce rates in our society because a spouse falls short of the expectations of their partner. While this may be a hard pill to swallow for some people, know that true love begins first with loving God before one can even love oneself and commit to loving others from God's perspective.

Similarly, it is impossible to claim to love God without loving human beings he made in his image. First John 4:20 says, "If someone says that 'I love God,' and hates his brother, he is a liar, for he who does not love his brother whom he has seen, how can he love God whom he has not seen?"

Your love toward other people reveals your love and heart conditions toward God. If you love other people a little, it indicates that you love God a little, and if you love others much, it is a sign that your heart condition toward God is much love.

Vignette

> Your love and care for people who are different from you and the poor is a litmus test of your heart conditions toward God, who created them in his image.

THE GOOD SAMARITAN PARABLE

Consider the parable of the good Samaritan and the illustration that Jesus provided about showing love and mercy to our neighbors in need. In this case, our neighbor is not necessarily a person who lives close to us but could be a total stranger. Thus, Jesus says:

> And behold, a certain lawyer stood up and tested Him, saying, "Teacher, what shall I do to inherit eternal life?" He said to him, "What is written in the law? What is your reading of it?" So he answered and said, "You shall love the Lord your God with all your heart, with all your soul, with all your strength, and with all your mind, and your neighbor as yourself." And He said to him, "You have answered rightly; do this and you will live." But he, wanting to justify himself, said to Jesus, "And who is my neighbor?" Then Jesus answered and said: "A certain man went down from Jerusalem to Jericho, and fell among thieves, who stripped him of his clothing, wounded him, and departed, leaving him half dead. Now by chance, a certain priest came down that road. And when he saw him, he passed by on the other side. Likewise, a Levite, when he arrived at the place, came and looked, and passed by on the other side. But a certain Samaritan, as he journeyed, came to where he was. And when he saw him, he had compassion. So he went to him and bandaged his wounds, pouring on oil and wine; and he set him on his own animal, brought him to an inn, and took care of him. On the next day, when he departed, he took out two denarii, gave them to the innkeeper, and said to him, 'Take care of him; and whatever more you spend, when I come again, I will repay you.' So which of these three do you think was neighbor to him

who fell among the thieves?" And he said, "He who showed mercy on him." Then Jesus said to him, "Go and do likewise." (Luke 10:25–37)

The parable was an illustration of a man traveling from Jerusalem to Jericho who was robbed, beaten, and abandoned to die. In this incident, a priest came by and saw the injured man; instead of helping, he sought another means to pass by. Surely, this priest must be a preacher of anti-social programs to his congregation. Then, a Levite came by, and instead of helping, he used another pathway to cross over. Indeed, that Levite must be a member of the priest congregation. From the scriptural standpoint, the priests and the Levites are knowledgeable about the word of God and his command to love, show compassion, and help the needy, yet they disobeyed biblical instructions concerning such a situation. The behavior of the pastors who are preaching socialism concerning government aid to the needy is equivalent to the behaviors of the priest and the Levite who avoided helping a man in a dying situation. But noticed what the good Samaritan did, one who was the least likely to show love and mercy and was considered, during that time, immoral and ungodly. He went above and beyond to do what the priest and the Levites could not do. Do you know the equivalent of the good Samaritan in our postmodern society, the Democrats that have been labeled immoral and ungodly? However, they have been the political party that has been pushing for equitable justice, economic opportunities for minority groups, and government aid to the poor and needy, while the Republicans and their fierce supporters, the Christian Evangelical pastors, are using the shouting of socialism as a different, yet deceptive pathway, to subvert government programs designed for the poor.

DENYING HELP TO THE POOR IS A REPROACH TO GOD

Proverbs 17:5 states, "He who mocks the poor reproaches his Maker; he who is glad at calamity will not go unpunished." Denying help to the poor, as well as opposing efforts to help the poor while lamenting "socialism," is a mockery to the poor and a reproach to God. It also suggests smirking over their poverty, which is an abominable act before God, and according to his word, a person who engages in such behavior will not escape punishment. Consider the parable of the rich man and Lazarus as illustrated by Jesus, in which he says:

> There was a certain rich man who was clothed in purple and fine linen and fared sumptuously every day. But there was a certain beggar named Lazarus, full of sores, who was laid at his gate, desiring to be fed with the crumbs which fell from the rich man's table. Moreover the dogs came and licked his sores. So it was that the beggar died, and was carried by the angels to Abraham's bosom. The rich man also died and was buried. And being in torments in Hades, he lifted up his eyes and saw Abraham afar off, and Lazarus in his bosom. Then he cried and said, "Father Abraham, have mercy on me, and send Lazarus that he may dip the tip of his finger in water and cool my tongue; for I am tormented in this flame." But Abraham said, "Son, remember that in your lifetime you received your good things, and likewise Lazarus evil things; but now he is comforted and you are tormented." (Luke 16:19–25)

Obviously, God is not against the rich because he is the one who gave them their wealth. So, the Scripture says, "Every good gift and every perfect gift is from above, and comes down from the Father of lights, with whom there is no variation or shadow of turning" (Jas 1:17). Another Scripture states, "And you shall remember the LORD your God, for it is He who gives you the power to get wealth" (Deut 8:18a). However, God's gift of wealth to an individual is not just for the person but an extension of God's arm in blessing others in need. Therefore, if Lazarus was "desiring to be fed with the crumbs which fell from the rich man's table," it implies the rich man's refusal to help Lazarus in his state of deprivation, which is a mockery against Lazarus and a reproach against God.

Furthermore, the rich man's refusal to assist Lazarus signifies a lack of compassion toward Lazarus but gloating over his poverty; therefore, he would not go unpunished according to Scripture. Proverbs 14:31 also states, "He who oppresses the poor reproaches his Maker, but he who honors Him [God] has mercy on the needy." One of the godliest ways to honor God is to use the blessing he has given you to show mercy on the needy. The rich man did not honor God with the wealth God had given him by showing mercy to Lazarus; instead, he was apathetic and unmerciful; therefore, he could not receive mercy from God and found himself in Hades. So, Jesus says, "Blessed are the merciful, for they shall obtain mercy" (Matt 5:7).

This type of behavior is prevalent among the Republican Party and some Christian Evangelical leaders, who often oppose programs that will help the poor and then lament "socialism." Some have built a doctrine out of one scripture that says, "If anyone will not work, neither shall he eat" (2 Thess 3:10), while simultaneously ignoring a host of other scriptures where God commanded us to help the poor unconditionally. Consequently, such actions are also making a mockery of the poor and a reproach against God, which are also abominations before God. It is not wise to use one scriptural verse to create a doctrine and then use the doctrine to contradict other scriptural verses.

Also, Jesus says, "On these two commandments hang all the Law and Prophets" (Matt 22:40). The fulfillment of the two commandments to love God and love your neighbor as yourself fulfills the requirement of all the laws God commanded humanity to obey through his prophets. As mentioned above, the ability to love others begins with cultivating love in one's heart for God. Suppose Democrats show love and acceptance to marginalized groups that the Republicans and some Christian Evangelicals may consider sinners, lazy, poor, and marginalized. In that case, they are more likely to enter the kingdom of God than the modern-day Pharisees. Because some Democrats are more likely to fulfill the two most essential commandments on which hang all the Law and Prophets, again, you cannot love humanity unless you love God first. You cannot love God without loving human beings he created in his image. Truth is based on the word of God, and it is practical; it is not based on bogus imagination or a false sense of belief. Jesus says, "You will know them by their fruits" (Matt 7:16). Those who do not love God will rather make excuses to justify their actions than obey God's commandment to love others. So, Jesus says "If you love Me, keep My commandments" (John 14:15). That commandment includes loving the poor, the marginalized, and all of God's creation equally. You cannot claim to love God while you hate human beings he made in his image because of their class or race. The evidence of your hate is the differential treatment of them because of their external traits.

The display of false moral superiority common among some Christian Evangelicals and the Republicans has its historical reality that can be traced back to the days of Jesus on Earth. The Pharisees labeled Jesus "a friend of tax collectors and sinners" (Luke 7:34) because he accepted and showed love to those condemned by the Pharisees. If Jesus were to be present today physically, he would also be labeled by these modern-day Pharisees as a "friend of sinners" and a "socialist." As the Pharisees in the days of Jesus were blinded to recognize that Jesus was the promised Messiah because their hearts were given to politics, fame, riches, and worldly affairs rather than the truth of God's word, so are these modern-day Pharisees blinded to recognize Jesus if he were to appear physically today. He would not come as a Republican, guaranteed, which would be a cause for his immediate rejection by these neo-Pharisees. Those who have formed an unholy coalition with the Republican Party and converted God's ministry into political preachings function outside the framework of God's purpose for their ministry. Like their predecessors, they have created religion without a relationship with Christ.

Consequently, they are ineffective in disseminating the greatest message to humankind: "For God so loved the world that He gave His only begotten Son, that whoever believes in Him should not perish but have everlasting life" (John 3:16). Furthermore, partisan politics is divisive, making it more challenging to serve God and mammon simultaneously. As Jesus said, "No servant can serve two masters; for either he will hate the one and love the other, or else he will be loyal to the one and despise the other. You cannot serve God and mammon" (Luke 16:13). Therefore, it is practically impossible to serve God and partisan politics at the same time.

Vignette

> The absence of reverential fear of God and the secularization of church doctrines promulgates secular humanism within the church. It alienates her from fulfilling her divine purpose of being the light and the salt of the world.

GOD DESIRES MERCY AND NOT SACRIFICE

In another incident, Jesus was confronted by the Pharisees, and they accused his disciples of picking grain to eat on the Sabbath (see Matt 12:1–2). Still, Jesus responded to them by saying, "But if you had known what this means, I desire mercy and not sacrifice, you would not have condemned the guiltless" (Matt 12:7). Many guiltless families who really need government assistance have been condemned because of their impoverished state. An important lesson for the modern-day Pharisees is that God does not desire your sacrifice and sanctimonious attitude but love and mercy. The fulfillment of public ceremonial activities without a notable change of heart that reflects God's love is hypocrisy. Gathering like-minded critics around your talk table or platform so that they will echo and applaud your criticism of government-sponsored programs to help the poor and to condemn those who are different from you is not the gospel of our Lord Jesus and does not reveal God's love. Anything done without the love of God profits nothing (see 1 Cor 13:3). People who do not have love in their hearts cannot accept those who are different from them but will always conjure up reasons to justify their condemnation of the guiltless, and such behavior is detestable before God.

ARGUMENTS AGAINST GOVERNMENT-SPONSORED SOCIAL PROGRAMS

Opponents of government-sponsored welfare programs argue about the government's legitimacy in taxing hard-working individuals to give to people who refuse to work. My question to them is, What data do you have to support your claims that people refuse to work when given the opportunity? While some concerns may be legitimate, one may question whether the welfare system is perfect. Of course not! Does it need reform? Chances are that reform may be necessary! Should the government stop the welfare programs for families who need help because the system is imperfect? Definitely not! Such a proposition will cause more harm than good.

Scripturally, the government is an approved social institution by God. It has taxing authority and redistributive power of society's resources, as long as it is done in a nondiscriminatory manner. As it is written, "Let every soul be subject to the governing authorities. For there is no authority except from God, and the authorities that exist are appointed by God. Therefore whoever resist the authority resists the ordinance of God, and those who resist will bring judgment on themselves" (Rom 13:1–2).

Consequentially, resisting government authority based on personal prerogatives rather than godly reasons is resistance against God's approved governing entity, and it is sinful. On the other hand, Christians submitting to government authority established by God to serve his purpose is righteous, except in a situation where one is asked to engage in ungodly behavior. For "we ought to obey God rather than men" (Acts 5:29). Nonetheless, the application of this Scripture is only valid if a government demands Christians to engage in behaviors that sharply contradict God's laws or standards, not because of individual biases or prerogatives.

It is essential to examine the biblical event that prompted similar questions with the Pharisees concerning government legitimacy to tax its citizens. However, in this episode, the Pharisees' motives were evil rather than knowing the truth. So, the Pharisees sent their disciples to ask Jesus this question, "Tell us, therefore, what do You think? Is it lawful to pay taxes to Caesar or not?" (Matt 22:17). Jesus responding to their question, the Scripture says:

> But Jesus perceived their wickedness, and said, "Why do you test Me, you hypocrites? Show Me the tax money." So they brought Him a denarius. And He said to them, "Whose image and inscription is this?" They said to Him, "Caesar's." And He said to them, "Render, therefore to Caesar the things that are Caesar's, and to God, the things that are God's." When they had

heard these words, they marveled, and left Him and went their way. (Matt 22:18–22)

Jesus' response clarifies lingering confusion regarding a governmental authority to impose and collect tax on its citizens. If he approved the Jews paying taxes to a Roman government, which was a foreign government, although a governing authority in Israel at that time, indeed, the US government has the legal power to tax its citizens and residents.

Throughout the Scripture, God has always commanded his people to support the governing authority through their financial contribution. Many Christian Evangelical leaders understand this principle and emphatically impose the concept on their followers; however, some have developed amnesia regarding God's position with the governing authority in our society.

God commanded the children of Israel through Moses to bring offerings, such as gold, silver, bronze, etc., for the building of the tabernacle (see Exod 35:4–9). Likewise, when the temple in Jerusalem was being built, the tribes of Israel gave precious stones, iron, bronze, silver, gold, etc., along with David's generous gifts, to build the temple (see 1 Chr 29:6–9). Furthermore, in Mal 3:8–11, God imposed tithes and offerings on his people to support the governing authority, the church, and feed the poor. In this instance, bringing one's tithes to the governing body was predicated on obedience to God's command that comes with more incredible blessings and protection of one's resources. The demands for tithes are equivalent to taxes that the government levy on all citizens and residents, which the government uses the tax proceeds to build infrastructures, pay its bills and the cost of doing business, and take care of the poor in society. Therefore, taxation is not theft, but the individual who refuses to pay tax is a thief. God asked the children of Israel this question, "Will a man rob God? Yet you have robbed Me! But you say, 'in what way have we robbed You?' In tithes and offerings" (Mal 3:8). Conceptualizing the same scenario in today's social context suggests that refusing to pay your tax or your fair share of the tax is stealing from the government and society. Such behavior is unpatriotic!

REALITY CHECK FOR CHRISTIAN EVANGELICAL LEADERS

Some Christian Evangelical leaders who are quick to speak ills of social programs in such a demeanor as if they have received a revelation from God need to examine their hearts. First, it is important to have a clear understanding of the differences between social programs and socialism.

Social programs do not constitute socialism, as discussed in chapter 1, so it is improper to call social programs socialism. Second, social programs are instituted throughout the Scripture, and you are currently practicing social programs in your church and ministry. Tithes and offerings are examples of social programs instituted by God, and many churchgoers have difficulty justifying why they should give their church the hard-earned money they need for their families. When a pastor is building a new church or adding more buildings to an existing church and he demands his members and outsiders to contribute toward the building, that is also a social program. Even though the pastor may claim that the church belongs to the members, in reality, we know whose name is on the deed. When people are not able to see their own errors except others, that is also hypocrisy. Third, revelation from God is always true and correct. God will not give any person an artificial and exaggerated revelation. The concept of a social program involves rendering a helping hand to those in need. When a pastor asks people to donate to his church or ministry, perhaps, to feed the poor, he is also promoting social programs. In this case, he is taking from those who have to help those who do not have. If the government decides to redirect the money it spends on the poor to those pastors who preach against socialism so that they can feed the poor in their churches, they will not reject such an opportunity. Rather they would shout "Glory be to God" instead of "socialism."

The preaching of partisan politics by Evangelical leaders has brought a sharp divide among Christians. It has minimized the impact of the gospel in saving souls and displaced the transformative power of God's word with partisan politics. A recent survey data revealed a decline in church attendance.[1] The survey indicated that 17 percent of Americans left their denominations because their church incorporated politics in their preaching, and 27 percent were disheartened about scandals with church leaders. Jesus says, "And I, if I am lifted up from the earth, will draw all people to Myself" (John 12:32). However, today's church leaders are lifting politics and themselves up rather than Christ, and the outcome has been people departing from Christ. Politics cannot save humanity because it is susceptible to human ideology, which is induced by classism, racism, and hate, to divide and categorize people.

---

1. Public Religion Research Institute, "Church Attendance," para. 1.

DECEPTIONS OF POLITICAL PREACHING OF SOCIALISM

I watched a television evangelist in September 2021 preach on socialism; it was the most convoluted, manipulated, and ungodly preaching, perhaps, I have ever heard. The irony is that this poli-preacher may have considered himself skilled to invoke scriptures unrelated to his concept of socialism to deceive many, but one thing he forgot is that he cannot deceive God, who knows his heart. It was inconceivable to me that one who was called to preach the gospel of the Lord Jesus would stoop so low and trade his calling to preach the Republican Party's political agenda. It also was uncomfortable listening to his preaching because of his lack of fear of God in manipulating God's word for political purposes. In his preaching on socialism, all the scriptures presented were unrelated to socialism. He could not give a single scripture to support his sermon on socialism because the social programs he deceptively called socialism originated with God. My position is not to attack the preacher, although his misinformation was outrageous. The point is to confront the ungodly spirit behind this type of deception. Presenting the word of God deceptively to align with the Republican Party agenda is as ungodly as the doctrine of Balaam. It is disturbing to see some Christian Evangelical preachers have fallen into this type of political trap, presenting the Republican Party as God's party or a political party approved by God. It is a lie from the pit of hell. The preaching against social programs to help the poor and falsely branding them as socialism is unmistakably a message from the pit of hell, not from God.

A typical behavior of people who engage in deception is to avoid being specific; rather, they will mix unrelated issues, making it hard for an unwitting mind to identify their schemes. The sermon was entitled "Socialism—A Cultural Prophecy." The preaching spiraled from racism to defunding of police, cancel culture, destruction of monuments, greed, selfishness, lust, violence, great stress and trouble, power control, one-world system of government, evil, the mark of the beast, anti-Christ, Noah's ark, and the return of Jesus to do away with socialism and Marxism. Any logical-thinking individual understands that all those terms and concepts do not have a direct correlation with socialism. However, to achieve his political agenda, this poli-preacher interjected all those unrelated concepts to generate a substantial fear of socialism. He did not provide any evidence or an explanation of how the concepts are directly connected to socialism.

Furthermore, this political preacher, in his overzealousness to disparage social programs for the poor, made statements that are exaggerated and incomprehensibly deceiving. For example, he suggested that socialism is tailor-made for the antichrist's appearance. He did not explain how socialism is tailor-made for the antichrist's appearance. However, the Scripture states otherwise about the type of economic system with the appearance of the antichrist. Revelation 13:17 says, "And no one may buy or sell except one who has the mark or the name of the beast, or the number of his name." This Scripture describes capitalism, not socialism. When individuals engage in an economic endeavor of buying and selling goods and services, it represents capitalism, not socialism. The Scripture did not say that no one would receive free gifts from the government without the mark of the beast, but rather, "no one may buy or sell."

After the preaching of socialism by this political preacher, I decided not to listen to his message again. It is ungodly for a preacher to label social programs for the poor and needy socialism and then paint a picture to link salvation to his anti-social programs rhetoric. Meanwhile, he justifies the social programs he receives in his parsonage and churches and condemns the one for the poor and needy. Based on his preaching, he must not be a believer in the Lord Jesus. Typical behavior of hypocrites, that is, to condemn others for the same thing they are doing.

Finally, this political preacher labeled socialism evil because Karl Marx, who promoted the concept of socialism, was anti-God. Because Karl Marx was anti-God does not necessarily mean that socialism is evil. Social programs you call socialism did not originate with Karl Marx; they originated with God. Moreover, there are a lot of inventions and discoveries made by atheists that have been beneficial to humanity. For example, Thomas Edison was one of the most profound inventors in human history. His inventions include the incandescent light bulb, electric power generation, motion picture camera, sound recording, and phonograph.[2] But he was an atheist, and because he was an atheist, should we condemn his inventions? Of course, not! We all have benefited from his inventions, and he made the following statements in expression of his disbelieve in the existence of God:

> I have never seen the slightest scientific proof of the religious ideas of heaven and hell, of future life for individuals, or of a personal God . . . So far as religion of the day is concerned, it is a damned fake . . . Religion is all bunk. . . I cannot believe in the immortality of the soul . . . I am an aggregate of cells, as, for instance, New York City is an aggregate of individuals. Will New York City go to heaven? . . . No; nature made us—nature did it all—not the gods of the religions.[3]

2. Christina, "Eight Secular Scientists," para. 10.
3. Christina, "Eight Secular Scientists," para. 5.

Another atheist includes Alan Turing, who was the founder of computer science and artificial intelligence.[4] The ability to send text messages and emails, surf the internet, do online banking, etc., was a result of his discoveries.

God does not discriminate in his blessings and gifts to the just and unjust. Matthew 5:45 says, "That you may be sons of your Father in heaven; for He makes His sun rise on the evil and on the good, and sends rain on the just and on the unjust." It is a mystery of God, and we have to respect God's indiscriminate disposition of his goodness and not condemn it.

EMBRACING THE TRUTH OF GOD'S WORD

Embracing the truth of God's word and objective facts will enable preachers to constructively disseminate the word of God to bear good fruit that will change lives for the better and avoid potential long-lasting disruptive effects of misinformation. The Scripture says, "My people are destroyed for lack of knowledge. Because you have rejected knowledge, I also will reject you from being priest for Me; because you have forgotten the law of your God, I also will forget your children" (Hos 4:6). The rejection of the knowledge of the word of God leads to destruction, which is not a godly position to embrace.

SCRIPTURES WITH GOD'S COMMANDMENT TO HELP THE POOR

Below is a list of scriptures not cited in this chapter with God's command to help the poor. Interestingly, there are no scriptures that state we should not have a program to help the poor because the poor will always be among us.

1. Leviticus 19:10: "And you shall not glean your vineyard, nor shall you gather every grape of your vineyard; you shall leave them for the poor and the stranger: I am the LORD your God."

2. Leviticus 25:35: "And if one of your brethren becomes poor, and falls into poverty among you, then you shall help him, like a stranger or a sojourner, that he may live with you."

3. Deuteronomy 24:14–15: "You shall not oppress a hired servant who is poor and needy, whether one of your brethren or one of the aliens who is in your land within your gates. Each day you shall give him his wages, and not let the sun go down on it, for he is poor and has set his

---

4. Christina, "Eight Secular Scientists," para. 2.

heart on it; lest he cry out against you to the Lord, and it will be sin to you."

4. Deuteronomy 24:19–22: "When you reap your harvest in your field, and forget a sheaf in the field, you shall not go back to get it; it shall be for the stranger, the fatherless, and the widow, that the Lord your God may bless you in all the work of your hands. When you beat your olive trees, you shall not go over the boughs again; it shall be for the stranger, the fatherless, and the widow. When you gather the grapes of your vineyard, you shall not glean it afterward; it shall be for the stranger, the fatherless, and the widow. And you shall remember that you were a slave in the land of Egypt; therefore I command you to do this thing."

5. Deuteronomy 26:12: "When you have finished laying aside all the tithes of your increase in the third year—the year of tithing—and have given it to the Levite, the stranger, the fatherless, and the widow, so that they may eat within your gates and be filled."

6. 1 Samuel 2:7: "The Lord makes poor and makes rich; He brings low and lifts up.

7. Psalm 9:18: "For the needy shall not always be forgotten; the expectation of the poor shall not perish forever."

8. Psalm 41:1: "Blessed is he who considers the poor; the Lord will deliver him in time of trouble."

9. Proverbs 14:21: "He who despises his neighbor sins; but he who has mercy on the poor, happy is he."

10. Proverbs 22:19: "He who has a bountiful eye will be blessed, for he gives of his bread to the poor."

11. Proverbs 22:22–23: "Do not rob the poor because he is poor, nor oppress the afflicted at the gate; for the Lord will plead their cause, and plunder the soul of those who plunder them."

12. Isaiah 61:1: "The Spirit of the Lord God is upon Me, because the Lord has anointed Me to preach good tidings to the poor, He has sent Me to heal the brokenhearted, to proclaim liberty to the captives, and the opening of the prison to those who are bound."

13. Zechariah 7:10: "Do not oppress the widow or the fatherless, the alien or the poor. Let none of you plan evil in his heart against his brother."

14. Luke 14:12–14: "Then He [Jesus] also said to him who invited Him, 'When you give a dinner or a supper, do not ask your friends, your

brothers, your relatives, nor your rich neighbors, lest they also invite you back, and you be repaid. But when you give a feast, invite the poor, the maimed, the lame, the blind. And you will be blessed, because they cannot repay you; for you shall be repaid at the resurrection of the just.'"

15. Galatians 2:10: "They [apostles] desired only that we should remember the poor, the very thing which I also was eager to do."

16. Ephesians 4:28: "Let him who stole steal no longer, but rather let him labor, working with his hands what is good, that he may have something to give him who has need."

17. Hebrew 13:16: "But do not forget to do good and share, for God is well pleased with such sacrifices."

18. James 1:27: "Pure and undefiled religion before God and the Father is this: to visit orphans and widows in their trouble."

19. James 2:14–17: "What does it profit, my brethren, if someone says he has faith but does not have works? Can faith save him? If a brother or sister is naked and destitute of daily food, and one of you says to them, 'Depart in peace, be warmed and filled,' but you do not give them the things which are needed for the body, what does it profit? Thus also faith by itself, if it does not have works, is dead."

20. First John 3:17: "But whoever has this world's goods, and sees his brother in need, and shuts up his heart from him, how does the love of God abide in him?"

SUMMARY

As presented in this chapter and chapter 1, there are vast numbers of the scriptures that unequivocally reveal God's heart toward the poor. As the Scripture says, "But without faith it is impossible to please Him" (Heb 11:6). I believe that without concerted efforts to help the poor, it is also impossible to please God. The rich young ruler who claimed to have kept all the commandments from his youth quickly was astonished by Jesus' response to his question, "If you want to be perfect, go, sell what you have and give to the poor, and you will have treasure in heaven; and come, and follow Me" (Matt 19:21). One may ask, Why give to the poor instead of the rich? Well, giving to the poor who cannot pay you back reveals your heart condition toward God. If you walk in the Spirit, you will understand this revelation. Even keeping the commandments could not make the rich young ruler perfect before God without cultivating sacrificial love in his heart toward the poor, having faith in God, not in his wealth, and following Jesus. Engaging in political maneuvers to denigrate and block programs to help the poor is an unwise position with God. The Scripture says, "Whoever shuts his ears to the cry of the poor will also cry himself and not be heard" (Prov 21:13).

While some churches, ministries, and organizations have done outstanding jobs in helping the needy, especially during the pandemic crisis, both here at home and abroad, others have converted their ministry to political platforms to disparage social programs that were designed to help the poor as ungodly with the shout of socialism. Some of them do not have a clear understanding of the concept of socialism or cannot differentiate socialism from social programs; however, socialism sounds evil enough to use to poison the minds of their followers, even though some of their followers depend on government-sponsored programs to alleviate their family's financial stress. Voters need to ask themselves these questions: What kind of loyalty do I get in return from a political party I pledged my support to? What actions have the leaders taken for my well-being and my family? How does the political party I support protect my financial interest? Just because Democrats initiated programs to help struggling families, which is consistent with biblical values, is not a valid reason to slander such programs as socialism. On the contrary, such action promulgates division in our society, which is ungodly.

Chapter 3

Abortion—A Political Punch Bag

Abortion is the most pervasive topic for some Evangelical preachers to use and demonize anyone who votes for Democrats. Although, from a realistic and moral standpoint, abortion is not a pro-choice issue; it is an ungodly practice. However, the notion that one is anti-abortion, which everyone in their appropriate state of mind should be, makes them a godly person is hilarious. Note: I chose to use "anti-abortion" rather than "pro-life" because both connote different meanings, which have often been overlooked. The differences in meaning are explained in this chapter. Just because one opposes abortion does not make him righteous, godly, or even less a sinner than the person who supports abortion. In addition, anti-abortion is not God's benchmark or blueprint for salvation and does not prove that one is a Christian or saved, as some Christian Evangelical preachers purport.

Moreover, not every Republican is against abortion; for example, these three Republican senators identified themselves as pro-choice, Shelley Moore Capito, Susan Collins, and Lisa Murkowski, and have voted for pro-choice legislation. Likewise, not every Democrat is pro-abortion; for example, Senators Bob Casey and Joe Manchin and Rep. Tulsi Gabbard even introduced two pro-life bills in the US House of Representatives in December 2020. Even the former president, Donald Trump, has not always taken a decisive position against abortion. Still, since it is a topic that is politically expedient for him, he gave the impression that he opposes abortion. In his 1999 interview with Tim Russert of *Meet the Press*, he said, "I just believe in choice . . . I am very pro-choice, and yet I hate the concept of abortion."[1] During the interview, Mr. Russert also asked Mr. Trump if he would ban

---

1. Russert, "I Am Very Pro-Life," 0:43–1:23.

partial-birth abortion, and Mr. Trump responded: "No. I am pro-choice in every respect and as far as it goes, but I just hate it." When it comes to abortion, you cannot be halfhearted about it; you are either pro-choice or anti-abortion, and there is no in-between. In addition, on May 15, 2023, Mr. Trump suggested that the governor of Florida DeSantis's six-week ban on abortion, is "too harsh," but at the same time, he refused to clearly state his stance on abortion.[2]

Furthermore, tens of millions of Democrats oppose abortion, and tens of millions of Republicans are pro-choice. According to a poll on values and beliefs between 2018 and 2020, 24 percent of Democrats identified themselves as pro-life, while 29 percent of Republicans identified themselves as pro-choice.[3] So, for those who are driven by partisan politics, how do you ratify such conflict that a significant number of Republicans are pro-choice, including their lawmakers, and a substantial number of Democrats are anti-abortion? Thus, for the conservatives who cannot see themselves voting for a Democrat because of their self-righteous demeanor about abortion, how do you justify yourself voting for a Republican who supports abortion instead of a Democrat who is against abortion? The same question goes for a Democrat who would not vote for a Republican because of their beliefs about abortion. While abortion is morally wrong, its politicization for political gains is equally morally wrong.

I watched a Christian program on January 25, 2021, and the wife of the network's owner made a shocking statement that infers the blood of aborted children is on someone's head if they vote for Democrats. I said to myself, "Wow, what a hypocrite!" In essence, she has failed to realize that out of her mouth, she has just condemned herself. Your sanctimonious or holier-than-thou attitude will not justify you before God. In a different scenario, another hypocrite made a similar comment in an outraged and hateful voice suggesting that people who vote for Democrats are bringing a curse upon themselves and their families and even a thousand generations. So, these hypocrites, out of their mouths, have condemned those who voted for Democrats as murderers of unborn babies. In contrast, unbeknownst to them, they have also condemned themselves as murderers of those who have been born but look different from them. Jesus says, "For by your words you will be justified, and by your words, you will be condemned" (Matt 12:37). Jesus also says:

> Judge not, that you be not judged. For with what judgment you judge, you will be judged: and with the measure you use, it will

2. Dorn, "Trump Avoids Definitive Stance," para. 1.
3. Gallup, "Pro-Choice or Pro-Life," para. 1.

be measured back to you. And why do you look at the speck in your brother's eye, but do not consider the plank in your own eye? (Matt 7:1–3)

However, hypocrites in their convoluted minds deceive themselves into believing that as long as they are using their anti-abortion rhetoric to condemn others and promote their political agenda, that makes them appear righteous. All sins are abominations before God. Also, the act of justifying yourself while condemning others is sinful before God. Jesus spoke of a parable concerning a Pharisee and a tax collector who went to the temple to pray:

> Two men went up to the temple to pray, one a Pharisee and the other a tax collector. The Pharisee stood and prayed thus with himself, "God, I thank You that I am not like other men—extortioners, unjust, adulterers, or even as this tax collector. I fast twice a week: I give tithes of all that I possess." And the tax collector, standing afar off, would not so much as raise his eyes to heaven but beat his breast, saying, "God, be merciful to me a sinner!" I tell you, this man went down to his house justified rather than the other, for everyone who exalts himself will be humbled, and he who humbles himself will be exalted. (Luke 18:10–14)

The two individuals above who condemned those who voted for Democrats and the biblical event illustrated by Jesus demonstrate a typical behavioral pattern among the Pharisees by creating a false sense of righteousness for themselves by condemning others. Interestingly, while some Christian Evangelical leaders are demonizing people who vote for Democrats, many of their church members have committed abortion and presently seek abortions. For example, research shows that in 2014, 13 percent of women whose religious affiliation was Evangelical Protestant sought abortions, 17 percent who sought abortion identified themselves as mainline Protestant, and 24 percent were Roman Catholic.[4]

REPUBLICAN PARTY ASSOCIATION WITH HATE GROUPS

The Republican Party has provided a platform for hate groups to express their innate racism. Some of them carry the Bible in their hands while justifying their racist views against other racial groups. Many church leaders have been silent and pretended to be unaware of systemic racism in the

---

4. Jerman et al., "Characteristics of U.S. Abortion," para. 6.

United States. However, their silence and passivity reflect their consent to the continuous function of systemic racism and murderous rampages of some racist White police officers against ethnic minority groups. They share a political platform with White supremacists and other hate groups. They even cast their vote and encouraged others to vote for a presidential candidate who refused to denounce these hate groups. Lest they forget the biblical position about hate, which says, "Whoever hates his brother is a murderer, and you know that no murderer has eternal life abiding in him" (1 John 3:15). Even though this is not a physical murder, it is a murderous act committed in a person's heart. The magnitude of this type of murder is not any less than abortion before God. For out of the heart proceeds every sin, including hate and murder (see Matt 15:19). Therefore, the support of a political party that houses racist groups and the silence about systemic racism in the United States is equally an abominable sin before God as abortion. The question then is, How can God endorse a political party that provides a platform for hate groups to express their hatred against God's creation? God cannot approve of such a party because he cannot contradict his word; neither will he endorse a political party that violates the core biblical principles as presented in every chapter of this book. Notably, those Christian Evangelical leaders who coerced their followers to vote for the Republicans cannot see the wickedness within the Republican Party because their behaviors are hypocritical. Hypocrites do not see their own sins but will climb to the mountaintop to shout loudly about other people's sins while masking theirs. Hypocrisy is not a Christ-like spirit but a deceptive spirit.

God is not a racist. He struck Miriam, the sister of Moses, with leprosy for opposing Moses's marriage to an African Black woman, an Ethiopian (see Num 12:1–15). One who hates does not have the Spirit of God in him but is born of the devil. First John 4:8 says, "He who does not love does not know God, for God is love." The Scripture also says that Satan is a liar, hater, and murderer (see John 8:44). One of the ways Satan carries out his evil acts is by using his children to hate and murder the creation that God loves. Those who know the truth but decline to call racism evil are no different from racist groups. James 4:17 says, "Therefore, to him who knows to do good and does not do it, to him it is sin." So, if the one who supports a political party that approves abortion is a murderer, in the same sense, the one who supports a party that houses hate groups is also a murderer. Therefore, both acts of murder are of exact equivalence of sin before God.

ANTI-ABORTION DOES NOT MEAN PRO-LIFE

It is hypocritical to claim you care for the life of the unborn when the same passion is not extended to the life of those who have already been out of their mother's womb but look different or are of a different social class. First John 4:20 says, "If someone says, 'I love God,' and hates his brother, he is a liar; for he who does not love his brother whom he has seen, how can he love God whom he has not seen?" If this biblical verse were to be translated to our contemporary society relative to abortion it would go in this manner: "If you are truly pro-life, the same passion you claim to have for the unborn babies whom you have not seen must be given to the lives of those you have seen, though they may be of a different look or social class from you." In reality, some people who claim to be pro-life are not pro-life, but only use pro-life rhetoric to advance their political agenda. To others, claiming to be pro-life serves as the most reasonable means for them to present themselves as godly and again advance their political jargon deceptively. Abortion is not a typical topic an average preacher will preach on a Sunday morning; the issue mostly comes up only when a preacher wants to coerce his followers to vote for Republican candidates and demonize Democratic candidates. The false emotional claims toward the life of the unborn, which are not extended to the life of those who are already born but of different races, classes, or moral states, are nothing short of counterfeit emotions toward human lives.

Often people who use abortion to defame others for voting for a Democrat will make a comment like, "I just can't vote for someone who supports the killing of the unborn." They make such a comment with a false sense of justification in their demeanor. Nevertheless, they vote for a party that colludes with hate groups and disenfranchises marginalized groups, which is also murder. While it is not godly to support the killing of the unborn, it is equally ungodly to support a political party that condones hate groups; for they are also murderers of those who are out of their mother's womb. Both murders are ranked the same before God.

However, as the Scripture says, our righteousness is unclean before God (Isa 64:6). Thus, you are not justified before God because you oppose abortion while you remain silent or concede to racist groups that dominate the Republican Party. All souls are mine, says the Lord (see Ezek 18:4). They are all equal in his eyes. Differential treatments based on race and social class are ungodly practices often tolerated by the Republican Party. Something is fundamentally wrong with a political party that its membership does not reflect the diversity of the population of our society or Christianity.

Vignette

In its true meaning, the concept of pro-life is not limited to the life of the unborn; it should encompass the protection and value of life at all stages. The sanctity of life should be extended to all human lives with the same levels of passion regardless of race, social class, gender, national origin, age, or moral state. It should encompass equal justice, love, care, and opportunities for all humans beings regardless of physical attributes. However, these are not the political priorities of the Republican Party, the so-called though misconstrued God's party. It is a political party of status quo and self-proclaimed righteous individuals.

It is disingenuous to use abortion to engage in political exploitation and psychological tactics to demoralize or subject one to a sense of guilt for voting for a Democrat as a support for the killing of unborn babies. Some Christian Evangelical leaders often exacerbate this type of political manipulation to vilify those who did not vote for Republican candidates. For example, I watched an interview on a CBN program in which a Black woman explained why she stopped voting for Democrats after she realized through the preaching of an Evangelical preacher that her vote for Democrats suggested her support for the killing of unborn babies. This type of induced false consciousness is very dangerous because she has unconsciously pledged her support to the very group that cares less about her, her unborn child, and her children outside her womb.

There is no demonstrated evidence to suggest that the Republican Party's anti-abortion position genuinely reflects care for lives that are different from theirs. Consider the reckless gun laws passed by Republican governors and legislators that contribute to between 38,000 and 45,222 firearm-related deaths yearly. When was the last time a Republican President's tax reform was designed to help the working class, except for the rich? When was the last time the Republican Congress initiated programs that genuinely elevated people from poverty? Therefore, I have a question for some Christian Evangelical leaders: How is the Republican Party God's party or a party whose agendas are endorsed by God? Is it because their leaders support programs designed to help the poor without decrying socialism? Is it because their leaders oppose the deportation of adults who grew up in the US because their parents brought them into the country illegally when they were young? Is it because they support universal background checks for gun purchases without falsely claiming an infringement of Second Amendment rights? Is it because they publicly condemn a police officer for killing an unarmed Black man who was not a threat to the officer and support policy reforms that will hold the police accountable? Is it because they publicly condemn hate groups that have infiltrated the Republican Party and denounce associations with them? Is it because they oppose a system of dominance and inequality perpetuated by the majority group in our society? Is it because they denounce the status quo and support equitable justice in our society? Is it because they oppose placing greater value on material assets over human lives? Is it because they oppose a stratification system that ranks members of society by class, race, gender, national origin, etc.? You see, the position of the leaders of the Republican Party on the above-mentioned social issues does not reflect God's value, not one. Therefore, how can anyone logically conclude that the Republican Party is God's party or endorsed by God based on biblical principles?

There is no such thing as an innocent bystander. You are guilty of murder, hate (which is also murder), and racism because you share the same political platform with racist groups and have not made conscientious and consistent efforts to condemn these racist groups publicly. Some have secretly conceived in their hearts the false ideology of White supremacy and have ascribed superiority to the White category to justify the dehumanization of other racial groups. Your silence is not only an endorsement of racism but a confirmation of your heart conditions.

ABORTION RATES IN THE UNITED STATES

Christian Evangelicals and Republicans' abortion rhetoric lacks synonymous effects in reducing abortion rates in the United States. Statistically, abortion rates in the United States have not been lower with a Republican president than a Democratic president, even when the Republican Party controls both houses of the legislative branch. After the landmark decision of the US Supreme Court in the Roe v. Wade case in 1973, which legalized abortion in the US, the total number of abortions increased significantly, topping the highest level at 1,429,577 in 1990 under Republican president George H. W. Bush. Then the total number of abortions began to decrease steadily, except in 1996, 2002, 2006, and 2018.[5] Three of the four times the total number of abortions increased from the previous year involved two Republican presidents. For example, in 2006, Republican George W. Bush was the president of the United States, and the Republican Party controlled both houses of Congress. Even though the Republican Party was in control of the executive branch, both houses of the legislative branch from 2003 to 2007, and with the majority of conservative-appointed Supreme Court

---

5. Herndon et al., "Abortion Surveillance," 4.

Justices, Roe v. Wade was not overturned, neither was there any drastic reduction in the total number of abortions. Instead, there was an uptick in the total number of abortions in 2006.

However, in 2017, the total number of abortions dropped, which was short-lived because there was an increase in the total number of abortions in the United States by 1 percent from 2017 to 2018.[6] During this time, the sitting president was a Republican, Donald Trump, and the Senate and House of Representatives were controlled by the Republican Party. These results suggest that the abortion rhetoric often promoted by some Christian Evangelicals and Republicans is irrelevant and has zero effect on the total number of abortions in the United States. According to CDC abortion records, the first time the total number of abortions in the United States was under one million (884,273) per year was in 1998, from the previous year of 1,186,039.[7] The sitting president in 1998 was a Democrat, Bill Clinton, although the Republican Party controlled both houses of the legislative branch during that year. In 2012, the abortion rate was lower than the 1973 abortion rate, and the largest decrease in the total number of abortions took place in 2013, under the presidency of Barack Obama, a Democrat. So, a decrease in the total number of abortions and abortion rates in the United States is more likely to happen under a Democratic president than a Republican president. Although, the decrease does not suggest direct influence from a Democratic president or any political party. However, almost half a century later, on June 24, 2022, the US Supreme Court overturned Roe v. Wade, ending abortion rights in the US. It will be interesting to see the future effects of Roe v. Wade being overturned on abortion rates in the US.

REASONS FOR ABORTION

There are several reasons a woman may choose to abort her unborn child, such as poverty, unplanned pregnancy, rape, health-related issues, etc. These reasons are by no means to undermine the gravity of abortion or to justify abortion but to highlight the complexities surrounding the decision-making trajectories with abortion. For example, studies revealed that a woman's financial state plays a significant role in her motivation to abort her unborn child. According to the Guttmacher Institute, a research organization on good reproductive health and policy, 75 percent of women who sought abortion had income below the federal poverty line.[8] In another

6. Kortsmit et al., "Abortion Surveillance," 2.
7. Herndon et al., "Abortion Surveillance," 4.
8. Jerman et al., "Characteristics of U.S. Abortion," 9.

study, financial difficulty (40 percent) was noted as the major reason for a woman to terminate her pregnancy.[9] These results suggest that a practical approach to combating abortion should include creating programs that will lift people out of poverty. However, any federal government efforts to create such programs will be sharply confronted by the same group that claims to be pro-life. They will demonize such efforts with the shouting of "socialism" and "overreach hand of big government." The Christian Evangelical leaders and the Republican Party's ambiguous positions about the sanctity of human life are classic examples of hypocrisy!

Poverty is a structural problem embedded in our social institutions. While we claim to subscribe to an open stratification system, opportunities have not been allocated equitably to all racial groups. Systemic racism still dominates and disproportionately affects some groups to a greater degree than others. A woman from a marginalized group may not have the same level of joy in raising a child in a society that is historically oppressive toward her group as you would find a woman from the majority group. No wonder women from minority groups are more likely to seek abortion than women from the majority.[10] Again, this is not to suggest that poverty and systemic racism justify abortion; however, they are social realities that cannot be ignored if we are truly pro-life. Poverty plays a role in abortion, and race influences a person's chances of upward mobility in the United States. Thus, systemic racism can reduce the quality of family life and cause an unbearable burden to a mother, even increasing the likelihood of committing an abortion or killing their child outside the womb. Imagine the degree of distress that will cause a mother to kill her beloved daughter because of racial injustice. In 1856, Margaret Garner, a slave woman, escaped from her slave master with her husband and four children. Before she was captured to be returned to the slave master, she slaughtered her youngest daughter with a butcher knife and made an unsuccessful attempt to kill the other three.[11] To Garner, it was better for her children to be dead than to suffer as slaves. The horrifying experience of Margaret Garner depicts the inhumanity of slavery, and the same inhuman behavior is still perpetuated differently today in the form of abortion and systemic racism.

9. Biggs et al., "Why Women Seek Abortion," 9.
10. Cohen, "Abortion and Women of Color," para. 1.
11. Carroll, "Margaret Garner," para. 2.

HISTORICAL PATTERNS OF DEHUMANIZATION IN THE UNITED STATES

The practice of today's abortion may have its connection to the United States' history. Abortion is a form of dehumanization, just like the slavery of Blacks and Native American genocide, and they formed the historical foundation of the disenfranchisement of certain cohorts of the US population. Thus, the practice of abortion may have been inexplicably intertwined with the dehumanization of Blacks during slavery and other forms of racial injustice in our society. As the unborn babies were dehumanized, so were the Blacks and Native Americans dehumanized. To advocate for the life of unborn babies without advocating for the lives of the marginalized groups in our society is incompatible with the concept of the pro-life crusade. The sanctity of life must be respected at all stages of life; otherwise, it is nothing short of hypocrisy or political rhetoric. Both aisles of the political spectrum have blood on their hands in one way or another. Any effort that will yield positive outcomes in reducing abortion rates in America will need to be affirmatively linked to concerted efforts to stop dehumanizing minority groups, respect for all human lives, and a push for equitable justice for all. The way to begin to reverse the killing of the unborn in America is by repenting, correcting, and stopping the dehumanization of members of minority groups. The act of dehumanizing and disenfranchising some members of our society is intertwined with reckless laws on abortion and firearms, and such behavior is ungodly and needs to stop. So many drops of innocent blood have been poured into this land. No political party wins when we marginalize and dehumanize others, either through abortion, careless gun laws, or social injustice. However, we all win and benefit when we treat all groups, including those inside their mothers' wombs and those outside their mothers' wombs, equally and ascribe the same degree of sanctity of life.

ERRONEOUS ASSOCIATION OF ABORTION TO WORSHIP OF MOLECH

While speaking against ungodly behavior such as abortion is essential, it is equally important to present the message in love and truth. It is the goodness of God that leads people to repentance (see Rom 2:4). Additionally, it is the Holy Spirit that convicts and draws people to repentance (see John 16:8). The job of Christians is to engage in the ministry of reconciliation (2 Cor 5:18), not the ministry of condemnation. The practice of the ministry of condemnation will inadvertently lead to sabotaging the purpose of the gospel of our Lord Jesus. When ministers of the gospel intentionally and overzealously misrepresent the word of God or misalign the truth for political purposes, they are as guilty as the one who commits abortion, the very individual they are trying to condemn. Some Christian Evangelicals have consciously concocted words and phrases to defame those who support Democrats as support to the worship of Molech, an ancient god.

Equating abortion to the worship of Molech is a flawed assertion or argument. Let us examine what the Scripture says, "And you shall not let any of your descendants pass through the fire to Molech, nor shall you profane the name of your God: I am the Lord" (Lev 18:21). Molech is an ancient deity of the Canaanites, Ammonites, and perhaps other surrounding nations to Israel. Two distinguishing factors separate how Molech is presented in the Bible compared to how some Christian Evangelicals present Molech for political gains. First, in several other scriptures where Molech was mentioned, they mostly refer to the sacrifice of children to a pagan god. The sacrifice may take place by passing through the fire or any other form to fulfill the sacrificial demands of their god, Molech. Women who seek abortion do not do so to sacrifice their unborn children to a deity but rather for some other reasons, such as financial difficulty, health issues, etc. Second, the sacrifice to a Molech involves children out of their mother's wombs, while abortion involves babies still in their mothers' wombs. Although both acts are grave sins and abominations before God, they are carried out for different reasons. If you claim that abortion is the worship of Molech, in the same manner, the assertion should be applied to the unjustified killing of Blacks by police officers, slavery, systemic racism, and reckless gun laws that kill tens of thousands of Americans every year as worship of Molech. The root of all these behaviors is hate, which the Scripture describes as murder (see 1 John 3:15). Moreover, all these hate groups' political affiliation is the Republican Party, supposedly God's party. But the Scripture says, "He who does not love does not know God, for God is love" (1 John 4:8). The position of Christians should always involve presenting the truth regardless of political affiliation rather than exaggerating or demonizing people for political purposes.

PERSONAL ANALYSIS OF EACH POLITICAL PARTY'S APPROACH TO ABORTION

Having examined both the Democratic Party and the Republican Party's position about abortion, I have come to the following conclusion. One group says that no matter how much it will cost you, do not let the "fetus" come out of your womb even if it has reached the fetal viability stage because it is not a human being. We will give you the financial support and all the help you need to abort the fetus if it is an inconvenience to you because it is your right to do so. But once you let that fetus come out as a human baby, no matter what he does, you cannot touch him, and you cannot even hurt his feelings for the sake of correcting or disciplining him. You should respect whatever decision he makes, even at the infant stage, because that is his right. Then the other party says, Oh no, that fetus is a human being and precious; you cannot abort it. We will fight and create laws to protect that fetus while in your womb. But if it makes a mistake and comes out wrong race or social class, we have several ways to frustrate and kill him for you. First, we will isolate him and marginalize him to the point he will wish he was never born. Second, we will ensure that he does not get the same opportunities as others, and we will stereotype, stigmatize, and blame him for not being successful. Third, if he dares to cross paths with a police officer, we will support the officer for killing him and even protect the officer from being held accountable. Although each political party will deny that the above statements represent their views about human life, their actions speak louder than their voice. If they engage in a more critical thought process, that is, removing their blindness and looking inside as an outsider, they will get a better picture of their short-sightedness. In a woman's womb, the fetus is a human being in its developing stages and created in God's image. Those outside their mother's womb with different physical attributes are also human beings created in God's image. They are all equal before God, and Jesus died to save every one of them. Know that God created one human race equally in his sight; it is the man who made racism and classism.

Vignette

Both the Democratic Party and Republican Party engage in some form of dehumanization of life at different stages based on hierarchical rankings. Those with greater power in society impose their will on others and justify their actions with flimsy excuses. However, none of their approaches represent the sanctity of life nor biblical values for human life because partisan politics are man-made systems with many frailties.

SUMMARY

Being antiabortionist does not represent or grant salvation nor suggest righteousness with God. On the other hand, the practice of abortion is reckless and unrighteous, and it is as reckless and murderous as some of the Republicans, GOP lawmakers, and entire hate groups who are anti-abortionists but engaged in hateful behaviors against God's creation because of their physical traits. Therefore, voting for the Republican Party will never make anyone righteous, justify someone before God, pave the way for salvation, or grant eternal life to anyone. So, what is the purpose of the heightened deceptions from Christian Evangelical leaders in presenting the Republican Party as a party approved by God when its practices and policies contradict biblical teachings? It simply indicates a lack of fear of God, and the practice of Balaam's doctrine, which includes working for money and self-benefit rather than God.

Furthermore, one may ask, does it mean that Christians should not vote since whichever political party one supports, he or she becomes a murderer by association? As American citizens, our civic duty is to select our leaders through our representative democracy. Therefore, we need to exercise our constitutional right by participating in the democratic process of selecting our leaders. However, it is deceptive to foster a belief that the only godly vote is to vote for the Republican Party. The people who create such false beliefs are false teachers. So, yes, Christians can vote for Democrats or Republicans, and it will not affect their Christianity or have adverse effects on their relationship with God.

Additionally, both political parties are worldly entities, and God did not create them. Neither party is perfect nor solely represents biblical standards or God's views. However, quantifying both parties' structural and functional policies shows that Democrats have more policies that reflect biblical principles than Republicans. This may sound shocking to some; however, I have carefully documented each party's position concerning social and political policies in this book. Reading the Gospels (Matthew, Mark, Luke, and John) reveals that the practices of the Republicans and some of the Christian Evangelical leaders reflect the exact traditions of the Pharisees that Jesus condemned. They have the laws, and they are divisive, self-righteous, and quick to condemn those who are different without expressing God's love for sinners that Jesus gave his life to save. Jesus came to save sinners, not self-righteous individuals (see Luke 5:32). If you listen to conservative radio or TV talk shows, divisive messages dominate the program, as well as distortion of facts and God's word. It is not the message of the cross nor the expression of God's love.

One may ask, Does this mean that Christians should not take a righteous position to condemn ungodly behaviors in our country? By all means, they should! Godly leaders have the mandate to confront and condemn ungodly practices in truth and love. They should confront behaviors that are incongruent with biblical principles, not based on political affiliation. They should be unbiased and take a neutral position in confronting ungodly practices from both parties. In the same manner and frequency, abortion is condemned; racism must also be condemned. Taking a political position to condemn one party while exonerating or concealing the ungodliness of another is deceptive; it does not reflect the Spirit of Christ, which is the Spirit of truth.

Thus, it is essential to vote for a candidate who has integrity and represents your views, biblical values, and issues of concern. But on the other hand, avoid voting for a candidate who lacks integrity because you are promoting fraud and dishonesty. Do not vote for a party; vote for individual candidates. Because God does not belong to any political party, and neither does he endorse any party. This view is not to suggest undermining the providence of God in the US elections, especially in presidential elections. Sometimes, his providence prevails for a particular candidate to win an election for a season and for a purpose, especially in the presidential election. This notion also underscores the significance of voting for a candidate as God leads you rather than a political party. However, when you start judging others for casting their votes for candidates because of political affiliation, you have opened the door for the same judgment upon yourself because both parties embrace practices that do not coincide with biblical teachings. Also, when you start politicizing and promoting one party while demonizing the other, you have inadvertently opened the door for judgment by association.

Lastly, it is an affront to God's faithfulness and sovereignty to think that the Republican Party gives Christians the right to worship, preach the gospel, and serve God in the United States. For those who hold such views, my question to you is, To what extent are you willing to compromise your faith by transferring God's sovereignty to your political party? In reality, the Republican Party cannot give the church the right to preach the gospel; neither will radical liberals stop Christians from declaring biblical truths. If you seek first the kingdom of God and his righteousness (not your political party), he will take care of the rest for you (see Matt 6:33). Moreover, Jesus says, "On this rock I will build My church, and the gates of Hades shall not prevail against it" (Matt 16:18b). The head of the church promises protection over his bride; therefore, the bride's alliance and trust must be in him alone, not with a political party. If the bride (the church) will do what the Groom has commanded her to do, he is faithful to fulfill his promises. Furthermore, religious liberty is a constitutional right in the United States, and it is a gift from God. However, collusion with a worldly political party to subvert persecution makes the church look like the church of Sardis (see Rev 3:1–6). Jesus described the Sardis church as dead, and their works were not perfect before God. Unlike other churches, the Sardis church was not prosecuted because they were more like the culture of their society. When the bride forsook protection from the groom and sought protection from an imposter, that is adultery, just like the Israelites did with God. If the church conforms to the cultural orientations of the society to avoid persecution, it makes her a dead church. That explains why miracles and breakthroughs are no longer a desired theme of the churches today. However, the etiology of miracles, deliverance, and breakthroughs are in persecutions, in which Christ is glorified.

Chapter 4

Social Justice

Social justice is a divisive concept in our society, primarily due to the influence of political affiliations. Thus, the interpretation of social justice has taken on different meanings depending on the political lens one uses. However, if the influence of partisan politics is excluded from the interpretation process, and a more critical approach is taken, especially from the biblical and constitutional perspectives, a clearer pathway is possible for higher levels of consensus on the meaning and significance of social justice. Democrats and Republicans have opposing views on important social, political, and economic issues. This chapter examines the differences between the two political parties in disseminating social justice in social situations relative to biblical standards.

WHAT IS SOCIAL JUSTICE?

Oxford Reference defines social justice as "the objective of creating a fair and equal society in which each individual matters, their rights are recognized and protected, and decisions are made in ways that are fair and honest."[1]

I will describe social justice as an honest and compassionate treatment of others that encompasses equal rights, opportunities, freedom, and respect for life regardless of external characteristics. Social justice embodies treating others in the same manner you would want to be treated. It is necessary for creating a sense of fairness, peace, love, morality, stability, rendering help to the weak, and respect for human life, especially in a culturally diverse society like the United States.

1. Oxford Reference, "Social Justice."

DECLARATION OF INDEPENDENCE ON JULY 4, 1776

The concept of social justice is highlighted in the Declaration of Independence, which states: "We hold these truths to be self-evident, that all men are created equal, that they are endowed by their Creator with certain unalienable Rights, that among these are Life, Liberty, and the pursuit of Happiness." The Declaration of Independence recognizes the indispensable rights bestowed upon all human beings by God to receive fair and equitable treatment in all social situations regardless of external criteria. The challenging question is, How many Americans genuinely believe that all men are created equal and endowed by their Creator with certain unalienable rights without regard to their physical traits? If indeed we believe and practice that all men are created equal, the political fight about social justice will be unnecessary and nonexistent in the United States.

BIBLICAL VIEWS ON SOCIAL JUSTICE

Although some Christian leaders oppose the concept of social justice based on their perceived notion that it is different from biblical justice, such a view is flawed because social justice is innately embedded in the concept of biblical justice. Those who hold such views are influenced by their political association rather than the truth of God's word or genuine desire for the implementation of social justice. Reviews of biblical texts indicate higher levels of parallel relationships between both.

Justice is an integral aspect of God's kingdom, for the Scripture says, "Righteousness and justice are the foundation of your throne; mercy and truth go before your face" (Ps 89:14). Also, Zechariah declared the word of the LORD to the Jews concerning God's expectations of their social relationships with one another, and especially their treatment toward the marginalized groups in the society:

> Thus says the LORD of hosts: "Execute true justice, show mercy and compassion everyone to his brother. Do not oppress the widow or the fatherless, the alien or the poor. Let none of you plan evil in his heart against his brother." (Zech 7:9–10)

The above Scripture summarizes the bolts and nuts required for both biblical justice and social justice, which includes the demonstration of mercy and compassion to others and the forbidding any mistreatment of the disadvantaged in our society. Additionally, if you notice from both scriptures above, they indicate how mercy and truth are heavily associated with the dissemination of justice. So, if someone struggles to implement equitable justice, it is an indication of the absence of mercy and truth in the person.

Vignette

Social justice is the core tenet of American democracy. It constitutes distributive justice, such as equitable social and economic benefits to all without regard to physical attributes. It promotes equal opportunity for all in our political structure and other social institutions.

OPPORTUNITIES FOR POLITICAL ADVANCEMENT

Democrats are more likely to promote social justice, while Republicans are more concerned with maintaining the status quo. Historically, the Democratic Party has been a more inclusive party than the Republican Party, embracing the concept of social justice, such as equal rights and opportunities for all. Minority groups in the United States have been able to achieve political success through the Democratic Party than the Republican Party. For the sake of clarifying what constitutes the membership of a "minority group" and its application in our social institutions, I will begin by asking a question: Which of the following groups would you consider to belong to minority groups in the United States? (A) African Americans, (B) American Indians and Alaska Natives, (C) Asian Americans, (D) Hispanics, (E) Black and Hispanic Women, (F) Asian Women, or (G) White Women. If you select the first six groups, you are partially correct; however, the correct answer is all seven choices. Because the correct description of a minority group is not always limited to numerical data but a reference to a group with less power structure in society. The members of a minority group always have less power and control over their lives regardless of their demographic size. Historically, women of all races, including White females, have not had control over their lives in the United States. Thus, everyone in the United States is a minority except White males.

So, moving forward, here are some political positions that minority groups in the United States first achieved through the Democratic Party, and some of them have not been replicated with the Republican Party. Barack Obama, the first African American to be elected the president of the United States (2009–17); Hilary Clinton, the first woman to win a presidential nomination and head a major political party (2016–20); Nancy Pelosi, the first woman to hold the office of the speaker of the US House of Representatives (2007–11 and 2019–23); and Kamala Harris, the first female vice president of the United States. No member of a minority group has ever achieved any of the above political positions through the Republican Party, which suggests that the party does not embrace equitable opportunities. The following elected positions for minority groups were first accomplished through the Democratic Party before some minority groups could attain the same political positions through the Republican Party. For elected gubernatorial position, Lawrence Douglas Wilder was the first African American to be elected governor in the United States in the state of Virginia (1990–94).[2] Two other elected African American governors include Deval Patrick of Massachusetts, 2007–16, and the recently elected governor of Maryland on November 8, 2022, Wes Moore.[3] The first female governor in the United was a Democrat, Nellie Tayloe Ross of Wyoming, between 1925 and 1927,[4] and the second in the same year was also a Democrat, Miriam Ferguson of Texas, who held the governorship position on two non-consecutive times, 1925 to 1927 and 1932 to 1934.[5] Ella T. Grasso, a Democrat, was the first female elected governor (1975–80) without her husband being the previous governor.[6] Gary Locke was the first Asian American elected governor in American history in Washington State (1997–2005), and he was a Democrat. The Democratic Party initiating the first step to assimilate minority groups in all levels of the US political system, as shown above, indicates their acknowledgment that all men are created equal and their effort to execute true justice. As it is written in the Bible, "You shall love your neighbor as yourself" (Matt 22:39b). Those who love their neighbors as themselves are more likely to give them equal treatment, which is not a common practice among the Republicans.

Vignette

The proper application of social justice should imply equal justice for all. However, those who thrive on social categorization based on physical traits and political affiliations struggle to embrace social justice but would rather direct their efforts

---

2. Daniels, "Only Three Black Governors," para. 5.
3. Daniels, "Only Three Black Governors," paras. 1–6.
4. Mark, "First Female Governor," para. 1.
5. Scott, "Texas First Woman Governor," para. 2.
6. Zorthian et al., "50 Women," para. 24.

to rationalize injustice. This approach has enabled the sustainability of social injustice in the United States.

PARTISAN POLITICS' EFFECT ON THE DEMONSTRATION OF MERCY AND COMPASSION ON SEXUAL ASSAULT AND DOMESTIC VIOLENCE VICTIMS

Perceptions and attitudes vary among the Republicans and Democrats in demonstrating affection and compassion for victims of sexual assault. Research shows that Republican men are less likely to believe victims of sexual assault and domestic violence and treat their cases as a myth than Democratic men.[7] Republican women are more likely to align their views with Republican men; likewise, Democratic women are more likely to side with Democratic men's views. An online survey conducted by *Time* shows that 93 percent of Democrats are more likely to believe the victims of sexual harassment compared to 79 percent of Republicans.[8] The survey also shows that 71 percent of Republicans and 74 percent of Democrats agreed that a Democratic congressman accused of sexual harassment should resign. However, if the accused congressman is a Republican, only 54 percent of Republicans believe that he should resign, and 82 percent of Democrats believe that the accused should resign. Even though both parties displayed disparity over who should resign when accused of sexual assault based on political affiliation, the gap was much larger with the Republican Party than the Democratic Party. This huge gap of 17 percent demonstrates a sense of lack of equitable justice, which is common among some members of the Republican Party. However, God admonishes us to render equitable justice as it is written in the Scripture, which says, "You shall not show partiality in judgment; you shall hear the small as well as the great; you shall not be afraid in any man's presence; for the judgment is God's" (Deut 1:17b).

Although both Democratic and Republican men have been accused of sexual assaults, most Democrats are more likely to demand that the alleged perpetrator resign from office or discourage him from running for political office, while the Republicans are more likely to claim that the allegation was politically motivated and least likely to hold the alleged perpetrator accountable. However, the Republicans will discourage the accused candidate from running for political office if they perceive that the accusation will hurt

---

7. Ortiz and Smith, "Social Identity Threat," 1318.
8. Alter, "Republicans Are Less Likely," para. 3.

the alleged offender's chances of winning. Democrats are more likely to hold their members accountable far more than Republicans. For example, in 2021, the governor of New York, Mr. Andrew Cuomo, was accused of multiple sexual misconducts, and he was pressured by a Democratic president, Joe Biden, Democratic Congress, and Democratic state legislatures to resign without the involvement of the Republicans. A Democratic attorney general, Letitia James, hired outside lawyers to investigate him, and the outcome of the investigation showed he indeed engaged in unlawful behaviors, such as initiating unwanted touching. The outcome of the investigation forced him to resign in August 2021. This type of action is less likely to happen with the Republican Party without a number of them rallying behind their accused member and claiming that the accusation was politically motivated.

In 2017, Republican Roy Moore ran for a senatorial position which he lost. During his campaign for the Senate, he was accused of sexual misconduct by several women when they were teenagers while he was in his thirties, yet the Republicans did not compel him to denounce his candidacy due to the allegations; rather several rallied behind him and claimed that the accusations were politically motivated. Compare that to Al Franken of Minnesota, who was pressured to resign from the Senate in January 2018 by his fellow Democrats due to sexual allegations. Considering the comparison of the two incidents: One was already a senator and was compelled by Democratic lawmakers to resign due to sexual allegations, and the other was trying to become a senator, but GOP lawmakers and the GOP president could not oblige him to withdraw his candidacy due to sexual allegations. Equitable justice is a challenging concept within the Republican Party. The Republican Party is more likely to practice differential justice and less likely to hold its members accountable, which violates the rule of equitable justice. Two Supreme Court justices nominated by GOP presidents were accused by multiple women of sexual assaults; nonetheless, the GOP senators confirmed them to the highest court for a lifetime position. In 1991, Clarence Thomas was accused of sexual harassment by Professor Anita Hill during the time she worked for him, and in 2018, Brett Kavanaugh was accused of sexual assault by Professor Christine Blasey Ford when both were in high school, and she was pinned down in a locked room. Even though these two women testified before the Senate Judiciary Committee, it did not restrain Republican senators from moving forward with the confirmation. Oh, it is important to mention that the GOP president, Donald Trump, who nominated Brett Kavanaugh, has been accused by more than a dozen women of sexual misconduct. His past comments and behaviors show little or no respect for women.

During the 2016 presidential campaign, a 2005 video from "Access Hollywood" about Mr. Trump's derogatory statement about women was made public. In the video, Mr. Trump was heard bragging about his sexual assaults on women. For example, he said: "You know I'm automatically attracted to beautiful, I just start kissing them. It's like a magnet. Just kiss. I don't even wait. And when you're a star, they let you do it . . . You can do anything. Whatever you want. Grab them by the p****. You can do anything."[9] In the same video, Mr. Trump was also heard bragging about his effort to have an affair with a married woman. His behaviors indicate a lack of morality and respect for women and marriage. Those words came to haunt Mr. Trump in a defamation and battery case filed against him by E. Jean Carroll. So, on May 9, 2023, a jury found Mr. Trump liable for sexual battery and defamation, and Ms. Carroll was awarded $5 million in damages.[10] After the jury verdict, as usual, Mr. Trump claimed that the case was a political witch hunt. My two cents about such a comment are that the secret to averting a political witch hunt is staying away from criminal, immoral, and unethical behaviors. I challenge you, Mr. Trump, with all due respect that if you try this secret, you will notice the gradual disappearance of all the so-called political witch hunts against you. It is that simple! Because we are a country of the rule of law, and when people do not adhere to societal standards concerning moral and ethical issues, as well as compliance with the laws of the land, we hold them accountable. A core component of US social justice is that nobody is above the law, including a president or former president.

A common denominator for GOP-appointed and elected officials accused of sexual assault is to claim political witch hunts as a defense mechanism instead of admitting their wrongdoings. In some cases, some of them take a more aggressive response toward the victims by victimizing them again, making the second victimization more traumatic. But the silence of the Republican Party supporters in sexual assaults and other immoral or criminal behaviors is disturbing. More specifically, it makes one wonder, what is going on with a party that Christian Evangelical leaders have falsely propagated as God's party that reflects biblical values? There is no biblical support for this type of injustice. For God spoke to the children of Israel saying, "Learn to do good; seek justice, rebuke the oppressor, defend the fatherless, plead for the widow" (Isa 1:17). God did not say to defend the oppressor at the expense of the victim. Rebuking and holding the oppressor accountable and defending the victim is a true example of justice. Although

---

9. Fahrenthold, "Trump Recorded," paras. 1–2.
10. Schonfeld, "Sexual Battery," paras. 1–2.

I believe that sexual assault accusations should be thoroughly investigated to establish the legitimacy of the accusations, botched investigations, like the type that happened during the confirmation of Brett Kavanaugh, are unacceptable. Our elected officials and those appointed to high-ranking positions should be people of integrity.

Another incident, although not related to sexual assault, involved a GOP-elected official whose resume, family life, and career were based on fabricated information. George Santos, a US representative for New York's third congressional district, created stories about his life that were inconsistent, such as claiming that he graduated from college when he did not, working for Citigroup or Goldman Sachs, when he did not, and being a landlord of multiple properties, which was untrue.[11] He deceived voters who elected him to the US House of Representatives, which is fraudulent behavior, yet most GOP lawmakers would not demand his resignation. On May 10, 2023, Mr. Santos was indicted on thirteen federal charges, which included money laundering, lying to Congress, wire fraud, and public fund theft.[12] There were no unified and concerted efforts from the GOP lawmakers to sanction Mr. Santos until a year later before he was expelled from Congress. The present-day Republican Party has become a party that tolerates, as well as embraces, falsehoods, as we have seen how they have embraced the dishonest behaviors of the former president, Mr. Trump. Therefore, it is impossible for God to be a Republican or endorse GOP practices, as falsely promoted by some Evangelical preachers. Compare Mr. Santos's incident to a New Jersey senator, Bob Menendez, who was indicted on charges of bribery by federal prosecutors on September 22, 2023. Even though he stepped down as the chair of the Senate Foreign Relations Committee, several Democratic senators, representatives, including the New Jersey governor, Phil Murphy, and other Democratic leaders demanded that he resign hours after he was indicted.[13] It is a type of action that does not exist among the Republicans, to hold their members accountable for breaking public trust.

---

11. Gold and Ashford, "George Santos Admits to Lying," paras. 1–5.
12. Stieb and Hartmann, "George Santos," para. 1.
13. Friedman, "This Is Horrifying," para. 1.

GOP IS LESS LIKELY TO HOLD ITS MEMBERS ACCOUNTABLE FOR CRIMINAL AND UNETHICAL BEHAVIORS

For the Republican Party to investigate one of its members for sexual assault or other types of crimes will depend on other sensitive factors besides seeking justice for the victims. Such sensitive factors might include financial loss and how close the victim is to them. For instance, the Texas GOP–controlled House of Representatives impeached Republican State Attorney General Ken Paxton on May 27, 2023. While I applaud such a rare move to impeach one of their own because of extensive records of corruption, the motives behind the impeachment were unrelated to his corrupt, criminal, and unethical behaviors. The charges against Paxton include bribery and abuse of power to help a friend and political donor, Nate Paul, by using the attorney general's office to intervene in a lawsuit between Mr. Paul and charity, while Mr. Paul, on the other hand, helped Mr. Paxton keep his extramarital affair secret by hiring the woman involved in the affair in exchange for legal protection.[14] Other charges include securities fraud and firing of whistleblowers, which is a violation of the Texas Whistleblower Act. The impeachment charges are not new; they have been around for years, including the securities fraud in which Paxton was indicted in 2015 and had used his position to delay the trial. The move to investigate and impeach Paxton took place after, in February 2023, Mr. Paxton reached a settlement of $3.3 million with the whistleblowers in a lawsuit brought against him. With the Senate approval, the settlement has to be funded by Texas taxpayers rather than Mr. Paxton, which triggered an investigation by the Republican-led State House of Representatives. The investigative committee made this statement, "We cannot over-emphasize the fact that, but for Paxton's own request for a taxpayer-funded settlement over his wrongful conduct, Paxton would not be facing impeachment by the House."[15] This is shocking that, despite the abundance of Mr. Paxton's corruption, he would receive criminal immunity from the state Republican lawmakers as long as he did not become a financial burden to the taxpayers. What about the whistleblowers who were unjustly fired by Mr. Paxton? What kind of justice does the Republican-led State House of Representatives and Senate offer them? These cohorts of godless Republican Party members have zero sense of justice for victims of crime, the disadvantaged, the poor, and the innocent; it is all about the status quo. This is

---

14. Despart and Barragan, "Texas AG," paras. 35–48; Vertuno and Bleiberg, "Why Texas GOP-Controlled House," paras. 5–10.
15. Vertuno and Bleiberg, "Why Texas GOP-Controlled House," paras. 5–10.

the group that Evangelical preachers are deceptively pushing their followers to vote for when their ways are unbiblical. Psalm 82:3 states, "Defend the poor and fatherless; do justice to the afflicted and needy. Deliver the poor and needy; free them from the hand of the wicked." The Republican Party members would not honor such biblical command because their primary concern is to protect their members of higher status who violate the laws of the land to the detriment of the weak. It is a party that some members propagate a false sense of conservatism but cannot live up to its purported postulation.

The Texas House Republican impeachment of Mr. Paxton led to his automatic suspension as Texas attorney general until the Senate trial. Mr. Paxton never admitted any wrongdoing but, in his defiance, made the following statement:

> The sham impeachment coordinated by the Biden Administration with liberal House Speaker Dade Phelan and his kangaroo court has cost taxpayers millions of dollars, disrupted the work of the Office of Attorney General, and left a dark and permanent stain on the Texas House." The weaponization of the impeachment process to settle political differences is not only wrong but also immoral and corrupt.[16]

Interestingly, people who engage in immoral and corrupt behaviors are calling the system or the people who investigate them immoral and corrupt. Furthermore, why is it that Republicans who violate the law of the land and engage in unethical behaviors never admit their wrongdoings? Rather they shift the blame on the Democrats who had nothing to do with their criminal behaviors. It was the House Republicans who impeached Mr. Paxton and those who testified against Mr. Paxton including his former senior official. How did President Biden's administration become the scapegoat for Mr. Paxton's corruption? Nevertheless, on September 16, 2023, Texas Republican senators acquitted Mr. Paxton of all sixteen articles of impeachment.[17] What a travesty of justice!

According to the *Texas Tribune*, Mr. Paxton has a long history of Texas political scandals in his twenty-one years of public office ranging from felonies to unethical practices. Notwithstanding being acquitted by the Republican Senate, he still faces security fraud charges dating as far back as 2015, and he is under federal investigation that was brought against him by his senior officials.

16. Despart and Barragan, "Texas AG Ken Paxton," para. 4.
17. Despart, "Texas Attorney General," para. 1.

Reviewing the history of Texas, there had been only two times the GOP State House had impeached one of their own, and guess what the cause of the impeachment was? Financial improprieties. First was Governor James Ferguson in 1917 because of embezzlement, misuse, and diversion of public funds, and the second was Judge O. P. Carrillo in 1975 due to filing a false financial statement and diverting public funds and equipment for personal use.[18] So, for the GOP members who lean toward corruption, the line you do not want to cross is tampering with public funds. Otherwise, you will receive immunity from the GOP State House, Senate, and other GOP members who condone corruption at the expense of your victims. For clarification, some GOP members are honest and God-fearing people; however, the party had been infiltrated by hateful, corrupt, and godless people, who want to destroy the unity of our country, democracy, peace, and equitable justice.

Recently, the Republican Party, under the leadership of Donald Trump, has been converted into a cult rather than a political party. Some honest GOP members attest to the conversion of the party into a cult. For example, former GOP senator Alan Simpson and former GOP representatives Denver Riggleman, Liz Cheney, and Joe Walsh all acknowledged that the Republican Party had become a cult. The same political maneuvering has dominated multiple criminal cases and ethical violations against former president Donald Trump, and most GOP members have declined to hold him accountable, even in the face of the most obvious and appalling behaviors unexpected of a president. Mr. Trump could not have survived as a president under the Democratic Party because the Democratic lawmakers and their voters would have removed him from office a long time ago. Instead of the GOP lawmakers taking a bold step to remove Mr. Trump, they have rather cowardly succumbed to his intimidations and even harassed the legislative body and judicial systems for investigating Mr. Trump's obvious criminal and unethical behaviors.

SOCIAL JUSTICE IS ASSOCIATED WITH TELLING THE TRUTH

Conservative news media is extremely biased and promotes divisive and distorted messages; it is no surprise that a recent poll rated Sean Hannity of Fox News as the least trusted news anchor by 30 percent and Lester Holt of NBC as the most credible news anchor by 32 percent.[19] Additionally, out of forty-six countries surveyed in global media trust, the US media ranked the

---

18. Vertuno and Bleiberg, "Why Texas GOP-Controlled House," paras. 1–9.
19. Clark, "Most and Least Trusted," paras. 1–7.

lowest, and the ranking of local TV news shows that a conservative news media, Fox, was rated the least media outlet to trust at 46 percent.[20] A Public Religion Research Institute (PRRI) survey in 2021 shows that 68 percent of Republicans still believe in Mr. Trump's big lie that the 2020 election was stolen from him, even though there has not been any iota of evidence to support the baseless claim. The survey also reveals that 82 percent of Republicans who watch Fox News and 97 percent of Republicans who trust far-right news believed that the election was stolen from Mr. Trump, compared to 44 percent of Republicans who consume mainstream media. The results of these polls are not unexpected or a surprise to those who have carefully considered high levels of media distortion within conservative media outlets.[21]

On April 18, 2023, Fox News reached a $757.5 million settlement with Dominion Voting Systems, an election technology, for promoting false conspiracies about their voting machines redirecting votes for Mr. Trump to Mr. Biden in the 2020 election.[22] During the pretrial of the defamation suit, a plethora of evidence through text messages, emails, and deposition revealed that Fox executives and hosts knew that the false conspiracies about the 2020 presidential election were illogical, yet they continued to promote the falsehoods because that is what they believe their audience wants to hear. After the settlement, Justin Nelson, the attorney for Dominion Voting Systems, made the following statements, "Truth matters. Lies have consequences. Today's settlement of $787,500,000 represents vindication and accountability. Today represents a ringing endorsement for truth and for democracy."[23] Indeed, lies have consequences, and truth matters regardless of false impressions portrayed by Fox hosts to normalize inaccurate information in order to entertain their audience. It is interesting that Fox hosts believe that their audience prefers to hear lies rather than the truth; therefore, they feed their audience with false conspiracies. It takes a dishonest heart to desire lies (see Prov 17:4). The desire to listen to lies has become a common behavioral pattern among some fierce GOP supporters. Even when one listens to Christian TV or radio programs, often you have interjection of career politicians propagating falsehoods that any reasonable individual would know lacks credibility. They will discourage their followers from listening to mainstream media so that they will not discern the truth for themselves.

20. Newman et al., "Reuter's Digital Report," 113.
21. Public Religion Research Institute, "'Big Lie.'"
22. Dickson, "Dominion, Fox News Settle Defamation," para. 1.
23. Taylor, "Fox News Reaches $757.5 Million Settlement," para. 1.

Another conservative organization located in Houston, Texas, known as True the Vote, has been accused of promoting false conspiracies, especially about the 2020 election. The organization claims that its goal is to stop voter fraud; however, its approach to stopping voter fraud is by promoting unsubstantiated claims and false allegations. On October 31, 2022, the founder, Catherine Engelbrecht, and another leader of the organization, Gregg Phillips, were jailed by a federal judge for contempt of court. They failed to release the name of a supposed FBI confidential informant in a defamation lawsuit to support their voter fraud conspiracy theories involving China.[24] Both Engelbrecht and Phillips have also been accused of directing donations to their nonprofit organization for personal use.[25] On June 5, 2023, a nonprofit watchdog organization, Campaign for Accountability (CfA) asked the Texas attorney general's office and the IRS to investigate True the Vote leaders concerning issuing personal loans to Catherine Engelbrecht and disproportionately providing financial support to General Counsel Jim Bopp's law firm and a longtime director Gregg Phillips's business.[26] These financial transactions were improperly reported on their tax returns. Interestingly, this right-wing organization titled its name True the Vote when it actually operates on false conspiracies, which is misrepresenting falsehood to be truth, just like Mr. Trump's social media is called Truth Social when he has been described by many as a pathological liar. This type of behavior is ungodly, manipulating the truth to deceive unaware individuals, which is an aspect of injustice. However, God hates lies and wants us to tell the truth, practice justice, and live in peace. So he declares:

> These are the things you should do: Speak each man the truth to his neighbor; give judgment in your gates for truth, justice, and peace. Let none of you think evil in your heart against your neighbor, and do not love a false oath: for all these are things that I hate, says the LORD. (Zech 8:16–17)

Promoting lies, false conspiracy theories, and distortion of facts to manipulate and destroy truth and people's lives has become a familiar playbook for some conservative extremists in the recent decade. While these vicious behaviors have caused severe harmful effects on their victims, the majority of Republicans and Christian Evangelical leaders have not taken decisive steps to condemn and disassociate themselves from extremist groups.

---

24. Huseman, "True the Vote Jailed," para. 1.
25. Jaramillo, "True the Vote Accused of Using Donations," paras. 1–3.
26. Clauw, "Watchdog Requests IRS Investigate," para. 1.

Silence in situations that deserve public condemnation has become their modus operandi.

Consider the callous behavior of right-wing conspiracy theorist Alex Jones, who used his media platforms to proclaim that the Sandy Hook Elementary School shooting that took place on December 14, 2012, was a hoax, propagated on behalf of those who oppose the Second Amendment.[27] A horrendous incident in which twenty children and six adults were killed shocked the nation and was aired on every major media outlet, yet he used his lying skills to deceive some unwitting individuals into believing his lies. His noxious false conspiracy added unbearable pain to the parents who lost their children in the massacre and subjected them to death threats and harassment. On October 12, 2022, a Connecticut jury ordered him to pay $965 million to families who suffered from his false claims about the Sandy Hook Elementary School shooting.[28] In another defamation lawsuit, a Texas jury in August 2022 also ordered him to pay $49 million to two parents of Sandy Hook victims. It is expensive to engage in reckless false conspiracies against innocent people. The urgent question in situations like this is, Why is it so easy for some of these conservatives to promote and embrace lies even in the face of indisputable facts and absolute truths? Proverbs 17:4 says, "An evildoer gives heed to false lips; a liar listens eagerly to a spiteful tongue." Thus, listening and embracing lying lips indicates an ungodly heart condition, according to God's word. A corrupt heart will most likely embrace falsehoods, as well as engage in spreading lies. Such behaviors are ungodly, contrary to what some Christian Evangelical preachers have falsely promoted about GOP platforms. It has become a common practice among some conservatives to embrace falsehoods, and the outcome of such ungodliness is increased spread of evil among the people because they do not know God, as the Scripture says, "And like their bow they have bent their tongues for lies. They are not valiant for the truth on the earth. For they proceed from evil to evil, and they do not know Me,' says the LORD" (Jer 9:3).

Scripturally, Jesus is the Truth and Satan is the Liar (see John 14:6, 8:44). The deception of some Christian Evangelical leaders using the GOP abortion rhetoric to persuade their members to support a political party that is dominated with lies, injustice, hate groups is ungodly. There is no biblical example that God asked his people to form partnerships with liars, haters, and people who promote injustice against marginalized groups. Neither is there any example in the Bible where God used manipulations

---

27. Maxouris and Joseph, "Alex Jones," para. 3.
28. Queen and Thomsen, "Alex Jones Must Pay," paras. 1–3.

and deceptions to accomplish a goal, as dominated by the Mr. Trump-led Republican Party.

Furthermore, lies have been a destructive path to deny justice to the disadvantaged and to promote perennial division, as evidenced in the big lie disseminated by one man about the 2020 presidential election that has created a sharp divide in our country. This type of lie has been targeted to undermine the voting rights of racial and ethnic minority groups in our democracy. It has now become a model for some GOP candidates who lost elections to generate unsubstantiated claims to challenge election results. For example, immediately after the 2022 midterm election, some GOP candidates who lost the election filed frivolous lawsuits to overturn the will of the voters. In Arizona, Republican candidates for governor Kari Lake, secretary of state Mark Finchem, and attorney general Abraham Hamadeh, who lost to their Democratic opponents, filed lawsuits seeking to overturn the election results.[29] All these three Republican candidates spawned ridiculous falsehoods and asked courts to certify them as winners of elections they clearly lost. Among the three, Kari Lake was frivolously persistent with her false claims all the way to the state Supreme Court with no evidence to support her false claims. During the process, a court fined her lawyers $2,000 for making false claims that over 35,000 votes were inserted in the ballot. On May 22, 2023, a judge finally dismissed her case for failure to provide evidence to support her false claims. This is disturbing in that if one loses an election, he or she makes up false stories and strives to use the court to overturn the will of the people. These individuals are trying to undermine the democratic process of electing leaders as dictated by the Constitution and to use the court to counteract the will of the voters. This type of behavior is aimed at creating an unequal social justice system; that is, if a Democrat wins an election, we will accuse him or her of election fraud, and perhaps some judge will empathize with us to overturn the result. Thank God we still have judges who refused to compromise their oaths of office and render unbiased rulings. As the Scripture says, "Open your mouth and judge righteously and plead the cause of the poor and needy" (Prov 31:9). God will bless those judges who refuse to compromise and judge righteously.

It is also disturbing that some GOP extremists do not believe in equitable justice and treatment. Their sense of justice is perverted in that the scale of justice has to be twisted to tilt in their favor to convey justice to them. Such a mindset is childish, barbaric, and repugnant. A further illustration of inequitable justice with the GOP extremists was demonstrated on April 6, 2023, when the Tennessee House GOP expelled two Black Democrats

---

29. Schonfeld, "GOP Legal Challenges," para. 3.

for violation of the chamber's rules on decorum while sparing the third Democrat, who is White.[30] It makes one question the moral reasoning behind such differential treatment, in which three Democrats were involved in gun violence protest, the two Blacks received expulsion, and a third, a White woman, escaped expulsion by one vote. It is shameful, distasteful, and immoral behavior. A compelling question about this behavior is, How can members of society coexist peacefully with each other when some people hold such absurd views of differential justice based on race, social class, and political affiliation? Contrary to the misrepresentations of some Christian Evangelical leaders, such behaviors do not reflect biblical teachings, and God cannot endorse a political party or individuals who clearly violate God's commandment to love your neighbor as yourself.

VIEWS ABOUT DIVERSITY IN AMERICA

According to a PRRI survey in 2021, Democrats are 82 percent more likely to believe that diversity makes the United States stronger than the Republicans at 47 percent, and 16 percent of Republicans believe that diversity makes the country weaker compared to 3 percent of Democrats.[31] Concerning racial diversity, 30 percent of Republicans say they would prefer that the country be made up of different races, while 64 percent of Democrats would prefer racial diversity in America. The same survey shows that 51 percent of Americans believed that the Republican Party had been taken over by racism, including 55 percent of Independent voters.[32]

A study by two political science professors showed that racism was a significant motivating factor for Trump voters.[33] Mr. Trump's association with racist groups and the refusal of Christian Evangelical leaders to condemn such behavior is a covert expression of racism. Also, editorial analysts concluded that the White Evangelicals are the supporters of Mr. Trump's big lie about the 2020 election, which is influenced by racism.[34] Even though the false claims of a stolen election by a pathological liar have been tried in courts of law all the way to the Supreme Court, no evidence was found about the stolen election, yet 60 percent of White Evangelicals chose to believe lies.[35] These people chose to believe lies instead of the truth because

30. Wolf and Razek, "Democrats in Retaliation," paras. 1–8.
31. PRRI, "Competing Visions of America," para. 27.
32. PRRI, "Competing Visions of America" para. 19.
33. Hooghe and Dassonneville, "Explaining the Trump Vote," 528.
34. Marcotte and Salon, "Evangelicals Are the Backbones," para. 1.
35. PRRI, "Ahead of Anniversary," para. 4.

their behaviors are consistent with the biblical Pharisees and hypocrites, as Jesus stated in John 8:44:

> You are of your father the devil, and the desires of your father you want to do. He was a murderer from the beginning and does not stand in the truth because there is no truth in him. When he speaks a lie, he speaks from his own resources, for he is a liar and the father of it.

In addition, God despises liars and embraces truth. Proverbs 12:22 declares, "Lying lips are an abomination to the LORD, but those who deal truthfully are his delight." If dealing truthfully is God's delight, shouldn't a political party portrayed by some Christian Evangelical leaders as a party whose agendas are endorsed by God operate in truth rather than promoting lies?

People who hate God's creation because of their race, national origin, or any other external characteristics are murderers, and eternal life does not abide in them (see 1 John 3:15).

Survey data shows that only 30 percent of White Republicans believe that Blacks experience discrimination in America, as opposed to 74 percent of White Democrats,[36] a substantive difference between both parties about embracing the societal realities of racism, which also reflects one's heart about embracing facts or lies.

Vignette

> The external manifestation of racism reflects the internal structure of the mind and self-concept of the racist. Thus, racism becomes an outlet for a more serious internal crisis.

RACISM IS A FORM OF SOCIAL INJUSTICE

Racism is the belief that one's race is superior to others. When someone holds such a belief, it manifests in their attitude and treatment toward people of different races, such as dehumanization, inequity, and differential justice. Racist individuals often engage in confirmation bias—that is, focusing only on the information that will confirm their racist beliefs while evidence that might contradict their racist views is ignored. The Republican Party has been described by several people, including its members, as a racist party. In his farewell speech, GOP representative Adam Kinzinger

---

36. Demby, "America's View on Discrimination," para. 5.

described the GOP as a party that "shelter[s] the ignorant and the racist."[37] A former GOP strategist, Stuart Stevens, described the Republican party as a racist party that embraces the hatred and bigotry of Trumpism.[38] The Republican Party attracts racist and hate groups, and the hate groups have been the core covert members of the party. During the presidential debate in October 2020, President Trump refused to denounce association with a racist group that supports his campaign and presidency but rather made this statement: "Proud Boys stand back and stand by."[39] Interestingly, they complied with Mr. Trump's request and were part of the Capitol rioters who wanted to overthrow the US government on January 6, 2021. A dozen other racist groups also participated in the Capitol riot, such as QAnon, militiamen, White supremacists, Oath Keepers, etc. Even though these hate groups have been an integral part of the Republican Party, the Christian Evangelical preachers have not publicly condemned their association with the party. Rather, they deceptively pretend as if the Republican Party's association with the hate groups does not exist and continue to deceive their followers with the preaching of socialism and abortion. The practice of hate and association with hate groups is an abomination in the sight of God. So, the Bible teaches that we are all one and of the same value to God in Christ Jesus. Galatians 3:28 says, "There is neither Jew nor Greek, there is neither slave nor free, there is neither male nor female; for you are all one in Christ Jesus." God does not judge or evaluate human beings based on physical characteristics. When God asked Samuel to anoint one of Jesse's sons, and when he saw Jesse's first son, Eliab, he said, "Surely, the LORD's anointed is before Him" (1 Sam 16:6). But God responded to him by saying, "Do not look at his appearance or his physical stature, because I have refused him. For the LORD does not see as man sees; for man looks at the outward appearance, but the LORD looks at the heart" (1 Sam 16:7). It was David, the one that Jesse, his father, considered unqualified that God chose to be the king of Israel.

Vignette

Racism is a type of idol worship that displaces the preeminence of God and undermines his purpose and sovereignty in the life of his creation. It forms the basis of an improper approach to judging and treating others rather than the set standard of the

---

37. Reed, "'We Shelter the Ignorant,'" para. 1.
38. Corn, "Republican Party Is Racist," paras. 1–13.
39. Farivar, "More Than a Dozen Extremist Groups," para. 23.

word of God. The practice of racism is not a social issue but a spiritual matter that makes a mockery of God concerning his creation. Additionally, it is not a sinless behavior nor a victimless sin.

Furthermore, the Scripture teaches that everyone should receive equal treatment regardless of their race/national origin: "The stranger who dwells among you shall be to you as one born among you, and you shall love him as yourself; for you were strangers in the land of Egypt: I am the LORD your God" (Lev 19:34). Thus, regardless of one's race, national origin, social class, or gender, all shall receive equal treatment, according to God's law and also according to the United States law. Those who violate the laws of our country and God's law concerning equitable justice and treatment are taking unwise risks with God. In addition, as God reminded the Israelites that they were once a stranger in Egypt, the same is applicable to all Americans except the Native Americans. Everyone in the United States or their ancestors were once strangers in the US, and that is more reason why everyone should be treated equally.

Vignette

The practice of racism is cancerous and a euphemism for death, subtly structured to function and destabilize peace, trust, and unity in society, with the ultimate goal of societal destruction without remedy. It is not Russia, China, or any other country that will destroy the United States of America; the United States will destroy itself. The lethal weapon for destruction is racism, which originates from hateful hearts.

Interestingly, at the center of decades and centuries of political divide and hatred in the United States is racism. Racism and discrimination in the United States have not been dealt with in a punitive manner to discourage the continuum of the behaviors. To some extent, they have been normalized and treated as if it is the right of the perpetrators to discriminate against and dehumanize other racial and ethnic groups. Any behavior or action carried out to the detriment of another person's freedom cannot be treated as a right issue but a violation of human rights and freedom. Due to the poisonous nature of racism, there would *never* be any positive outcomes from such practice but accumulations of God's judgment on the perpetrators.

Racism is based on hindering ignorance and reinforced by social norms. The debilitating ignorance associated with racism leads to differential treatment, social injustice, prejudice, stereotyping, and unfounded fear of other racial and ethnic groups. Social norms have strong direct and indirect influence in perpetuating the fear of outside groups. In reality, the group that poses the greatest threat to us is not the outside group but our ingroup, which is the group you belong to and interact with more frequently. According to FBI records, in 2017, about 88 percent of Black victims were killed by Black offenders, and about 80 percent of White victims were killed by White offenders.[40] However, we have been socialized to fear members of outgroups and only trust ingroup members. In reality, we are more likely to be victimized by members of our own group than outgroup members. This does not suggest letting your guard down for either ingroup or outgroup members, but to treat people on an individual basis because there are both good and bad people in every race and ethnic group.

SOCIAL INJUSTICE IN REDISTRICTING

The ideal purpose of redistricting is to ensure equitable representation and political power for all racial and ethnic groups, which coincides with the concept of democracy and social justice. Both Democrats and Republicans practice redistricting; however, Republican states flagrantly use redistricting to weaken the voting power of minority groups. For example, in Louisiana, 58 percent of the adult population (eighteen years and above) are Whites, and 33 percent of the adult population (eighteen years and above) are African Americans, but due to unfair redistricting tactics known as gerrymandering, the voting power of African Americans was reduced to 17 percent, while the voting power of Whites was increased to 83 percent.[41]

Also, in Texas, even though 90 percent of the population growth was people of color, according to the 2020 US census, the lawmakers did not draw legislative maps to ensure a fair and equal representation of the people of color communities.[42] After the 2020 election, some states like Louisiana, South Carolina, Arkansas, and Alabama have embraced racially gerrymandered maps, and some of them have been ruled by the court as unconstitutional. Racial gerrymandering has become a modus operandi for Republican states to disenfranchise the voting power of racial and ethnic minority groups in the US, even though such impropriety violates the Voting Rights Act (VRA) of 1965. It is also a detestable behavior before God, as the Scripture says, "Dishonest scales are an abomination to the Lord, but a just weight is His delight" (Prov 11:1). The question remains, What is wrong

40. Federal Bureau of Investigation, "2017 Crime."
41. Wiley, "Why Race Matters," para. 6.
42. Howard, "Racial Gerrymandering," para. 8.

with equitable justice and treatment of all people without regard to race and external factors? How do inequitable justice and mistreatment of minorities bring joy to a person's heart? If someone is driven by differential justice based on race, it suggests much bigger problems within the person than can be perceived outwardly. The root cause of inequity and maltreatment is hatred, which originates from Satan. People who hate other people also hate truth and justice, and they also have no reverence for God. There is nothing good that can come out of racism but destruction.

Vignette

> The dehumanization of minority groups as a result of racism, sexism, classism, and ethnocentrism represents the root cause of all social injustice and inequities. Furthermore, the continuum of systemic social injustice in the United States is evidenced in the disenfranchisement of minority groups' economic and political opportunities.

On the other hand, the Bible teaches us to love one another because God is love, and, for those who belong to him, their hearts are inescapably filled with his love toward all human beings he created in his image. Pay careful attention as you read these scriptural verses about love:

> Beloved, let us love one another, for love is of God, and everyone who loves is born of God and knows God. He who does not love does not know God, for God is love. In this, the love of God was manifested toward us, that God has sent His only begotten Son into the world, that we might live through Him. In this love, not that we loved God, but that He loved us and sent His Son to be the propitiation for our sins. Beloved, if God so loved us, we also ought to love one another. No one has seen God at any time. If we love one another, God abides in us, and His love has been perfected in us. By this, we know that we abide in Him, and He in us, because He has given us His Spirit. And we have seen and testify that the Father has sent the Son as Savior of the world. Whoever confesses that Jesus is the Son of God, God abides in him, and he in God. And we have known and believed the love that God has for us. God is love, and he who abides in love abides in God, and God in him. Love has been perfected among us in this: that we may have boldness in the day of judgment; because as He is, so are we in this world. There is no fear in love, but perfect love casts out fear because fear involves torment. But he who fears has not been made perfect in love. We love

> Him because He first loved us. If someone says, "I love God," and hates his brother, he is a liar; for he who does not love his brother whom he has seen, how can he love God whom he has not seen? And this commandment we have from Him: that he who loves God must love his brother also. (1 John 4: 7–21)

According to the above Scripture, those who cannot love are not born of God, and God does not abide in them because God is love. There is no fear in love, no racism in love, and no social injustice in love. Those who hate and discriminate against others because of their race or national origin do so because the love of God is not in them, and they also hate God. If the love of God abides in them, then it will be a natural transition to love those who are different from them. Also, understand that God's standard to measure genuine love is the love rendered to people who are different from you, not to people who are like you. Thus, Jesus says:

> For if you love those who love you, what reward have you? Do not even the tax collectors do the same? And if you love your brethren only, what do you do more than others? Do not even the tax collectors do so? Therefore, you shall be perfect, just as your Father in Heaven is perfect. (Matt 5:46–47)

The above scriptural verses do not suggest that you should not love and do good things for your loved ones or those who are like you. However, when you extend your love and kind treatment to those who are different from you, even in the same capacity as you render to your loved ones, you score high marks of love with God, which brings generational blessings.

GOP DOUBLE STANDARD ABOUT SOCIAL JUSTICE

Republicans always brag about being tough on crime, and it appears that their toughness on crime is only the crime committed by a group different from them or non-party members. They make false claims about supporting the blue, especially when Blacks protest about the killing of an unarmed Black man by a police officer. However, when it comes to the police opposing state gun laws that make it easier for criminals to have access to guns, GOP lawmakers will turn their back on the blue in favor of the NRA–backed reckless gun laws. Furthermore, a more despicable example of the GOP's inconsistent claim of backing the blue involved the January 6, 2021, insurrection at the Capitol in which 150 Capitol police officers and hundreds of workers were injured during the attack, four people died in the crowd that day, and afterward, five police officers who served on the Capitol on January 6, 2021, died.[43] Officer Brian D. Sicknick died on January 7 as a result of the attack by the mob. Officer Howard S. Liebengood committed suicide four days later, Officer Jeffrey Smith, who received a blow to the head, committed suicide nine days later, and Officers Gunther Hashida and Kyle DeFreytag committed suicide in July 2021. Imagine the extent of emotional trauma these police officers must have endured to lead them to commit suicide. This is disturbing—police officers carrying out their honorable duties became victims of mob attacks that were incited by a US president and condoned by the majority of GOP lawmakers. A shocking aspect of the whole episode is the complicity of some GOP lawmakers and even labeling the insurrection as "a legitimate political discourse" instead of a deadly coup on the US government.

On the other hand, Democratic lawmakers have actively lobbied so that the deaths of police officers who committed suicides will be classified as line-of-duty deaths for the purpose of their families receiving benefits.[44] Shouldn't the GOP lawmakers who always portray themselves as being tough on crimes and supporters of the police be the ones actively involved in what the Democratic lawmakers are doing? Rather they all rescinded and kept silent because the GOP has become a cult, and its lawmakers are devoid of a sense of justice. On January 6, 2023, when the law enforcement officials were honored for protecting the lawmakers during the Capitol riot, only one GOP lawmaker, Rep. Brian Fitzpatrick, attended the ceremony.[45] This type of behavior is disturbing, in that GOP lawmakers lacked integrity to honor police officers who risked their lives to protect them. Because the perpetrator of the Capitol riot was the GOP president, therefore, the victims of Donald Trump's criminal behavior have to be victimized again. This is a dangerous cult mentality, where the victims are penalized for doing their jobs, and the criminal perpetrator is exonerated.

GOP lawmakers have not demonstrated integrity or consistency with issues relating to truth and social justice. Their sense of justice depends on who committed the crime and who is the victim. They flip-flop at will and are terrified of Donald Trump. They are afraid of holding Mr. Trump accountable for his criminal behaviors; thus, a violent coup that was carried out against our democratic republic government that resulted in the loss of lives should not be investigated, and the perpetrators should not be prosecuted. This is a double standard for a party that claims to be tough on crimes. Because this violent coup involved a former GOP president,

43. Cameron, "Capitol Riot," paras. 1–8.
44. Cameron, "Capitol Riot," paras. 1–8.
45. Dorman, "DC Metropolitan Police," paras. 1–2.

therefore, a deadly crime should not be investigated, and the offenders should receive criminal immunity. Interestingly, on January 6, 2021, when the Capitol riot took place, the majority of GOP lawmakers expressed their disapproval of what happened, and even some blamed President Trump. However, within a few weeks later, most of them flipped, retracted their narratives, and aligned themselves with Donald Trump. On February 4, 2022, the Republican National Committee voted to censure Representatives Liz Cheney of Wyoming and Adam Kinzinger of Illinois for partaking in the House Committee investigation of the Capitol riot.[46] Thus, on December 6, 2022, during the congressional gold medal ceremony, the family of the fallen officer of the January 6 riot, Officer Brian Sicknick, snubbed the GOP lawmakers because "they're just two-faced" and lacked "integrity" as the mother of Officer Sicknick described GOP lawmakers.[47] The Republican Party, under the headship of Donald Trump, has structured itself to lies and deceptions, as the Scripture states, "'And like their bow, they have bent their tongues for lies. They are not valiant for the truth on earth. For they proceed from evil to evil, and they do not know Me,' says the LORD" (Jer 9:3). Indeed, these two-faced GOP lawmakers who support Donald Trump in his ungodly efforts to destroy our God-given democracy and the unity of the nation do not know God, contrary to the illusion propagated by some Christian Evangelical preachers.

In all these, one may wonder, What were the positions of Christian Evangelical leaders concerning the deadly attack on the US government? They were mostly silent and lacked the integrity to condemn the violence in the Capitol publicly. A few did, some of them as a result of fulfilling an obligation that they did speak against the violence on Capitol Hill rather than making concerted efforts to condemn the act on a consistent basis. However, most of them have directed the attention of their followers to the preaching of socialism while discouraging them from consuming mainstream media. For, as long as they are able to deter their followers from watching mainstream media and reading the internet, they continue to push their convoluted messages to create hate and a sharp divide in our country. Again, your silence is complicity, and your alliance with the Republican Party, your deception in promoting its agendas as biblical, is not a sinless behavior. Your friendship with a political party that promotes division instead of unity, injustice against marginalized groups, hate against different races, and distortion of truth is enmity with God (see Jas 4:4). When people do not feel resentment in their spirit for engaging in behaviors that support

---

46. Weisman and Epstein, "G.O.P. Declares," paras. 1–7.
47. Duster, "Family of Fallen January 6 Officer," paras. 5–7.

the mistreatment of minority groups, calling evil good and good evil, and keeping silent in ungodly behaviors that should have been condemned, it is an indication of being devoid of the Holy Spirit because Holy Spirit is a Spirit of truth. There are no biblical examples of some of the Christian Evangelical leaders' behaviors and collusion with the GOP that can be found with any of the true biblical priests, prophets, and apostles except the Pharisees, false prophets, and priests. Again, as Jesus says, you cannot serve God and mammon simultaneously (see Matt 6:24); therefore, the Evangelical preachers who align themselves with partisan politics cannot serve God and the Republican Party at the same time.

THE POLARIZATION OF POLITICS

Politics divides and undermines Christ's teaching to love your neighbor as yourself. Both political parties use politics to treat members of another political party as enemies rather than fellow Americans. The extremists have directed their loyalty and patriotism to the country as American citizens to their political party. In essence, an idealistic and patriotic approach is loyalty to your country, its well-being, and values over a political party. It is concerning to the degree that partisan politics is destroying the unity of our country, and the church, which is supposed to be the light for such a time as this, has become an enabler in breeding the division.

LIBERATION THEOLOGY

Liberation theology proposes the role of churches in liberating marginalized groups from their oppressors. It emphasizes the use of political efforts by churches to fight for and defend the oppressed, poor, women, and immigrants. Liberation theology advocates for equitable justice and equal access to societal economic resources. The concept of liberation theology is consistent with God's commandment to his people for righteous judgment and to protect the marginalized groups in our country. For example, God sent Jeremiah to declare the following commandment to the king of Judah: "Execute judgment and righteousness and deliver the plundered out of the hand of the oppressor. Do no wrong and do no violence to the stranger, the fatherless, or the widow, nor shed innocent blood in this place" (Jer 22:3). This scripture suggests that Christians have a godly obligation to fight for the poor, fatherless, widows, immigrants, and women and to deliver them from their oppressors. In essence, a realistic approach to moral reasoning compels one to embrace internal ethical principles in rendering equitable justice for all, regardless of external characteristics. An even more significant influence is the commandment of the Lord Jesus, to love your neighbor as yourself (see Matt 22:39).

However, contrary to God's commandment, some Evangelical preachers have consistently engaged in deceptive political tactics that promote oppressive messages against the very group that God warns us not to mistreat. They intentionally avoid mentioning or preaching scriptures that contradict their political messages. They have inadvertently chosen mammon over God's word. However, the will of God on how we should treat the disadvantaged is expressed in the Scripture, which states: "Learn to do good; seek justice, rebuke the oppressor; defend the fatherless, plead for the widow" (Isa 1:17). In reality, the effective implementation of liberation theology could help to avert or minimize social injustice, poverty, racism, and discrimination in our society. An example of liberation theology involves an exemptional effort made by a Christian group to collect signatures to eject Tennessee House Speaker Cameron Sexton for his role in expelling the Black lawmakers.[48] The role of the house speaker and other Republicans in expelling the two Black Democrats and sparing the White Democrats for the same behavior is despicable. Anyone with a sense of justice should not keep silent, seeing or knowing about such social injustice. Thus, Christian groups and churches have a godly obligation as a group to consistently fight for the rights of minority groups in the United States and promote equitable justice for all. Disappointingly, a number of them have done the opposite.

SUMMARY

If God were to reveal your heart to you now, what would your heart conditions show concerning your views on racism, social injustice, and disenfranchisement of minority groups in the US? You do not have to commit a violent act against another person because of their race to be a racist. If you hold the false notion that your race is superior to other racial groups, you are racist because God created all men equal in his image (see Gen 1:26–28). If you give preferential treatment to people of your race, you are a racist because God does not show partiality (see Acts 10:34). Know that God created one race, the human race; it is men who created racism. Racism often begins with the mindset that "my race is superior to other races," which escalates into conscious acts of such false belief. The root of such false beliefs and actions is hate, not love, but we have been commanded by our Lord Jesus to love our neighbors as ourselves (see Matt 22:38). Our neighbor is not

---

48. Balevic, "Christian Group," para. 3.

limited to people who are like us or live close to us, but it can be someone different from us, as illustrated in the parable of the good Samaritan.

Compassion, mercy, truth, and love toward other people are the foundations of social justice. Thus, narcissists, self-righteous individuals, haters, and people with inflated self-concepts cannot show compassion and mercy toward other people because there is no love or truth in them, and they cannot understand the necessity of social justice. The basis of their interpretation of social justice is the individual's external characteristics rather than the biblical standard of equitable justice for all. Regrettably, the perversion of justice, distortion of truth, and differential treatment based on party affiliation and external traits have become normalized under Donald Trump's Republican Party. All these are inconsistent with biblical teachings; therefore, the Republican Party's agendas could not be endorsed by God as falsely promoted by some Christian Evangelical leaders.

Apostle Paul asked the Galatians, "Who has bewitched you?" The same question is being asked today to the Christian Evangelical leaders who support the ungodly practices that exist with Donald Trump's Republican Party; who has bewitched you? Your actions are not approved by God, which is why your phony prophecies and prayers resulted in negative outcomes. It is important for you to take a critical look at the potential effects of your support and actions instead of using mental heuristics in dealing with spiritual issues that require deep spiritual and thought processing. Such a deeper look at your behavior will enable you to foresee the long-term effects of your actions because you cannot eat your cake and still have it. The divisive messages and preaching of the Republican Party's oppressive policies and practices are far more destructive to our nation than the things the Democrats are being accused of doing. Evangelical leaders' partnership with the Republican Party and the persuasion of their followers to vote only for the GOP candidates will further enhance social injustice and divide our country to destruction—nothing good will come out of it because God is not a part of the wicked alliance. Developing trust in a political party rather than God has prevented God from intervening, but if Christians put their trust in God instead of a political party, they will see that God is able to transform the United States of America because he cares for America's well-being, too. The Scripture says:

> Behold, the LORD's hand is not shortened that it cannot save, nor His ear heavy that it cannot hear. But your iniquities have separated you from your God; and your sins have hidden His face from you so that He will not hear. For your hands are defiled with blood, and your fingers with iniquity; your lips have

spoken lies, your tongue has muttered perversity. No one calls for justice, nor does any plead for truth. They trust in empty words and speak lies; they conceive evil and bring forth iniquity. . . . The way of peace they have not known, and there is no justice in their ways; they have made themselves crooked paths, and whoever takes that way shall know no peace. . . . Justice is turned back, and righteousness stands afar off; for truth is fallen in the street, and equity cannot enter. So truth fails, and he who departs from evil makes himself a prey. The Lord saw it, and it displeased Him that there was no justice. (Isa 59:1–4, 8, 14–15)

Chapter 5

Gun Laws and Firearms-Related Violence

Gun control in relation to violence is another polarizing topic in the United States. It is also one of the most pervasive social issues that dominates our political discourse and create sharp divides between the Republicans and Democrats. Dialogue about the issue suggests obvious structural differences between the two political parties; while one sees gun ownership as a constitutionally protected right and, therefore, opposes any restriction that will prevent people from owning guns since such an effort would be deemed unconstitutional, the other pushes for universal background checks for gun purchases, to avert criminals, violent, and mentally ill individuals owning guns. Given the two opposing views, the overarching query is the relationship between guns and murder rates. Another intriguing matter to consider is the relationship between guns and violent criminal acts in the United States. This chapter reviews the effects of the proliferation of gun ownership for self-defense, as claimed by one group, and the impact of universal background checks in reducing gun violence, as implied by another. It also assesses biblical views on firearms.

GUN VIOLENCE IN THE UNITED STATES

The proliferation of guns and the tendency to misuse guns make the United States a very violent nation compared to other high-income countries. A study that compared firearms-related deaths in the United States and other high-income countries found that almost 97 percent of firearm deaths of children from birth to four years happened in the United States.[1] Addi-

---

1. Grinshteyn and Hemenway, "Violent Death Rates," 20.

tionally, the study showed that nearly 92 percent of gun-related deaths of women took place in the United States, and approximately 84 percent of all gun-related deaths happened in the United States. In 2022, more than six thousand children's deaths and injuries were related to gunfire.[2] Gun violence is the leading cause of death of American children, surpassing car accident deaths.[3] Evidently, access to guns at home does not make homes safe, and neither does the abundance of firearms outside the home make the public safe.

There are more firearms in the hands of Americans than the actual population of the US. It is estimated that Americans own 393 million firearms, greater than twenty-four countries combined, with the highest civilian gun ownership.[4] Additionally, more than one hundred gun-related deaths and more than 230 shootings and injuries due to gun violence occur daily in the United States.[5] Approximately 39,707 gun-related deaths took place in 2019; 60 percent of the deaths were suicides, and 36 percent were firearm homicides.[6] In the United States, the highest number of gun violence deaths and firearms-related homicides in the past twenty years occurred in 2020, with a total record number of 43,598.[7] An updated report by the CDC in May 2022 shows 45,222 firearm deaths occurred in 2020, which translates to 124 firearm-related deaths every day.

Gun violence does not only have tremendous costs to human lives but is financially very costly. On average, it costs the federal, state, and local governments $34.8 million daily for gun violence.[8] Also, every year, it is estimated to cost taxpayers, communities, employers, victims of gun violence, and their families $280 billion. Thus, making it easier for criminals and at-risk individuals to have access to guns has not saved lives; instead, it has been very costly to human lives and finances.

STAND-YOUR-GROUND LAWS OR CASTLE DOCTRINE

Stand-your-ground laws, nicknamed "shoot first" laws, permit people to use deadly force to eliminate their opponents if they reasonably believe

2. Gun Violence Archive, "GVA 10-Year Review."
3. Gebeloff et al., "Childhood Greatest Danger," paras. 1–2.
4. Karp, "Estimating Global Civilian-Held Firearms," 4.
5. Gun Violence Archive, "GVA 10-Year Review."
6. Educational Fund to Stop Gun Violence, "Data Reveals," para. 2.
7. Gun Violence Archive, "GVA 10-Year Review."
8. Gun Violence Archive, "GVA 10-Year Review."

their opponents threaten their safety. Although the laws support the use of lethal means for people to defend themselves, the application of the laws has been very deceptive. It encourages violence under the presumption of self-defense and, at the same time, discourages retreating or engaging in a conscientious effort to de-escalate violence. Thirty-eight states have enacted stand-your-ground laws as of January 2024,[9] and the majority of the states are in the red states or Republican states. Florida was the first state to ratify such laws in 2005, which was promoted by the National Rifle Association (NRA).[10] By 2012, gun-related deaths due to stand-your-ground laws have increased by over 200 percent in Florida.[11] With the stand-your-ground laws, more people started using the laws as a license to kill, even in situations that presented no reasonably perceived threat. The shooting of Trayvon Martin, on February 26, 2012, an unarmed Black teenage boy, by a self-appointed neighborhood crime watcher was a classic example of how someone can commit murder and use stand-your-ground laws to escape punishment from the criminal justice or receive criminal immunity.

In a research study by two Texas A&M University professors to examine the effects of stand-your-ground laws on homicides, they found that stand-your-ground laws increased the total number of homicides by 8 percent, which is an additional six hundred deaths per year within the twenty-three states in their study.[12] Additionally, they explored the efficacy of stand-your-ground laws in preventing violent crimes. The results showed that they did not have any effect in preventing aggravated assault, burglary, and robbery. The states with stand-your-ground laws also have the highest gun sales in the United States. Texas tops the list of gun purchases in 2020 at 1,870,075, followed by Florida at 1,658,434.[13] The only two groups benefiting from stand-your-ground laws are the NRA and the Republican Party because of the financial support GOP lawmakers receive from the NRA at the expense of American lives. What a shame!

In examining the relationship between stand-your-ground laws and the number of gun-related deaths in the United States, it is interesting to note that stand-your-ground laws strongly correlate with gun deaths in the United States. There are eighteen states with the highest number of gun-related deaths ranging from thirteen to over twenty per one hundred thousand people, and they all have stand-your-ground laws. Alaska topped the

9. Wikipedia, "Stand Your Ground Law," para. 28.
10. Tabachnick, "Stand Your Ground," paras. 7–10.
11. CBS Miami, "Stand Your Ground," para. 1.
12. Cheng and Hoekstra, "Does Strengthening Self-Defense Law?," 844.
13. Security.org Staff, "Gun Country," 4.

list, and all the states are Republican states except Nevada, which is a swing state. On the other hand, I also noticed that the seven states with the lowest number of gun-related deaths do not have stand-your-ground laws, and all are Democratic states. All of this shows that stand-your-ground laws have dangerous and deadly consequences and should be eradicated to reduce gun-related deaths and homicides in the United States. The data presented challenges one to question how can the Republican Party be a party endorsed by God when its practices and policies facilitate the killing of people created by God. The Evangelical leaders who use their abortion rhetoric to persuade their followers to vote for the Republican candidates will not share this type of information about gun-related deaths in the United States with their followers because it will violate their Faustian bargain (deal with the devil) they have with the Republican Party.

REPEALING BACKGROUND CHECK INFLUENCES GUN VIOLENCE

Repeal of background checks in gun purchases positively correlates with gun violence. For example, Missouri saw a 14 percent increase in murder rates and a 25 percent increase in homicide rates from 2008 to 2012 after it repealed its permit-to-purchase (PTP) handgun law in 2007.[14] This increase in gun violence as a result of the repeal represents forty-nine more murders each year from 2008 to 2012 and sixty-eight more firearm-related homicides each year from 2008 to 2012. In addition, the rate of gun-related deaths in Missouri increased by 35 percent, and firearm-related homicide increased by 65 percent between 2014 and 2019.[15]

The weakening of gun laws also poses a significant threat to public safety by allowing criminals who should have been in prison to be set free. On January 20, 2020, a man opened fire on a group of people outside the 9ine Ultra Lounge nightclub in Kansas City, Missouri, killing a woman and leaving fifteen people wounded.[16] The property security guard killed the shooter. Reviewing the criminal background of the shooter, the Jackson County prosecutor admits the shooter should have been in prison for previous unlawful use of a firearm, if not the Missouri gun law that was weakened in 2016. Congressional Republicans' opposition to universal background checks, because they claim they want to make it easier for people to have guns to protect themselves, has been counterproductive. The outcomes of

---

14. Webster et al., "Effects of the Repeal," 298.
15. Educational Fund to Stop Gun Violence, "Missouri Gun," para. 1.
16. Nozicka and Schwers, "At Least 15 Reported Wounded," paras. 1–2.

repealing background checks create the pathway for easy access and an abundance of guns in the hands of criminals, which empowers them to commit more gun violence against law-abiding citizens.

The question one must ask is, What are the motives for congressional Republicans to always oppose universal background checks, an approach that saves lives? This is a party that claims to be pro-life, and obviously, there is nothing in their policy about gun laws saving lives other than to increase preventable deaths and injuries.

GUN ACCESSIBILITY INFLUENCES GUN VIOLENCE

Gun violence is influenced by easy access to guns rather than a person's mental health and personality traits according to research conducted by University of Texas Medical Branch, Galveston, Texas professors.[17] In their study, they examined three variables in relation to gun violence, namely, gun access and ownership, mental illness, and personality traits. The outcome of the research showed that gun access and ownership were the catalysts for gun violence, including mass shootings that have cut many lives short in the United States. Having access to guns also increased the likelihood of a person threatening another individual with a gun by 18.15 times. In addition, hostile and at-risk individuals were more likely to be more vicious and dangerous if they had access to guns. According to the researchers, the outcomes of their research work could significantly influence legislators in passing gun laws that will save lives. One will hope that to be true with the congressional Republicans, who have always pushed for the proliferation of guns in society. Furthermore, individuals who own guns were 5.22 times more likely to take guns outside their homes, and individuals with access to guns were 4.74 times more likely to take guns outside their homes.[18] As more people are taking their guns outside their homes, it is more likely they will use their guns to shoot others, even in situations that do warrant the use of firearms.

GUN ACCESSIBILITY INCREASES DOMESTIC VIOLENCE

The combination of guns and domestic violence is dangerous in a relationship; thus, the availability and accessibility of guns increase domestic

---

17. Lu and Temple, "Dangerous Weapons," 1.
18. Lu and Temple, "Dangerous Weapons," 1.

violence substantially. In most cases, women are disproportionately affected by gun violence in intimate partner relationships. According to The Educational Fund to Stop Gun Violence, a woman is five times more likely to be killed if her partner has access to a gun; about 4.5 million women have been harassed, coerced, and terrorized with a gun; and almost a million women are victims of intimate partner gun violence. About 72 percent of murder-suicide involves intimate partners, and a large number of them are women (94 percent) who were killed by their partners using guns.[19]

Vignette

The proliferation of guns has created a culture of gun violence in our society. It normalizes killing one's opponent as an acceptable means of settling squabbles. It defiles cordiality, civility, and patriotism and desensitizes compassion and value for human life. It also creates a noxious culture of barbarism, the survival of the fittest, and a wild, wild west mentality that glamorizes violence and political campaigns of dehumanization.

PUBLIC OPINION ON STRICTER GUN LAWS

A Pew Research Center survey in 2020 found that 60 percent of Americans want stricter gun control laws, which is an increase from 52 percent in 2017.[20] Additionally, the desire to make gun laws less strict has dropped from 18 percent in 2017 to 11 percent in 2020.[21] The survey also found that the support for banning high-capacity magazines has increased from 65 percent in 2017 to 71 percent in 2019. Another survey focusing on Evangelical leaders shows that 58 percent of them own guns, and 55 percent favor stricter gun laws.[22] Interestingly, the group that is supposed to understand the sanctity of human life from God's perspective holds a similar view of the world.

---

19. Langley and Pasternack, "American Roulette," 5.
20. Schaeffer, "Share of Americans," paras. 2–3.
21. Schaeffer, "Share of Americans," paras. 2–3.
22. National Association of Evangelicals, "Evangelical Leaders Own Guns," para. 1.

GUN LAWS AND MASS SHOOTINGS

On February 14, 2018, a nineteen-year-old man shot and killed seventeen students with a semi-automatic rifle at his former high school, Marjory Stoneman Douglas High School, in Parkland, Florida. The deadly incident, in which seventeen other students were also wounded, sparked a national outrage among middle and high school students. I watched with intense interest as many students walked out of classrooms for days and weeks in a nationwide protest demanding stricter gun laws, keeping guns out of the hands of at-risk individuals, and protecting public schools. It was believed that the shooter had a mental health condition, and the FBI had been alerted six months before the shooting concerning his posting on YouTube to shoot a high school; therefore, he should have not been allowed to have access to guns. On March 24, 2018, the students, along with the support of thousands of other people, took their protest to Washington, intending to confront the lawmakers and the president about the necessity to modify gun laws to keep guns out of the hands of at-risk individuals and to make school campuses safe.

As the "March for Our Lives" crusade was unfolding, I was particularly interested to see how the Republican president and Republican Congress would react to the plea of these teenagers, who took courageous steps to petition the president and Congress for stricter gun laws and safer school campuses. In this incident, these high school students, the future American leaders, were disappointed, as they found out that the congressional Republicans' loyalty was to the NRA, not to their safety or the American public. During a meeting with the Republican senators, even former President Donald Trump told them, "You are afraid of NRA" to respond to the students' petitions. Although Donald Trump signed a bill that made minor adjustments to background checks and provided funds to improve school safety, the changes fell short of the students' expectations. It was disappointing that the legitimate petitions of the students were snubbed as if they did not matter. The irony of the whole episode is that some of the parents of the students continue to vote for congressional Republicans, who did not care for the safety of their children. The question still remains, How can God endorse a party that is more interested in the NRA making money at the expense of the safety of precious lives that God created?

With the rising number of mass shootings in the United States, 2021 experienced the highest number of mass shootings at 690, with 645 people killed and 3,267 people shot during the mass shootings.[23] In 2022, there

---

23. Gun Violence Archive, "GVA 10-Year Review."

were 648 mass shootings in the United States, killing 637 people and injuring over 2,500, while mass shootings in 2020 were at 610, with 521 people killed and 2,541 people wounded.[24] Interestingly enough, gun sales were at an all-time high of approximately 22 million in 2020,[25] and second highest in 2021, with approximately 17.4 million guns sold.[26] The total number of gun-related deaths from 2020 to 2022 was at an all-time high; interestingly, the years that experienced the highest number of gun sales also experienced the highest number of gun-related deaths. For example, in 2020, there were 43,710 firearm deaths; in 2021, there were 45,096 gun-violent deaths; and in 2022, 44,265 gun-related deaths.[27] These data suggest that the availability and accessibility of guns, especially at the hands of at-risk individuals and criminals, exacerbate gun violence. The question is, Are we going to adhere to the facts or subjective views that are unrelated to the facts, as promulgated by the Republican lawmakers and NRA? What will it take for our society to wake up and reclaim power?

While mass shootings reached a historical record in 2021, states controlled by the Republican Party continue to enact laws that will flood society with more guns, making our society less safe. On June 16, 2021, the permitless carry bill was signed into law in Texas, and the effective date was September 1, 2021. House Bill (H.B.) 1927 allows Texas residents to carry a handgun to the public without requiring a license to carry guns, as long as they are not prohibited either by the federal or state government to carry guns. Guess who was present when the bill was signed into law? The NRA president. What a mockery of our democracy, a for-profit organization influencing elected officials in passing bills that affect the safety of the mass populace. Before the bill was signed into law, a majority of Texas voters (59 percent) opposed a bill that would allow people to carry a gun without a license.[28]

Additionally, many Texas police departments opposed House Bill 1927, including the Fort Worth police chief, making a direct appeal to the chairman of the Texas Senate Committee on Constitutional Issues via mail, expressing their opposition to H.B. 1927.[29] Yet, public opinion and police departments' appeals were ignored. This is clear evidence that the Republican lawmakers do not care for the well-being of the citizens, except for

24. Boschma, "Mass Shootings," paras. 3–10.
25. Security.org Staff, "Gun Country."
26. Safe Home, "Gun Sales in the U.S.," paras. 2–3.
27. Gun Violence Archive, "GVA 10-Year Review."
28. Ramsey, "Majority of Texans Oppose," para. 13.
29. Dearman, "Texas Law Enforcement," paras. 1–5.

themselves and the rich. Their action contradicts their pretentious claims that they support men and women in blue, which often comes up when a mass protest occurs due to a police shooting a member of a minority group. However, with H.B. 1927, the Republican lawmakers ignored the appeals of many police departments and chose money at the expense of police safety. This type of betrayal of public trust and hijacking of our democracy will continue until the voters decide to vote out these self-serving politicians. Even if you must vote Republican, please support the Republican candidates during the primary election who are committed to serving the public's interest, not themselves. With many mass shootings that have taken place in the US, there remain to be seen heroes emerging out of the active shooting scene with their guns to stop the mass shooting from taking place, a lie promulgated by congressional Republicans and the NRA.

Interestingly, it is not a coincidence that in the past eight years, five out of the ten deadliest mass shootings in the US happened in Texas.[30] On May 24, 2021, the hearts of many Americans were broken, seeing the merciless killing of nineteen children and two adults at Robb Elementary School in Uvalde, Texas. The eighteen-year-old gunman, Salvador Ramos, barricaded himself in a classroom killing defenseless children and their teachers. The mass shooting presented a shocking reality about police cowardliness in a dire situation to protect the vulnerable at a time most needed. Even though there were at least forty armed lawmen on the scene, they waited over an hour before confronting and killing the gunman, but, before then, twenty-one lives had been lost. The Robb Elementary School shooting was the deadliest school shooting in Texas and the second deadliest school mass shooting in the US after the Sandy Hook Elementary School shooting in Newton, Connecticut, on December 14, 2012. However, the deadliest mass shooting (not school-related mass shooting) in Texas history happened on November 5, 2017, at First Baptist Church in Sutherland Springs, in which twenty-six people were killed, and the gunman was chased, and he crashed his vehicle and died as a result of a self-inflicted gunshot.[31] Texas has the highest registered gun ownership in the US. In intimate partner relationships, 67 percent of women murdered by their male partners in Texas were by firearms.[32]

---

30. Tucker, "Gun-Loving Texas," para. 1.
31. Sanchez, "Timeline of Texas Mass Shootings," paras. 1–5.
32. Texas Council of Family Violence, "Honoring Texas Victims," paras. 4–5.

FOOD FOR THOUGHT

If you are like me, perhaps you may have asked yourself this question: Why do the Republican lawmakers adamantly oppose universal background checks for gun purchase and push for gun laws that encourage the abuse of guns at the expense of human lives? Furthermore, why do the Republicans have this devious partnership with the NRA that is costly to American lives? Although most Americans support stricter gun laws, the NRA invests millions of dollars yearly in the gun rights lobby to undermine the people's will. Ninety-six percent of NRA donations went to the congressional Republicans,[33] which has been a significant reason for their opposition to passing common-sense gun laws that will reduce gun deaths and firearm suicides. In addition, when Donald Trump was running for the presidential election in 2016, the NRA spent more than $30 million in his campaign and invested more than $50 million in the Republican Party in the 2016 election.[34] Does this explain why the GOP lawmakers and governors pass reckless gun laws to increase the sales of guns while claiming the Second Amendment right? These are the same people that Evangelical leaders use the abortion rhetoric to portray as people of high moral integrity.

Democracy is our identity as a nation, and arguably the United States is the oldest practicing democratic society in the world. Democracy is what makes us unique, as a nation. If we lose our democracy to a few economically elite individuals or groups, we will lose our identity and will no longer be unique and different from other nations of the world. Over the past few decades, democracy, which is the government of the people, has gradually been slipping away from the hands of the people into the hands of a few economically elite groups. A study conducted at Princeton University and Northwestern University found that average American citizens have little or zero influence on US government policy, while the economic elites and organized interest groups have a significant impact on US government policy.[35] This is a dramatic shift of power from the citizens to a few economic elites. It is the responsibility of the citizens to reclaim the political power that belongs to them by voting out politicians, both Republicans and Democrats, who partner with for-profit interest groups. For the sake of preserving the efficacy of democracy for future generations, political actions are needed by this present generation; otherwise, our society will entirely turn into an oligarchy and eventually into totalitarianism. What a nightmare that will be!

33. Spies and Balcerzak, "NRA Place Big Bets," para. 1.
34. Spies and Balcerzak, "NRA Place Big Bets," paras. 1–6.
35. Gilens and Page, "Testing Theories of American Politics," 564.

Vignette

It should be illegal for elected or government officials to form a partnership or be influenced by a for-profit organization. The only guaranteed outcome of such a relationship is corruption, undermining our democracy, and subtle transfer of power from the people to a few economic elites and organized interest groups, making our government system an oligarchy instead of a democracy. Moreover, it is unpatriotic, immoral, and a betrayal of public trust for elected officials to partner with a for-profit organization at the expense of public safety. Thus, it is the civic duty of the citizens who cherish life, liberty, and the pursuit of happiness to vote out those elected individuals who have compromised the integrity of our democracy and their oaths of office by forming profane alliances with the economic elite and organized interest groups.

GUN CONTROL LAWS VERSUS SECOND AMENDMENT

Whenever the issue of introducing stricter or safer gun laws is mentioned, one who opposes such action will immediately respond in a defiant voice, saying, "That is an infringement of the Second Amendment right." Such a response, which often comes from congressional Republicans, is illogical and deceptive. Creating stricter gun control laws does not constitute an infringement of people's constitutional right to own a gun. The approach could be likened to the Department of Motor Vehicles creating stricter laws to make driving safe. For example, creating laws that forbid drunk drivers from getting behind the wheel, suspending the driver's license of convicted drunk drivers, making texting and driving illegal, and not issuing driver's licenses to people who failed the driving test. The purpose of such driving laws, including stricter gun laws, is not to infringe on people's right to drive or own guns but to create an environment where people can coexist safely. One would think that lawmakers would understand the rationale behind the need to create stricter gun laws, except they are controlled by special interest groups. The ambiguity in this argument is that the very same group that opposes stricter gun laws that save lives turns around and passes stricter voting bills to infringe on citizens' constitutional right to vote. A gun is often related to death, while voting is related to the exercise of freedom. A logical approach to both issues would suggest restrictive laws for that which kills and less restrictive laws for that which liberates.

GUNS DON'T KILL PEOPLE; PEOPLE KILL PEOPLE ARGUMENT

Some people claim that guns do not kill people. Indeed, guns themselves do not kill people; it is people who kill other people; however, guns have become the most lethal means they use in killing. You do not need to be a rocket scientist or do a statistical analysis to understand that guns' availability and easy access to people, especially to quick-tempered individuals, mentally ill, criminals, or someone who lacks self-control, make it easier for them to murder other people. A common trait among states with high gun violence is the accessibility of guns. States with more guns have more gun deaths.[36] There are more registered firearms in Texas than in any other state, and according to the US Centers for Disease Control and Prevention, approximately four thousand gun-related deaths take place in Texas every year. It makes sense because the easier it is for people to have access to guns, the more likely they will use them. The road rage that led to gun violence, in which someone was killed, could have not been possible if the killer did not have a gun with them while driving, because there are no possible means for the outraged driver to jump out of his car while driving on the highway to kill his opponent, except if he has a gun with him in the car. The mass shooters were able to kill many people quickly because of their access to assault weapons and high-capacity ammunition magazines to kill many people effortlessly. The ability to kill many people without being subdued by their victims is made possible because of the high capacity of the guns they have with them. The child who picks up a gun, not knowing its lethal effect, and shoots another child is made possible because of the availability and easy access to the gun.

People become drug addicts because of easy access and availability of drugs to them, and if the drugs are not available to them, there will be no drug to use to make them drug addicts. For the same reason, if guns are not available and easily accessible to hostile and at-risk individuals, firearm homicides and firearm suicides will be drastically reduced. People become alcoholics because of the availability and easy access to alcohol, and in the absence of alcohol, they are sober. If the law holds bartenders and bars accountable for serving alcohol to someone perceived to be drunk, which consequently leads to the individual causing an accident, why can't the law hold lawmakers responsible for passing reckless laws that promote the easy access of guns to criminals and mentally ill individuals, who later commit violence with the guns they were allowed to purchase?

---

36. Wolf, "States with the Most Gun Violence," para. 3.

Vignette

The easy access and availability of guns make preventable violence and deaths inevitable. It is common sense that since guns have been made easily accessible to people, there has been an increase in gun deaths and firearm homicides.

The deadly mass shooting at Covenant School, a private elementary school in Nashville, Tennessee, on March 27, 2023, resuscitated the argument for stricter gun laws in the United States. This shooting, which resulted in six deaths—three nine-year-olds and three staff members—was the one hundred and thirtieth mass shooting within the first three months of 2023, which tracks the year to possibly become one of the deadliest years of mass shootings in the US. There had been a total of 9,998-gun violent deaths as of March 27, 2023, which is in track with 44,287 total gun-related deaths in 2022.[37] Even though the twenty-eight-year-old female, Audrey Hale, used three of the seven guns she purchased legally in the attacks, she had been in treatment for an emotional disorder.[38] Selling guns to a person with an emotional disorder is a dangerous act, as evidenced in the death of three elementary school children and three staff members. However, with stricter gun laws, gun-related deaths could have been prevented.

Just like previous massacres, this mass shooting drew much empathy as well as criticisms concerning gun laws that make it easier for criminals and mentally and emotionally unstable individuals to purchase guns and commit gun violence. Whenever suggestions for stricter gun laws are mentioned, some GOP lawmakers will oppose such a move. For example, after the massacre at the Covenant School in Nashville, Tennessee, a GOP lawmaker from Tennessee, Rep. Tim Burchett, resisted suggestions for gun legislation that would create a safer society. He said, "If you want to legislate evil, it is just not going to happen. We need a real revival in this country."[39] The same thing could be said about abortion; we do not need legislation; rather, we need revival. Nevertheless, both need legislation to avoid wasting human lives.

Another GOP lawmaker, Rep. Clay Higgins, in his response about stricter gun laws after the Nashville elementary school shooting, states, "There's no such thing as gun violence. There's only human violence. It's intellectually unsound to state otherwise."[40] In essence, Rep. Higgins, what

---

37. Gun Violence Archive, "GVA 10-Year Review."
38. Hernandez, "What We Know," para. 35.
39. Nobles et al., "Tennessee Rep. Burchett," para. 3.
40. Edwards, "GOP Rep.," para. 4.

is intellectually unsound is the baseless claim that "there's no such thing as gun violence." It is equivalent to saying that there are no such things as cybercrime, armed robbery, road rage, cyberbullying, and poisonous deaths. All these involved instruments used to commit aggressive, violent, and deadly crimes. The absence of the associated instruments will drastically reduce the probability of such aggressive and violent acts occurring.

The problem with the GOP's phony position on abortion is that it is not about a concern for human lives; it is a political tactic to gain Christian votes. A genuine concern for human lives is not limited to lives in mothers' wombs but lives outside mothers' wombs. As long as they are receiving financial support from the NRA in gun sales to the detriment of human lives, they will continue to oppose restricted gun laws. Some argue that stricter gun laws will not reduce gun violence or save lives. Such an argument is flawed because the same logic can be applied to abortion, whereby one can argue that stricter abortion laws will not save unborn babies' lives. In reality, stricter gun laws and abortion laws will increase the probability of saving lives. Disappointedly, both parties, Democrats and Republicans, are guilty of systemic dehumanization at different stages of human life span.

It is common sense to know that guns will lead to unwarranted gun violence in the wrong hands. Similarly, it is common sense to understand that power in the hands of self-centered politicians will lead to enacting self-benefiting policies. The Republican Party's abhorrent partnership with the NRA is self-serving. When the Republican lawmakers repeal background checks to make it easier for guns to be sold to at-risk individuals and criminals, it results in financial benefits for the NRA, and they are, in return, financially supporting Republican Party political campaigns. The whole episode simply represents placing monetary value over human lives. That is immoral and unbiblical!

RECOMMENDATIONS TO REDUCE GUN VIOLENCE

The waiting period seems to be one of the most effective methods to reduce gun violence, especially for at-risk and hostile individuals. The waiting period refers to the time frame between gun purchase and actual gun possession. Thus, waiting period laws delay the final acquisition of a purchased gun by some days. The waiting period serves as a "cooling off" period to prevent impulsive gun violence. The extant study demonstrates a positive relationship between waiting periods and a reduction in gun violence. The waiting period reduces firearm homicides by 17 percent and by 7 to 11 percent for firearm suicides each year.⁴¹ In addition, studies show that stricter gun laws reduce gun violence. Based on the yearly analysis of the Giffords Law Center, more stringent gun laws save lives; states with stricter gun laws have fewer firearm fatalities than states with loose or fewer gun laws.

On the other hand, less strict gun laws increase gun fatalities. For example, Alaska has the highest number of gun-related deaths than any other state in the country and has one of the worst gun laws. It does not have universal background checks on firearm sales, a waiting period, or a ban on high-capacity ammunition. Stand-your-ground is part of Alaska gun laws, which exacerbate gun violence in the state. Banning high-capacity ammunition can effectively reduce the number of gun casualties that might occur within a short period. A for-profit organization should be prohibited from partnering with elected officials and influencing legislation that affects the masses. The natural outgrowth of such a relationship is corruption, and it is an affront to our democracy. Other factors include restricting at-risk individuals' access to guns, reducing substance abuse, and increasing employment.⁴²

BIBLICAL PERSPECTIVE ON GUNS

The issue of guns and gun control was not discussed in the Bible since guns were not in existence during the days of the Bible. However, other types of weapons, which may be considered prototypes of modern-day firearms, such as swords, bows, arrows, and spears, were discussed and used heavily in battles. It is essential to distinguish how weapons were used in the days of the Bible versus the promotion and the use of guns today in the United States. Most biblical instructions about the use of weapons were primarily focused on the Jewish militia fighting against their enemies, usually foreign countries, not slaughtering their fellow citizens. Nonetheless, no biblical instruction forbids people or Christians from owning weapons to protect themselves and their family members. It may be necessary for some people to own guns for self-defense at home, especially those who feel comfortable owning guns, considering our postmodern crime-ridden society. This view is not the same as bearing arms in public, where abundant evidence shows the increase of unwarranted gun violence.

There seems to be a misunderstanding about Jesus' instruction to his disciples. "Then He said to them, 'But now, he who has a money bag, let him take it, and likewise a knapsack; and he who has no sword, let him sell his

---

41. Luca et al., "Handgun Waiting," 12162.
42. Campbell et al., "Risk Factors," 1093–95.

garment and buy one'" (Luke 22:36). Jesus' speech was a symbolic expression of how future events, primarily satanic attacks, and the world system, will be intensified against his disciples and believers, which will require a greater degree of spiritual preparation. He was not speaking about buying weapons for physical battles since our warfare is not physical battles. "For the weapons of our warfare are not carnal but mighty in God for pulling down strongholds" (2 Cor 10:4). The Scripture did not advocate for Christians to engage in physical combats since the root of our battles is spiritual. "For we do not wrestle against flesh and blood, but principalities, against powers, against the rulers of the darkness of this age, against spiritual hosts of wickedness in the heavenly places" (Eph 6:12).

Furthermore, to confirm that Jesus was not speaking about buying man-made weapons, he rebuked Peter for drawing out his sword and cutting off the high priest servant's ear. Matthew 26:52 states, "But Jesus said to him, 'Put your sword in its place, for all who take the sword will perish by the sword.'" The inevitable outcome of bearing arms in public is more gun violence and firearm shootings. Contrary to the illusions promulgated by the congressional Republicans and the NRA, the accessibility of guns does not help people defend and save their lives, but in essence, it destroys lives, as supported by research evidence. The people who keep amassing more guns, including assault weapons and high-capacity magazines, are usually at-risk individuals and criminals, the very individuals who should not have access to firearms. A more rational approach should be to get guns out of the hands of at-risk individuals and criminals instead of empowering them with more assault weapons. Another important scripture to consider, which is often taken out of context, states:

> If a thief is caught breaking in at night and is struck a fatal blow, the defender is not guilty of bloodshed; but if it happens after sunrise, the defender is guilty of bloodshed. Anyone who steals must certainly make restitution, but if they have nothing, they must be sold to pay for their theft. (Exod 22:2–3 NIV)

I chose to use the New International Version (NIV) with these scriptural verses for the sake of clarity because NIV presents a clearer picture of the two verses than the King James Version or the New King James Version. In verse 2, there are two possible scenarios in which a defender (homeowner) may not be guilty of striking a thief who is breaking into his house at night with a fatal blow. First, night presents a greater challenge for the homeowner to see and identify the thief, so the homeowner may strike the thief in his effort to defend himself and his castle, which may result in the thief's death. Second, a thief who chooses to break into someone's home at night may have a violent intention other than to steal things. In this scenario, the homeowner has the right to defend himself and his family, which may also result in the thief's death. Nevertheless, the biblical verses should not be misinterpreted as a license to kill a thief who breaks into your home when there are other possible means to avoid killing the thief. It is the intent of your action that will ultimately justify you before God, not the legal system. Even if the criminal justice system refuses to prosecute or acquit someone of murder, that does not mean that God has acquitted the person of murder. God disapproves of murder, especially when it is avoidable. For all souls belong to him, and they are precious to him.

However, if the killing occurs during daylight, the homeowner or defender is guilty of bloodshed. Furthermore, because the homeowner can see the thief during the day than at night, it gives him a greater chance of avoiding confrontation or killing the thief. Nonetheless, I do believe if an armed robber breaks into your home, regardless of the time of the day, you have a God-given right to use whatever means necessary to defend and protect yourself and your family.

QUESTIONS FOR THE CHRISTIAN EVANGELICAL LEADERS

Why is it that the Christian Evangelical leaders who are politicizing abortion do not talk about forty thousand gun-related deaths every year, and most of these deaths are preventable? Why are they silent about the reckless gun laws passed by the Republican lawmakers and governors that have escalated firearm suicides and homicide in the United States? The Evangelical leaders' silence and refusal to publicly declare their support for stricter gun laws that would have saved human lives is hypocritical and absurd. Their silence about the Republican Party's vile partnership with the NRA is also hypocritical and ungodly. Yet many of the Evangelical leaders work so hard to compel unwitting individuals to view the Republican Party as a party endorsed by God, as well as coerce their followers to vote only for Republican candidates. Other than the Republican Party's anti-abortion political position, their position on other social issues is unbiblical.

For the Evangelicals who promote the Republican Party as God's party, it is duplicitous to use its anti-abortion position as a reason to justify the ungodly practices that go on within the party and even to justify your support for the party. If you care for the life of the unborn, you should equally care for the life of the mother, father, and siblings of the unborn. All souls belong to God, and they are equally valuable to him. If you must talk about abortion, you must also obligate yourself to talk about less restrictive gun laws promulgated by the Republican Party, which have intensified gun-related deaths in the US. You cannot show favoritism; you must be upright, as God demands of us.

SUMMARY

As presented in this chapter, a plethora of research and documented evidence creates a strong prima facie case for the significance of stricter gun control laws to minimize gun-related deaths and firearm suicides in the United States. The egregious misinterpretation of the Scripture can be misleading. The New Testament believers were not called to bear arms in public, as there were no approved examples from Jesus, the apostles, and the early church concerning armbearing. Jesus rebuked Peter for using his sword, and of course, if you take a weapon to the public, you are more likely to be tempted to use it. However, Christians are called to be peacemakers, and so Jesus says, "Blessed are the peacemakers, for they shall be called sons of God" (Matt 5:9). So, packing up guns in public has not resulted in peacemaking but violence.

The use of stand-your-ground law to kill another person, especially when such killing is unnecessary, is murder in God's law. Exodus 21:12 states, "He who strikes a man so that he dies shall surely be put to death." Furthermore, Exod 21:14 says, "But if a man acts with premeditation against his neighbor, to kill him by treachery, you shall take him from My altar, that he may die." Life is precious before God, and when a man or woman kills another, God demands justice, contrary to the view of those who support the proliferation of guns in public.

Those who are staunch supporters of the Republican Party and always voting for Republican Party candidates need to take a deep look to assess how the Republican Party cares about your well-being. You may have developed an innate distaste for the political views of the Democrats that you have purposed in your mind that on no condition can you vote for a Democrat. If you hold such views, be sure that you are not supporting corrupt politicians who placed greater values on their selfish interests rather than the safety of the public. Furthermore, you need to take a profound analytical approach in assessing how each party directly affects you and the well-being of your family. Some Democrats may support policies like abortion, which is ungodly; however, as discussed in chapter 3, not all Democrats are pro-abortion; in the same manner, not all Republicans are anti-abortion; actually, 29 percent of Republicans are pro-abortion. Democrats may support policies they perceive to promote human rights, while non-Democrats may see such policies to contradict their values. Nonetheless, if you carefully consider the policies of the Democrats, you will see that they do not have direct negative effects on you and your family's safety and financial well-being. On the other hand, the Republican Party's position on a lot of political issues, such as social programs, social justice, and guns, has direct negative effects on the safety of average American life and well-being. The congressional Republican Party's interest is primarily focused on protecting the interest of the elite and special interest groups, not of the average Americans.

Chapter 6

Immigration Laws and DACA

Immigration plays a crucial role in shaping American history of citizenship, with the genealogy of nearly all US citizens being traced back to immigration, except the Native Americans. This reality is captured in the adage, "We all are immigrants," underscoring the nation's roots. If you're not a recent immigrant, you are most likely a descendant of earlier generations of immigrants. Given this historical backdrop, the United States should possess a profound understanding of immigration issues, and their complexities, and a compassionate stance toward new arrivals. However, immigration remains a divisive issue in American politics, with different ideological approaches embraced by the two dominant political parties.

Both Democrats and Republicans hold conflicting views on the structural approach to immigration policy. In this chapter, I will explore the biblical perspectives on immigration and then delve into how these views align or clash with the immigration policies of each political party. To illustrate these points, I will provide some examples and data that shed light on the complex relationship between immigration and politics in the United States.

BIBLICAL ORIGIN OF IMMIGRATION WITH GOD'S COVENANT PEOPLE

The concept of immigration originated with God, which he initiated with the man he made a covenant with and blessed the whole world through him. Genesis 12:1 states, "Now the LORD had said to Abram: 'Get out of your country, from your kindred and from your father's house to a land that I will show you.'" Thus, Abram, later named Abraham, emigrated from his native country and migrated with his wife Sarah to several countries. In his journey from country to country, there was a sovereign shield of protection over Abraham and his household; God rebuked and plagued leaders like pharaoh, king of Egypt, and Abimelech, king of Gerar, for Abraham's sake because they attempted to take his wife from him. So, the Scripture says:

> When they went from one nation to another, from one kingdom to another people, He permitted no one to do them wrong; yes, He rebuked kings for their sakes, saying, "Do not touch My anointed ones, and do My prophets no harm." Moreover He called for a famine in the land; He destroyed all the provision of bread. (Ps 105:13–16)

God also revealed to Abraham what would happen to his descendants by saying, "Know certainly that your descendants will be strangers in a land that is not theirs, and will serve them, and they will afflict them four hundred years" (Gen 15:13). So, the Israelites, the descendants of Abraham, were enslaved immigrants in Egypt four hundred years. Additionally, the Israelites were immigrants for forty years in the wilderness before they finally possessed the Promised Land by the sovereign hand of God. Immigration has been an integral part of Jewish history, including prominent Jewish figures such as Jacob, Joseph, and Moses. All these migrated to foreign countries, although not always voluntarily. Similarly, multiple Jewish migrations to foreign countries have been involuntary in most cases, but God was always with them. The historical accounts of the Jewish immigration experience and God's instructions to the Israelites on how to treat foreigners present an ideal model for other nations of the world on how to implement immigration policies, especially for America, whose historical immigration experience could be likened to that of the Jews.

For the most part, America has been a promised land for the first cohorts of immigrants and subsequent immigrants. The first settlers who fled from Europe in search of religious freedom, including the Pilgrims and Puritans, came to the United States with the same view that America was their promised land, a land of freedom and economic opportunities. Likewise, America has been a land of great hope for many; thus, the primary motives of recent immigrants into the United States have been in search of better economic opportunities and freedom.

BIBLICAL TEACHING ON HOW TO TREAT IMMIGRANTS

Deuteronomy 10:18–19 reveals God's love toward immigrants and his commandments for the host country to love the immigrants in their country. "He [God] administers justice for the fatherless and the widows and loves the stranger, giving him food and clothing. Therefore love the stranger, for you were strangers in the land of Egypt." This instruction to love strangers (immigrants) is also relevant to Americans to love the immigrants in their country, for all were once directly or indirectly immigrants, except the Native Americans. Therefore, xenophobia and jingoism are ungodly practices and should be treated as despicable behavior. God understands the vulnerability of immigrants in their host country and how easily they could be exploited by the wicked, so he warns them not to mistreat them. So, God says:

> And if a stranger dwells with you in your land, you shall not mistreat him. The stranger who dwells among you shall be to you as one born among you, and you shall love him as yourself; for you were strangers in the land of Egypt: I am the LORD your God. (Lev 19:33–34)

GOD COMMANDS JUSTICE FOR THE IMMIGRANTS

It is ungodly to deny justice to the immigrants and citizens of different national origin for it provokes God's judgment on those who engage in such practice. Deuteronomy 27:19 states, "Cursed is the one who perverts the justice due the stranger, the fatherless, and widow. And all the people shall say, 'Amen!'" God also demands that a foreigner should not be mistreated, and neither should he receive unequal justice because he is a foreigner. Exodus 22:21 says, "You shall neither mistreat a stranger nor oppress him, for you were strangers in the land of Egypt." So, God demands that immigrants receive equal justice just as the citizens. "One law shall be for the native-born and for the stranger who dwells among you" (Exod 12:49). For people who think it is their civic duty to deny and pervert justice due to an immigrant or people of different national origin, you have a chance to repent and stop such ungodly practice. God sees everything that people do and knows the heart of everyone, and that is why he is described as omnipotent, omniscient, and omnipresent God. The Scripture also says that he watches and performs his word (see Jer 1:12). The truth of God's word is not subject to people's acceptance or acknowledgment, because God's word is settled in heaven forever (see Ps 119:89–91).

According to God's word, immigrants should also be allowed to partake in cultural and religious activities as much as they are willing and meet the set criteria. Numbers 9:14 states, "And if a stranger dwells among you, and would keep the Lord's Passover, he must do so according to the rite of the Passover and according to its ceremony; you shall have one ordinance, both for the stranger and the native of the land." In addition to having the same privilege in participating in cultural and religious activities, the above scripture also implies equal protection of the law for all and equal accountability for the violation of the law.

Interestingly, God uses the same lens of justice for immigrants as for other marginalized groups, such as the fatherless, widow, and poor. In Zechariah 7:10, God says, "Do not oppress the widow or the fatherless, the alien or the poor. Let none of you plan evil in his heart against his brother." The person who has the propensity to oppress a widow also has the same inclination to oppress the fatherless, the alien, and the poor. It takes an ungodly heart to oppress and mistreat marginalized groups. Such ungodly behavior is not limited only to the disadvantaged, for the perpetrator is also more likely to plot evil against his family members, friends, and neighbors. How someone treats immigrants, widows, fatherless, and the poor indicates their heart conditions toward others, including family members and friends. Furthermore, it indicates whether they have a fear of God in them or not and their heart conditions toward God, who created the marginalized groups. It is not wise or safe to mistreat a group of people who are at the center of God's heart, for he vows to avenge and render judgment. God says:

> You shall neither mistreat a stranger nor oppress him, for you were strangers in the land of Egypt. You shall not afflict any widow or fatherless child. If you afflict them in any way, and they cry at all to Me, I will surely hear their cry; and My wrath will become hot, and I will kill you with the sword; your wives shall be widows, and your children fatherless. (Exod 22:21–24)

The above scriptural verses are very serious and should capture the attention of people concerning how they treat marginalized groups. For God says if they (marginalized groups) cry out to him, he will hear them and, in his anger, will render judgment that includes making the wives and children of the perpetrators widows and fatherless. The Christian Evangelical preachers who are drawn to preaching socialism should also present these types of scriptural verses to their followers because of the serious consequences associated with the violation of the above scriptures. It is important to take the word of God seriously and not based on convenience because, God says, "So shall My word be that goes forth from My mouth; it shall not return unto Me void, but it shall accomplish what I please, and it shall prosper in the thing for which I sent it" (Isa 55:11). Also, know that all Scripture is given by inspiration of God (see 2 Tim 3:16).

Vignette

> The mistreatment of immigrants and people of different national origins is a type of sin that does not go unpunished by God, even for generations. It reveals the wickedness of the heart of the person toward God's creation and a debilitating heart condition toward God. It is an abomination before God that elicits generational iniquities. God's set standard of a righteous heart is based on how you treat marginalized groups and people different from you, not on how you treat people like yourself (see Matt 5:46–48).

Know that if you do good, you bless yourself, your children, and future generations, but if you mistreat the vulnerable, you have brought God's judgment upon you, your children, and future generations. Do not be deceived by anyone telling you otherwise; even when sins are forgiven, some of the consequences remain. The choice is yours!

God is always mindful of the immigrants, widows, and fatherless and looks after them, for the Scripture says, "The LORD watches over the strangers; He relieves the fatherless and widow; but the way of the wicked He turns upside down" (Ps 146:9). He also fights and defends the cause of this group and commands that they should be helped. "And if one of your brethren becomes poor, and falls into poverty among you, then you shall help him, like a stranger or a sojourner, that he may live with you" (Lev 25:35). It is ungodly for employers to take advantage of the immigrants and the poor; thus, God commands that they should not withhold the wages of immigrants, poor, and needy. Therefore, he instructed the Israelites by saying:

> You shall not oppress a hired servant who is poor and needy, whether one of your brethren or one of the aliens who is in your land within your gates. Each day you shall give him his wages, and not let the sun go down on it, for he is poor and has set his heart on it; lest he cry out against you to the LORD, and it be sin to you. (Deut 24:14–15)

God also reveals his heart of compassion toward the immigrant, fatherless, and widow. He commands farm owners to intentionally leave some produce behind during harvest for the immigrant, fatherless, and widow to gather.

> When you reap your harvest in your field, and forget a sheaf in the field, you shall not go back to get it; it shall be for the stranger, the fatherless, and the widow, that the Lord your God may bless you in all the work of your hands. When you beat your olive trees, you shall not go over the boughs again; it shall be for the stranger, the fatherless, and the widow. When you gather the grapes of your vineyard, you shall not glean it afterward; it shall be for the stranger, the fatherless, and the widow. And you shall remember that you were a slave in the land of Egypt; therefore I command you to do this thing. (Deut 24:19–22)

There is a plethora of scriptures that clearly illustrate God's position and passion toward immigrants and how the host country should treat them. The Scriptures are sufficient for any country, especially the United States of America, to create comprehensive immigration laws based on God's standards. The argument that the Bible did not talk about immigration laws as an excuse to exonerate those who create inhumane immigration policies is flawed and illogical. God explicitly revealed his heart condition toward immigrants in the Scriptures, which presents sufficient guidelines to create immigration laws based on biblical principles. Let us examine some immigration policies that each political party has enacted and compare them with biblical teachings.

DEFERRED ACTION FOR CHILDHOOD ARRIVAL (DACA)

DACA is an executive order initiated by President Barack Obama on June 15, 2012. It was an immigration policy designed to protect individuals brought to the United States illegally by their parents as children. The policy protects them from deportation as long as the individual is not a threat to national or public safety and does not have felonies, significant misdemeanors, or three or more other misdemeanors.[1] In addition, the recipient must be at least fifteen years old, and it is renewable every two years. Although DACA is not a legal status, it does give eligible recipients work authorization in the

---

1. US Citizenship and Immigration Services, "Consideration for Deferred Action," para. 15.

United States. There are approximately 636,390 active DACA recipients as of December 31, 2020.[2]

However, the Trump Administration announced its rescission from the DACA program on September 5, 2017. The action ensued multiple legal battles that resulted in a United States district court judge ruling on December 4, 2020, which implied that Chad Wolf, the acting secretary of the Department of Homeland Security, lacked the authority to block the DACA program. The judge issued an order obliging the Department of Homeland Security to reestablish the DACA policy that was in existence before September 5, 2017.[3] Prior to the ruling on December 4, 2020, the United States Supreme Court ruled (five to four) on June 18, 2020, that the Trump administration's effort to terminate DACA violates the Administration Procedure Act (APA) because the agency did not present a reasonable explanation for its actions, nor present alternative options to address the DACA program after it was deemed illegal by then-Attorney General Jeff Sessions.[4] Donald Trump and most GOP lawmakers' policy to deport DACA recipients is inconsistent with biblical values, which is another example that the Republican Party's agendas contradict biblical standards and cannot be a party endorsed by God.

By necessity, it should be the moral obligation of a host country to protect, provide, and care for immigrant children as one of their own, who, not by their own doing, were brought illegally to the United States by their parents. The question that my heart ponders is: What is the moral justification for penalizing and deporting children or adults for the crimes of their parents? For some of these DACA recipients, known as Dreamers, their primary language is English, and to deport them to a country of unfamiliar language and culture is inhumane. Like any one of you reading this book, if you or one of your children is expatriated to a foreign country with an unfamiliar language and culture, imagine the difficulty of surviving under such conditions. The deportation of Dreamers also contradicts God's instructions on how to treat immigrants. God says, "The stranger who dwells among you shall be to you as one born among you, and you shall love him as yourself; for you were strangers in the land of Egypt: I am the LORD your God" (Lev 19:34). The root of this type of inhumane and ungodly treatment is a lack of love toward people who are different, which congressional Republicans, presidents, and people with strong Republican Party affiliation often promulgate. The absence of love is hatred, and the benchmark of

2. US Citizenship and Immigration Services, "Count for Active DACA," 1.
3. Romo, "Judge Orders Trump Administration," para. 3.
4. Morse et al., "U.S. Supreme Court Ruling," para. 1.

love is to love those who are different from you. The irony of this ungodly treatment of immigrants is the silence and/or support from some Christian Evangelical leaders and their followers. The same group of individuals who are very vocal and quick to politicize abortion now pretends to be unaware of the ungodly policies promulgated by the Republican Party against immigrants, which is a type of inhumane treatment.

The American Dream and Promise Act was passed by the US House of Representatives along the party line after the Democrats took control of the House in 2019, creating the pathway for permanent residence for eligible DACA recipients. However, the act was not considered in the Senate because of the opposition of Republican senators.[5] There is nothing righteous or godly for congressional Republicans to block the pathway for eligible Dreamers to receive permanent residency. This is a political party the Christian Evangelical leaders promote as God's party when their political position on social issues prodigiously contradicts God's values.

Once again, crosschecking both parties' political positions on social issues, the Democrats' approach and policies are more likely to conform to biblical teachings, while the Republicans' policies sharply contradict biblical principles. The question then is, Why do the majority of the Christian Evangelical leaders overwhelmingly support a political party whose policies regarding respect for human lives contradict the teaching of our Lord Jesus to love your neighbor as yourself? The Lord Jesus has set a test that the hypocrites and some Republicans cannot pass, that is:

> You shall love the LORD your God with all your heart, with all your soul, and with all your mind. This is the first and great commandment. And the second is like it: You shall love your neighbor as yourself. On these two commandments hang all the Law and the Prophets. (Matt 22:37–40)

It is impossible for the extreme conservative group found among the Republican Party to please God. All their behaviors and policies are inconsistent with biblical values, except abortion. And, of course, abortion has been turned into a political punch bag since there is no demonstrated evidence in their policies to indicate they care for the average Americans except for the rich.

By all accounts, the Dreamers, the very group the Republican president and some of the congressional Republicans want to deport, qualify to be fellow American citizens. They grew up in the United States, have jobs, and pay their taxes. There are an estimated 29,000 Dreamers who are frontline

---

5. Kumar, "Trump Voters Want," para. 21.

health workers, such as doctors, registered nurses, medical assistants, and personal care aids; 14,900 are teachers, and 142,100 work in restaurants, grocery stores, farms, and the agriculture industry.[6] Their occupational positions are essential, especially during the 2020 and 2021 coronavirus pandemic. The deportation of DACA recipients will most likely pose some challenges to replace critical positions they hold in our society. The practice of extreme politics can lead to inhumane treatment, which is countercultural to American values, as well as dangerous to society's sustainability.

Those who mistreat others have no love in their hearts, which makes it hard for them to show love or mercy to people different from them. Furthermore, God says to the Jews, "For I desire mercy and not sacrifice, and the knowledge of God more than burnt offerings" (Hos 6:6). Jesus re-emphasizes the same scriptural verse by saying, "But if you had known what this means, I desire mercy and not sacrifice, you would not have condemned the guiltless" (Matt 12:7). If you pay attention to Evangelical preachers who promote the Republican Party agendas and congressional Republicans who talk about immigration, social programs, social justice, and gun violence, there is no mercy to human lives in their tones but excuses, condemnation, and self-justification. In addition, it takes a heartless and unmerciful cohort of individuals to block the DACA program and to block efforts to create policies that will enable eligible DACA recipients to become citizens. Such behavior is ungodly and indicates one's heart condition toward God. To have faith in the grace offered to us by the Lord Jesus requires obedience to his command, and the fruit of the obedience is love toward another person regardless of race, ethnicity, nationality, class, gender, age, and moral state. Jesus says, "If you love Me, keep My commandments" (John 14:15). Christian Evangelicals whose political affiliation is Republican have moral and godly obligations to condemn their party's policies that contradict biblical teachings. They should challenge the Republican Party to enact laws on social issues that reflect biblical standards to continue receiving their support and votes.

PUBLIC OPINION ON DREAMERS

A majority of American registered voters, both Democrats and Republicans, do not want DACA recipients deported but support the idea of allowing them to stay in the United States. Sixty-one percent of Americans support eligible Dreamers to become citizens, 17 percent approve of eligible

---

6. Svajlenka, "Demographic Profile of DACA," paras. 6–8.

Dreamers receiving legal residency, and 12 percent approve of their deportation.[7] Another poll conducted by the Pew Research Center reveals that 74 percent of Americans favor granting legal residence to Dreamers, while 24 percent oppose such a move.[8] The poll also indicates that 91 percent of Democrats support granting permanent residence to Dreamers; only 54 percent of Republicans agree with the same. Since most Americans support granting permanent residence to Dreamers, the congressional Republicans need to stop opposing the people's will through their inaction or repealing of the DACA program.

FAMILY SEPARATION AT THE US BORDER

Family separation practices at the US–Mexico border, a policy adopted by the Trump administration during the 2018 "zero tolerance" period, created traumatic experiences for vulnerable immigrant families fleeing from the hardship of their home countries. The unbearable horror of parents suddenly losing the custody of their children and children forcibly being separated from their parents, and perhaps never seeing each other again, is incomprehensible and questions a person's moral state to make such an inhumane policy. The outgrowth of this cruel policy has been devastating for immigrant families, resulting in avoidable deaths. For example, Marco Antonio Munoz, a thirty-nine-year-old father, committed suicide in a detention cell after being separated from his wife and child.[9] In two other incidents, a seven-year-old girl, Jakelin Caal Maquin, died from a bacterial infection known as streptococcal sepsis while in the custody of US Border Patrol after she was separated from her family,[10] and an eight-year-old, Felipe Gomez Alonzo, died in Border Patrol custody of an influenza infection after being separated from his family.[11]

An immigration policy that undermines the significance of family bonds raises concerns about both short- and long-term mental and emotional damage to family units. Separating children from their parents poses potential serious mental health problems, suicide ideation, post-traumatic stress disorder (PTSD), and depressive disorder to children of immigrants.[12] Parents are equally affected traumatically when their children are separated

7. Kumar, "Trump Voters Want," para. 5.
8. Krogstad, "Americans Broadly Support," para. 2.
9. Miroff, "Family Was Separated," paras. 1–7.
10. Sanchez, "Guatemalan Girl," para. 2.
11. Boyette et al., "Guatemalan Boy," paras. 1–2.
12. Cardoso, "Running to Stand Still," 143.

from them, as seen with Mr. Munoz, who took his life after being separated from his family and put in the immigration cell. Some parents are more likely to experience anxiety, high depression, and PTSD due to forcible separations from their children.[13] The "zero-tolerance" policy is un-American and contradicts our legal and social values. It is a policy that kills and destroys families.

BORDER WALL

The building of the US–Mexico border wall has been an ongoing sociopolitical debate topic that has generated polarizing views between the Republicans and Democrats. Politicizing social issues suppresses efforts to enact a sound policy or reach a consensus that benefits everyone. Therefore, social problems requiring commonsense resolutions have taken a complicated path due to diverging political discourse. Personally, I believe that building a border wall is a necessary undertaking for several reasons. The intention is not to stop immigration but to control a seemingly chaotic situation at the US–Mexico border. The building of a border wall is essential in enhancing national security and minimizing the influx of criminal activities, such as drug smuggling, human trafficking, illegal movement of weapons, terrorist groups, and unlawful entry. Congressional Democrats' opposition to building secure border walls is equally as superficial as Republican senators' inaction to creating policy that will enable Dreamers to become citizens. It is incomprehensible why anyone would oppose the building of border walls seeing the degree of criminal activities that take place on the US–Mexico border. Immigrants also have a responsibility to honor the country's law; they seek asylum by going through the approved port of entry rather than using an illegal entrance. In the absence of necessary border walls, the immigration crisis at the borders, as we have seen with President Biden's administration, will continue to rise even though the administration refuses to acknowledge the crisis's existence. On average, each day, Border Patrol agents seized 4,657 pounds of narcotics and $3.7 million worth of products with Intellectual Property Rights violations in 2018.[14] Border walls may not stop illegal migration, especially for those who are desperate, but they are most likely to cut down the number of illegal migrants and other criminal activities. For example, the number of people trying to cross the San Diego border illegally in the early 1990s dropped from 600,000 to 39,000 in 2015

13. Habbach et al., "You Will Never See," para. 7.
14. U.S. Customs and Border Protections, "On a Typical Day," paras. 2–10.

after building a fence and increasing Border Patrol presence.[15] Additionally, there was a significant increase in drug seizures, such as methamphetamine, fentanyl, and marijuana, at the San Diego border. The drug smugglers were forced to use ports of entry, where it was easier to catch them.[16] The depth of drug and smuggling activities was drastically reduced in the El Paso sector, including areas with new border walls. Again, a border wall may not stop illegal immigration and criminal activities but will allow Border Patrol agents to have better control of the daily activities at the border with enhanced technology and manpower.

SUMMARY

God's position and policy on treating immigrants are clearly delineated in the Scripture, which should serve as a model for the US immigration policy. A bipartisan effort is necessary to create comprehensive immigration laws that reflect biblical standards. Such immigration laws should include securing our national borders. The border wall is essential for national security and to control the influx of illegal immigration, which creates a substantial financial burden on the economy. The annual cost of illegal immigration in the United States is approximately $116 billion.[17] The money could be directed to more productive endeavors, including investment in countries with the highest number of illegal immigrants in recent years, to help their economy and discourage people from emigrating from their home country to seek economic opportunities in the United States. While there are no official methods to calculate the number of people who successfully cross the border illegally, the number of apprehensions can give a clue about yearly illegal immigration. According to US Customs and Border Protection, annual apprehensions were high in 2000 at 1.68 million and dropped to approximately 404,142 in 2018 but increased again in 2019 to approximately 860,000. The US cannot sustain the whole world, nor the massive number of illegal immigrants who want to flood the country, making border walls necessary. In addition, the border wall will reduce the degree of human crises at the border and the inflow of criminal activities. Reformed immigration legislation is essential, one that should create the pathway for DACA recipients to become citizens; it should be a moral obligation, not a political punch bag.

15. McFadyen, "Weighing the Pros and Cons," para. 20.
16. Department of Homeland Security, "Border Wall System," paras. 3–15.
17. O'Brien et al., "Fiscal Burden," para. 4.

PART 2

Evangelical Leaders and Trumpism

Chapter 7

Evangelical Leaders and Trump's Chaotic Presidency

DONALD TRUMP'S FOUR-YEAR PRESIDENCY

The presidency of Donald Trump was surrounded by Christian Evangelical leaders, such as Dr. Robert Jeffress, Paula White-Cain, Samuel Rodriguez, etc. Many Christian Evangelicals have elevated the former president, Donald Trump, as their savior. Some considered him the modern-day Cyrus, specifically because of his role in recognizing Jerusalem as the capital of Israel. A simple explanation of Cyrus is that he was Persian king from 539–530 BC; he made a decree that freed the Jews and allowed them to return to Jerusalem to rebuild the temple (see Ezra 1:1–11; 6:3–5). The Evangelical leaders visited Mr. Trump at the White House and prayed for him on several occasions. In 2016, when Pastor Mark Burns welcomed the then-presidential candidate, Mr. Trump, to his congregation, he introduced him as a man who believes in Jesus, when, in fact, he has repeatedly refused to ask God for the forgiveness of his sins because, according to Mr. Trump, he has not made any mistake in his life. That is blasphemy! A man who had not made a mistake, let alone sinned, cannot believe in Jesus or receive him as his Savior. Romans 3:23 says, "For all have sinned and fall short of the glory of God." Also, the Scripture says, "For this is my blood of the covenant, which is poured out for many for the forgiveness of sins" (Matt 26:28). Therefore, if the Scripture states that all have sinned and Jesus poured out his blood to save sinners, someone cannot be a believer in Jesus if they reject what Jesus represents and his covenant of salvation.

Even though Mr. Trump's presidency was marked by high levels of scandals, instability, and dishonesty, the Christian Evangelicals who supported

Mr. Trump defended him while some remained silent. Such behavior of some Christian Evangelicals is unbiblical and immoral. The GOP lawmakers also defended Mr. Trump in his reckless behaviors, as discussed in this chapter. Most of Mr. Trump's actions resulted in self-inflicted wounds, even though he and his allies remain in denial and refuse to accept accountability for his actions. On August 18, 2020, a bipartisan report from the Senate Intelligence Committee revealed a series of interactions between Donald Trump's 2016 campaign and Russian government operatives.[1] The report indicated several occasions in which Mr. Trump's campaign manager Paul Manafort secretly shared campaign information with Russian intelligence officer Konstantin Kilimnik. According to the report, the Trump administration and his close allies refused to cooperate with the investigation. The findings of the Senate Intelligence Committee were not a surprise to many because, during the 2016 campaign, Donald Trump made a public plea to the Russians, saying: "Russia, if you are listening, I hope you are able to find the 30,000 emails that are missing."[2] Such a statement raises questions about Trump's ties with Russia and his willingness to do anything, no matter how shrewd or unethical it may be, to win an election. It is uncharacteristic for a US presidential candidate to seek help from a foreign country, especially a country that has reinvigorated a cold war with the United States, to investigate his political rival. In 2017, President Trump repeatedly said that the Russian election interference was a "hoax" and a "made-up story."[3] However, a bipartisan Senate Intelligence Committee report proved that President Trump was lying.

Furthermore, unlike any US president, Mr. Trump, on July 16, 2018, at a Helsinki, Finland, summit, publicly sided with the Russian president, Vladimir Putin, over US intelligence agencies concerning Russia's meddling with the 2016 election. In his self-serving effort, he contradicted the FBI and said he had no reason not to believe Putin. This is disturbing; a president who is willing to discredit the US intelligence agency that our country relies on for selfish gain is definitely a dangerous president. His comment elicited rebukes from both Democrat and Republican lawmakers. Paul Ryan, who was then the US house speaker, made this statement: "There is no moral equivalence between the United States and Russia, which remains hostile to our most basic values and ideals."[4] He concluded by suggesting "no question" Moscow had interfered in the 2016 election. John McCain

---

1. Mallin et al., "Senate Report Details," paras. 1–2.
2. Wertheimer and Eisen, "Trump Illegally Asked Russia," para. 2.
3. Gerth, "With His 10,000 Lies," para. 23.
4. BBC, "Trump Sides with Russia against FBI," paras. 7–8.

also stated it was a "disgraceful performance" by a US president. "No prior president has ever abased himself more abjectly before a tyrant," Senator Chuck Schumer, a Democrat, stated on Twitter, "In the entire history of our country, Americans have never seen a president of the United States support an American adversary in the way Donald Trump has supported President Putin." In another tweet, he stated, "For the president of the United States to side with President Putin against American law enforcement, American defense officials, and American intelligence agencies is thoughtless, dangerous, and weak. The president is putting himself over our country."[5]

In addition, former CIA director John Brennan stated on Twitter, "Donald Trump's press conference performance in Helsinki rises to & exceeds the threshold of 'high crimes & misdemeanors.'"[6] He also tweeted, "It was nothing short of treasonous. Not only were Trump's comments imbecilic, he is wholly in the pocket of Putin. Republican Patriots: Where are you???" I ask the same question, Where are the Republican patriots? The present cohorts of Trump-supported Republicans have destroyed the image of the Republican Party and its integrity. They do not seek integrity, truth, and honesty but lies and dishonesty, even if it means destroying our democracy. They are willing to undermine the legitimacy of our electoral process and democracy. If Mr. Trump would miraculously change today to be a selfless and honest person, the same fierce supporters that portray him as their savior would back away from him because he no longer represents their radical and dishonest views. As the saying goes, "Birds of a feather flock together." For some strange reason, an honest, law-abiding, and godly person does not appeal to this present-day cohort of Christian Evangelicals and fierce GOP supporters. The group that portrays itself as conservative, law-abiding, and godly is more devilish than the group they condemn. Mr. Putin would not even stoop that low to betray his country for Mr. Trump.

Then in 2019, Mr. Trump initiated another underground activity by pressuring Ukraine to investigate and provide damaging information about his political rival in the 2020 presidential election, Joe Biden, and his son Hunter.[7] Furthermore, he blocked the $400 million military aid to Ukraine in his desperate effort to secure a quid pro quo deal with Ukraine's president Volodymyr Zelenskyy. The scandal became a public issue in September 2019 due to an anonymous government worker who filed a complaint against the president. The complaint indicated a concerted effort from White House staffers to engage in a cover-up. It appears the only type of relationship

---

5. BBC, "Trump Sides with Russia against FBI," paras. 11–12.
6. Nussbaum, "Trump Publicly Sides with Putin," para. 14.
7. Wolf, "Trump's Ukraine Scandal," para. 1.

Donald Trump could have with other people is a corrupt relationship. You have to be a criminal-minded person, willing to compromise your integrity and tell a bunch of lies, to work for Mr. Trump. The Ukraine scandal led to his impeachment in December 2019; he was convicted by the Democratic-led House of Representatives and acquitted by the Republican-led Senate in January 2020.[8]

With the emergency of COVID-19 in 2020, Mr. Trump downplayed the deadliness of the virus on several occasions. In February 2020, he publicly stated that COVID-19 is less dangerous than the flu while at the same time privately telling the journalist Bob Woodward that the virus was "more deadly than even your strenuous flu."[9] His deceptions and mismanagement of the COVID-19 pandemic were not harmless acts, as the virus caused more deaths in the US than in any other country. The rapid spread of the virus and many of the COVID-19-related deaths in the United States could have been possibly prevented or reduced if we had a president who put the safety of the citizens ahead of his political aspirations. Of course, no matter what President Trump did, the Republican lawmakers and some Christian Evangelical leaders would not hold him accountable. They have called evil good, and some pretended as if the evil and ungodly behaviors of Donald Trump were only an imagination; they did not happen. So, the majority of Americans said they had had enough of his dishonesty behaviors and voted him out. Therefore, he and his allies conjure up more lies by saying, "The election was stolen."

Additionally, Mr. Trump has presented more lies and misinformation than any other president in US history. For example, on May 2, 2019, a *Courier-Journal* article headline read, "With his 10,000 lies, President Trump is the most dishonest politician ever."[10] The article presented several instances where Mr. Trump lied or made false claims, from Stormy Daniels to lies about the Mueller investigation, his taxes, immigration, etc. As reported by *Forbes*, PolitiFact assessed the statements made by President Obama, President Trump, and President Biden in their first one hundred days in office to see who told the most lies. Out of the twelve statements made by President Obama that qualified for assessment, only one was false. Out of the twenty-nine statements from President Trump that were eligible for assessment, seventeen statements were false. President Biden had two false statements out of four assessed statements.[11] So, President Trump engaged in more de-

---

8. Murse, "Biggest Donald Trump Scandals," paras. 2–3.
9. Gangel et al., "Trump Admits to Concealing," paras. 2–5.
10. Gerth, "With His 10,000 Lies," para. 1.
11. Markowitz, "Who Lied More," para. 8.

ceptive lies than President Obama and President Biden combined in his first one hundred days in office. President Trump made a total of 30,573 false or misleading claims during his presidency, and almost half took place during his fourth year.[12] With this degree of false claims and misinformation, President Trump met the criteria of a pathological liar.

Trump's "zero tolerance" policy at the US–Mexico border that sanctioned the separation of children from their parents was an inhumane approach to solving immigration problems. The forcible separations of families at the border created traumatic experiences for vulnerable immigrants and resulted in at least two preventable deaths if the children had been with their parents.

Trump's administration was marred with turbulence and instability, unlike his recent predecessors. It was like a revolving door, and Cabinet and other White House positions were short-lived due to people being fired or individual decisions to resign. Within the first two and a half years of his presidency, he had more Cabinet turnover than any of the five previous presidents in their first four years.[13] The Cabinet turnover was unprecedented since no other president at the beginning of their presidency had such quick turnover in the past one hundred years.[14] This is a clear indication of a man who is unstable in every aspect of his life. He undoubtedly transferred his turbulent life, as evidenced in his relationships and business, to his administration. Additionally, in less than fourteen months, there were more turnovers among Trump White House senior aids than in the first two years of the last four presidents.[15] Furthermore, on June 19, 2023, Mr. Trump was interviewed by anchor Bret Baier on Fox News, and Mr. Baier reminded him of the claim he made during his 2016 campaign that he would only hire the best in his administration. Mr. Trump responded by saying, "Well, I did do that!" Then Mr. Baier told him many of the best individuals he hired do not support him to be president again, and that includes the following:

1. "This time, your Vice President Mike Pence is running against you. Your ambassador to the United Nations, Nikki Haley, she's running against you. Your former Secretary of State, Mike Pompeo, said he's not supporting you."

2. "You mentioned National Security Adviser John Bolton. He's not supporting you, either. You mentioned Attorney General Bill Barr. Says

---

12. Kessler, "Trump's False or Misleading Claims," paras. 1–4.
13. Joung, "More Cabinet Turnover," para. 1.
14. Keith, "Trump Cabinet Turnover," para. 1.
15. Keith, "White House Staff Turnover," para. 4.

you shouldn't be president again. Calls you 'the consummate narcissist' and 'troubled man.' You recently called Barr a 'gutless pig.'"

3. "Your second defense secretary is not supporting you. Called you irresponsible. This week, you called your White House Chief of Staff John Kelly 'weak and ineffective' and 'born with a very small brain.' You called your acting White House Chief of Staff Mick Mulvaney a 'born loser.' You called your first Secretary of State, Rex Tillerson, 'dumb as a rock,' and your first Defense Secretary, James Mattis, 'the world's most overrated general.' You called your White House press secretary Kayleigh McEnany 'milquetoast.'"

4. "And multiple times, you've referred to your Transportation secretary, Elaine Chao, as 'Mitch McConnell's China-loving wife.'"[16]

Did you notice Mr. Trump's unruly personality in name-calling ("born with a very small brain," "born loser," "dumb as a rock," "milquetoast," etc.) to individuals who did not succumb to his corruption? Where have you seen such disorderly behavior with an American president ever? Would you like to work for a manager who belittles you and blasts you with name-calling before your coworkers? Would you marry a person who engages in outbursts of name-calling because you did not do things the way they wanted you to do them? Most normal people are more likely to say "No" to any of the above questions. If that is the case, the question still remains, Why do Evangelical leaders pledge their unquenchable support to a man who does not live by biblical standards?

The assessment of Mr. Trump by some top national security officials, such as former Defense Secretary James Mattis, former Director of National Intelligence Dan Coats, and former Secretary of State Rex Tillerson, is concerning. Mr. Mattis called Mr. Trump "dangerous" and "unfit" to be commander-in-chief.[17] A warning that the nation should take seriously. All the warning signs about Mr. Trump are crystal clear; however, people are blindly and unwisely supporting a man whose goal is self-elevation to the detriment of other people's lives, our democracy, and the stability of our country at large.

---

16. Grindell, "Donald Trump," paras. 4–7.
17. Gangel et al., "Trump Admits to Concealing," para. 9.

DIVISIVE PRESIDENT

Examining the roles of presidents to enhance their relationship with the citizens shows that past presidents obliged themselves to unite the nation once sworn into office; however, the contrary was the case with Donald Trump. The country was further divided under President Trump, and partisan polarization grew larger. Political scientists of the Brookings Institution rated President Donald Trump the most polarized US president by a substantial margin.[18] In 2020, 60 percent of Americans believe that President Trump caused the nation to be more divided, and only 12 percent thought he has tried to unite the country.[19] In addition, in 2017, according to a Quinnipiac University National Poll, 59 percent of American voters believed that President Trump's behavior encourages racist groups to express their racist views publicly.[20] Indeed, this is a president that had caused more harm than good in our country, and one might ask, what is the reason behind the fierce support of Christian Evangelicals to a president who has consistently, in every conceivable standard, violated biblical teachings, without repentance?

Additionally, President Trump never achieved an approval rating up to 50 percent during his presidency; it hovered around 38 percent and 47 percent.[21] During his final weeks in office, his approval rating dropped to 29 percent, partly because of his alleged role in the Capitol Hill riot.[22] President Trump was a very controversial, divisive, and belligerent president. Moreover, he was the only president in recent decades of whose job performance most Americans did not approve. In fact, 54 percent of Americans disapprove of his job performance as a president. If more Americans disapprove of President Trump's job performance than approve of his performance, the question then is, How did he expect to win the 2020 presidential election? Did he expect some aliens dropped from the sky to vote for him? President Trump's reelection chances were very slim, considering his chaotic presidency, dishonesty, and that the polls were not in his favor. Therefore, the only fraud in the 2020 presidential election is the person making false claims of voter fraud, and he is the only fraud that needs to be investigated.

So, it is not logical for anyone to think that President Trump won the 2020 election. The facts and the evidence are lacking. The majority of Americans do not like him or want him to be their president, and that is

---

18. Eady et al., "Comparing Trump," para. 3.
19. Moreno, "Majority Thinks Trump," para. 1.
20. Quinnipiac University National Poll, "Trump Is Dividing the Country," para. 4.
21. Fearnow, "Trump Never Received a Majority," para. 6.
22. Pew Research Center, "Biden Begins Presidency," para. 2.

why he never won the popular votes either in the 2016 or 2020 presidential elections. According to the Quinnipiac University National Poll in 2018, 59 percent of American voters say they do not like President Trump.[23] The Republicans and some Christian Evangelical leaders may want him as their president and even exalt him to a demigod position. However, the rest of the country has had enough of the four years of Donald Trump's divisiveness and chaotic presidency. His older sister, Maryanne, described Donald Trump as a man who lacks a moral compass and will only attend church if the cameras are there. Maryanne was also surprised to see the level of support Donald Trump received from Evangelical Christians. Maryanne, you are not alone; most people are equally surprised that Evangelical Christians will support a man who continually violates just about every biblical moral standard and causes more division in our country than any individual.

PRESIDENT AS A CHIEF CITIZEN

One of the roles of a US president is known as a chief citizen, which suggests that the president is a moral leader while representing the interest of the citizens.[24] However, these expected roles of a president were foreign concepts to Mr. Trump; rather, he expects the citizens and social institutions to serve him and his own interests. The irony of Mr. Trump's presidency is that he has no regard for a person's freedom and autonomy because of the structure of his immoral mindset that everyone must serve for his selfish interest. If something is not good for Donald Trump, it then means it is not good for the nation. That is a dangerous pre-operational cognitive function that does not recognize the individuality of US citizens. My question to the Evangelicals who believe that Mr. Trump is their God-sent leader is, How is that consistent with the roles of biblical leaders approved by God? Mr. Trump is fighting to consolidate power for his benefit and his family. What are you fighting for yourself and your family? Mr. Trump also does not understand that people do see things differently from him. If you notice, very often, Mr. Trump will viciously attack his opponents and even his close allies who do not yield to his corrupt moves. Mr. Trump does not see people as independent, autonomous free-will beings but rather as instruments or means to accomplish his goals and will violently dispose of any individual, as one would dispose of untuneful instruments, if they do not yield to his corruption.

23 Quinnipiac University National Poll, "U.S. Voters Dislike Trump."
24. Assets Pearson's School, "President's Job," 1–4.

Evangelical Leaders and Trump's Chaotic Presidency

The expected duties of a US president include protecting democracy, serving the welfare of the citizens, and upholding the US Constitution, laws, and orders. Under the presidency of Mr. Trump, all these critical expected duties of a president were bulldozed. Even on December 4, 2022, he proposed the termination of the US Constitution in order to overturn the 2020 presidential election and declare the loser the president of the United States of America. Mr. Trump was a self-serving president whose ultimate goal was to establish a monarchy for himself and his lineage to rule the US with an iron hand.

GOP LAWMAKERS' VIEWS ABOUT DONALD TRUMP

Senator Ted Cruz made the following statements about Donald Trump during the 2016 presidential primary election news conference, saying that he is a:

> Pathological liar, utterly amoral, a narcissist at a level I don't think this country's ever seen, and a serial philanderer. This man is a pathological liar; he doesn't know the difference between truth and lies . . . in a pattern that is straight out of a psychology textbook, he accuses everyone of lying. Whatever lie he's telling, at that minute, he believes it . . . the man is utterly amoral.[25]

Mr. Trump had not changed since 2016, when Senator Cruz painted an accurate picture of him, for Senator Cruz to support President Trump in his fraud election claims and acquit him of two impeachments. Thus, Senator Cruz has become all that he called Mr. Trump in 2016; since he pledged his unswerving support to a man he described as a pathological liar and amoral. As the saying goes, "birds of a feather flock together," so it is with the GOP lawmakers who endorse Mr. Trump's corruption. Moral and ethical individuals do not compromise their integrity; certainly, not for an amoral president.

Senator Marco Rubio described Donald Trump as a dangerous con man who would shatter the Republican Party if he became the nominee.[26] How accurate he was in portraying Donald Trump; however, like Senator Cruz, he would later support Donald Trump and acquit him of two impeachments. These two senators, including other GOP congressmen and women, knew much about Mr. Trump; yet they continuously surrendered to a dangerous con man to continue dividing the country and destroying

---

25. Wright et al., "Cruz Unloads with Epic Takedown," para. 1.
26. O'Keefe, "Rubio Called Trump a Dangerous 'Con Man,'" para. 1.

our democracy. It indicates their lack of integrity and cowardice. It is unnatural for a man to lay down in cowardice for another man to walk all over him, as the GOP congressmen have done with Donald Trump. They have stabilized unethical behaviors as if it is the norm. History books will not have any heroic narratives about the present cohort of GOP lawmakers. They have bowed down to an unruly bully and have given him a free pass to do whatever he wants without accountability in fear of retaliation if they oppose him. They are afraid that Donald Trump will campaign against them and they will lose their reelection bid. What a cowardly approach to dereliction of duty. These cowards have put their short-term selfish gain above the country's safety and democracy; it is a betrayal of their oaths in office and the nation at large. While they are yielding in fear to an amoral president because they do not want to lose their reelection bids, there are brave men and women in the military surrendering their lives daily to protect our country and democracy. There are also courageous police officers risking their safety every day to keep our communities safe. Still, the GOP Congress could not fathom the thought of losing reelection for the sake of upholding integrity. What a disgrace! What has become of the recent cohort of GOP lawmakers? Have they forgotten that the United States is a country of the braves and not of the cowards? What happened to brave men like Patrick Henry, who said, "Give me liberty or give me death"? Mr. Henry's speech on March 23, 1775, appealed to the emotions of the people of his state, Virginia, to support the Revolutionary War for American independence.[27] So, for GOP lawmakers, if you are so terrified of Mr. Trump that you cannot stand up for truth, liberty, and integrity, you are not worthy of being a lawmaker, and your constituency has an obligation to vote you out.

According to CNN reporters, Mitt Romney, before he became a senator, made this comment about Donald Trump, saying:

> Here's what I know: Donald Trump is a phony, a fraud. His promises are as worthless as a degree from Trump University. He's playing members of the American public for suckers: He gets a free ride to the White House, and all we get is a lousy hat.[28]

Senator Romney further said, "Dishonesty is Donald Trump's hallmark." Senator Romney's description of Donald Trump would later prove to be accurate. Senator Romney has been a lone ranger in condemning the unethical and dishonest behaviors of Mr. Trump and even that of some GOP

---

27. National Constitution Center, "Patrick Henry's Most Famous Quote," para. 1.
28. Bradner and Treyz, "Romney Implores," paras. 2–3.

lawmakers, while others have surrendered themselves to be controlled and manipulated by Mr. Trump. What a shame!

Vignette

The current cohort of Trump-supported GOP lawmakers and governors presents a historical threat to US democracy. The danger associated with this radical group is the cognitive limitation to foresee the potential consequences of their actions to themselves and their families and the inevitable disaster to the unity of the Republican Party specifically and the nation at large. Indeed, every action must produce an effect, and the inescapable effect of their actions is a nationwide disaster.

MR. TRUMP'S ABUSIVE RELATIONSHIP WITH GOP LAWMAKERS

The relationship between President Trump and GOP lawmakers is toxic, controlling, and intimidating. Just like an abusive relationship between a woman and her controlling husband, the GOP lawmakers are paralyzed with fear, unable to stand up against Mr. Trump or even seek help to break away from the abuse. Two times help came in the form of impeachments to enable them to free themselves from Mr. Trump, but they unwisely rejected such opportunities. Just like an abused woman would not allow police to arrest her abuser, GOP lawmakers declined to cut ties with Donald Trump. The two impeachments against President Trump were gifts from the House Democrats; since GOP lawmakers declined to accept the gifts, they will soon find out that if they do not stand up against a bully, the bully will not respect them nor stop bullying them. The irony of this controlling relationship is that men, generally, are not socialized to be wimpy and allow another man to control them with intimidation, especially in a free world like the United States of America.

Vignette

The inevitable outcome of Mr. Trump's leadership of the Republican Party is the ultimate destruction of the party. The continuum of gradual dissemination of the party's core tenets as a result of corruption and perversion of truth and facts will facilitate the party's demolition, although it would not happen without chaotic outcomes within the party and society. However, the ensuing outcome will be good prevailing over evil.

On the other hand, Christian Evangelical leaders have craftily discouraged their followers from consuming public media, which will prevent them from knowing the truth about Mr. Trump. At the same time, they intertwined their preaching of the gospel with the preaching of abortion and socialism. While preaching against abortion is a righteous endeavor, the politicization of it is as sinful as the act itself.

SUMMARY

The Evangelical leaders have become enablers of Mr. Trump's corruption and ungodly behaviors. They have not taken a firm position to condemn his unbiblical behaviors, and their refusal to condemn his ungodly behaviors gives false impressions about the God of the Christians and biblical teachings as if the kingdom of God promotes corruption and lies. Moreover, God does not condone a self-serving, self-promoting, arrogant, prideful, and unforgiving man. One of the significant Christian principles and biblical teachings is forgiveness. However, Mr. Trump is extremely retaliatory and lacks the capacity to forgive. Thus, it is impossible for God to approve such a man because he cannot contradict his word.

Mr. Trump's effort to discredit the legitimacy of the FBI in publishing their unbiased findings is not patriotism. He was supposed to uphold the institution instead of trying to degrade it. Mr. Trump spent years in court battles for the release of his taxes, and now we know why he spent years fighting for the release of taxes. One who refuses to pay his fair taxes, especially a self-proclaimed billionaire who engages in unpatriotic behavior, does not need to be a president of the United States. A US president is expected to be a person of integrity, one who selflessly seeks the welfare of the citizens, the institutions, and the nation at large, and not one who tries to pervert everything for self-benefit.

Chapter 8

False Prophecies about the 2020 Presidential Election

The 2020 presidential election was an election unlike any other in recent decades. It was an election that generated a lot of emotions, prophecies, passion, division, anger, hate, illusion, and violence. Because of the illusion among some Christian Evangelicals that the Republican Party is a party endorsed by God, their unwavering support for Mr. Trump elicited many false prophecies. The Evangelical leaders' passionate and emotional attachment to their preferred presidential candidate influenced a plethora of false prophecies rather than the Spirit of Christ. Thus, their prophecies did not come true. Because their prophecies about the presidential election did not materialize does not necessarily mean that they are all false prophets. However, a number of them are certainly false prophets, especially those who try to articulate more prophecies to cover up the previous ones. Their prophetic utterances were more like fortune-telling and divination based on selfish desires, perceptions, and biases to influence others to vote for a particular candidate. So, Jeremiah declared to the Israelites, saying, "And the LORD said to me, 'The prophets prophesy lies in My name. I have not sent them, commanded them, nor spoken to them; they prophesy to you a false vision, divination, a worthless thing, and the deceit of their heart'" (Jer 14:14). In this manner, some of the prophecies about the 2020 presidential election resulted from false visions and deceptions; therefore, God frustrated them.

WHAT IS PROPHECY?

The Holy Spirit inspires true prophecy; it is a divine message, knowledge, or revelation outside the natural realm. Prophecy involves a declaration of God's word through a human agent, as one receives utterances from the Holy Spirit. It predicts a future event, gives hope, and warns of potential judgment if repentance is not sought. Prophecy will reflect the testimony, word, or witness of the Lord Jesus, as the Scripture says, "For the testimony of Jesus is the spirit of prophecy" (Rev 19:10). Thus, a prophet is an individual anointed by God to declare prophetic words about future events, warn people about God's impending judgment if repentance is not sought, and bring hope to heal the brokenhearted. A prophet is God's agent, representative, or spokesperson, to proclaim God's word to the people.

BIBLICAL WARNING ABOUT FALSE PROPHETS

False prophets, as well as false prophecies, are not anything new but have been in existence since the existence of prophecy. Satan is a master in counterfeiting God's gift and word and will use both witting and unwitting individuals to carry out his deceptions and lies. The Lord Jesus warns believers about false prophets by saying:

> Beware of false prophets, who come to you in sheep's clothing, but inwardly they are ravenous wolves. You will know them by their fruits. Do men gather grapes from thornbushes or figs from thistles? Even so, every good tree bears good fruit, but a bad tree bears bad fruit. A good tree cannot bear bad fruit, nor can a bad tree bear good fruit. Every tree that does not bear good fruit is cut down and thrown into the fire. Therefore by their fruits you will know them. (Matt 7:15–20)

Indeed, you will know who is a true or false prophet by their fruits. A true prophet is inspired by the Holy Spirit to declare God's word, and he is driven to please God without the fear of man. God spoke to Jeremiah, a man whom he ordained a prophet from his mother's womb, saying, "'Do not be afraid of their faces, for I am with you to deliver you,' says the LORD" (Jer 1:8). However, a false prophet will display the fear of man; therefore, he will compromise to please man. In his effort to please man, he will engage in false prophecies that will please a man's heart.

The Lord Jesus says, "For false christs and false prophets will rise and show great signs and wonders to deceive, if possible, even the elect" (Matt 24:24). The apostles also warn believers about false prophets. First John 4:1

says, "Beloved, do not believe every spirit, but test the spirits, whether they are of God; because many false prophets have gone out into the world." Second Corinthians 11:13–15 states:

> For such are false apostles, deceitful workers, transforming themselves into apostles of Christ. And no wonder! For Satan himself transforms himself into an angel of light. Therefore it is no great thing if his ministers also transform themselves into ministers of righteousness, whose end will be according to their works.

Interestingly, partisan politics have generated a lot of false prophets to present themselves as God's messengers and ministers of righteousness. But if you look carefully through the lens of the Holy Spirit, you will see that they seek to please man, not God, and they lack the fear of God in them. To help believers guard themselves against false prophets, God provided us a standard to know whether he is the one speaking through a prophet or not. For God says:

> And if you say in your heart, "How shall we know the word which the LORD has not spoken?" When a prophet speaks in the name of the LORD, if the thing does not happen or come to pass, that is the thing which the LORD has not spoken; the prophet has spoken it presumptuously; you shall not be afraid of him. (Deut 18:21–22)

During the 2020 presidential election, some people prophesied presumptuously and according to their hearts' desires, and not by the Spirit of God. They could not discern the time of the season, the writing on the wall, and the leadership of the Holy Spirit. Thus, they prophesied presumptuously, and God frustrated all their prophecies, and not a single one came true. Isaiah 44:25–26 says, "Who [God] frustrates the signs of the babblers, and drives diviners mad; who turns wise men backward, and make their knowledge foolishness; who confirms the word of His servants, and performs the counsel of His messengers." God has obliged himself to confirm the word of his prophets because the Spirit of God conceived the prophecies, but prophecies envisioned by fleshly desires will be unfulfilled by God. Several evangelists and televangelists falsely predicted that Mr. Trump would win the 2020 election. Such leaders include Pat Robertson, who prophesied falsely in the 2012 and 2020 presidential elections, and Paula White-Cain, who called on angels from Africa and South America to assist Trump in being reelected. Interestingly, the calling of angels from Africa and South America sounds more like someone invoking evil spirits because

God's angels descend from heaven. Making false prophecies in the name of the LORD is detestable behavior before God. Thus, God spoke through Jeremiah saying, "I have heard what the prophets have said who prophesy lies in My name, saying 'I have dreamed, I have dreamed!' How long will this be in the heart of the prophets who prophesy lies? Indeed, they are prophets of the deceit of their own hearts" (Jer 23:25–26). Indeed, all the so-called prophets who prophesied that Donald Trump would win the 2020 election, including those who prophesied and elevated the Republican Party as a party endorsed by God, are prophets of the deceit of their own hearts.

BIBLICAL EXAMPLES OF FALSE PROPHETS

Several incidences of false prophets and prophecies took place in the days of the Bible. A notable example was Ahab, the king of Israel, when he desired to go to war against Ramoth Gilead. So, he asked Jehoshaphat, the king of Judah, to go with him. Jehoshaphat agreed but requested that King Ahab first inquire from the LORD. So, the Scripture says, "Then the king of Israel gathered the prophets together, four hundred men, and said to them, 'Shall we go to war against Ramoth Gilead, or shall I refrain?' So they said, 'Go up, for God will deliver it into the king's hand'" (2 Chr 18:5). Jehoshaphat, a man of God, was not impressed with what he saw, so he said, "Is there not still a prophet of the LORD here, that we may inquire of Him?" (2 Chr 18:6).

It is important to note that Ahab was a wicked king who surrounded himself with self-appointed false prophets who prophesied to him according to his heart's desires. Much of what we saw in the 2020 presidential election was a leader who surrounded himself with people who prophesied to him what he wanted to hear, but not according to God. Ahab's response in 2 Chr 18:7–10 states:

> So the king of Israel said to Jehoshaphat, "There is still one man by whom we may inquire of the LORD; but I hate him, because he never prophesies good concerning me, but always evil. He is Micaiah the son of Imla." And Jehoshaphat said, "Let not the king say such things!" Then the king of Israel called one of his officers and said, "Bring Micaiah the son of Imla quickly!"

While the messenger has gone to bring Micaiah, the true prophet of God, the other four hundred false prophets of Ahab continue to prophesy lies to boost Ahab's ego. In one accord, they all prophesied that the king should prosper by going to war against Ramoth Gilead. It is very dangerous when men forsake God's way to choose an easy and ungodly path, which often results in disaster. So, when Micaiah came, "Then he said, 'I saw all Israel scattered on the mountains, as sheep that have no shepherd.' And the Lord said, 'These have no master. Let each return to his house in peace'" (2 Chr 18:16). The king of Israel, Ahab, was not happy with Micaiah's prophesy and accused him of prophesying evil against him. Apparently, Ahab had ears that itch for lies and abhorred truth. Just like those who have made lies an acceptable way of life, they will always reject the truth and pursue falsehoods. However, a true prophet of God will always prophesy what God shows or tells him, not what is suitable for men's ears. Micaiah went further to explain to the king what he saw in the spirit:

> Then Micaiah said, "Therefore hear the word of the Lord: I saw the Lord sitting on His throne, and all the host of heaven standing on His right hand and His left. And the Lord said, 'Who will persuade Ahab king of Israel to go up, that he may fall at Ramoth Gilead?' So one spoke in this manner, and another spoke in that manner. Then a spirit came forward and stood before the Lord, and said, 'I will persuade him.' The Lord said to him, 'In what way?'" So he said, 'I will go out and be a lying spirit in the mouth of all his prophets.' And the Lord said, 'You shall persuade him and also prevail; go out and do so.' Therefore look! The Lord has put a lying spirit in the mouth of these prophets of yours, and the Lord has declared disaster against you." (2 Chr 18:18–22)

Ahab commanded that Micaiah be put in prison and be fed with bread and water of affliction because he did not prophesy what he wanted to hear. He commanded that Micaiah remain in prison until he came back from the war with Ramoth Gilead. Of course, as God spoke through his prophet Micaiah, Ahab was killed in the war, and Jehoshaphat nearly lost his life, but he cried out to the Lord, and God saved him. An important lesson here: First, if you are a man or woman of God, it is unwise and unsafe to enter into a covenant or committed relationship with someone who does not have a committed relationship with Christ. Second, if you are God's prophet or prophetess, do not compromise the integrity of your office as a prophet or prophetess to please men or leaders, just like Balaam did (see Num 22–24). You cannot serve God and mammon at the same time (see Luke 16:13). Third, avoid a relationship with leaders who choose lies over truth unless you are willing to prophesy lies (see Deut 18:1–31).

Ahab did not like the prophecies of Micaiah because they were not fitting to his fleshly desires, so he sought prophets who would prophesy to him what he wanted to hear. The outcome of the prophecies he received from his false prophets was his death. True prophecy is not predicated on numbers but comes from the Spirit of God, who knows the end of a thing from the beginning.

PROPHECIES IN THE 2020 PRESIDENTIAL ELECTION

The prophecies during the 2020 presidential election reveal how easily some Christians can be deceived or deviate from God's path to please a man. Of course, the man they want to please is a man whose ego is not submitted to Christ, just like Ahab. Four hundred false prophets prophesied to Ahab what he wanted to hear, while Micaiah was the only true prophet of God, and he was struck for speaking the truth. Second Chronicles 18:23 says, "Then Zedekiah the son of Chenaanah went near and struck Micaiah on the cheek, and said, 'Which way did the spirit from the Lord go from me to speak to you?'" In the same manner, if there had been a true prophet of God and he prophesied otherwise, he would have been struck by one of the Trump fanatics. There were a lot of so-called prophets during the 2020 presidential election, and they echoed each other in their false prophecies that President Trump would win the election. Although, as I have mentioned above, not everyone who prophesied incorrectly about the election is a false prophet, I hope the election's outcome served as a teachable moment for those who are truly God's prophets. However, some people's heart conditions are not right nor subject to the Holy Spirit; therefore, they cannot accept the truth but prophesy more lies. Imagine this self-proclaimed prophet, Pastor Robin Bullock—not only did he prophesy falsely that Mr. Trump would win the 2020 presidential election, but he also went further by prophesying that the prophets will call Mr. Trump back to the White House for three terms.[1] He also admonished his congregation not to recognize Joe Biden as the president of the United States; otherwise, they would enter into sin.[2] The behavioral pattern represents common characteristics of false prophets from biblical standards; they try to undermine reality by engaging from one false prophecy to another to deceive their followers. But their prophecies are not from God, so God frustrated them.

Thus, the Scripture warns us saying, "Do not listen to the words of the prophets who prophesy to you. They make you worthless; they speak a vision of their own heart, not from the mouth of the Lord" (Jer 23:16). The false prophecies about the 2020 presidential election came from Trump supporters, who want to use their prophecies to persuade people to vote in a particular manner. Therefore, they prophesied lies and visions of their

1. Lemon, "Christian Pastor Claims," para. 1.
2. Villarreal, "It's a Sin to Recognize Joe Biden," paras. 1–5.

hearts. Interestingly, none of these false prophets received any revelation from God that the 2020 election results would be rigged in favor of Joe Biden. A true prophet would have received such revelation from God; however, these false prophets immediately switched to support Mr. Trump's false claims about stolen elections, to cover up their false prophecies.

On the other hand, consider one, Jeremiah Johnson, who has the fear of God, and repented for his inaccurate prophecy about the 2020 election. Although he accurately predicted Mr. Trump's win in 2016, he missed the 2020 election. Surprisingly, 90 percent of people who responded to his repentance were negative responses.[3] Apparently, some Christian Evangelicals prefer to hear more false prophecies than truth, and it explains why a majority of them support Mr. Trump's false claims about the 2020 election results.

BALAAM'S UNHOLY ASSOCIATION WITH BALAK

Numbers 22 reveals the uncontrollable desire of a man endowed with the gift of prophecy from God to seek fame and create a relationship with an ungodly king. Balak, the king of Moab, and his people were exceedingly afraid to see the children of Israel around their border because they knew they were next in line to be destroyed by the Israelites. So, Balak sought help from Balaam to come and curse the children of Israel. Thus, the Scripture states:

> So the elders of Moab and the elders of Midian departed with the diviner's fee in their hand, and they came to Balaam and spoke to him the words of Balak. And he said to them, "Lodge here tonight, and I will bring back word to you, as the LORD speaks to me." So the princes of Moab stayed with Balaam. Then God came to Balaam and said, "Who are these men with you?" So Balaam said to God, "Balak the son of Zippor, king of Moab, has sent to me, saying, 'Look, a people has come out of Egypt, and they cover the face of the earth. Come now, curse them for me; perhaps I shall be able to overpower them and drive them out.'" And God said to Balaam, "You shall not go with them; you shall not curse the people, for they are blessed." (Num 22:7–12)

Balaam's initial action was the right step to take by every prophet or child of God, that is, to seek God first, to know his will, for every significant undertaking. God honored his action by appearing to him and then asking him this question, "Who are these men with you?" Whenever God asks a

---

3. Lemon, "Christian Pastor Claims," para. 7.

person a question in a critical situation like Balaam, in most cases, it suggests that either the person's motive is not right or he/she is out of the will of God in that situation. Then God responded to Balaam's presumptuous pursuit by saying, "You shall not go with them; you shall not curse the people, for they are blessed" (Num 22:12). For someone with an honest motive, God's response should have settled the matter for him permanently. However, Balaam's motives were fabricated, which were revealed in his subsequent actions. When Balak increased his pressure on Balaam with promises of more fabulous gifts and fame, Balaam succumbed to the pressure and went back to God to ask for the same thing God had already said "No" to him in his first request. This behavior was illogical, radical, and had unintended consequences. God responded to Balaam's second request in this manner, which states, "And God came to Balaam at night and said to him, 'If the men come to call you, rise and go with them; but only the word which I speak to you—that you shall do'" (Num 22:20). The word "if" is a conditional phrase, suggesting that it is not God's perfect will for Balaam to go with the men. Although God's permissive will in this situation allowed Balaam to go with the men, he was angry with Balaam because his way was perverted before God. Thus, an angel of the LORD stood against Balaam to kill him, but his donkey's sensitivity and actions saved him; nevertheless, Balaam still went to Balak. Balaam did not curse the Israelites because God warned him; however, he provided Balak with distorted means to cause a stumbling block for the children of Israel, which the Scripture called the "doctrine of Balaam" (see Rev 2:14). Balaam's actions caused him an eternal separation from God.

Balaam's undoing was his quest for riches and fame with Balak, the king of Midian. A prophet's desire to please an ungodly king rather than God often has a downward spiral effect on his relationship with God. As the Scripture says, "Do you not know that friendship with the world is enmity with God? Whoever therefore wants to be a friend of the world makes himself an enemy of God. Or do you think that the Scripture says the following in vain, 'The Spirit who dwells in us yearns jealously'?" (Jas 4:4–5).

Careful observation of the roles of the so-called prophets around President Trump's camp during the 2020 presidential election revealed similar characteristics of the biblical prophets who traded their righteous position with God for worldly fame. Just like Balaam showed a greater passion for honoring a king than God, so did some of these so-called prophets and prophetesses who demonstrated greater passion publicly for Mr. Trump than for the Lord Jesus. Some even idolized him as another savior, undermining Christ's exclusivity as the world's Savior. As a Christian, you could not help but be shocked and outraged. How can God bless a man whom some of these so-called prophets and prophetesses have idolized and exalted to the place of Christ? God is a jealous God (see Exod 20:5; 34:14) and will not share his glory with another (see Isa 42:8). He will strike down a leader that the people try to exalt as God. Acts 12:21–23 states:

> So on a set day Herod, arrayed in royal apparel, sat on his throne and gave an oration to them. And the people kept shouting, "The voice of a god and not a man." Then immediately an angel of the Lord struck him because he did not give glory to God. And he was eaten by worms and died.

In addition, some people have exalted former President Trump and treated him as a demigod; therefore, he presents himself as a prideful man with a boisterous ego. He did not give glory to God for winning the 2016 presidential election, even though there were several odds against him. Rather he boasted of self-effort for his victory. However, according to the Scripture, "God resists the proud, but He gives grace to the humble" (Jas 4:6). Thus, any prideful person or leader is subject to God's opposition. Mr. Trump exhibited unruly and prideful behaviors, along with deceptions during the 2020 presidential election, which did not please God. Strangely, the Christian Evangelical leaders have not mustered any guts to confront Mr. Trump to repent of his wicked ways; rather, they falsely present him as a righteous man. So, God spoke to the Israelites through Jeremiah saying:

> Thus says the LORD of hosts: "Do not listen to the words of the prophets who prophesy to you. They make you worthless; they speak a vision of their own heart, not from the mouth of the LORD. They continually say to those who despise Me, 'The LORD has said, "You shall have peace"'; and to everyone who walks according to the dictates of his own heart, they say, 'No evil shall come upon you.'" (Jer 23:16–17)

Many Evangelical preachers have pushed their false prophecies giving the false impression that all is well with the wickedness that exists within the Republican Party and Donald Trump when, in fact, it is not true. It is a dangerous role to play, that is, granting immunity and salvation to an unsaved person. God's standard for salvation is the same for all, as stated in the Scripture. Mr. Trump has not humbled himself before God to repent and ask for forgiveness because of his pride and ungodliness. The Evangelical leaders have given false impressions to anyone who identified themselves with the Republican Party as a righteous person, even in the face of some of them engaging in ungodly and inhumane behaviors. They prophesy falsely to them that they shall have peace and evil will not come upon them for violating God's word. However, according to the Scripture, "Though they join forces, the wicked will not go unpunished; but the prosperity of the righteous will be delivered" (Prov 11:21). Additionally, the Scripture asserts that God renders judgment to everyone according to their deeds (see Rom 2:6).

For those who had previously prophesied falsely about the 2020 presidential election and other incidents, learn from your false prophecies, and also take note of this: If you are prophesying from the realm of your consciousness, chances are it is not inspired by the Holy Spirit. If you are prophesying to impress or exalt a man, chances are that is outside the realm of the Spirit of prophecy. If you are prophesying from your preconceived notions and desires, chances are it is not from God.

Vignette

> Several prophecies about the 2020 presidential election were influenced by false visions, lies, and deceptions, and God did not send the so-called prophets. For some of them, the reality was disillusioning when their prophecies did not come true; therefore, they uttered more false prophecies to mask the previous prophecies. The basis of their disillusion is the falsified notion propagated by Christian Evangelical leaders to portray the Republican Party as God's party or a party endorsed by God, but nothing could be further from the truth.

Those who are believers in the Lord Jesus are forbidden from falling in love with worldly fame and riches, and those who love worldly things do not have the love of Christ in them. First John 2:15–17 says:

> Do not love the world or the things in the world. If anyone loves the world, the love of the Father is not in him. For all that is in the world—the lust of the flesh, the lust of the eyes, and the pride of life—is not of the Father but is of the world. And the world is passing away, and the lust of it; but he who does the will of God abides forever.

GOD'S PROVIDENCE IN ELECTING US PRESIDENTS

Some have argued about the providence of God in electing US presidents. I was shocked by a comment made by a Christian network owner, who made a statement in this manner, suggesting that he used to believe that God selects US presidents, but after this election (the 2020 presidential election), he did not believe that anymore. Such a statement is unwise and undermines God's sovereignty; because something did not happen according to your expectations does not mean it excludes God's influence in the process. God speaking to the children of Israel declares the following, "For My thoughts are not your thoughts, nor are your ways My ways, says the LORD. For as the heavens are higher than the earth, so are My ways higher than your ways, and My thoughts than your thoughts" (Isa 55:8–9). So, because one does not understand God's way or his plan for a particular situation or season does not indicate an absence of his divine order. Judges 14:1–3 illustrates how Samson's parents objected to his desire to marry a Philistine lady. The Philistines were enemies of the Israelites, and they were uncircumcised and pagan worshipers. Therefore, the Israelites were forbidden to marry the Philistines. However, the parents of Samson did not know that it was God who was behind Samson's desire to marry the Philistine woman. Judges 14:4 says, "But his father and mother did not know that it was of the LORD—that He was seeking an occasion to move against the Philistines. For at that time, the Philistines had dominion over Israel."

I sincerely believe in God's providence in electing US presidents due to the global influence they have. Even though God's providence prevails for one to be elected a president, he will still reject a president and replace him if he is dominated with a spirit of pride and insubordination without repentance like Saul.

Back in 2008, Kim Clement (considered a true prophet by some Christians, who passed away on November 23, 2016) had prophesied that a Black man would become the president of the United States after the presidency of George Bush. The truthfulness of such prophecy remained questionable in the minds of many since the chances of such prophecy being fulfilled were very remote. However, it takes one who truly hears from God to make such a bold prophetic statement that contradicts popular views. On April 10, 2008, Kim Clement released this prophecy about Obama for the 2008 presidential election:

> For they have unfairly spoken against an African man, and I'm not talking about Jeremiah Wright; I'm talking about Obama. For God said, "Even though you may think this or that, there is an element of righteousness inside of him to reach out for Jesus. Therefore, I will sway it next week," says the Spirit of God, "and I will cause My man, My power—to exalt in the White House what is necessary to declare victory. For this time, I shall rise

up and I shall make known who I am in a way that I have never done in this nation," says the Lord.[4]

Furthermore, in 2008, CBN published one of the prophecies of Kim Clement concerning the 2008 presidential election in which he prophesied on June 17, 2008, saying:

> A president that I will bring into the White House, and they will say "He is ungodly." They will say, "He does not know God." Even as Jesus disguised Himself at the great feast, so I have disguised this man's heart. When he comes to the White House, not only shall he be mine, but he shall pray as a man who has never prayed in the White House.... Fear not, for he shall sit in that seat in the White House, and suddenly my Spirit will come on him and baptize him with fire and with the anointing, says the Spirit of the Lord.[5]

So, Kim Clement declared the will of God for Mr. Obama to become the US president; many Evangelicals who are pro-Republican immediately labeled him a false prophet because it is inconceivable for them that God would allow a pro-abortion Democratic presidential candidate and a Black man to win the presidential election. This type of sanctimonious or holier-than-thou spirit dominated the Pharisees and they could never accept Jesus as the Messiah because he did not fit in or meet the standards of the tradition of the elders. The very group the Pharisees looked down on and condemned was the same group that Jesus hung out with and performed miracles in their lives. Today's Evangelicals who are pro-Republican Party are exactly like the Pharisees of the Bible, and God has blinded them because their hearts are not right, and the love of God does not exist in them. If you notice, whenever they are confronted with social situations that are perceived to be inconvenient to them concerning choosing the word of God or the Republican Party agenda, they cunningly and easily manipulate their way to embrace the Republican Party agenda over God's word. Their security and identity are found in the social group they belong to, not in Christ. Subconsciously, they value their social belonging to their group as far more important than their spiritual belonging to Christ. To them, the only reasonable criteria for evaluating a true Christian is one who meets the standard of their social group. That is why miracles are not happening with them. Their anointing is limited to the tone of their voices and the seven and twelve steps protocols, but not any manifested miracles as with Jesus and his disciples.

4. Clement, "Obama Prophecy," para. 3.
5. Buseck, "Prophetic Voices," para. 10.

In the same manner, there was a prophecy about Donald Trump's presidency. On September 11, 2015, a Dallas, Texas, pastor prophesied about Donald Trump winning the 2016 presidential election. He said, "There will be cleansing in the land with the new president, but the cleansing is not toward destruction but cleansing toward unity. And God will enable the new president to bring healing amongst all the people . . . and righteousness will begin to radiate across America."[6] The descriptions presented about Donald Trump in this prophecy do not reflect Mr. Trump, before his presidency, during his presidency, or after his presidency. Nonetheless, just like President Obama, President Trump had no chance of winning the 2016 presidential election; yet God prevailed for him. However, neither president gave God credit for winning the election.

There was also a prophecy about Joe Biden winning the 2020 presidential election by Apostle Johnson Suleman, a senior pastor of Omega Fire Ministries International. Apostle Suleman said that God revealed to him that Donald Trump would lose the 2020 presidential election, Joe Biden would win and be impeached, and the vice president would replace him and become the president.[7] The prophecy of Joe Biden becoming the president was fulfilled; however, only time will tell if the second part of the prophecy will come to pass.

Now, visiting President Obama and President Trump's prophecies, you will notice that even though both prophecies came true, neither of them yielded themselves to be used by the Holy Spirit to fulfill the second portion of the prophecies. President Obama never submitted himself for the Holy Spirit to come upon him and baptize him with fire but embraced extremely radical views. President Trump did not bring cleansing toward unity and healing to the nation; rather, he brought disaster and division to the nation as a whole.

It is not uncommon when God had made someone a king for that individual to walk in disobedience or engage in a lifestyle inconsistent with God's laws. For example, Samuel anointed Saul to be the first king of Israel. Even though the children of Israel rejected God as their leader, they wanted to have their own king like other nations; therefore, God commanded Samuel to anoint Saul to be the king of Israel (see 1 Sam 9:15—10:1). However, Saul did not obey God's commandment concerning the destruction of the Amalekites; therefore, God rejected him from being the king of Israel (see 1 Sam 15:1–35). God instructed Prophet Samuel to anoint David to replace Saul (see 1 Sam 16:1–13). Then the Spirit of the LORD departed from Saul,

6. Dhinakaran, "US Presidential Election," 1:30–2:30.
7. Sunday, "Trump's Defeat Confirms," paras. 1–3.

and he became obsessed with evil desires to kill David. He was also obsessed with maintaining his position as the king of Israel and passing the kingdom to his descendants. Even when Saul gave his daughter, Michal, to David as a wife, his purpose was to use his daughter as a snare to David (see 1 Sam 18:20–29). Saul's obsession to kill David escalated such that he hunted for David from country to country and even executed priests because they did not contact him when David came to the temple (see 1 Sam 21:1–10; 22:9–23). Does this type of rage and obsession to remain a ruler to the detriment of people's lives remind you of a leader in our country? Prophet Samuel mourned at length for Saul when God rejected him as the king of Israel (see 1 Sam 16:1), just as some Christian Evangelicals mourned desperately when God rejected Donald Trump from being the president of the United States, as demonstrated in the 2020 presidential election. Now the Philistines warred against Israel (see 1 Sam 31:1–13), and I believe God set up the war to destroy Saul and establish his covenant with David as the king of Israel. In that war, Saul and his three sons were killed, which opened the pathway, over time, for David to ascend to the throne as the king of Israel.

Even when God calls and anoints a person, and they depart from obeying God without repentance, he will withdraw his Spirit from that person, and the spirit of torment will overtake that person. It is inconsistent with the biblical doctrine that one can live like the devil, disobey God's laws, and still have the Spirit of God in them. Moreover, if the Spirit of God is not in you, it indicates that you do not belong to him. Because those who have his Spirit hear his voice and a stranger they will not follow (see John 10:26–30). I am strongly convinced that God has blinded the present-day Pharisees from perceiving or conceiving the truth. There is a huge spiritual and cognitive blockage that they cannot trespass, limiting their spiritual ability to understand God's way. Just as it was in the days of Jesus the Pharisees could not conceive that Jesus was the long-anticipated Messiah that God promised them because God blinded them and their hearts were not right with God, so it is with the present-day Pharisees. To them, being anti-abortion and being a Republican are God's standards for salvation and righteousness, which is untrue. There are far more ungodly behaviors levied against people of different national origin, race, and social class from the Republicans than the Democrats, and such practice is murder before God (see 1 John 3:14–15). The Evangelicals and the Republicans who practice and condone the mistreatment of these marginalized groups can never please God because these groups are the center of God's heart. Search the Scripture for yourself and see if you will find otherwise. Moreover, the use of denialism as a scapegoat does not alter the seriousness of the social injustice against marginalized groups before God.

There was also another incident in the Bible in which God instructed a prophet known as Ahijah to anoint a man known as Jeroboam, who would later become the first king of the northern kingdom of Israel (consisting of ten tribes, besides Judah and Benjamin) after Solomon had passed away. Jeroboam was a mighty man of valor and a servant of Solomon. Because of Solomon's disobedience of God's laws concerning idol worship, God decided to make Jeroboam the first king of the northern kingdom of Israel after the death of Solomon. So the Scripture states:

> Now it happened at that time, when Jeroboam went out of Jerusalem, that the prophet Ahijah the Shilonite met him on the way; and he had clothed himself with a new garment, and the two were alone in the field. Then Ahijah took hold of the new garment that was on him and tore it into twelve pieces. And he said to Jeroboam, "Take for yourself ten pieces, for thus says the LORD, the God of Israel: 'Behold, I will tear the kingdom out of the hand of Solomon and will give ten tribes to you, but he shall have one tribe for the sake of My servant David, and for the sake of Jerusalem, the city which I have chosen out of all the tribes of Israel.'" (1 Kgs 11:29–32)

Then God made a promise of an everlasting covenant with Jeroboam if he would obey his commandment as David did:

> So I will take you, and you shall reign over all your heart desires, and you shall be king over Israel. Then it shall be, if you heed all that I command, walk in My ways, and do what is right in My sight, to keep My statutes and My commandments, as My servant David did, then I will be with you and build for you an enduring house, as I build for David, and will give Israel to you. (1 Kgs 11:37–37)

King Solomon sought to kill Jeroboam after he heard about the prophecy of Jeroboam becoming the king of Israel. So, Jeroboam fled to Egypt until Solomon passed away. After the death of Solomon, the ten tribes had a serious conflict with Rehoboam, the son of Solomon, about the tax burden that caused them to reject Rehoboam as their king and crown Jeroboam as their king. So, Rehoboam became king of two tribes: Judah and Benjamin. Now, here is the focal point of this narrative: Jeroboam was a man who did not have a royal background and thus had no chance of becoming the king of Israel, but God showed great grace to him and anointed him to be king of Israel and made a covenant with him of building an enduring house if only he did what was right before God and obeyed his commandments. You would think this man would be grateful unto God, obey his commandments, and do what is right before God, as God commanded him. Surprisingly, that was not the case for Jeroboam, for he did not acknowledge or honor God, who made him king, but rather devised crafty ways to turn the Israelites from worshiping God to worshiping idols. Jeroboam was so traumatized about losing his position as king of Israel that he decided to use deception and lies to coerce the Israelites to worship idols instead of the God of Israel. Does this behavioral pattern sound familiar to someone you know as a president? Now here is what Jeroboam spoke in his heart:

> And Jeroboam said in his heart, "Now the kingdom may return to the house of David: If these people go up to offer sacrifices in the house of the LORD at Jerusalem, then the heart of this people will turn back to their lord, Rehoboam king of Judah, and they will kill me and go back to Rehoboam king of Judah." Therefore the king asked advice, made two calves of gold, and said to the people, "It is too much for you to go up to Jerusalem, here are your gods, O Israel, which brought you up from the land of Egypt." And he set up one in Bethel, and the other he put in Dan. Now this thing became a sin, for the people went to worship before the one as far as Dan. He made shrines on the high places, and made priests from every class of people, who were not of the sons of Levi. (1 Kgs 12:26–30)

This king changed God's established protocols for the priesthood, which was supposed to be of the Levi lineage; instead, he selected those loyal to him and made them priests of his pagan gods. Even with the prophet's warning, he did not repent; therefore, God rejected him as the king of Israel. God used the same prophet that anointed him, Ahijah, to declare judgment upon Jeroboam and his lineage to cut off their existence and kingship in Israel. The judgment was also extended to the Israelites, for God uprooted and scattered them outside the land of Israel (see 1 Kgs 14:7–18). Now, the judgment of God came upon Israel because Jeroboam made the people sin against God. The Scripture says, "And He [God] will give Israel up because of the sins of Jeroboam, who sinned and made Israel sin" (1 Kgs 14:16). So, it is important to be prudent that the citizens of a nation do not compromise to sin against God because of the sins of their king or president, because when God judges that king or president, he will also judge the nation as a whole. Going along with the big lie of a stolen election and your silence, which is complicity and calling evil good because of political affiliation, are all an abomination before God.

Lessons to grasp from these two kings, Saul and Jeroboam, include:

First, God can ordain someone to be a president, yet he will reject him if he does not honor or obey God's commandments.

Second, because God anointed someone to be a president does not mean a guaranteed righteousness, immunity, or a free pass to sin without God's judgment.

Third, when God rejects someone from being a king or president, it means it is time for the supporters to move on; otherwise, you will be fighting against God, which is not a safe position to be in with God.

Fourth, when God rejects someone, an evil spirit often overtakes them, and they will engage in chaotic behaviors, such as influencing others to sin against God and violently going after their perceived opponents. They also always engage in crafty, ungodly, and violent behaviors to preserve their kingship or presidency and for their lineage.

Fifth, because someone was anointed to be a king or president does not mean you should ignore the warning signs and ungodly behaviors and say in your heart, well, God knew about this person before he anointed him to be a president; therefore, his behaviors must be approved by God; then you intentionally or unintentionally partake in or condone the ungodly behaviors. God will also judge you because you know better and know the word of God. The children of Israel knew God's commandment concerning idol worshiping, yet they yielded to the urgings of Jeroboam to worship idols, which brought the judgment of God upon them and their generations. The same type of ungodly behavior is manifesting today with Donald Trump and Evangelical Christians, especially their leaders. They know the word of God, and they know the position of God concerning lies, division, prideful spirit, unbalanced scale, injustice, unforgiveness, hate, etc., of which all these ungodly behaviors are associated with Mr. Trump; yet some Christian Evangelicals and their leaders continue to support and present Mr. Trump as their savior instead of Christ, the blessed Savior!

Remember, as it is written, "Pride goes before destruction and a haughty spirit before a fall" (Prov 16:18). Therefore, when individuals who had no chance of being a king or president, and God in his mercy opened the door for them to become king or president, instead of acknowledging God for the blessed opportunity, exalt themselves as if it was their efforts and skills that gave them the position; God will certainly demote that person because he hates prideful spirit.

Remember also that God is a Spirit, and the word of God was written under the inspiration of God (see 2 Tim 3:16), and those who worship God must worship him in spirit and truth (see John 4:24). Outside the influence of the Holy Spirit, you are more likely to serve him carnally, and will not be under the influence and leading of the Holy Spirit, which is a key component in relationship with God.

The ex-president, Mr. Trump, displayed a lot of Saul's characteristics after God rejected him as the president of the United States, contrary to some Evangelical preachers' claims, such as Pat Robertson and Robin Bullock, who presented President Biden as Saul and gave the impression that Mr. Trump was David, which is biblically unsound and untrue. It is important to note that both prophesied incorrectly about the 2020 presidential election and, after their prophecies did not come true, they switched to the misapplication of scriptural events. The extent to which some Evangelical preachers are willing to compromise to misinterpret the Scripture for partisan politics is disheartening. They did not provide any clear explanation of how Joe Biden could represent Saul and Donald Trump represent David. Nevertheless, here are some reasons why Mr. Trump could not be King David but King Saul. And, of course, this does not suggest President Biden to be David, for he is not.

First, Saul became a king before David, and due to his disobedience to God's commandments, God replaced him with David. Mr. Trump became a president before Mr. Biden, and due to Mr. Trump's prideful spirit and all manner of sinful behaviors, such as lies, unforgiveness, retaliation, hatred, deceptions, corruption, dishonesty, manipulations, etc.—distasteful before God—God has to replace him as the president of the United States of America.

Second, Saul was a self-absorbed king, and when God rejected him as the king of Israel, he became violent and killed priests and went after anyone who did not sympathize with him in his pursuit to kill David. He chastised his son Jonathan and his daughter Michal for not helping him capture and kill David. Both saved David's life from Saul's obsession to kill David. He engaged in ungodly behaviors to keep himself as the king of Israel and to pass on the kingship to his descendants. A similar experience happened with Mr. Trump after he lost the 2020 election; he became violent, as witnessed in the January 6 riot, and he used all manner of corruption to keep himself as the president, which included persuading election officials to overturn the election results to his favor and creating fake state electors. He aggressively went after his close allies who did not sympathize with him in his corrupt moves to retain his presidency, such as the vice president, Mike Pence, and the US attorney general, William Barr.

THE DECEPTION OF MINGLING THE GOSPEL WITH POLITICS

It is deceptive for one to present themselves as a messenger of Christ while engaging in a divisive political discourse. Partisan politics, by nature, is divisive and corrupt; however, the gospel of the Lord Jesus is a message of hope, love, grace, and salvation, and it is highly deceptive and ungodly to mix both together. However, some people have converted their podiums to preach the gospel of our Lord Jesus for their selfish political gains and to promote their preferred political party's agendas. The Scripture warns believers about such ungodly people: "For certain men have crept in unnoticed, who long ago were marked out for this condemnation, ungodly men, who turn the grace of our God into lewdness and deny the only Lord God and our Lord Jesus Christ" (Jude 1:14). Much of this type of ungodly behavior has dominated some media outlets and churches in recent years, whereby these ungodly men and women craftily turn the gospel of our Lord Jesus into personal political benefits. They turned the grace of God into profanity and permission to sin without consequences. Also, they subscribe to another companion and savior besides the Holy Spirit and the Lord Jesus. In addition, Paul warned the Roman church to avoid corrupt individuals who cause division among believers:

> Now I urge you, brethren, note those who cause divisions and offenses, contrary to the doctrine which you learned, and avoid them. For those who are such do not serve our Lord Jesus Christ, but their own belly, and by smooth words and flattering speech deceive the hearts of the simple. (Rom 16:17–18)

These individuals masterfully transform themselves as messengers of the cross, but their ultimate goal is to coerce people into their political party. Their subliminal messages include promoting their political views and candidates while pretending to care about the gospel of Jesus Christ. I suggest that believers disassociate themselves from individuals, ministries, and churches that blend the gospel of the Lord Jesus with partisan politics. Our Lord Jesus is clear about such intermixing by saying, "No one can serve two masters; for either he will hate the one and love the other, or else he will be loyal to the one and despise the other. You cannot serve God and mammon" (Matt 6:24). Partisan politics is mammon, divisive, corrupt, and unable to save a soul. Therefore, it is practically impossible to serve the two juxtaposed institutions at the same time. Anyone who attempts to serve both institutions simultaneously practices the doctrine of Balaam and, by default, serves partisan politics, not God. As believers, we are obligated to strictly adhere to the groundwork of the gospel, as modeled by our Lord Jesus Christ and the apostles. The Lord Jesus has not modified or changed his mind about the Great Commission:

> And Jesus came and spoke to them, saying, "All authority has been given to Me in heaven and on earth. Go therefore and make disciples of all nations, baptizing them in the name of the Father and of the Son and of the Holy Spirit, teaching them to observe all things that I have commanded you; and lo, I am with you always, even to the end of the age." (Matt 28:18–20)

The commandment from our Lord Jesus is to make disciples and baptize them in the name of the Father, the Son, and the Holy Spirit, not in the name of a godless political party. My questions to those who intermingle the gospel with partisan politics are: How do your political endeavors demonstrate the message of the cross that God so loves the world? How many souls have you saved with your divisive political jargon? Your political mumbo jumbo is more likely to drive people away from the kingdom of God than to save them. Perhaps, you do not care about the degree of the damage your divisive politics is causing in the body of Christ because your work is of the flesh and not of the Spirit.

The group Jesus repeatedly rebuked in the Bible were the Pharisees, and he called them "hypocrites." This was the same hypocritical group that convoluted the word of God into political gains, as these modern-day Pharisees are melding the word of God with partisan politics. Apparently, not much has changed since then in terms of the behaviors of the Pharisees during the days of Jesus' ministry and today's Pharisees. Interestingly, it was not the prostitutes, tax collectors, and whoremongers that Jesus rebuked, not because he approved of their lifestyles, but because they were the ones who needed help, and he came to save them. However, those who claim they are not blind or have no sin in them do not need help; therefore, their sins remain. John 9:41 says, "And Jesus says, 'For judgment, I have come into the world, that those who do not see may see, and that those who see may be made blind.'" I believe that those who combine the preaching of the gospel and partisan politics have been blinded by the Lord Jesus so that they cannot see.

Vignette

The intermingling of the preaching of the gospel of Jesus Christ with partisan politics is an anti-Christ spirit that tries to undermine and displace the work of the cross. It subliminally conveys the notion of a secondary savior and an alternative way to God besides the Lord Jesus.

DECEPTIONS AND FALSE PROPHECIES

Many Evangelical Christian leaders, GOP lawmakers, and their followers have repeatedly misaligned the word of God with their political movements to deceive their followers. A right-wing ReAwaken America Tour event in Batavia, New York, on October 7, 2022, was organized by former National Security Adviser General Michael Flynn, in which Clay Clark (the head of the ReAwaken America organization) made this statement: "I want you to look around, and you will see a group of people that love this country dearly," he said. "At this ReAwaken America Tour, Jesus is King [and] President Donald J. Trump is our president."[8] This statement clearly indicates a lack of fear of God and an ungodly effort to undermine the work of the cross and what Christ represents. It implies merging Christ with a man who promoted false claims about the 2020 election and a fusion of the heavenly kingdom and earthly political party. In this event, attendees were invited to be baptized and recruited to join the so-called "army of God." What a deception! Evil, hateful, and wicked political groups deceive people into presenting themselves as God's representatives. This type of evil behavior, which is based on the absolute lack of fear of God, will not go unpunished by God. As reported by *Newsweek*, on February 2, 2023, one of the attendees of the ReAwaken America Tour event, a pro-Trump prophet, Pastor Julie Green, posted a video in which she claimed that God told her:

> A bunch of Democrats are going to be arrested. You will see them step down, you will see them completely walk away, you will see them resign and you will see many die. These are days of great judgment the earth has never seen. I made sure to destroy their gods before their faces but now you will see me judge. Now you will see judgments be poured out like never before. You will see things in front of your face, you never thought you would see. You will see many being hauled out of places in government buildings. You will see them be handcuffed and walked out. You will see them being marched out because I will make sure the world sees them fall.[9]

---

8. Lardner and Smith, "Michael Flynn's ReAwaken," para. 16.
9. Kaonga, "Donald Trump Prophet," paras. 1–12.

I can tell you right off the bat that God did not speak to this self-appointed prophetess. These pro-Trump and pro-GOP prophets/prophetesses prophesy lies because they are always hallucinating. If you noticed, all their prophecies are either hateful toward Democrats or delusional favor toward Republicans. They do not hear from God; neither does God speak to them. That is why none of their false prophecies have come true. Again, God spoke through Jeremiah saying, "And the LORD said to me, 'The prophets prophesy lies in My name. I have not sent them, commanded them, nor spoken to them; they prophesy to you a false vision, divination, a worthless thing, and the deceit of their heart'" (Jer 14:14). Because of the deceptions in their hearts, they prophesy lies and worthless things; therefore, God frustrates them. It has been over eleven months since the false prophecy was declared, and none of it has come to pass. In a more realistic view, it has been the opposite that has happened. The root of these false prophecies is the illusion that God endorses the Republican Party's agendas. As Apostle Paul asked the Galatians, "O foolish Galatians, who had bewitched you that you should not obey the truth, before whose eyes Jesus Christ was clearly portrayed among you as crucified?" (Gal 3:1). The same question could be asked today, O irrational Trump supporters, who have deceived you into aligning your political party lies with the gospel of Jesus Christ? Deceiving people with false prophecies is distasteful before God, for he says:

> Behold, "I am against the prophets," says the LORD, "who use their tongues and say, 'He says.' Behold, I am against those who prophesy false dreams," says the LORD, "and tell them, and cause My people to err by their lies and by their recklessness. Yet I did not send them or command them; therefore they shall not profit this people at all," says the LORD. (Jer 23:31)

Unbeknownst to Trump supporters, it is God who removed Mr. Trump from office, as he removed Saul from being the king of Israel. By the same total number of electoral votes, 306, that God allowed Mr. Trump to be elected as president of the United States in 2016, he also used to elect his rival, Joe Biden, in 2020 and remove Donald Trump from office. In spite of all the secret and wicked plots of Mr. Trump and his allies to steal the 2020 presidential election, God frustrated all their efforts and exposed them. Believe it or not: It is God who makes it possible for one to be elected as president of the United States.

Vignette

There is absolutely zero evidence to support the postulation that God approves Republican presidents over Democratic presidents. Nor is there any evidence to suggest that the Republican Party agendas are approved by God. The Republican Party practices and the Evangelical leaders' rhetoric represent the practices of biblical Pharisees, and their rhetoric and practices were often condemned by Jesus, as shown throughout the Gospels.

CRITICAL LESSONS TO GRASP

A disturbing aspect of these so-called prophets, who mysteriously only receive prophetic utterances about Republican candidates, is that they never learn from their past false prophecies. One who had previously uttered false prophecy about presidential elections made this statement in the form of a prophetic expression, "The Republican will win more elections in 2022 to become the majority in Congress; mark my word." Anyone who understands the historical records of midterm elections knows that the president's party almost always has a bad midterm election. So, it was not anything prophetic to expect the Republican party to become the majority in both the House of Representatives and the Senate in the 2022 midterm election. Past data revealed that the president's party often loses, on average, twenty-eight House and four Senate seats.[10] However, since he treated it as something prophetic by saying, "Mark my word," I marked his word to verify the accuracy. It turns out that the Republican party did not have the majority in Congress: they only had a slight majority in the House of Representatives, and the Democrats had the majority in the Senate, even with the economic downturn and inflation. The Republicans fell short of expected outcomes, again, even with the bad economy. I pray that God will open the spiritual eyes of these political preachers to understand that there is no partiality with God. He is not a Republican nor does he endorse the ungodly practices and policies of the Republican party, nor does he support any unbiblical policies and practices of the Democrats.

The same individual, after the 2020 election and after Joe Biden had been declared president-elect, and with tons of frivolous lawsuits from Mr. Trump and his allies, frequently said, "I am praying," and I said to myself, praying for what? Perhaps, he hoped the judges would reverse Joe Biden's victory. He was so obsessed with the 2020 presidential election results that it

---

10. Woolley, "2020 Midterm Elections," para. 1.

was distasteful hearing him always talking about the election. I was shocked and grieved when he mocked President Biden for stumbling on Air Force One steps. That day, I decided not to watch the program again. I withdrew my monthly support for the ministry to help the poor and transferred it to another ministry that also helps needy families but is not involved in preaching politics. Another shocking comment he made happened around September 2020 when President Trump nominated Amy Coney Barrett for Supreme Court justice, and he said perhaps she would help to overturn the election results if Joe Biden won. This is not only ungodly but immoral and criminal thoughts and reasoning. How can someone who called himself a man of God engage in such evil and ungodly thoughts to pervert our country's democratic process? Before the election took place, there was already a secret plot from Mr. Trump and his allies to overturn the election results if he lost the election. How can God be a part of such a corrupt group of people and a political party? Dishonest behaviors are distasteful before God, for the Scripture says, "Dishonest scales are an abomination to the Lord, but a just weight is His delight" (Prov 11:1).

Shockingly, these political preachers have misrepresented who God is and biblical doctrines in their godless pursuit of mammon, in this case, partisan politics. God gave us democracy, and he honors the will of the people, as he guides by his providence who becomes the president of the United States. God loves our country, and he cares for America's well-being and will not allow Mr. Trump and his allies to destroy our country and democracy.

For those who are still struggling to accept Joe Biden as your president, take heed from what God spoke to the children of Israel who were carried away captive to Babylon: "Seek the peace of the city where I have caused you to be carried away captive and pray to the Lord for it; for in its peace you will have peace" (Jer 29:7). My suggestion is enough fighting against the will of God for choosing Joe Biden over Donald Trump. Even if it is still a mystery to you why God chose Joe Biden, you just have to trust God. Faith in God is amplified when you do not understand yet you trust him. Also, pray for God's peace, wisdom, and Spirit to guide President Biden in his presidency and to make righteous policies, for in these, we all have peace. Furthermore, for those whose hearts are right with God and want to do the will of God, here is a warning from God to guard your heart against false prophets:

> For thus says the Lord of hosts, the God of Israel: Do not let your prophets and your diviners who are in your midst deceive you, nor listen to your dreams, which you caused to be dreamed.

For they prophesy falsely to you in My name; I have not sent them, says the LORD. (Jer 29:8)

SUMMARY

False prophets and false prophecies exist today as they were in the Bible days, and the promulgators are in the body of Christ. As Jesus declares, "You will know them by their fruit" (see Matt 7:16). Because a good tree will produce good fruits, and a bad tree will produce bad fruits (see Matt 7:17). The pursuit of partisan politics, worldly riches, and fame drives one away from God, for no one can serve two masters. The love of worldly things indicates that one does not have a love of God in them (see 1 John 2:15). Because someone has a platform, which they are supposed to use to preach the gospel, but they use it to engage in divisive political babbles, it does not mean you should listen to them. Walk away from them or change your TV channel. Partisan politics divide families, friends, churches, organizations, and nations because it is not from God. Those who use their podium to preach partisan politics and spread hate and division are not of God because the message of the cross is love, grace, forgiveness, peace, and hope. If you pay careful attention to those who use their ministry platform to dialogue about politics, you will notice that they mostly portray one party as an evil party that wants to convert society into socialism. Meanwhile, they and their family members, church/ministry, and church members benefit from the social programs they dubbed as socialism. At the same time, the ungodliness in another party (the Republican Party) is exonerated or covered as if it does not exist, which is typical behavior of hypocrites. Nevertheless, God has no partiality, for he will judge both Democrats and Republicans with the same standard (see Rom 2:11; Col 3:25).

There is no reward in heaven for converting people to the Republican Party or Democratic Party. We receive rewards for bringing souls into the kingdom of God, not converting them to a political party. There are no biblical examples from our Lord Jesus and the apostles for mixing the gospel of the cross with partisan politics. It was the Pharisees who perverted the word of God with their traditions, politics, and pursuit of riches and fame. The modern-day Pharisees are doing the same thing today. They have converted God's house into a place for buying and selling goods, and the dominant good today is politics. Again, separate yourself from religious leaders who mingle the preaching of the gospel with partisan politics, for they are hypocrites and out of the will of God. The Scripture warns us by stating, "But know this, that in the last days, perilous times will come: For men will be lovers of themselves, lovers of money, boasters, proud, [and] blasphemers" (2 Tim 3:1–2). By their fruit, as Jesus declares, you shall know them. It is also important to remember the warning from our Lord Jesus:

> Not everyone who says to Me, "Lord, Lord," shall enter the kingdom of heaven, but he who does the will of My Father in heaven. Many will say to Me in that day, "Lord, Lord, have we not prophesied in Your name, cast out demons in Your name, and done many wonders in Your name?" And then I will declare to them, "I never knew you; depart from Me, you who practice lawlessness!" (Matt 7:21–23)

The above Scripture applies to people who are in the church, not outsiders. Lawlessness in this situation implies to those who know God's word and will, yet they choose to pursue worldly riches and fame and practice the doctrine of Balaam. It includes those who willfully disobey God's laws and the commandment of the Great Commission by our Lord Jesus; instead of winning souls for the kingdom of God, they are winning souls for a political party. Christians should have the right to vote for any candidate, as they are guided by the conviction of their heart, without being persuaded or condemned by some religious leaders who turned politicians.

Chapter 9

Was the 2020 Presidential Election Stolen?

A nineteenth-century philosopher and theologian, Søren Kierkegaard, said, "There are two ways to be fooled. One is to believe what isn't true; the other is to refuse to believe what is true."[1] Surprisingly, many people today in our society have opted to believe what is not true, as well as to refuse to believe what is true about the 2020 presidential election results. Therefore, they have unconsciously turned their minds to lies and deception.

Whether the 2020 presidential election was stolen or not is a rhetorical question that any honest and logical-thinking individual should affirmatively know the answer to be "No." However, to simple-minded individuals, it creates an illusion in their minds to believe what is not true and alludes to the need to solve a mystery that does not exist. Yet, to others, the acceptance that the election was stolen relinquishes them of the mental burden to logically analyze the possibility of such widespread voter fraud taking place in a country arguably known as the world's oldest democracy. It takes a simple-minded individual and a heart conditioned for falsehood to believe lies. Proverbs 14:15 says, "The simple believes every word, but the prudent considers well his steps." The simple quickly fall for fallacy without taking essential steps to logically evaluate the reality of what they hear. And it is a shocking reality to see that a large number of people fell for baseless claims about widespread voter fraud in the 2020 presidential election, as propagated by Donald Trump and his fierce allies. None of them produced any logical evidence for the courts or the public to support their unfathomable fictitious claims.

---

1. Patterson, "Two Ways to Be Fooled," para. 2.

CHRISTIAN EVANGELICALS ARE SUPPORTERS OF TRUMP'S BIG LIES ABOUT THE 2020 ELECTION

Records indicate that Christian Evangelical leaders and their followers have promoted the false claims of Mr. Trump about the 2020 presidential election. According to a PRRI survey in 2021, six of ten White Evangelical Protestants believe that the 2020 presidential election was stolen from Donald Trump.[2] In April 2022, thousands of Evangelical leaders and followers gathered at Oral Roberts University in Oklahoma, and Pastor Gene Bailey made the following statements after his prayer: "There's one thing that I know for sure, and this is the raw truth: The raw truth was on Nov. 3, 2020, President Donald J. Trump won the election. That election was rigged. It was stolen. We're still waiting on the election to be corrected, and we're not going anywhere."[3]

I have news for you Pastor Bailey, you will be waiting forever for the election to be corrected because there is nothing to be corrected about the election, except the actual fraud about the stolen election was everyone who made false claims that did not exist. The false belief that God endorses the Republican Party has led to the illusions in the minds of some Evangelical preachers to propagate falsehood about the 2020 election results. The behavior of some of these political preachers is distasteful in that they are so morally debased, illogical, and spiritually devoid that they cannot distinguish lies from truth or facts from fiction. I believe that these political preachers are either not called by God or have totally abandoned their calling in pursuit of worldly gains. Jesus warns Christians about false prophets by saying:

> Not everyone who says to Me, "Lord, Lord," shall enter the kingdom of heaven, but he who does the will of My Father in heaven. Many will say to Me in that day, "Lord, Lord, have we not prophesied in Your name, cast out demons in Your name, and done many wonders in Your name?" And then I will declare to them, "I never knew you; depart from Me, you who practice lawlessness!" (Matt 7:21–23)

A preacher using the pulpit God gave him to preach politics instead of the word of God to save souls is a practice of lawlessness, and I believe that God has given some of these political preachers over to a debased mind, to do things that are not fitting (see Rom 1:28). You have been warned by the Holy Spirit several times, yet you resisted him, and if you claim that Holy Spirit

---

2. Public Religion Research Institute, "Big Lie," para. 4.
3. Mantyla, "There Is a Payback Coming," paras. 3–4.

has not warned you about the preaching of the Republican Party politics instead of the gospel, it then means you are never his from the beginning.

There has never been a time in the history of mankind that God's people gathered many times and called upon the name of God hundreds of times about a particular issue that God did not answer them speedily, except in this case of a fabricated stolen election. All the prophecies from the so-called prophets were false about the 2020 presidential election. None of these self-proclaimed prophets received any revelation from God that the election results would be stolen by Joe Biden. So, what does it take to get the message that God is not with your baseless claims and in your pursuit of mammon and practice of lawlessness?

Let us take some logical steps to review some issues and facts concerning the 2020 presidential election and examine the background of the man who promulgated the claims about election fraud. A person's background is an irrefutable, integral aspect of their identity because it reveals who they are and their character and predicts what they are capable of doing presently and in the future. Some employers conduct background checks on their potential employees to better understand the person they are about to hire. The same is true in this situation, knowing the background of a man who promoted election fraud in the 2020 election to understand what he is capable of doing presently and in the future.

FAMILIAR PATTERNS OF CONSPIRACY THEORIES WITH DONALD TRUMP

The first time Donald Trump ran for a presidential election in 2016, he campaigned on repeated ambiguous narratives that the US elections are rigged and that the only way he will lose in Pennsylvania is "if cheating goes on."[4] Such a claim is uncharacteristic of previous presidential candidates, but for Donald Trump, it was setting the stage to cast doubt on our electoral process if the election results did not favor him. He was also setting the stage to use the court system to overturn the will of the people and appoint himself the president of the United States. Even after mysteriously winning the election in 2016, although not by popular votes, and after Hilary Clinton had conceded, he still promoted another unsubstantiated claim by saying, "I won the popular votes if you deduct the millions of people who voted illegally." So, a voting integrity commission created by the Trump administration investigated and produced no evidence of widespread voter fraud.[5] How-

---

4. Smith and Siddique, "Trump Claims 'Cheating,'" para. 1.
5. Villeneuve, "Trump Commission Did Not Find," para. 1.

ever, the commission was later dissolved by executive order. So, making baseless claims about rigged elections has been Donald Trump's strategy to cast doubt on our democratic electoral process, which is one of the most secure election systems in postmodern societies. Even during the Republican primary election in 2016, he accused Senator Ted Cruz of stealing the Iowa caucuses and demanded nullifying the result because Ted Cruz won the caucus. He also cried foul play saying the system was "rigged" against him after Ted Cruz won the Colorado caucuses. Speaking to his followers in Albany, he claimed that Mr. Cruz's campaign bribed voters and that the Republican primary election process was "a rigged, disgusting, and dirty system."[6] Interestingly, a crooked man called our system crooked. Have you ever seen or heard a US president derogating our system and falsely accusing the citizens of selfish gain? It is shocking to me that people are listening to a man who has no ability to tell the truth. Remember the birther conspiracy promulgated by Donald Trump against the then-Senator Barack Obama, who was a Democratic Party presidential nominee in 2008? He also used the same playbook against Ted Cruz in 2016, saying he was not eligible for the presidency because he was not a "natural-born citizen." Then comes the 2020 presidential election; seeing that the poll was not in his favor, as well as the mass populace, Mr. Trump started sounding the false alarm repeatedly about a rigged election months before the election took place. His false alarm resonated with his like-minded supporters, who have no regard for the rule of law but would do anything to topple our democracy. In sum, false claims about election fraud and conspiracy theories are a familiar stock-in-trade of Mr. Trump, as he has done several times in the past.

POST-ELECTION LAWSUITS

Then, seeing that he lost the presidential election on November 3, 2020, he and his corrupt allies filed over fifty lawsuits in local, state, and federal courts alleging voter fraud, and all the lawsuits were dismissed, dropped, or ruled against Trump for lack of evidence, except one. The only one ruled in Trump's favor was a minor case that affected only a few people regarding ID confirmation of first-time voters in Pennsylvania. However, the Pennsylvania Supreme Court later overturned the ruling.[7] Federal judges, including the ones appointed by President Trump and the Supreme Court, rejected all the frivolous lawsuits brought by President Trump and his allies due to lack of evidence. Thank God that we have a judiciary system that works. Our

6. Jacobs, "Trump Protests," paras. 1–5.
7. Shamsian and Sheth, "Trump and His Allies," para. 7.

God-given democracy came close to being hijacked by a psychopath and his criminal-minded allies.

Vignette

> The unrelenting, aggressive efforts to use the judicial branch to overturn legitimate presidential election results was a close call to calamity and a test of the fortitude of our democracy.

Trump's attempted coup was, perhaps, the greatest assault on our democracy since its existence. Donald Trump hoped to find a sympathizer among the judges or a court ruling that would grant him a substantial victory among his fifty-plus lawsuits, enabling him to legitimize his position to nullify or overturn the election results. His goal was to topple our democratic process of electing presidents and reinstate himself as the reelected president. Disappointingly, some people unwisely supported him in his selfish quest to destroy our democracy. Sometimes, people may not have a good grasp of the value of what they have until they lose it. If the attempted coup had succeeded, that would have been the end of democracy in the United States, and we would have lost our identity as a nation. The government would no longer belong to the people; instead, the people would become slaves to the government, including those who unwisely supported the coup. Imagine, if we become a nation where the politicians are no longer elected by the will of the people but rather by the judicial branch based on who can conjure the most outrageous lies, what a disaster that would be to our beloved nation and democracy. That would be very dangerous to our republic, liberty, and Constitution. Without any moral or ethical restrictions, our nation would become a banana republic, where corruption and self-serving dictators dominate.

Furthermore, the Supreme Court is the highest federal judiciary branch in the land and, thus, the final arbiter of the law. For people seeking justice through the judiciary system, the Supreme Court is their last resort. The decisions of the Supreme Court on any controversial case are final. However, it was not so for a man that several Christian Evangelical leaders and Republicans promoted as running on the premises of protecting the integrity of the law. Apparently, when it comes to respecting the law, the standard changes depending on the perpetrator and the victim. Differential methods in applying the law are not a form of justice and do not reflect biblical values or our Constitution. President Trump demonstrated no respect for our proven democratic electoral process and the rule of law as established by the judiciary system. His actions tarnished our image and moral authority globally concerning the free and fair election process. So much of the campaign slogan, "Make America Great Again!"

FACTS SURROUNDING THE 2020 PRESIDENTIAL ELECTION

Even with all the evidence showing that Joe Biden won the election and had been declared president-elect, President Donald Trump continued his baseless claims about a fraudulent election. Some honest people from his camp objected to his false claims; for example, on November 12, 2020, the head of the Cybersecurity and Infrastructure Security Agency (CISA), Christopher Krebs, stated that the 2020 election was "the most secure in American history."[8] Then on November 18, 2020, Trump fired him for speaking the truth. Sadly, President Trump, some GOP lawmakers, and their fierce supporters have engaged in disorderly conduct to harass and penalize anyone who spoke the truth. The expectation is for everyone to jump onto Mr. Trump's bandwagon and promote his lies and deceptions, or at least say nothing that will contradict his lies. On December 1, 2020, Trump-appointed Attorney General William Barr, who has been very loyal to President Trump, said his justice department did not find any evidence of widespread voter fraud that could change the election outcomes. Mr. Barr also said during an interview, "My attitude was: It was put-up or shut-up time. If there was evidence of fraud, I had no motive to suppress it. But my suspicion all the way along was that there was nothing there. It was all bullshit."[9]

Although, according to the Justice Department policy, it only investigates election fraud after election certification, not before it is certified, for the purpose of prosecuting crimes, not to influence election outcomes.[10] However, Mr. Barr, a Trump loyalist, permitted his department to conduct an informal investigation on some allegations made by Mr. Trump and his fierce allies, perhaps to please the president and set the record straight. One of the investigations involved the allegation of counting machines switching Trump's votes to Biden, which produced no evidence. After his inquiry, he concluded that the evidence would have manifested when the ballots were counted by hand if the counting machines had been rigged.[11] Yet, Mr. Barr was vilified by Trump for speaking the truth, which perhaps may have led

8. Sanger and Periroth, "Trump Fires Cybersecurity Official," paras. 1–10.
9. Karl, "Inside William Barr's Break Up," paras. 1–7.
10. Karl, "Inside William Barr's Break Up," para. 15.
11. Karl, "Inside William Barr's Break Up," para. 21.

Was the 2020 Presidential Election Stolen?

to his resignation as the US attorney general. In his attacks against Mr. Barr, President Trump said:

> Bill Barr was a disappointment in every sense of the word. Instead of doing his job, he did the opposite and told people within the Justice Department not to investigate the election. Just like he did with the Mueller report and the cover-up of Crooked Hillary and RUSSIA RUSSIA RUSSIA, they don't want to investigate the real facts. Bill Barr's weakness helped facilitate the cover-up of the Crime of the Century, the Rigged 2020 Presidential Election![12]

Vignette

The danger of working in Donald Trump's administration is that you have to become a liar, deceiver, and manipulator to succeed in his administration. You cannot stop once you start lying and covering up for him because his whole life revolves around dishonesty. Therefore, our society needs to honor those who did not succumb to Donald Trump's pressure to compromise their integrity but stood up for the truth. Their courage to stand up against a bully saved our democracy, which is the type of bravery we need in our society. In the same manner, those who forsook their oaths of office to serve a man's interest rather than for the country's welfare should be penalized and voted out of office. It is vital to send a clear message that we are people of integrity by severely sanctioning behaviors that contradict integrity; otherwise, a more egregious future attempt to topple our democracy is inevitable.

On January 27, 2021, the Maricopa County Board of Supervisors collectively chose to verify the authenticity and security of election equipment used in Maricopa County, Arizona. As a result, a certified public accounting firm, BerryDunn, was hired to examine the county's contract with Dominion Voting System and verify the contract was performed with integrity and per the county's procurement requirements and procedures.[13] The investigation result indicated an "absence of conflict of interest." In addition, Maricopa County hired two independent voting system testing laboratories, Pro V&V and SLI Compliance, to carry out the following tasks:

---

12. Samuels, "Trump Calls Barr 'a Disappointment,'" para. 2.
13. BerryDunn, "Maricopa County," para. 1.

- Analyze election equipment software and hardwares' hacking vulnerability.
- Verify that no malicious malware was installed.
- Test that tabulators were not sending or receiving information over the internet.
- Confirm that no vote-switching occurred.

According to Maricopa County Directors of Election Day and Emergency Voting,[14] the forensic audit of the Dominion Voting Systems tabulation equipment and software produced the following results:

- Pro V&V and SLI Compliance found that all software and equipment inspected were using certified software and were not modified.
- Pro V&V and SLI Compliance found no instances of malicious software or hardware installed on the tabulators or system.
- Pro V&V and SLI Compliance found no evidence of internet connectivity.
- Pro V&V found no evidence of vote switching and concluded that the equipment tabulated and adjudicated ballots accurately.

Another GOP personnel who repeatedly rejected Donald Trump's false claims about election fraud was Georgia Secretary of State Brad Raffensperger. In an interview with the *Atlanta Journal-Constitution*, he said:

> I'm a Republican. I understand the disappointment on my side. We verified the results. We had the first run of what the total was. Then we did a 100 percent hand retally of all 5 million ballots. Then we ran those ballots again through the scanner. All three times the results were very similar.[15]

Yet another Republican election official with the Georgia Secretary of State office, Gabriel Sterling, refuted Trump's claims of election irregularities by presenting line-by-line and detailed information about the election.[16] His presentation mitigated election fraud claims in Georgia, as promoted by President Trump and his allies.

The judiciary branch, independent entities, and honest Republicans have investigated claims made by Mr. Trump and his lawyers multiple times. Yet, there was no iota of evidence produced, nor did the outcomes of

---

14. Jarrett and Valenzuela, "Update on Forensic Audit," paras. 3–5.
15. Wickert, "Raffensperger Disputes Fraud Claims," para. 7.
16. Parks, "Georgia Election Official," para. 1–3.

the investigations support their false claims. It is a disgrace to human intelligence to continue to believe false claims in spite of abundant evidence that suggests otherwise. One of the most significant distinctions between human beings and animals is intelligence. Human beings are equipped with the intellectual ability to cognitively process and analyze information logically, while animals operate on a limited level of intelligence or intuition. One refusing to use his brain and objectively process information is an insult to humanity. Refusing to accept the truth and opting for lies is an immoral and debased life; thus, the nation's welfare should outweigh one's selfish desire in their quest for their preferred presidential candidate to win an election.

Furthermore, some honest Republicans took a bold stand to resist Mr. Trump's malicious lies about the election. Like Senator Mitt Romney said on January 6, 2021, after the insurrection, "The best way we can show respect for the voters who are upset is by telling them the truth."[17] In essence, the truth is that Donald Trump lost the election. One of the Republicans who took a bold stand to refute Donald Trump's lies was Rep. Liz Cheney, from Wyoming; she was number three in GOP House leadership, and she demonstrated admirable courage and boldness to denounce Donald Trump's lies. She also resisted the pressure from her party and offered a more direct rebuke to Trump's bogus claims about the 2020 election by making these statements:

> Millions of Americans have been misled by the former president. They have heard only his words, but not the truth, as he continues to undermine our democratic process, sowing seeds of doubt about whether democracy really works at all . . . Those who refuse to accept the rulings of our courts are at war with the Constitution . . . Our duty is clear. Every one of us who has sworn the oath must act to prevent the unraveling of our democracy. This is not about policy. This is not about partisanship. This is about our duty as Americans. Remaining silent, and ignoring the lie, emboldens the liar.[18]

Another Republican from Wisconsin, Paul Ryan, former US House of Representatives speaker, during an interview with Milwaukee's *WISN* TV, said this about the election: "It was not rigged, it was not stolen, Donald Trump lost the election, Joe Biden won the election, it's really clear."[19] However, Mr. Ryan also warns the Republican Party for their continued support of President Trump, which is dividing the party, by saying this, "I think it's a

17. Narea, "Romney Just Urged Republicans," para. 3.
18. Larson, "'Our Election Was Not Stolen,'" paras. 1–10.
19. Wainscott, "Donald Trump Lost the 2020 Election," para. 5.

big mistake for the Republican Party to be a party about a person or personality. And I think we'll just keep losing if we wrap ourselves around one person. We have not lost this much this fast in a long, long time." Also, a GOP lawmaker, Dan Crenshaw, an ally of Donald Trump, rejected the claim that the 2020 presidential election was stolen as claimed by Mr. Trump and his allies.[20]

THE DESPERATION OF A DESPERATE PRESIDENT

With the judiciary system not working in Mr. Trump's favor due to lack of evidence, and a few individuals in his camp countering his false claims, President Trump resorted to more desperate crafty approaches to stay in power. He started making calls to multiple states' election officials, asking them to either find fictitious votes for him or block certifying Joe Biden's win. For example, he called Georgia Secretary of State Brad Raffensperger and asked him to "find" 11,780 votes to overturn Joe Biden's victory in Georgia.[21] He displayed an unimaginable erratic and psychopathic behavior uncharacteristic of past US presidents. In essence, his motive for the election fraud claim is not to uncover facts because the facts are unequivocally before him but to flex his muscle in subverting the US democratic process for selfish gain. Generating false conspiracy theories has been a familiar modus operandi for Donald Trump. For Mr. Trump, the end justifies the means, and it does not matter how he gets to the end.

After Joe Biden had taken the oath of office of the presidency, more reports have emerged of the uncanny desperate efforts of Donald Trump to overturn the 2020 presidential election. For example, the former acting attorney general in Trump's administration, Jeffrey A. Rosen, told the congressional investigators how Donald Trump wanted to use the Justice Department to overturn the election. Mr. Trump had said to the department officials, "Just say the election was corrupt and leave the rest to the R. Congressmen and me."[22] One may wonder why Donald Trump would have so much confidence in the Republican congressmen to defend his lies. These GOP lawmakers have abdicated their oaths of office and have inadvertently chosen to serve in the interest of a dishonest president instead of the country's interest. In another episode, Mr. Trump criticized Mr. Rosen by saying, "One thing we know is you, Rosen, aren't going to overturn the election," as he contemplated replacing Mr. Rosen with the acting assistant

20. Relman, "Republican Rep. Dan Crenshaw," para. 1.
21. Fowler, "Trump to Georgia Election Officials," para. 14.
22. Herb, "Trump to DOJ," para. 3.

attorney general, Jeffrey Clark.[23] According to the report, Mr. Clark was willing to do Donald Trump's bidding; thus, Mr. Trump considered replacing Mr. Rosen's position with Mr. Clark. Such a suggestion elicited threats of a mass resignation from the Justice Department and White House.

The thought of invoking martial law was floated in the Oval Office meeting on December 18, 2020, to enable Donald Trump to remain in power.[24] The former national security advisor, Michael Flynn, whom President Trump pardoned, first initiated the idea during his appearance on a conservative television network, Newsmax.[25] He suggested that President Trump impose martial law to override the 2020 election results. Although some have argued that Donald Trump does not have such constitutional authority to declare martial law, the idea of using military power in a democratic election process is troubling. Anyone who cherishes our democracy should find such a thought awful!

Nonetheless, the irony of the entire episode is the silence and support of the majority of the congressional Republicans and Christian Evangelical leaders concerning the unparalleled attacks on our democracy by Mr. Trump and his falsehoods. They also endorsed either openly or silently the lies of President Trump about election fraud. These people are supposed to uphold the truth but have deliberately called evil good because of their lack of integrity. Proverbs 17:4 says, "An evildoer gives heed to false lips; a liar listens eagerly to a spiteful tongue." It takes a corrupt heart to believe Donald Trump's lies and naughty tongue. Donald Trump's record is shrouded with clouds of dishonesty and mischievousness. Most congressional Republicans and Christian Evangelical leaders are not unaware of his questionable record, yet they continue to push for the support of a corrupt president. As reported by the *Arkansas Times*, Mr. Trump is not only the most corrupt president but the most amoral president and political leader in American history.[26] The report suggested that no other president or political leader come close to the scale of Mr. Trump's corruption and immorality.

---

23. Lucas, "Senate Report Details," para. 5.

24. Goodwin, "Trump's Talk of Martial Law," paras. 1–7; Kristian, "What Would Actually Happen," para. 1.

25. Goodwin, "Trump's Talk of Martial Law," paras. 1–7.

26. Dumas, "Donald Trump Corrupt Legacy," para. 1.

PRESIDENT TRUMP'S FALSE CLAIMS ABOUT ELECTION FRAUD CREATED POTENTIAL ACTS OF VIOLENCE

President Trump's amplified misinformation has generated a lot of threats to election officials in the swing states where he lost to Joe Biden. For example, Georgia Republican Secretary of State Brad Raffensperger, Georgia voting system manager Gabriel Sterling, and other election officials, including their family members, were subjected to constant threats of violence because they disagreed with President Trump. Thus, Mr. Sterling pleaded with President Trump to stop promoting threats of violence against election officials with his false claims about the election, as reported by the *New York Times*, saying, "Mr. President, it looks like you likely lost the state of Georgia. Stop inspiring people to commit potential acts of violence. Someone is going to get hurt; someone is going to get shot; someone is going to get killed. And it's not right."[27]

Furthermore, Mr. Sterling, who is a Republican, asked the two Republican senators to intervene and ask President Trump to stop his baseless claims about the election fraud. But, instead of the senators intervening, they asked Mr. Raffensperger to resign. Their chosen solution to the problem generated by Donald Trump was disturbing. Is this the type of society we want to create, punish those who spoke the truth, and reward liars? How does this type of behavior reflect God's values when lies are an abomination before him? These questions are also for the Christian Evangelical leaders who have been deceiving their followers by promoting the Republican Party as God's party and dishonest GOP lawmakers and presidents as God's approved candidates. Your behavior is ungodly, and you are contributing to the destruction of our country and democracy. Furthermore, the threats of violence from Mr. Trump's supporters escalated, and on January 6, 2021, Mr. Trump's supporters laid siege to the US Capitol. The violent attack was the final effort of Donald Trump and his supporters to overthrow the US government and democracy. It was a shocking and distasteful event, one never expected to happen in the US.

Vignette

Mr. Trump's false claims about the 2020 election will negatively impact the US political landscape for several years to come. It

---

27. Fausset, "Georgia Election Official Lashes Trump," para. 1.

serves as a model for future election candidates who lost the election to promote false claims about their lost election.

THE HOUSE COMMITTEE INVESTIGATION OF THE JANUARY 6 RIOT

The deadly insurrection on Capitol Hill on January 6, 2021, was an act of domestic terrorism that was fermented by one of the most dishonest presidents in the history of the United States. Mr. Trump's role in the violence led to his impeachment on January 13, 2021, and the House Select Committee initiated an extensive investigation of the January 6 attacks on the United States Capitol. The investigation was a bipartisan effort, consisting of nine members of the House of Representatives and chaired by Rep. Bennie Thompson. The committee interviewed over twelve hundred witnesses; collected thousands of text messages, emails, and documents; and issued more than one hundred subpoenas.[28] The committee investigation lasted eighteen months and their findings showed desperate efforts of the former president to overturn his 2020 election loss to President Joe Biden. The committee unanimously voted to report Mr. Trump to the Department of Justice for criminal charges. There were four criminal referrals recommended by the committee against Mr. Trump, which include (1) obstruction of an official proceeding, (2) conspiracy to defraud the United States, (3) conspiracy to make false statements, and (4) inciting, assisting, or aiding and comforting an insurrection.[29] In all this, the political preachers did not condemn Mr. Trump's efforts to destroy our democracy, rather some helped him by promoting the false conspiracy of a stolen election and others remained silent. What a disgrace!

TRUMP'S LONG HISTORY OF LEGAL AFFAIRS

Donald Trump is not a stranger to legal battles. In fact, he is a master in legal maneuvering. He had aggressively used lawsuits in his business dealings to intimidate his opponents and to swing the scale of justice in attempts to favor himself. The purpose of providing the information about President Trump's background is for educational purposes and to shed light on the moral character of a man who cried foul play in the 2020 presidential election. It is important to better understand President Trump before jumping

28. Wong et al., "Jan. 6 Committee Report," para. 23.
29. Alemany et al., "Jan. 6 Committee," para. 2.

into the bandwagon of sympathy that falsely claims that the election was stolen. Donald Trump and his business have a long record of being involved in over four thousand legal cases in the course of his business endeavors.[30] His legal battles include cases against his niece, business partners, and journalists whom he claimed under-reported his wealth. In addition, he had filed six corporate bankruptcies for his companies.[31] The question still remains, How can Mr. Trump be a proficient steward of the US economy, when he could not demonstrate such skills with his business?

TRUMP'S PERSONAL BACKGROUND

In July 2020, President Trump's niece, Dr. Mary Trump, released a book titled *Too Much and Never Enough: How My Family Created The World's Most Dangerous Man*. According to the *New York Times* report, she alleged that President Trump cheated on the SAT college entrance exam to gain admission to the Wharton School of the University of Pennsylvania.[32] The allegation is that Mr. Trump paid someone to take the SAT for him, which enhanced his admission chances into the Wharton School. However, while Mr. Trump has a shady record regarding his college admission, he regularly challenged President Obama to release his college records. One time he made this comment, "I heard he was a terrible student. I am certainly looking into it. Let him show his records."[33]

Nevertheless, when President Obama's academic record was released, it showed that he graduated with honors—magna cum laude from Harvard Law School. It is an unparalleled comparison between one who graduated magna cum laude from Harvard Law School and one who cheated to gain admission into the Wharton School of the University of Pennsylvania on a shady academic record that he does not want anyone to see. The latter has no chance of achieving an acceptable score on the LSAT to attend law school, let alone being admitted into Harvard Law School and graduating magna cum laude. This type of behavior is consistent with hypocrites, masking their inadequacies while accusing one better than them. In his statement, he claimed that he heard but did not provide the source of what he heard. Does that sound familiar? Indeed, it should! Remember all the false claims about the 2020 presidential election fraud without a shred of evidence.

---

30. Welker, "Donald Trump Settlement and Lawsuits," para. 7.
31. Murse, "Why Donald Trump's Companies Went Bankrupt," para. 6.
32. Haberman and Feuer, "Mary Trump's Book Accuses the President," paras. 1–9.
33. Fouhy, "Terrible Student," para. 3.

While President Trump was demanding that President Obama release his grades, he directed his attorney, Michael Cohen, to send letters to his high school, college, and college board, threatening them with lawsuits if they released his grades and SAT scores to a third party without his written permission.[34] What a hypocrite! For recent and past presidents, President Bush, President Obama, and President Biden, academic records were made public, but they never boasted or taunted anyone about releasing their records. But the one with shady academic records is the one making accusations against another president. President Trump's problems are self-imposed, not the media or the Democrats, as often claimed by him and his supporters. He is a prolific liar and dangerously dishonest, which is driven by his untamed selfish ego. Moreover, it takes a very dishonest person to believe the lies of President Trump or defend his questionable character.

President Trump had always bragged he was a stellar student but had not provided any academic record to validate his claims. According to a *Politico* report, from 2018, while President Trump was introducing the new secretary of state, Mike Pompeo, Trump touted his unsubstantiated claims of academic prowess by saying this:

> You know I heard that rumor a long time ago. I thought it was a rumor. I've heard it so many times. I've also heard I was first in my class at the Wharton School of Finance. And sometimes, when you hear it, you don't say anything; you just let it go. But I heard it with him. And being first in your class at West Point, because I know, that's a big deal.[35]

Although he has shielded his academic records with threats of lawsuits against his alma mater, other reliable sources have been used in an attempt to verify his claims. For example, in 1968, when Donald Trump graduated, his name was not on the list of students who graduated with honors in the program commencement.[36] In addition, his name was not on the dean's list published in 1968 by the *Daily Pennsylvanian*. If Donald Trump was the first in his class as he claimed, why is it that the University of Pennsylvania's Wharton School did not include his name on the list of students who graduated with honors? Why is it that his name was not on the dean's list that the *Daily Pennsylvanian* published in 1968 when he graduated? For a man who files lawsuits at the drop of a hat, shouldn't this be a more legitimate reason for him to file lawsuits against the University of Pennsylvania for denying him the honor of his name being listed on the dean's list and graduating

---

34. Jaschik, "Trump Threatened Colleges," para. 1.
35. Lima, "Trump Touts Renewed," para. 12.
36. Valania, "Fact Checking All the Mysteries," para. 23.

with honors? Instead, he objected to making his academic record public and resorted to making threats of lawsuits against his alma mater if his academic record was released to the public. Donald Trump is a man who lacks the innate ability to distinguish truth from lies. A man whose mind is so convoluted that telling lies has become his natural language and a way of life. The *New York Times*, in 2019, reported that President Trump's sister, Maryanne Trump, described him as someone who sees people "in monetary terms" and uses "cheating as a way of life." That sounds all too familiar to those who are honest about the ambiguous character of Mr. Trump.

Additionally, unlike both present and past presidents in recent decades who made their tax returns public, President Donald Trump was the only one who did not reveal his taxes; rather he spent years in legal battles to prevent releasing his tax returns to the public. One might wonder what he is hiding to invest so many resources in legal battles to keep his tax returns data secret. As recent previous presidents have done, he should have voluntarily released his tax returns data to the public if he had nothing to hide. Honest citizens pay their fair taxes, and they do not spend their time and resources in legal battles to keep their taxes a secret. Paying your fair taxes is an act of patriotism, and it is only traitors who would avoid paying their fair taxes. When his legal battle about the release of tax returns to Congress reached the Supreme Court on November 22, 2022, the Supreme Court, with no dissents, rejected his request to block the Congressional Committee (House Ways and Means Committee) from obtaining his tax returns from the IRS.[37] This rejection was after the unanimous ruling of an appeals court panel in August 2022, that granted the House Ways and Means Committee access to Mr. Trump's tax returns. Now, reviewing Mr. Trump's tax returns confirmed what most people had suspected and revealed why he spent years in court battles to prevent Congress from having access to his tax returns. Mr. Trump had lied many times and, on several occasions, said that he was under IRS audit, which was the reason why his tax returns were not released. The truth is that he did not have any ongoing IRS audit as he claimed. Reports showed that Mr. Trump had questionable business losses that were rolled over year after year to reduce his tax burdens.[38]

Furthermore, the Trump organization was subject to multiple investigations for tax evasion. In July 2021, New York state prosecutors charged the chief financial officer of the Trump Organization, Allen Weisselberg, for evading taxes with employee perks.[39] On August 18, 2022, Mr. Weis-

37. Cheney, "Supreme Court Backs House Effort," para. 1.
38. McIntire et al., "Paid $0 in 2020," para. 1.
39. Hemel, "Trump Organization Is in Big Trouble," para. 1–2.

selberg pleaded guilty to fifteen felonies and agreed to pay nearly $2 million in back taxes and serve five months in prison.[40] In addition, according to CNN, the Trump Organization was allegedly under investigation for property value inflation and deflation to pay lower taxes.[41] A New York jury found the Trump Organization guilty of altering business records and tax fraud.[42] Then, Justice Juan Merchan of the Manhattan Criminal Court fined the organization $1.6 million on January 13, 2023, which is the maximum allowable by law. It is inconceivable that the United States would elect a cheating, unpatriotic, lawless, and self-serving man as a president. Yet, some people pledged their unwavering support to him. What is the driving force for such steadfast support to a man who lacks integrity and is very divisive? Chapter 11 of this book explains the driving force behind the support of Mr. Trump, despite his dishonesty. According to PolitiFact, an organization that rates the statements made by politicians for accuracy, only 11 percent of President Trump's statements are true and mostly true. This suggests that if President Trump's mouth is moving, most of the time, he is lying. While most of his statements are lies, he was busy accusing the media's reports of being "fake news." In essence, the only fake news is the one who made the accusation of a false election. It is shocking that Christian Evangelicals would pledge their unwavering support to a man who lacks integrity in every conceivable measure. Mr. Trump's lifestyle contradicts every biblical value, and that should be a turnoff for Christians, not an attraction. How can God endorse a political party that embraces lies, deceptions, hate, division, and self-centeredness as a way of life, when he condemns such behaviors as written in the Bible?

President Trump, just like President Biden, had several draft deferments from Vietnam. They both never served in the military; although they played football, they received deferments as students, and eventually, medical exemptions for bone spurs and asthma, respectively.[43] However, Joe Biden's son Beau joined the Delaware Army National Guard after the September 11, 2001, terrorist attacks, and he later served in Iraq.[44] In 2015, he passed away due to brain cancer while holding the position of Delaware attorney general. But Mr. Trump or any of his children did not serve in the military. Donald Trump dodged being drafted into the military. Still, he

---

40. Scannell, "Former CFO of Trump Organization," paras. 1–3.
41. Moghe and Scannell, "Westchester County District Attorney," paras. 1–5.
42. Yousif, "Trump Organization Fined $1.6 Million," para. 1.
43. Caldera, "Received Multiple Draft Deferments," paras. 1–4; Lauria and Albright, "If Biden Were a President," paras. 1–3.
44. Milford and Starkey, "Remembering Beau Biden," paras. 1–4.

had the audacity to insult an American war hero, Senator John McCain, a much better man than him. Mr. Trump made a derogatory statement about Senator McCain's war record, saying, "He's not a war hero. He's not a war hero because he was captured. I like people who weren't captured."[45] Only an illogical coward would howl such an insulting statement to a war hero. A war hero who indeed paid an immeasurable price serving our country. Senator McCain paid his fair taxes and was a true patriot with integrity. Mr. Trump could have at least joined the military to demonstrate to the country how to go to war and avoid being captured. But he did not! It is shocking to see that people will support a man who would not make any sacrifice for our country, like joining the military, but has taken advantage of our system to his benefit, such as dishonest business practices, tax evasion, bankruptcies, and frivolous lawsuits. Indeed, there are no conceivable comparisons between Senator John McCain and Donald Trump in terms of the quality of a man. President Trump has no relationship with past presidents, either Democratic or Republican presidents. They know that Donald Trump's dishonest and belligerent behaviors are an insult to the office of the presidency. He represents the lowest of our country's experience with a president in modern America's history.

With the brief background information presented about President Trump, my question is, Would you hire a candidate with such a background if you are an employer? Please, understand that the question is, Would you hire a candidate, not Mr. Trump, with such a questionable background? Chances are, you would not. Would you comfortably enter into a business contract or partnership with someone who has dubious business records? Again, most likely, you would not. If you were a parent, would you want a man with such questionable character as Donald Trump to marry your daughter? Hopefully, you would say no, if you care for the stability and well-being of your daughter's marriage. If you would not hire a candidate with such a dubious background or enter into a business partnership with a man who files countless lawsuits if he does not have his way, why would you want him to be the United States president? No wonder 60 percent of American voters believe that President Trump lacks a moral compass to lead the nation, 61 percent do not think he is honest, which overshadows his leadership skills, and 62 percent believe he has divided the country.[46]

---

45. Martin and Rappeport, "Donald Trump Says John McCain," paras. 1–3.
46. Quinnipiac University National Poll, "Trump Is Dividing the Country," para. 1.

PSYCHOLOGICAL ANALYSIS OF LIARS

Lying takes place when someone purposefully makes claims that are exaggerated, fabricated, misleading, and misaligned with the intent to deceive. The act of lying poses a significant danger to social harmony, complicates relationships, and obscures credibility issues. Furthermore, past research findings demonstrate compelling evidence that certain personality traits have a higher probability of telling certain types of lies and engaging in antisocial behaviors. For example, researchers have linked the Dark Triad traits, Machiavellianism, narcissism, and psychopathy, to various dark actions, such as lying, sexual infidelity, academic cheating, dishonesty, aggression, bullying, and criminality.[47] In addition, individuals needing approval have been linked to dishonesty and deceptive behaviors. Although people lie for several reasons, the urge to lie for personal benefit is motivated by one's decision to deceive others within a particular social and situational context. Thus, a person who engages in vindictive and self-serving lies does so with the intent to undermine a competitor, promote his status, make false claims, cause harm, and gain an advantage in the situation.[48] For example, a dishonest politician's implicit political aspirations will elicit vindictive and self-serving lies to undermine his opponent for personal gain. Such behavior is consistent with Mr. Trump's false claims of voter fraud in the 2020 presidential election. His uncontrollable ego drives him to consistently engage in vindictive and self-serving lies to promote his status.

BIBLICAL VIEWS ABOUT LIES

The decision to deceive others elicits the temptation to lie for personal benefit. The danger of lying is that it creates a culture of illusion and manipulation and destroys relationships and trust. The act of lying undermines the reality, and the truth of who God is and his word and glorifies Satan, who is the father of all lies (see John 8:44). From the beginning, Satan has been a liar, and thus, he deceived Eve in the garden of Eden with his lies and then Adam (see Gen 3:1–7). The act of telling a lie or believing a lie is a behavior that is biblically condemned. Proverbs 17:4 says, "An evildoer gives heed to false lips; a liar listens eagerly to a spiteful tongue." Listening to and believing in false lips is inherently associated with being an evildoer and being a liar enhances the natural propensity to adhere to the vindictive, mischievous

---

47. Azizli et al., "Lies and Crimes," 34; Jonason et al., "What a Tangled Web," 117.
48. Muris et al., "Malevolent Side of Human Nature," 183.

tongue. An evil spirit from Satan influences people to lie because he is the source of all lies.

Consequently, absorbing lies as truth is also an evil spirit from Satan, displacing God's word with falsehoods. In the garden of Eden, Eve knew the word of God, yet she made a conscious decision to displace God's word with Satan's lies and ate the forbidden fruit and gave the fruit to her husband to eat (see Gen 3:1–7). Therefore, those who choose to believe the lies of a prolific liar, a man who cannot distinguish truth from lies, a man who launched the false claims of voter fraud, are also, by nature, liars, and deceivers. It takes an evildoer and a liar to believe false lips. The majority of the people who believed the lies of Donald Trump about election fraud knew the truth, but because they chose not to retain the truth in their hearts, God gave them over to a debased mind to believe things that are not fitting (see Rom 1:28). Those who knew the truth but kept silent, their silence is also their endorsement of those who practice lies and evil (see Rom 1:32). And their silence or discreet approval of the lies and misinformation about voter fraud in 2020 presidential is not sinless behavior. They are just as guilty as those who promote falsehoods about the election results. I believe God has given them over to a debased spirit of lies, and that is why they often prophesy falsehoods, especially with election results.

Everyone who knows Donald Trump knows that lying has been his stock-in-trade. The plethora of evidence presented in this chapter also affirms that lying is Donald Trump's natural language. Now, if God detests lying, he cannot possibly endorse a man and party that practices lying and deception. Therefore, it is utter deception to present Mr. Trump as a man approved by God to be president, when God had rejected him. It is also deceptive to present the Republican Party as God's party when most of their practices and positions on social issues sharply contradict biblical standards. God is holy, and he hates all manner of sins, including lies and false witnesses. The Scripture says:

> These six things the LORD hates, yes, seven are an abomination to Him: A proud look, a lying tongue, hands that shed innocent blood, a heart that devises wicked plans, feet that are swift in running to evil, a false witness who speak lies, and one who sows discord among brethren. (Prov 6:16–19)

Those who practice the above-mentioned sins lack the fear of God in them, and God cannot endorse a person or party that violates God's commandment. Under the regime of Donald Trump, our country suffered an unprecedented level of division, even within the Republican Party. Lies, false witnesses, and devices of wicked plans have become the order of the day. The danger of normalizing lies and deceptions as an acceptable practice in our country is the willingness of some people, especially some preachers, to compromise their integrity for the sake of political affiliation. Jeremiah 6:13 says, "Because from the least of them even to the greatest of them, everyone is given to covetousness; and from the prophet even to the priest, everyone deals falsely." This Scripture mirrors the false dealings of some Christian Evangelical leaders about the 2020 presidential election and their intentional misrepresentation of the Republican Party as God's party. So, God warns that people who deal in falsehood do not know him. Jeremiah 9:3 says, "And like their bow they have bent their tongues for lies. They are not valiant for the truth on the earth, for they proceed from evil to evil, and they do not know Me, says the LORD." Indeed, preachers who have left their calling of preaching the truth of God's word but have chosen to bend their tongues to proclaim lies about partisan politics do not know God. Not much has changed, if anything, since the days of the Bible with the Pharisees, false prophets, and preachers. Today's Pharisees, false prophets, and preachers have taken a more buoyant posture under the auspices of grace. But they forgot what the Scripture says, "Do not be deceived, God is not mocked; for whatever a man sows, that he will also reap. For he who sows to his flesh will of the flesh reap corruption, but he who sows to the Spirit will of the Spirit reap everlasting life" (Gal 6:7).

Continuous efforts to mislead people by presenting a political party as God's party is sowing to the flesh. Someone using the ministry God gave him to promote the agenda of a political party rather than advancing the message of the cross is also sowing to the flesh. Silently supporting the lies and deceptions of a political party is sowing to the flesh. The question then is, If a Democratic president had done the things Donald Trump has done, would you also be silent? Of course not! This is an indication that you practice hypocrisy. If you claim that you are giving grace to Donald Trump because he is a human being, why don't you give the same grace to a Democratic president? God is an impartial God. Additionally, if the wickedness that has taken place within the Republican party had happened with the Democrats, would you also be silent? Of course not! However, God uses the same standards to judge all elected officials regardless of political party affiliation. Romans 2:11 says, "For there is no partiality with God." Furthermore, Deut 10:17 says, "For the LORD your God is God of gods and Lord of lords, the great God, mighty and awesome, who shows no partiality nor takes a bribe." God does not use different standards with the US presidents and politicians because of their political affiliations, and those conceived by his spirit should not use different standards either. Proverbs 20:10 says, "Diverse weights and diverse measures; they are both alike, an abomination to the Lord." When those who call themselves Christians engage in differential justice based on political affiliation and other exterior characteristics, their actions are an abomination before God.

Promotion and endorsement of falsehoods are synonymous with the Pharisees. When their expected result is not achieved, their natural reaction to counteract the outcomes is the publicity of lies. A similar event took place in the Bible when the Pharisees propagated falsehood to suppress the truth about Jesus' resurrection. For example, in Matt 28:11–15, the Pharisees paid a large sum of money to the soldiers who were supposed to watch the grave where Jesus was buried. They gave the soldiers the money to spread a false rumor that Jesus' disciples stole his body at night while the soldiers were asleep to deny his resurrection (see Matt 28:11–14). Furthermore, the Scripture says, "So they [soldiers] took the money and did as they were instructed, and this saying is commonly reported among the Jews until this day" (Matt 28:15). So, spreading false rumors when things did not work out for the Pharisees has been their stock-in-trade. The Pharisees' false narratives about Jesus' resurrection had a strong negative effect on Jews in believing that Jesus was the promised Messiah. If it had been established for the Jews that Jesus was resurrected from the dead, that would have been a strong piece of convincing evidence for them to believe that Jesus was the Messiah. It is shocking that 60 percent of Christian Protestants believed the lies of Donald Trump, and a significant number of Christian Evangelical preachers promoted the lies of Mr. Trump of a stolen election with their silence and public declaration, as it was with the Pharisees in the days of the Lord Jesus. Caution, the analogy here is strictly about the promotion of falsehood, which is a common practice among the Pharisees, not about Jesus' resurrection and the 2020 presidential election results.

If you as a preacher use your pulpit to promote and condone lies, you are contributing to shaping our society to falsehoods. Lies, deceptions, and the pursuit of evil deeds will become the order of the day if repentance does not take place. Evangelical preachers should use their pulpit to promote the truth of God's word in love, not based on political affiliation, which often reflects hate, division, and deception. In the absence of repentance and revival, our country will become a society dominated by hate, lies, division, and corruption, even as the Scripture states:

> Everyone take heed to his neighbor, and do not trust any brother; for every brother will utterly supplant, and every neighbor will walk with slanderers. Everyone will deceive his neighbor, and will not speak the truth; they have taught their tongue to speak lies; they weary themselves to commit iniquity. Your dwelling

place is in the midst of deceit; through deceit, they refuse to know Me, says the Lord. (Jer 9:4–6)

People use deceptions and lies to deny the existence and sovereignty of God, and if you are a preacher and use your position to facilitate such ungodliness, God will hold you accountable for your role. Falsehood is detestable before God, and he encourages us to be truthful. Proverbs 12:22 says, "Lying lips are an abomination to the Lord, but those who deal truthfully are His delight." God does not and cannot contradict his word; thus, he cannot support or endorse a man who made a living lying and could not distinguish truths from lies. In the same manner, God cannot endorse or be a part of a political party that has provided platforms for those who engage in abominable behaviors of speaking lies, bearing false witnesses, devising wicked plans, deceiving unwitting hearts, and sowing seeds of division. The problem is that some have elevated their group's social norms above the truth of God's word. Whenever the word of God made them uncomfortable with their social norms, they immediately denounced biblical values. It is not a safe place to be for anyone who claims to be a Christian.

TRUTH AND LIES

I want to expand more on this Scripture, which says, "Lying lips are an abomination to the Lord, but those who deal truthfully are His delight" (Prov 12:22). A critical question about this verse is, Why will God consider lying lips an abomination and truthfulness a delight before him? Using other scriptures to address this question, you see that truth and love are interconnected, while lies and hate are entwined. Thus, you cannot love without loving truth, and neither can you love the truth without having love in your heart. Love and truth go together, and both are the foundation of justice and righteousness. The Scripture says God is love (see 1 John 4:16), and Jesus is the truth (see John 14:6). Psalm 89:14 says, "Righteousness and justice are the foundation of Your throne; mercy and truth go before Your face." Thus, the above scriptures suggest that love, mercy, and truth are inextricably intertwined with God's kingdom.

On the other hand, people who do not have love in their hearts often hate the truth and are drawn to lies and deceit. Those who hate other people do so because they hate the truth. The Truth is that God created all human beings in his image and loves them all equally. Thus, hate and lies go together and form the foundation of Satan's kingdom. So, Jesus describes the Pharisees in this manner, saying:

> You are of your father the devil and the desires of your father you want to do. He was a murderer from the beginning and does not stand in the truth, because there is no truth in him. When he speaks a lie, he speaks from his own resources, for he is a liar and the father of it. (John 8:44)

Therefore, the root of truth and justice is love, and the root of lies and injustice is hate. Know that haters are murderers, according to 1 John 3:15. People who are not of God cannot receive the truth because the love of God is not in them. Therefore, the practice of lies indicates rejection of the truth (Christ) and acceptance of lies (Satan), who is the father of all lies. Those who are silent about lies have also silently rejected the truth and endorsed the kingdom of darkness. If the Spirit of Christ dwells in you, every aspect of your being will scream loudly against lies and injustice because they are not of Christ. Being silent about lies suggests you are a witness to falsehoods, and so the Scripture warns, "A false witness will not go unpunished, and he who speaks lies, shall perish" (Prov 19:9). The righteousness of God demands punishment for individuals who engage in or support falsehoods.

Just as Jesus rebuked the Pharisees over two thousand years ago, so is he rebuking today's Pharisees, who have aligned themselves with partisan politics to deceptively promote a political party that its members are divisive, hateful, and pathological liars as God's party. They have forsaken the call of God upon their lives and have traded the mandates of the great commission for political proselytization.

Proverbs 17:15 says, "He who justifies the wicked, and he who condemns the just, both of them alike are an abomination to the LORD." To justify or present a lying, hateful, and divisive person or party as God's endorsed or righteous is an abomination to the LORD. To talk about the wickedness that exists in one party and not talk about the wickedness in another party is deceptive and a form of justifying the wicked, which is an abomination to the LORD. Furthermore, the Scripture says, "A disreputable witness scorns justice, and the mouth of the wicked devours iniquity" (Prov 19:28). God is a God of justice, and he has given those who belong to him a sound mind. The sound mind enables believers to disseminate truth and justice equitably without regard to political affiliation, race, gender, social class, etc. Those with the Spirit of Christ have the spirit of truth and justice in them.

SUMMARY

Mr. Trump instigated several false conspiracy theories about the 2020 election, mostly in swing states where Joe Biden won, including Georgia, Arizona, Wisconsin, Pennsylvania, and Nevada. However, these states have recounted the ballots multiple times, and there was no evidence of widespread fraud. Moreover, GOP officials in most of these states reached the same conclusion, asserting that no voting irregularities were found that could have altered the outcome of the election. These GOP officials voted for Republican candidates, yet they were honest in taking a stand to protect our God-given democracy from being destroyed by a dishonest president and declared that the "election was not stolen." The judicial branch examined all litigations brought by Trump and his allies, and the judges, including judges appointed by President Trump, reached the same conclusion that there was no evidence of voter fraud, and some of the cases were dismissed or dropped. Other sources, such as the polls, the number of voters for each party, etc., indicated that the odds were against Donald Trump winning the election against Joe Biden. He knew that he could not win against Joe Biden; that is why he pressured Ukrainians to initiate an investigation against Joe Biden and his son Hunter Biden. With the lack of evidence from every conceivable avenue concerning the 2020 election fraud claims, why are Donald Trump and his allies still propagating false claims about the election? If his supporters believe that the media, judicial branch, and mass populace are against President Trump, in that case, it stands to reason that he did not have the purported voters to reelect him as president of the United States. This means he clearly lost the election. The more significant concern is why so many Christian Evangelicals and their leaders endorse this type of dishonest behavior when the Bible clearly states that God despises liars. It is time to repent and align your behaviors and practices to biblical truth if you are a true believer in Christ Jesus.

Chapter 10

The Hidden Blessing of the Capitol Riot

As devastating and painful as the Capitol Hill riot on January 6, 2021, was, the overall outcome has a somewhat hidden blessing. The assertion is not to undermine the tragedy and loss of human lives. However, the January 6 insurrection was necessary to save our country and democracy. It was the most significant event that subdued the will of a dictator and compelled him to surrender to the results of the 2020 presidential election. As more revelations have emerged through the House Committee investigation, the evidence suggests that Donald Trump was determined to remain in power under any circumstances. His fierce supporters were equally determined to carry out whatever illegal activity necessary to keep him in the White House. Thus, the January 6 insurrection was a much lesser evil to save our country and democracy from potentially much bigger catastrophic events. The devastation and loss of lives on Capitol Hill on January 6, 2021, triggered fearful emotional reactions among his inner-circle allies to compel him to yield to the election results even though he did not concede to have lost the election. It was never the will of God for Donald Trump to remain the president of the United States, regardless of the false prophecies from some Evangelicals. God loves America, and God cares for America's well-being that he would not allow the evil spirits controlling Donald Trump to destroy our country and democracy. I am convinced that Mr. Trump regretted later yielding to the pressure of vacating the White House before January 20, 2021, without exhausting all other destructive options. Mr. Trump's niece, Mary Trump, made an apocalyptic statement on November 7, 2020, about Donald Trump after the election. She said, "This is what Donald's going to do: he's not going to concede . . . All he's got now is breaking stuff, and he's going to do that with a vengeance. I've always known how cruel he can be."[1] She was indeed very accurate in her statement that Donald Trump would not concede but would rather engage in destructive behavior before leaving the White House.

Furthermore, Dan Scavino, the former deputy chief of staff under Trump's administration, in his conversation with Jenna Ellis, a former attorney for Mr. Trump during the 2020 election, told her, "The boss is not going to leave under any circumstances, we are just going to stay in power."[2] The "boss" in this case was Mr. Trump, as his loyalists call him, and it was obvious to Mr. Trump's loyalists that he would *never* accept his loss nor leave the White House without severe traumatic events. It was the January 6 riot with pressure from his close allies that forced Mr. Trump out of the White House. The irony of Trump's madness is that there are people who are aiding and abetting him in his vengeance to destroy our democracy.

MONARCHY

Unbeknown to many, I believe the ultimate goal of President Trump was not necessarily winning the reelection but to institute a monarchy for himself and his family. However, winning the 2020 election was critical for him to establish a monarchy and autocratic government. While the statement may sound shocking to some, I will try to put the pieces together using Nicaragua's narratives about lost democracy for you to see the picture, hopefully clearly. Chapter 9 of this book revealed the interesting, though questionable, background of Donald Trump, a man whose familiar playbook involves lying and cheating to achieve his goals. This is also a man whose relationship with others is based on corruption for personal gain. Once a loyalist falls short of Trump's expectations or fails to comply with his evil motives, the person deserves immediate destruction in Mr. Trump's views. In examining Donald Trump's presidency and especially during his failed bid for reelection, those loyalists who refused to comply with his corrupt moves to overthrow our democracy became his vicious enemies instantly. In a nutshell, if Mr. Trump cannot use one to achieve his ruthless goals, the individual is of no value to him but deserves to be destroyed. For the present loyalists of Mr. Trump, learn from the experience of the past loyalists, from lawyers to cabinet members and vice president, how they were treated as enemies once they refused to comply with his corrupt aspirations. You will become his hitman, including killing your family members and friends; otherwise, Trump will destroy you. Preachers who are already labeling Trump as Cyrus,

1. Ankel, "Mary Trump Says Her Uncle," para. 1.
2. Culliton, "Jenna Ellis Was Told," para. 1.

the Persian king, and have elevated him to a position as your "deliverer," it will be a natural transition for you to use your pulpit to preach about him and ascribe godship to him. Otherwise, you would not retain the right to preach. You will be subjected to Trump's dictatorial leadership all the days of your life, losing your constitutional rights and freedom. Your children and grandchildren will serve Trump's family all the days of their lives, being denied the opportunity to be presidents, governors, etc., and without reaching their full potential in life. While the previous generations passed down democracy to you, you will be handing over to the future generations an autocracy because of your unwise decision to support a man's selfish desire to seize power and rule over you at the expense of our country's democracy and stability. The MAGA movement is a repulsive and unintelligent crusade because it contradicts what America represents. It does not make America great, but it promotes a self-serving dictator. It is disingenuous to perceive the MAGA movement as the Republican crusade against the Democrats because MAGA is a selfish undertaking by a dictator, who wants to destroy our democracy and establish a monarchy for himself and his family. Anyone who cares for the well-being of our country and our democracy should oppose such a movement. Please, know that we are a democratic society, and we do not serve a man because absolute power corrupts. Protect our democracy; it is our identity and the hope of other nations.

If you think the above statements are incomprehensible, let me ask you these questions, and I will suggest that you evaluate your honest responses to the questions. Have you ever imagined that it is possible in American democracy that there will be a president in our contemporary society who is so corrupt as to boldly call state election officials to overturn the election results in their states to his favor; who will persuade his vice president to lie and certify him as the winner of the election, instead of his opponent, who actually won the election; who will coax the US Justice Department to lie and say that the election is rigged and leave the rest of the lies for him and congressional Republicans; a president that the GOP lawmakers are so afraid of that they will never hold him accountable and will always be willing to comply with his corruption to the detriment of our country's solidarity; a president who would sway the White House staff into his corrupt biddings about the election results; and a president who would incite domestic terrorism on the US Capitol in his desperate effort to remain in office? If you were told ten years ago that this would be possible in America today, you would most likely not believe it. Again, assuming ten years ago, did you ever think Americans would be electing a man to the office of the presidency who had openly confessed his sexual assaults to women by grabbing them and kissing them in public without their permission? Did you ever imagine that we will elect someone to be a president who runs businesses that practice tax cheating? Did you ever think that Evangelical Christians would be so loyal and committed to a man whose life is 100 percent contradicting Christ's teachings that they are more loyal and committed to him than they are to Jesus, who died for them? If the degree of Evangelical Christians' loyalty to Mr. Trump had been given to the Lord Jesus, billions more people would have been saved, and we would have a much better and God-fearing country and world than what we have today.

Also, do you think that Mr. Trump's desperation to remain in office was just to serve another four years as the US president? You better think again, and this time more logically. All the warning signs are clearly written on the walls, but some people choose to ignore them until it is too late. It is time to depart from the fantasy world and cognitive limitation that suggests that "unless I see it happen physically, or else I won't believe it."

It may sound strange for some to perceive or label Mr. Trump as a dictator; however, he displays all the characteristics of a dictator, as illustrated in this chapter. Some people do acknowledge Mr. Trump as a dictator but fall short of taking the threat of dictatorship to our democracy seriously. Such a callous approach is dangerous because the consequences of having a dictator as the president of the United States include the loss of your rights and freedom as an American citizen, loss of freedom of speech, to protest, to sue your boss for violating your rights, endangering your safety or terminating your employment without legitimate cause. Every benefit you have enjoyed as an American citizen would vanish in thin air overnight because dictatorship does not acknowledge individual rights. For some, the thought of losing their rights is inconceivable because they have never experienced such before. However, to ignore evidence surrounding the possibility of something hypothetically taking place is a serious cognitive limitation. During an interview with CBS, Liz Cheney also raised the alarm that the US is "sleepwalking into dictatorship" if Donald Trump is reelected.[3] While all the warning signs about Mr. Trump are visible and all around us, some people tend to ignore them until it is too late with no point of return. Even though Mr. Trump denied being a dictator if elected again except on day one during an interview with Sean Hannity at a Fox News town hall, he has vowed to engage in vengeful "retribution" for his supporters. Also, he swore to go after the press, IRS, FBI, Department of Justice, and other federal agencies.[4] Is this a normal aspiration for a person seeking for presidency to destroy established societal institutions for doing the jobs they were created to do,

---

3. Remnick, "Sleepwalking into Dictatorship," para. 3.
4. Remnick, "Sleepwalking into Dictatorship," para. 5.

except for a person who is a dictator? This is a typical ambition for dictators, as also displayed by Daniel Ortega of Nicaragua.

Furthermore, have you ever wondered why Donald Trump is attracted to world dictators that other US presidents would not have a relationship with? For example, no recent past or even present president will cultivate a relationship with the North Korean dictator, Kim Jong Un, let alone meet with him multiple times and call him a good man. Likewise, the past or present US presidents will not develop a kosher relationship with Russian dictator Vladimir Putin, let alone call him a friend and ask his administration to investigate a political opponent. As the saying goes, "Birds of a feather flock together." Mr. Trump is drawn to these dictators because their totalitarian system of government represents his political aspirations.

NICARAGUA'S LOSS OF DEMOCRACY

Perhaps, we can learn from the experience of Nicaragua and how they lost their democracy to a dictator, Daniel Ortega, to avert the same happening in the US. In 1984, Daniel Ortega won the presidential election in Nicaragua. However, when he sought a second term in 1990, he lost to his liberal opponent, Violeta Chamorro. Furthermore, he suffered two more defeats in subsequent presidential elections in 1995 and 2001. Nevertheless, Daniel Ortega's slick moves, such as asserting statements like, "Jesus Christ is my hero now," and supporting efforts to ban abortion, all appealed to the populous religious group to give him victory in the 2006 election.[5]

After winning the presidential election in 2006, Daniel Ortega quickly consolidated power; he persuaded the Supreme Court to modify the Constitution, allowing him to run for election multiple times.[6] Does the modification of the Constitution for the benefit of a person sound familiar? Then, in 2019, Mr. Ortega nominated his wife, Rosario Murillo, as his running mate. Also, to silence his opponents, he locked them up in prison. Before the November 7, 2021, election, his administration invaded major media organizations and imprisoned thirty-nine leaders considered his enemies and seven presidential candidates.[7] As the protest against Ortega's dictatorship ravaged the nation, three hundred people were killed as a result.[8] For those who are pushing to reelect Mr. Trump, is this what you desire for our country? I would guess that your answer would be "No," especially, if you

5. BBC News, "Nicaraguan President Daniel Ortega," para. 14.
6. BBC News, "Nicaraguan President Daniel Ortega," para. 16.
7. Schifrin and Quran, "How Daniel Ortega Demolished Democracy," para. 9.
8. BBC News, "Nicaraguan President Daniel Ortega," para. 15.

care for the well-being of our country and its democracy. Mr. Trump has already vowed to go after the media, government institutions, and individuals considered his enemies and modify the Constitution, just exactly what Mr. Ortega did in Nicaragua. But this is not how the US political system works; you only see that type of practice in uncivilized minds and societies.

Mr. Ortega's second and subsequent terms were marred with increasing anti-democratic activities and policies, such as decreased civil liberties, pension system reform, journalists' arrests, unethical constitutional changes, political rivals' imprisonment, and violent oppression against protesters.[9] Moreover, in his pursuit to consolidate power, Mr. Ortega disannulled Nicaragua's democratic institutions and controlled major branches of the government, including the military, police, and state institutions.[10] In addition, he alienated and imprisoned his former allies, who opposed his corrupt government. Indeed, as the saying goes, "absolute power corrupts," so his dictatorial government became corrupt.

IMPORTANT LESSONS TO LEARN FROM NICARAGUA

After Mr. Ortega lost the election in 1990, he still controlled and maintained a dominant influence over his party and supporters. Many of his supporters believed he was the savior of their country, just like what we see today with fierce supporters of Donald Trump. Even after losing the election, GOP lawmakers and governors are still intimidated by Mr. Trump, which is an unhealthy relationship. They sanctioned anyone who disagreed with his lies about a stolen election, even within their party, just like what they did to Liz Cheney.

"Everything Will Be Better" was Ortega's campaign slogan, and of course, everything got worse during his regime, including the economy, civil liberties, etc. Does the slogan remind you of a similar one? Well, consider a familiar one since 2016, "Make America Great Again." However, America's image and democracy were shattered and made worse globally during Donald Trump's presidency. Our country had been so divided with inconceivable hatred toward outgroup members with the appearance of Mr. Trump on the political scene. Prior to Mr. Ortega's 2006 presidential election win, Mr. Ortega had crafted a streamlined approach to gain the religious organizations' support. His campaign speeches and images were directed at giving thanks to God and taking a formidable opposition to abortion. The church

---

9. Schifrin and Quran, "How Daniel Ortega Demolished Democracy," paras. 5–15.
10. Human Rights Watch, "Nicaragua Events of 2018," paras. 1–2; Rogers, "Unraveling of Nicaragua," para. 10.

in Nicaragua ignored his background and pledged their support to him. The same is also happening with Christian Evangelicals in the US today. However, it is essential to remember that a leopard cannot change its spots. A dictator is powerless without willing participants, and some Christian Evangelicals and their leaders and some Republican Party members have become willing participants in this scenario for Mr. Trump. As the saying goes, "A fish rots from the head down"; it has been a matter of fact with the Republican Party since 2016. Today's Republican Party is not the same party as under the leadership of President Ronald Reagan, President George H. W. Bush, Senator Bob Dole, President George Bush, Senator John McCain, and Senator Mitt Romney. Today's Republican Party is like a mobster, perverting the truth, engaging in divisiveness, and promoting violence and antidemocracy because of the direct influence of their corrupt leader, Donald Trump. Those with upright hearts have an obligation to denounce what is happening in the party to reclaim the Republican Party.

The 2018 protest, which demanded that Mr. Ortega step down and return to democracy, resulted in the killing of 120 people within seven weeks, mostly students.[11] In addition, Mr. Ortega's party Sandinista paid youth paramilitary to drive around in pickup trucks and attack protesters. The implementation of his zero-tolerance policy against civil unrest is antidemocracy. According to the Latin American editor for *Fusion*, a student told him, "We weren't ready for the massacres. We never thought the government was going to kill us. We never thought being a university student would be a crime in Nicaragua."[12] The US is not immune from this type of tyranny if the madness within the Republican Party to elect a dictator does not stop.

Vignette

Parents who are supporting Mr. Trump need to think twice about their actions and how they are endangering the lives of their children. Most of these parents can attest that their children's worldviews are different from theirs, which means their children would most likely protest against Mr. Trump's authoritarian system of government. Since Mr. Trump has zero tolerance for dissenting views, his hate groups (Proud Boys, QAnon, Oath Keepers, etc.) will openly execute protesters, and Mr. Trump will exonerate them. If you think your support for Mr. Trump will preserve the White race, you will end up destroying

11. Rogers, "Unraveling of Nicaragua," para. 1.
12. Rogers, "Unraveling of Nicaragua," para. 6.

the White race and the entire country. Hate of outgroup members is the most dangerous weapon to destroy America and it is the root of our political polarization.

Please know, electing a dictator to the White House is dangerous for our democracy, regardless of party affiliation, and the only group that attracted Mr. Trump are people who hate outgroup members. Proverbs 29:2 says, "When the righteous are in authority, the people rejoice: But when a wicked man rules, the people groan."

Our country has never experienced so much chaos, division, corruption, and perversion of truth in recent decades until Mr. Trump got into the political arena and became president. Religious organizations like the Roman Catholic Church supported and voted for Mr. Ortega because he said what they wanted to hear; however, they are not only groaning today but the leading critics of his autocratic government. Because someone says he is anti-abortionist or attended church once should not be the only criterion to earn unwavering support from religious organizations. Many have used the abortion rhetoric to gain support from conservative voters, and by the time their true nature is revealed, it is too late. Mr. Trump is not really an antiabortionist, as he confessed out of his mouth when asked if he would ban partial-birth abortion, and he responded: "No. I am pro-choice in every respect and as far as it goes, but I just hate it."[13] He also condemns Governor Ron DeSantis's six-week abortion ban by making the following statement, "He [Ron DeSantis] signed six weeks, and many people within the pro-life movement feel that was too harsh."[14] He also said that the abortion ban was "too harsh." But he had used the abortion rhetoric in his campaign to gain the support of the Evangelicals since such a move is politically expedient and rewarding to him. Indeed, the children of the world are wiser than the children of the light (see Luke 16:8). Because someone says what you want to hear and recognizes Jerusalem as the capital of Israel should not be a reason to undermine other warning signs and pledge unwavering support to the person. According to the Scripture, the antichrist will make a seven-year peace treaty with Israel, and he will deceive many (see Dan 9:27). Therefore, it is vital to examine the background and motives of politicians seeking your support. As the Scripture says, "Beloved, do not believe every spirit, but test the spirits, whether they are of God; because many false prophets have gone out into the world" (1 John 4:1). In the same token, many deceivers who are controlled by evil spirits have gone into the world to deceive many.

13. Russert, "I am very Pro-life," 0.43–1:23.
14. Goldiner, "Trump Dings Gov. Ron DeSantis," para. 3.

One should not ignore that a crucial behavioral pattern with dictators is their selfish and unquenchable quest for power. Honest leaders will accept defeat and respect the will of the people. However, a power-grabbing, self-serving dictator will not accept defeat or allow others to lead but will invoke all manner of dishonest and unscrupulous tactics to re-appoint himself to a leadership position. As a result, his second time around is far worse than the first. Another significant factor to note about dictators is that they do not transfer power to another person, except to a family member at the point of their death. If Mr. Trump had succeeded in his attempt to overturn the 2020 election results, there would be no other American to become president again, except the Donald Trump family.

After Mr. Ortega lost the 1990 election, he relentlessly pursued the office of the presidency again in multiple future elections. He also resorted to manipulative political endeavors, having absolute control over his party and influencing religious organizations, just like Mr. Trump. These groups helped to elect him in the 2006 election, and perhaps, by now, are regretting their role in electing him after his true nature is revealed. Nobody is safe with a dictator, including close allies, family members, and friends, because a minor misstep or skepticism spells one's doom. Mr. Ortega imprisoned former allies, and Kim Jong Un of North Korea executed loyalists, including a family member, and Vladimir Putin of Russia under his regime has had several allies, including top military individuals and millionaires and billionaires who criticized him, vanish or die mysteriously. Also, remember Mr. Trump's attraction to Vladimir Putin, and even supporting him over the federal government agencies. My question to those pushing for Mr. Trump's reelection: Is this what you want for our country? Like Mr. Ortega, Donald Trump has maintained a dominant influence on the Republicans, and Evangelical Christians have laid down their guard for him and even pushed for a third presidential run. Please, be wise and assess the cost of your action and the future of America. Mr. Trump is a dictator, and his actions align well with the characteristics of a person who might be a precursor of the antichrist. He is not the antichrist but a precursor and he displays similar characteristics of the antichrist.

Mr. Trump is not the only president who lost reelection. President Jimmy Carter lost to President Ronald Reagan in the 1980 election, and he devoted his time to humanitarian ventures. President George H. W. Bush lost to President Bill Clinton in the 1992 presidential election, and he treated the man who defeated him as a son and developed a relationship with him. The actions of these two presidents portray an accurate image of America and should be represented on the global stage. The divisive political tactics of Donald Trump, a man who has spent years and perhaps millions of dollars in legal costs, to avoid showing his taxes, are inconsistent with America's image globally.

If Mr. Trump had succeeded in his coup attempt, the second term would have allowed him to consolidate power and establish a monarchy and totalitarianism. Trump's four-year presidency was a trial period in that he tested the water and flexed his muscles with the GOP lawmakers, and he realized that they were afraid of him. They are scared of Mr. Trump campaigning against them during their reelection bid, as he has done against others, and they lost the election.

CAPITOL RIOT

The January 6, 2021, insurrection was the height of the antithesis of democracy, a politically motivated criminal act to undermine the people's will in a presidential election. It was one of the darkest days in American history, and a sober reality of the incident is that the violence was fomented by one of the most incompetent presidents in the history of the United States, Donald Trump. A president who had abandoned his oath of office in pursuit of selfish gains. His presidency unleashed a heightened level of division, hatred, corruption in our country, and disregard for the rule of law. In essence, when the head is corrupt, the rest of the body is subject to corruption also. Thus, the January 6 incident was an indication that some of Mr. Trump's loyalists had been contaminated by his corruption and had developed a disregard for the rule of law in our country, which led them to engage in domestic terrorism to overthrow the US government and destroy our democracy. The culmination of this incident was Mr. Trump fanning the flame of election fraud months before the election took place. The big lie about the 2020 election fraud had been embraced and promoted by some GOP lawmakers, some Christian Evangelicals, and members of extremist and White supremacist groups. Interestingly, GOP lawmakers and Christian Evangelicals who embraced Mr. Trump's big lies are in coalition with satanic hate groups for a political party that has often been mischaracterized and promoted to represent God's values. What a blasphemy! Some of the mob supporters of Mr. Trump that invaded the Capitol building also carried signs that read "Jesus is my savior and Trump is my president," "In God we trust," and "Jesus saves."[15] Their actions are heresy! Shockingly, people are breaking the law of the land and using the name of Jesus and God to justify their evil activities. Christian Evangelical leaders should set the record straight and disassociate themselves from a candidate who appeals to racist and violent

15. Ciliberto and Russell-Kraft, "They Invaded the Capitol," para. 9.

mobsters. They also have an obligation to disassociate themselves from racist groups and force them out of the Republican Party. They are unbelievers, and Christ's followers should have no relationship with those who practice evil. Apostle Paul declared to believers in Christ saying:

> Do not be unequally yoked together with unbelievers. For what fellowship has righteousness with lawlessness? And what communion has light with darkness? And what accord has Christ with Belial? Or what part has a believer with an unbeliever? And what agreement has the temple of God with idols? For you are the temple of the living God. As God has said: "I will dwell in them and walk among them. I will be their God, and they shall be My people." Therefore "come out from among them and be separate," says the Lord. "Do not touch what is unclean, and I will receive you. I will be a Father to you, and you shall be My sons and daughters," says the LORD Almighty. (2 Cor 6:14–17).

Haters practice lawlessness; they are unclean and are children of Belial. Those who promote one race instead of the human race as a whole are idol worshipers and children of Satan and not of God. They are doing the work of their father, Satan, who is a liar, and destroying God's creation.

The insurrection on January 6, 2021, led to the House Committee investigation, and their findings revealed collaborative efforts by Mr. Trump and his allies to steal the 2020 presidential election while at the same time promoting the big lie of election fraud. Now, with the Republican-led House of Representatives, they have begun to show their true nature of dishonesty and disruption of facts. The violent attacks on the Capitol on January 6, 2021, that the whole world saw and led to nine deaths, are being twisted and manipulated as a peaceful event, as presented by Fox News. These are belligerent, immoral, disgraceful behaviors that lack common sense. The whole world is watching and seeing the stupidity of such unscrupulous behaviors. History books will have nothing positive to say about this godless, amoral cohort of deceivers, and genuine Republicans need to cut ties with those who want to destroy our country and destroy the image of the Republican Party. There is not even an expression of compassion to those who lost family members as a result of this avoidable violent attack on January 6, 2021.

Vignette

> It is disingenuous to infer the January 6 riot was a battle between the Democrats and Republicans. The heart of the insurrection is a battle between dictatorship and democracy, corruption versus

honesty, truths versus lies, disrespect for the rule of the law versus respect for the rule of the law, evil versus good, and wrong versus right. If the GOP lawmakers believe that they embrace dictatorship, corruption, lies, evil, and disrespect for the rule of the law of our country as a fundamental precept of their party, then the natural inclination is the misinterpretation of the January 6 riot as a political battle between the Democrats and the Republicans.

An essential question for GOP lawmakers is, If a Democratic president had done what Donald Trump did on January 6 that led to the violent attack on Capitol Hill, would you have presented one-sided videos and claimed that the incident was a peaceful event? Most likely, you would not. Thus, it is important to understand that we are a country of equitable justice, and all criminal acts are treated the same regardless of who is the vigilante and the victim. The audacity of House Republicans investigating the House Committee for investigating the Capitol riot is a dangerous precedence. The House Republicans forgot to realize that the witnesses, informants, and whistleblowers in both House Committee and FBI investigations are Republicans, White House employees during Mr. Trump's presidency, Cabinet members, and Mr. Trump's close allies and even family members. They were not Democrats or independent voters but those who voted Republican. Most of them were honest individuals who knew that the things Mr. Trump was doing were unconstitutional and illegal.

Vignette

If the actions of Mr. Trump and his allies concerning their efforts to distort the 2020 election results, including the January 6 rioters, are not criminal behaviors, it then means we, as a society, do not have a clear definition of what is a crime, and all the people in prison need to be released until we reach a consensus of behaviors that constitute a crime in the US and can be applied equitably to all regardless of political affiliation, race, and external factors.

In contrast to the GOP lawmakers' unprecedented support of Mr. Trump's corruption, on August 14, 2023, eleven prominent members of the Republican Party, including judges and high-ranking senior federal officials, submitted an amicus brief supporting a speedy trial and the proposed trial date by Special Counsel Jack Smith in Mr. Trump's case.[16] The charges against Mr.

---

16. Preza, "11 Prominent Republicans File Amicus Brief," para. 1.

Trump include his corrupt effort to overturn the 2020 presidential election results. Furthermore, a group of six Republicans filed a lawsuit against Mr. Trump and Colorado Secretary of State Jena Griswold, a Democrat, to prevent Mr. Trump from running for the 2024 presidential election.[17] While Mr. Trump was pushing to delay the trial date, these elite members of the Republican Party suggested that the trial date should not be delayed for the sake of Mr. Trump's third election bid in 2024. On December 19, 2023, the Colorado Supreme Court ruled that Mr. Trump is ineligible to run for the presidency again due to his role in the Capitol riot on January 6, 2021.[18] According to the US Constitution clause, Mr. Trump was disqualified for violating Section 3 of the Fourteenth Amendment, which forbids a president, vice president, member of Congress, military, civil, or judicial officer who took an oath to support the Constitution but engaged in insurrection against the US government and the Constitution. However, Mr. Trump had vowed to appeal the ruling.

Considering that the House Republicans initiated an investigation of the House Committee for investigating the Capitol Hill riot raises some concerns: Would their next move involve investigating federal judges and Supreme Court justices for not ruling in favor of Mr. Trump? Would they also investigate those who testified against Mr. Trump? These House Republicans, in their unpatriotic efforts to please a corrupt president, are initiating dangerous precedence into our political and legal systems. The constituencies that elected these Mr. Trump puppets to office have a civic responsibility to vote them out of office to protect our country from being devoured by corrupt politicians. It is evident that you cannot be a Trump loyalist and be loyal to our country and democracy simultaneously. Both concepts severely contradict each other; therefore, you can only be one or the other, not both.

Interestingly, the majority of GOP lawmakers and Republicans accuse the office of the US attorney general of a political witch hunt for charging Mr. Trump for inciting mobsters to attack the Capitol on January 6, 2021, and taking classified documents to his Mar-a-Lago residence and refusing to return the documents. Their defense of Mr. Trump is not that he did not do what he was indicted for, but their position is based on their convoluted perception that Mr. Trump is above the law and cannot be held accountable. However, that is not a logical approach to defending someone indicted for a criminal case in the US because nobody is above the law in the US. The indictments should be left in the hands of the jury to decide Mr. Trump's fate based on the evidence presented during the trial. The GOP lawmakers

17. Woodruff, "'Unprecedented' Threat," para. 1–4.
18. Astor, "Trump Is Disqualified," 2.

can direct their defense of Mr. Trump more constructively by being honest with him and letting him know that nobody is above the law in the US and that there are consequences for his actions. Apparently, no one has been courageous and honest with Mr. Trump to advise him to be mindful of his actions and to consider their potential consequences. While some GOP lawmakers and Republicans may see Mr. Trump as their savior, the rest of the country sees him as a corrupt ex-president. If a Democratic president had done one-tenth of Mr. Trump's criminal behaviors, the same group of people who are defending Mr. Trump would have been screaming from the mountaintop that our country had gone to hell because of the corruption of a Democratic president. Equitable justice is an unacceptable concept for right-wing extremists like some of the GOP lawmakers.

The defenders of Mr. Trump's lies and criminal behaviors are the true enemies of our democracy and social justice. The use of a political witch hunt as a defense for Mr. Trump's indictment is a disgrace to human intelligence. The challenging question is, Which of the following actions of Mr. Trump is a political witch hunt? (1) The phone call Mr. Trump made to Georgia Secretary of State Brad Raffensperger when he asked him to find 11,780 votes for him so that he would be declared the winner in Georgia instead of Joe Biden. Is there any dispute that it was not Mr. Trump's voice that was on the recorded tape or that Mr. Trump did not make such a phone call? Did anyone set up Mr. Trump to make the phone call? Is it how past presidents behaved when they lost an election to seek corrupt options to declare themselves the winner of the election? So, how is this a political witch hunt? Thus, the use of political witch hunts as a defense mechanism is unintelligent. Making up lies in the face of indisputable facts is far more stupid than the actual acts. Both the liar and supporters of the lies are a disgrace to human decency and integrity. (2) Mr. Trump's pressure on the vice president, Mike Pence, to illegally reject certifying Joe Biden as the president in the 2020 election. Is there any dispute that Mr. Trump did not pressure Mike Pence from certifying Mr. Biden as the winner of the 2020 election? If Mr. Trump did not do the things he was being charged for, then he can legitimately claim a political witch hunt. Otherwise, other people who engage in corrupt and criminal behaviors like bribery, embezzlement, fraud, cybercrime, etc., can also claim a political witch hunt when prosecuted for violating US laws. (3) The fake electors from the seven states that Mr. Trump lost: Arizona, Georgia, Michigan, Nevada, New Mexico, Pennsylvania, and Wisconsin, in which Mr. Trump allies with his knowledge conjured fake certificates to subvert the election results. The question is, How do all these actions shift from criminal behaviors to political witch hunts?

The act of blaming President Biden and Democrats for Mr. Trump's criminal behaviors is illogical and ludicrous. Did the Democrats and President Biden trick Mr. Trump into engaging in criminal behaviors? Obviously, Mr. Trump and his allies are on a mission to pervert truth and justice in our country for their selfish gain. Those who are supporting and voting corrupt politicians into office whose effort is to serve a man rather than the welfare of our country will soon become their victims. There are no limitations to victimization by corrupt politicians, especially if you are not of higher economic status.

Vignette

> The behavior of Mr. Trump and those who support his criminal acts reflect the characteristics of a cult that is involved in organized crime with secret vows to protect each other and never to relent from their criminal endeavors and with the intent to destroy the US democracy and establish autocracy for themselves. Even though Mr. Trump's actions are shameful from a decent human behavior perspective, those who support his criminal behaviors are shameless in their bold support of his corruption.

Thus, cult mentality with conscientious efforts to engage in organized crime dominated the Republican Party led by Mr. Trump. No matter the type and depth of crime committed by Mr. Trump, he will still receive support from his supporters. They cherish his shameless and bold criminal behaviors to destroy the US Constitution and laws. Mr. Trump's corrupt behaviors reflect the secret desires of some of them; therefore, Mr. Trump could never be wrong based on their loyalty to him. These corrupt and hate groups desire to take the country back to the time of slavery. The progress the country has made in terms of race relationships and equality in social justice since the 1960s civil rights movement is distasteful to them. Therefore, by whatever means necessary to unthaw our democracy and social justice, they are willing to take such a route. It takes a criminal to support another criminal, and it takes a hater to form a coalition with hate groups. Again, birds of a feather flock together. The shocking aspect of this cult movement is the membership of some Christian Evangelicals, who are supposed to be wiser based on biblical teachings and the leadership of the Holy Spirit, to disassociate themselves from such cult movements. Just because Mr. Trump mentioned God in his speech or said that he supports Christians does not mean he acknowledges God in his life. My question to Christian Evangelicals is: Does any of Mr. Trump's behavior reflect compliance with biblical teachings and love for God? Christians should not be deceived because of Mr. Trump's speech that he supports Christians. Such speeches are directed to gain the support of Christian Evangelicals to vote for him just like what Daniel Ortega, the dictator, did to gain support from the Christian community to vote for him to become Nicaragua's president. So, Christian Evangelicals need to be wise and not be fooled by partisan politics. There are other GOP presidential candidates whose behaviors are closer to biblical standards you can vote for if you believe you must always vote Republican.

APOCALYPTIC WARNINGS

For those who have pledged their unwavering support to Mr. Trump, my question to you is, What is in there for you and your family? Mr. Trump is fighting for the benefit of himself and his family. If Mr. Trump ever becomes president again (God forbid), a guaranteed outcome is the destruction of our democracy and the establishment of an authoritarian monarchy for his family. However, it will result in unprecedented violence, corruption, instability, and the death of many, and you will be responsible for such tragedy. The warning signs about Mr. Trump are as clear as daylight. The outcome of Mr. Trump's monarchy is that your children and future generations will serve Mr. Trump's children forever. Your unwise actions will deny your children and future generations any chances of becoming the president of the United States or pursuing any political aspirations they may have. Shockingly, people living in autocratic societies are willing to risk their lives for democracy, and those who have democracy are foolishly trading their democracy for autocracy. Remember, nobody is safe with a dictator, including his close allies. All it takes is to disagree with a dictator once, and you will be eliminated. Again, look at Mr. Trump's history with his loyalties like Mike Pence and William Bar, with one-time refusal to carry out his corrupt bidding, in Mr. Trump's mind, the individual deserves to be eliminated. Everything Mr. Trump does is for his and his family's benefit. The political candidates that Mr. Trump endorsed, which some Republicans are voting into office as if they cannot determine on their own who is the right candidate to represent them, is to solidify Trump's loyalties. Mr. Trump expects payback from these individuals to carry out his corrupt bidding. Mr. Trump does not render a favor without a payback; he strongly believes in the quid quo pro concept. These individuals endorsed by Mr. Trump are obligated to yield to Mr. Trump's desire to destroy our Constitution or reconstruct it to Mr. Trump's favor. So, my question to Mr. Trump's loyalists is, Have you seen Mr. Trump forgive anyone he considered to have offended him? I have one more question: Do you want to trade our freedom and democracy to be like the Russians under Vladimir Putin? The continued unintelligent MAGA movement will ultimately put the US in a worse situation than Russia.

If Mr. Trump ever becomes president again (God forbid), the US Constitution would be at risk of being destroyed, as he alluded to in his comment in December 2022. His statement concerning "the termination of all rules, regulations, and articles, even those found in the Constitution"[19] was a warning sign of what he would do as a president, just like the election fraud statements he proliferated months before the election even took place. He would most likely influence Republican lawmakers to draft a new Constitution, and the focal points and contents would be structured around him and to benefit him. Judges and even Supreme Court justices would be subject to threats of violence and death if they did not rule in favor of Mr. Trump, just like prosecutors who indicted Mr. Trump have been subjected to threats of violence, as well as judges who did not rule in favor of Mr. Trump.

Furthermore, some Republican lawmakers have taken unprecedented steps to seek to remove prosecutors who indicted Mr. Trump from their office for doing the same job they have always done, which is a job they took an oath to do. A second chance of being president for Mr. Trump (God forbid) would empower all the racist groups, such as the Proud Boys, Oath Keepers, etc., to stand by armed and ready to carry out Mr. Trump's corrupt and violent bidding. Mr. Trump would endeavor to replace the leaders of social institutions in our country with his loyalists, and they all will be corrupted and serve Donald Trump and not the citizens of the United States. The concept of justice would be destroyed except for what Mr. Trump declares to be justice. Mr. Trump will rig elections to keep himself in office, just like what Mr. Putin is doing in Russia today. He would make one of his children the vice president and become the president when he is dead. He would establish a monarchy in the United States. Congressional elections, gubernatorial elections, and state house elections will be rigged in favor of Donald Trump's loyalists. Political opponents of Mr. Trump would be subject to imprisonment and death. Freedom of speech would be destroyed; journalists and media outlets would no longer publish facts but lies to elevate Mr. Trump, even far worse than what you see with Fox News. Corruption, lies, deception, and violence would dominate our society, as there would be no safe haven for anyone. Mr. Trump would be involved in multiple wars with other countries, and your teenage and adult children's lives would be interrupted and destroyed because they would be forced to go to war, just like what Mr. Putin did in Russia, forcing several men to

---

19. Holmes, "Termination of the Constitution," paras. 1–2.

abandon their families and flee out of Russia. Congress would not restrain Mr. Trump because the majority of the members of Congress would be his loyalists. These apocalyptic warnings to the United States of America should not be taken lightly because they are inevitable outcomes if Mr. Trump ever becomes a president again. Again, God forbid! For those who doubt the possibility of these apocalyptic warnings, to some extent, it would make more sense for you to experience the consequences of your actions, to get a taste of the madness of your support to a corrupt dictator; however, the consequences are too severe for our blessed nation, that it is not worth taking such risk. I pray that someday Mr. Trump himself will confirm these apocalyptic warnings to be true, and they indeed reflect his hidden agendas. For the doubters of these apocalyptic warnings, my questions to you are: (1) Did you ever imagine before January 6, 2021, that seemingly professional and intelligent people would risk their lives, careers, marriages, and integrity to partake in a violent coup to overthrow our democratic government because they believe the lies of Mr. Trump? If some people are willing to risk their lives for a dishonest dictator, what would stop them from becoming the hitmen of the dictator? (2) Did you ever imagine the possibility that a president who clearly lost an election would be able to summon so many people, including elected officials and Evangelical preachers, to promote his lies and engage in a plot to destroy our democracy that is the backbone and identity of the United States of America because of one man, who has a long history of lies and corruption? If there are people who are willing to engage in such behavior, that reveals the moral state of some people in our country and their willingness to carry out Mr. Trump's unethical bidding, and that is disturbing. (3) Did you ever imagine that elected officials of a party would be so scared of a president that they willingly compromised their integrity to conform to the president's immoral behaviors? If elected officials are so terrified of a president in the land of the free and brave and willing to surrender their integrity when there are no perceived physical threats, certainly, they will easily lay down cowardly to him with the presence of physical threats against them for their refusal. In essence, what happened with Mr. Trump's presidency reveals debilitating moral states of some members of our society that were previously perceived as inconceivable. The day the eyes of the fierce supporters of Donald Trump will be opened to reality, they will have a great appreciation of the democracy that God gave us.

If Mr. Trump had consolidated power (God forbid), preachers would be compelled to preach that Mr. Trump is god and the savior of the United States, and those who will not comply will lose their right to preach and be prosecuted. Those who falsely prophesied about Mr. Trump winning the 2020 election will become his false prophets to engage in more dubious prophecies, deceiving the nation and promoting Mr. Trump as a deity. God has set Mr. Trump to test their hearts and to know those who are Christ-followers and those who would rather follow a man than Christ.

Vignette

> The absence of spiritual discernment in the church today suggests disloyalty of the bride to the Groom, which is disconcerting! Preachers who have portrayed Mr. Trump as their God-sent savior, their behavior is consistent with the Scripture that says "Who exchanged the truth of God for lies, and worshipped and served the creature rather than the Creator, who is blessed forever. Amen" (Rom 1:25).

Donald Trump is a pathological liar, as established by studies, judicial system, and editorial and observable facts. Those who claimed to be Christians and continue to support Mr. Trump have exchanged the truth of God for Mr. Trump's lies. It is practically impossible to be a Christian led by the Holy Spirit and support Mr. Trump. Jesus says in John 4:23-24, "But the hour is coming, and now is, when the true worshippers will worship the Father in spirit and truth; for the Father is seeking such to worship Him." Anyone possessed by the lying spirit is possessed by the devil, and the evidence of a person being possessed by an evil spirit includes a life of manipulations, lies, deception, division, hatred, hate speeches, promotion of violence, unforgiveness, retaliation, inability to repent or love others, selfish and self-centeredness, and lack of fear of God, and all these are dominant characteristics of Mr. Trump.

SUMMARY

Although Mr. Trump's attempted coup on our democracy was a failure, he did demonstrate that our democracy is not invincible or immune from destruction as many, including myself, have thought. In essence, it does not require an external adversary, such as Russia or China, to demolish our democracy; the enemy is actually within. The presidency of Donald Trump reveals the worst of humanity. People with integrity did not survive in his administration, and people on the borderline of honesty had to be forced to become dishonest to work in his administration. Trump's presidency presents a shocking revelation of the degree to which people are willing to compromise and betray our democracy to fulfill the selfish unpatriotic desire of a man. It also reveals that the United States is more seriously divided than we had imagined, and there are still unresolved latent issues among the members of our society. We are not as united and civil as we thought, and some are not law-abiding citizens as they purport. Although society is technologically advanced, it does not indicate the civilization of its members' minds. The January 6 insurrection was a barbaric and incomprehensible act, and those who try to protect the perpetrators are equally barbaric in their position.

All of these underline the significance of protecting our democracy even more than ever before. The US democracy is at the crossroads of testing its efficacy. We cannot afford to let our democracy be destroyed, for that will indicate the downfall of America. The concept of justice, for some, is to compromise with corruption to the detriment of the larger society. We must strive to implement equal justice for all.

Chapter 11

The Danger of Falling into Mr. Trump's Corrupt Bidding

The success of the wicked in their corrupt activities is the collaboration of the unwise or unwitting individuals, who have little or no direct benefits in the activities. The consequences of their unwise partnership with the wicked often outweigh any potential benefits they could have received. It is a mystery why some people risk their lives, jobs, families, and reputations to assist the corrupt in pursuit of their criminal endeavors. Furthermore, it is also a mystery why seemingly educated people would forsake the principle of evaluating the cost and benefit of their actions, to engage in behaviors detrimental to themselves and the country at large. It puts one on the edge of not knowing who to trust.

Examining Mr. Trump's relationship with other people, including those in his administration, revealed that the relationships have not been normal or involved doing something good for humanity, other than people having to compromise their integrity and bend over backward in their behaviors to engage in actions that benefit Mr. Trump. As a result, some have found themselves in an awkward situation where they were induced to do things they would not have done otherwise. Those who succumbed to Mr. Trump's corrupt bidding have had their records tarnished with criminal charges, felonies, jail sentences, loss of jobs, financial loss, etc. In recent decades, no other United States president has destroyed so many people's lives as Mr. Trump. Yet, people are unwisely disposing themselves to dangerous situations to a self-absorbed being to achieve his selfish goals. There is absolutely nothing normal about Mr. Trump's partnership with his supporters, including the associated insane behaviors in the relationship.

LIVES TUMBLE DOWN DUE TO THE JANUARY 6 RIOT

The following individuals' lives have been ruined because of their involvement in the January 6 riot, their partnership with Mr. Trump, and believing his lies of a stolen election. Kenneth Kelly, a Florida medical doctor, participated in the Capitol riot on January 6, 2021, and lost everything important in his life, including his job, his home, his marriage, and custody of his children because of believing Mr. Trump's lies about a stolen election, and acting upon Mr. Trump's bidding that his supporters should fight for their country. Dr. Kelly pleaded guilty and was sentenced to a one-year probation and two months of home detention and is living in his RV, which may require him to wear a GPS locator. During his sentencing, Dr. Kelly expressed regret for his actions and said to the judge, "I am a different man. I blame myself for what I did that day. I take full responsibility."[1] That is the danger of the insane MAGA movement, people engaging in destructive behaviors they will regret afterward. Jennifer Heinl, the wife of a Shaler police officer, lost her job and marriage because she participated in the January 6 Capitol riot.[2] She pleaded guilty and was sentenced to fourteen days in jail and ordered to complete fifty hours of community service. Lori Vinson of Morganfield, Kentucky, lost her job after posting her participation in the Capitol riot on social media.[3] Retired Air Force Lieutenant Colonel Larry Rendall Brock Jr. lost his job with Fort Worth–based Hillwood Airways, and an attorney from Frisco, Texas, Paul Davis, who was an associate general counsel at Goosehead Insurance in Westlake, was fired from his job because of his involvement in the Capitol Hill insurrection.[4] In addition, Mr. Davis lost his fiancée and friends, and during an interview with *Business Insider*, he said, "Everything that I'd worked hard for 10 years evaporated overnight. I just didn't want to go on. I mean, I wanted to die. I really did. I was in so much emotional pain. I was so lonely. I didn't know how to even move forward with my life."[5]

A former CEO of a tech company in Chicago, Bradley Rukstales, lost his job for his participation in the Capitol riot and was sentenced to thirty days in prison.[6] Robert Palmer, a business owner in Florida, was sentenced

1. Hartmann, "Bizarre MAGA Riot Case," para. 8.
2. Peacock, "MAGA Marriage Split," para. 11.
3. Payton, "Nurse Loses Job," para. 1.
4. Lee, "Trump Supporters Lose Jobs and Businesses," para. 2.
5. Dzhanova, "Texas Lawyer Says He Hit 'Rock-Bottom,'" paras. 7–8.
6. Billeaud and Kunzelman, "CEO Who Threw Their Chair," para. 1.

to more than five years in prison on December 17, 2022, for participating in the January 6 riot. While he was being sentenced, he fought back tears and said he was "horrified, absolutely devastated" by his actions. "I'm just so ashamed that I was a part of that."[7] My question is, Is it worth it for one to risk their life, job, or relationship because of a man who cared less about them but only wanted to use them to achieve his goals? None of the individuals convicted of the January 6 riot ever received financial or legal support from Mr. Trump, but suddenly, their lives were ruined by a pathological liar.

According to the Department of Justice, as of August 6, 2023, more than 1,100 people have been charged in connection with the January 6 rioting, 632 of them have pleaded guilty, and 110 have been convicted in court trials. On September 5, 2023, Enrique Tarrio, a former leader of Proud Boys, was sentenced to twenty-two years in prison by a federal judge due to his participation in the January 6, 2021, riot on the US Capitol. He was convicted of several felonies, including seditious conspiracy by a Washington, DC, jury, and he received the longest sentence as of September 2023.[8] Stewart Rhodes, the founder of Oath Keepers, also received one of the longest jail sentences of eighteen years for seditious conspiracy.[9] Joe Biggs, a Florida Proud Boys leader, was convicted of seditious conspiracy and was sentenced to seventeen years in federal prison, along with Zachery Rehl, who was a Philadelphia branch Proud Boys leader and was sentenced to fifteen years in prison.[10] Other long sentences include Peter Schwartz for fourteen years; Thomas Webster for ten years; Jessica Watkins for eight and a half years; Patrick McCaughey for seven and a half years; Albuquerque Cosper Head, seven and a half years; Kyle Young, seven years; Guy Reffitt, seven years; Thomas Robertson, a Virginia police officer, and Julian Khater for more than six years.

It is difficult to comprehend how people choose to ruin their lives for a pathological liar. The House Select Committee that investigated the US Capitol riot on January 6, 2021, released a transcript of Jason Miller's testimony, in which he acknowledged Mr. Trump was informed by his own campaign that he lost the election, yet he continued to push for false election fraud.[11] Mr. Miller was Mr. Trump's adviser. Also, on July 25, 2023, Rudy Giuliani, a former lawyer for Mr. Trump, acknowledged in his court filing about making false statements that Georgia election workers Ruby

---

7. Kunzelman et al., "Capitol Rioters Tears," para. 3.
8. Legare and Macfarlane, "Proud Boys Leader Sentenced," para. 1.
9. Frazier, "Jan. 6 Sentences Are Piling Up," paras. 1–2.
10. Frazier, "Jan. 6 Sentences Are Piling Up," paras. 1–10.
11. Brigham, "Here's How Jason Miller's," para. 6.

Freeman and Shaye Moss engaged in election fraud.[12] While election lies are being promoted, people's lives are being destroyed. On November 3, 2023, Federico Klein, who was a State Department official appointed by Mr. Trump, was sentenced to six years in prison by US District Judge Trevor N. McFadden for his role in the January 6 riot, and the judge ordered him to pay $5,000 in fines and restitution.[13] In addition, his co-defendant, Steven Cappuccio, was sentenced to seven years and one month in prison. Both of them were convicted on July 20, 2023, of eight felonies for Mr. Klein and six felonies for Mr. Cappuccio. In July 2023, former California police chief Alan Hostetter was convicted on four felony counts for his role in the January 6 riot, including conspiracy to obstruct an official proceeding and carrying a dangerous or deadly weapon onto Capitol grounds.[14] Then on December 7, 2023, he was sentenced to eleven years in prison and part of his sentence includes a fine of $30,000 and $2,000 restitution.

PEOPLE'S LIVES MUTILATED DUE TO UNLAWFUL SUPPORT OF MR. TRUMP

The following former associates of Mr. Trump have had their images, records, and lives ruined due to engaging in unlawful actions that directly or indirectly connected to Mr. Trump's benefit. Michael Cohen, a former personal lawyer for Mr. Trump, pleaded guilty to lying to Congress about his involvement in "hush money" payments to women who claimed to have had affairs with Mr. Trump, and he also lied to Congress concerning Mr. Trump's business dealings with Russia.[15] He also pleaded guilty to tax evasion and bank fraud. During sentencing, Mr. Cohen said, "It was my blind loyalty to this man that led me to take a path of darkness instead of light. It was because time and time again I felt it was my duty to cover up his dirty deeds rather than to listen to my own inner voice and my moral compass."[16] Mr. Cohen, who was visibly emotional, also said he had been "living in a personal and mental incarceration" since he started working for Mr. Trump. In response, US District Judge William Pauley III, who sentenced Mr. Cohen, said, "Our democratic institutions depend on the honesty of our citizenry in dealing with the government."[17] Indeed, our social institu-

---

12. Brumback, "Lawyer Kenneth Chesebro Pleads Guilty," para. 1.
13. Department of Justice, "Two Sentenced for Assaulting," para. 2.
14. Fry, "Former La Habra Police Chief Sentenced," paras. 2–3.
15. Reilly, "Former Trump Lawyer Michael Cohen Sentenced," paras. 1–3.
16. Reilly, "Former Trump Lawyer Michael Cohen Sentenced," paras. 1–3.
17. Orden et al., "Michael Cohen Sentenced to 3 Years," paras. 15–17.

tions depend on citizens' honesty because honesty is still a core value of our democratic-republic society, which Mr. Trump's supporters must understand. It is destructive aiding and abetting in Mr. Trump's corrupt bidding. Mr. Cohen was also ordered to pay $1.39 million in restitution, $500,000 in forfeiture, and fines of $100,000. Mr. Cohen's wife, son, daughter, parents, and in-laws were in court during the sentencing, which was a painful experience for all of them to witness. Guess what Mr. Trump's response to all these was? He tweeted and said Mr. Cohen is "weak." For the rest of you who are MAGA fanatics and willing to carry out Mr. Trump's corrupt bidding, think twice about your partnership with Trump's MAGA movement because what happened to others, as illustrated in this chapter, will mostly happen to you. The inevitable outcome is the devastation of your life for Mr. Trump. It is shocking how people are destroying their lives to benefit a man who cares nothing about their well-being, as if they are under the influence of controlled substances. For some, it is already too late by the time they come to their senses.

Allen Weisselberg, chief financial officer (CFO) of Trump Organization, pleaded guilty to fifteen felonies on tax fraud schemes and was sentenced to five months in jail.[18] The sentence includes paying $2 million in back taxes, interest, and other associated penalties. Michael Flynn, a former Trump national security advisor, pleaded guilty to lying to the FBI concerning his communications with Russia's ambassador. Nevertheless, President Trump's administration stated, "Nothing about the guilty plea or the charge implicates anyone other than Mr. Flynn." Moreover, Mr. Flynn said, "My guilty plea and agreement to cooperate with the Special Counsel's Office reflect a decision I made in the best interests of my family and of our country. I accept full responsibility for my actions."[19] However, before President Trump left the White House, he pardoned Mr. Flynn in November 2020.[20]

Paul Manafort, former Trump campaign manager, pleaded guilty to two counts of conspiracy and was sentenced to ninety months in prison.[21]

George Papadopoulos, a former campaign advisor for Mr. Trump, pleaded guilty because he made false statements concerning his Russian contacts to the FBI.[22] He was sentenced to twelve days in prison.

---

18. Scannell and del Valle, "Former Trump Org. CFO, Sentenced," paras. 1–7.
19. Herb et al., "Flynn Pleads Guilty to Lying to FBI," para. 10.
20. Pengelly, "Trump Pardons Former National Security Adviser," para. 1.
21. Basu, "Paul Manafort Sentenced," para. 3.
22. Britzky, "George Papadopoulos Ordered to Report," paras. 2–3.

Rick Gates, former Trump campaign deputy chairman, pleaded guilty to conspiracy and lying to the FBI.[23] His sentence includes forty-five days in prison, three years of probation, and three hundred hours of community service.

A federal jury convicted Roger Stone, Mr. Trump's associate, of obstruction of justice, lying to Congress, and witness tampering.[24] He lied to Congress about seeking information from WikiLeaks when it would publish damaging emails about Hillary Clinton, who was the 2016 political rival to Mr. Trump.

Steve Deace, a *Blaze TV* host, was emotionally struck upon learning that both Jason Miller, former Trump advisor, and Rudy Giuliani, former Trump lawyer, knowingly promoted election lies.[25] Mr. Deace unknowingly also helped to promote Mr. Trump's lies about a stolen election. While some people were innocent victims of Mr. Trump's lies, others were intentional participants in promoting his lies.

On August 18, 2023, Mr. Trump was indicted by a Georgia grand jury, along with eighteen other co-defendants, for their corrupt efforts to overturn the 2020 election results.[26] These are the names facing prosecution by Fulton County District Attorney Fani Willis:

Rudy Giuliani, who was the ringleader of Mr. Trump's effort to overturn the election outcomes. He pushed for fake electors in Georgia and six other states that Mr. Trump lost in his desperate effort to reverse the election results. He was indicted on thirteen counts in Georgia, including conspiracy to commit first-degree forgery, violating the state's racketeering laws, etc.[27]

John Eastman, one of Trump's lawyers was also indicted on nine counts in the Georgia case. In his effort to subvert the election outcomes, he crafted a scheme to use fake electors in the seven states Mr. Trump lost to Mr. Biden and coerced then Vice President Mike Pence not to certify Joe Biden as the president-elect, which Mike Pence refused to do.[28]

Sidney Powell was one of Mr. Trump's lawyers who crafted a number of baseless conspiracy theories about the 2020 election results, including an allegation that Dominion Voting Systems was rigged for Joe Biden and a claim that Georgia governor Brian Kemp and Georgia Secretary of State Brad Raffensperger, both Republicans, were bribed to enable Joe Biden's

---

23. Basu and Meier, "Rick Gates Pleads Guilty," paras. 1–3.
24. Fernandez, "All the Trump Associates Convicted," paras. 1–3.
25. Gettys, "Conservative Cries Bitter Tears," paras. 1–5.
26. Popli, "These Are the 19 People Charged," paras. 1–3.
27. Samuels and Beitsch, "Giuliani Hits New Low," paras. 1–4.
28. Popli, "These Are the 19 People Charged," para. 7.

win.[29] Her conspiracy theories were so extreme and illogical that Mr. Trump and some of his allies rejected her. In addition, she pushed for Mr. Trump to use his presidential authority to seize the voting machines for forensic analysis. She was indicted on seven charges and was the second defendant to reach a plea deal with the prosecutors in exchange for testifying against Mr. Trump and other co-defendants. She was fined $6,000 and given six years of probation.[30] Other conditions of her plea deal include writing a letter of apology to the Georgia citizens, turning over case-related documents, and paying $2,700 in restitution to the state of Georgia.

Mark Meadows was the White House chief of staff in Mr. Trump's administration, and he was indicted for his role in helping Mr. Trump's botched effort to overturn the 2020 election results. The two charges against him are violating Georgia's racketeering laws and solicitation of violation of oath by a public officer.[31] However, in a different case with federal prosecutors, he received immunity that he might testify against Mr. Trump.[32] Mr. Meadows claimed that Mr. Trump is being dishonest about losing the election to Joe Biden.

Ray Smith was one of Mr. Trump's campaign attorneys during the 2020 election. He was actively involved in Mr. Trump's effort to overturn the election results in Georgia by promoting unsubstantiated claims about election fraud, including accusing election workers. He participated in the process of appealing to the state lawmakers to generate fake electors that would bypass voting for Mr. Biden to Mr. Trump during the Electoral College.[33] He was charged with twelve counts of election interference in Georgia.

Kenneth Chesebro was indicted for felony racketeering, conspiracy to commit forgery, conspiracy to file false documents, and four other charges. He masterminded the fake electors' scheme to falsely declare themselves as state "duly elected and qualified" electors and to certify that Mr. Trump won the state of Georgia.[34] On October 20, he pleaded guilty and was sentenced to five years of probation. He was also required to pay $5,000 restitution, perform one hundred hours of community service, and write a letter of apology to Georgia.[35]

---

29. Popli, "These Are the 19 People Charged," para. 10.
30. Fausset and Hakim, "Sidney Powell Pleads Guilty," paras. 1–7.
31. Popli, "These Are the 19 People Charged," para. 9.
32. Lybrand and Rabinowitz, "Mark Meadows Received," para. 1.
33. Grabenstein, "What You Need to Know," paras. 1–5.
34. Durkee, "Kenneth Chesebro Takes Plea Deal," paras. 1–7.
35. Brumback, "Lawyer Kenneth Chesebro Pleads Guilty," para. 3.

The Danger of Falling into Mr. Trump's Corrupt Bidding

Robert Cheeley faces ten criminal charges in the Fulton County case, including conspiracy to commit filing false documents, conspiracy to commit forgery in the first degree, solicitation of violation of oath by a public officer, violation of the Georgia Racketeer Influenced and Corrupt Organizations Act, known as the RICO Act, etc.[36]

Shawn Still was a newly elected Georgia state senator in 2020. He promoted Mr. Trump's conspiracy theories about the 2020 election and presented himself as one of the state's duly elected and qualified electors, to overturn the election results.[37] He was indicted on seven criminal charges in his alleged effort to pervert the will of the people in the 2020 presidential election.

Cathy Latham was indicted on eleven criminal charges. According to the indictment, Ms. Latham was one of the sixteen Georgia fake electors who presented themselves as the state's duly elected and qualified electors in their attempt to certify Mr. Trump as the winner of the Georgia election.[38]

David Shafer was one of the three fake electors in an effort to overturn the 2020 presidential election results in Georgia. He faces eight criminal charges including two counts of first-degree forgery, criminal attempt to commit filing false documents, and three counts of false statements and writings.[39]

Stephen Cliffgard Lee is a Lutheran pastor in Chicago, Illinois. He was indicted on five criminal charges including his scheme to pressure Georgia election workers Ruby Freeman and her daughter Wandrea "Shaye" Moss, to falsely confess election fraud.[40] Rev. Lee went to Freeman's residence, knocked on her door, and challenged her three times to call the police.[41] His actions led a group named Faithful Americans, which opposed Christian nationalism, to demand his expulsion. According to the petition for his expulsion, "The credible charges against Rev. Lee are deeply troubling, expose an abuse of pastoral authority as well as a threat to American democracy, and contradict the Biblical values of justice and truth. Such charges should thoroughly disqualify Rev. Lee from serving as a spiritual and moral leader in the Lutheran Church."[42]

---

36. Popli, "These Are the 19 People Charged," para. 17.
37. Popli, "These Are the 19 People Charged," para. 20.
38. Lupiani, "Who Is Cathy Latham?," paras. 1–3.
39. Popli, "These Are the 19 People Charged," para. 19.
40. Slisco, "Thousands of Christians Call to Expel," paras. 1–5.
41. Popli, "These Are the 19 People Charged," para. 21.
42. Slisco, "Thousands of Christians Call to Expel," para. 4.

Trevian C. Kutti was accused of participating in an alleged plot to coerce Ruby Freeman to falsely admit to engaging in election fraud. She visited Ms. Freeman's house and presented herself as a crisis manager to demand Ms. Freeman confess to election fraud or be arrested.[43] Ms. Kutti faces three charges that include violation of the Georgia RICO Act, conspiracy to commit solicitation of false statements and writings, and influencing witnesses.

Scott Graham Hall was charged with seven counts of criminal acts in the Fulton County case, including conspiracy to commit computer trespass, conspiracy to commit computer invasion of privacy, two counts of conspiracy to commit election fraud, conspiracy to defraud the state, and violation of Georgia's racketeering laws.[44] He was the first to accept a plea deal with the prosecutors and pleaded guilty to five misdemeanors. The plea deal requires him to write a letter of apology to the citizens of Georgia, testify in further proceedings, have five years of probation, and be forbidden from participating in polling activities.[45]

Jeffrey Clark was a high-ranking attorney of the US Justice Department whom Mr. Trump considered to appoint to be the acting attorney general so that he could send his drafted letter to Georgia in which he claimed voting irregularities and demanded that Georgia lawmakers should consider disannulling Biden's win.[46] When other senior officials of the Justice Department threatened to resign, Mr. Trump held back from appointing him to the position of acting attorney general. He was charged with the violation of Georgia's anti-racketeering law and attempting to commit false statements.

Michael Roman was a senior staff member for Mr. Trump's campaign, and he was indicted for his unsuccessful efforts to use fake electors to block certification of Joe Biden's victory in the 2020 election.[47] He also promoted unsubstantiated claims of voter fraud to justify his actions for fake electors. He faces seven charges in Georgia, including two counts of conspiracy to commit forgery in the first degree, two counts of conspiracy to commit false statements and writings, conspiracy to commit filing false documents, conspiracy to commit impersonating a public officer, and violation of the Georgia RICO Act.

Harrison William Prescott Floyd was a former leader of Black Voices for Trump and was indicted for influencing a witness and conspiracy to

---

43. Dreier, "Trump Indictment in Georgia," paras. 1–3.
44. Popli, "These Are the 19 People Charged," para. 27.
45. Brumback and Thanawala, "Bail Bondsman Charged," paras. 1–3.
46. Aditi et al., "Trump DOJ Official Jeffrey Clark," paras. 1–5.
47. Lord, "Trump Indictment in Georgia," paras. 1–4.

commit solicitation of false statements and writings.[48] In his effort to subvert the 2020 election results, he arranged a meeting with Ruby Freeman, a Fulton County election worker, and Trevian Kutti, a publicist, in which Mr. Floyd and Ms. Trevian threatened Ms. Freeman of going to prison if she did not confess that she had committed voter fraud.[49]

Misty Hampton, also known as Emily Misty Hayes, was a former election supervisor in Coffee County, Georgia. She unlawfully allowed Mr. Trump's supporters to have access to voter data and ballot-counting equipment at the Coffee County election office.[50] She was indicted on seven charges, which include two counts of conspiracy to commit election fraud, conspiracy to commit computer trespass, conspiracy to commit computer theft, conspiracy to commit computer invasion of privacy, conspiracy to defraud the state, and violation of the Georgia RICO Act.

Jenna Ellis was one of Trump's campaign attorneys, and she collaborated with Rudy Giuliani to exert pressure on the state legislature to overturn the 2020 election results.[51] She allegedly advised Mr. Trump to pressure Mike Pence to block the certification of Joe Biden's victory. She was charged with violating Georgia's racketeering laws and solicitation of violation of oath by a public officer. She was the fourth person to reach a guilty plea with the Fulton County District Attorney Fani Willis. When she pleaded guilty during her court appearance, she was in tears and said, "If I knew then what I know now, I would have declined to represent Donald Trump in these post-election challenges." Her plead deal includes five years of probation, $5,000 payment in restitution, one hundred hours of community service, writing an apology letter to the citizens of Georgia, which she had already done before the sentencing, and fully cooperating with prosecutors as the case advances.[52] In addition, Ms. Ellis was the only defendant who pleaded guilty and asked the court for permission to apologize publicly. While she rose in tears for her statement, she said, "As an attorney who is also a Christian, I take my responsibilities as a lawyer very seriously." She admitted her mistakes of trusting the information given to her by other lawyers who were more experienced than her, and without verifying the validity of their claims. One of the common mistakes some people make is blind compliance; some blindly adhere to the information from their leaders or from people they perceive to have deeper knowledge than they do without

48. Fausset, "Last Defendant in Trump Election," paras. 1–10.
49. Szep and So, "Kanye West Publicist Pressed," para. 2.
50. Dreier, "Trump Indictment in Georgia," paras. 2–3.
51. Gerstein and Cheney, "Another Trump Lawyer," paras. 1–10.
52. Fung, "Jenna Ellis Breaks Silence," paras. 1–12.

verifying the accuracy of the information they receive from them. To Ms. Ellis's credit, her actions to apologize to the court without a mandate from anyone reflects genuine repentance, which is true Christianity.

Besides the eighteen Trump-aligned defendants facing criminal charges from Fulton County District Attorney Fani Willis, several other individuals who engaged in fake electors' schemes in some swing states have been indicted or under investigation for their role in keeping Mr. Trump in power. These so-called fake electors signed documents claiming they were "the duly elected and qualified" presidential electors from their states, in their despairing effort to overturn Mr. Biden's win in their states in favor of Mr. Trump. On July 18, 2023, Michigan State Attorney General Dana Nessel filed felony charges against sixteen fake electors who submitted false certificates that claimed they were legitimate state electors so that they could subvert Mr. Biden's win in the state for Mr. Trump.[53] The maximum penalty for the top charges is fourteen years in prison. Furthermore, on December 6, 2023, six fake electors were indicted by a Nevada grand jury, and according to Nevada Attorney General Aaron Ford, "We cannot allow attacks on democracy to go unchallenged."[54] In December 2020, the six fake electors sent signed certificates to Congress and the National Archives falsely claiming that Mr. Trump won in Nevada. They all face two categories of felonies, which carry penalties that range from one year up to four or five years in prison.

Shockingly, so many lives have tumbled down because of a man who never influences people to engage in humanitarian deeds but only corruption to benefit himself. Most likely, all these Mr. Trump conspiracy theorists about the 2020 election who did not reach a plea bargain with the prosecutors would be convicted of felony charges and sent to prison for years, just like the January 6 rioters. It makes one ask, What does it take for some people to get it and understand who Mr. Trump is? Succumbing to Mr. Trump's corrupt bidding is like someone meddling with a burning flame by which the person will surely get burned. You do not have to be a victim and destroy your life for the light bulb to come on after it is already too late and there is no chance of reversing the consequences of your actions. Be wise, stay away from corruption and corrupt people, and do not deceive yourself by saying, "Everyone is doing it," for that is a dangerous perspective for anyone to embrace. Holding such a view persuades you to condone or even engage in criminal behaviors. Encourage yourself to respect the law of

---

53. Cappelletti, "Michigan Charges 16 Fake Electors," paras. 1–2.
54. Stern, "Nevada Grand Jury Indicts," paras. 1–2.

the land; it feels better with profound peace of mind to do the right thing than to engage in dishonest and criminal behaviors.

FINANCIAL LOSS FOR PROMOTING MR. TRUMP'S ELECTION LIES

In addition, promoting Mr. Trump's lies and corruption has resulted in huge financial losses to his allies who sponsored his false conspiracies. One of the victims is Mike Lindell, the CEO of MyPillow. In his support for Mr. Trump's corrupt effort to overturn the 2020 elections, he made massive financial contributions to endorse the election lies, including financing a two-week bus tour that was labeled "March for Trump."[55] During an interview with CNBC, he extended the false election claims by postulating that China was involved in the election fraud. Furthermore, he stated, "We are in 44 states now. We're doing canvassing efforts. I'll give an example. In Florida, we canvassed 10,000 people's names, and 2,600 of them were phantom voters."[56] Phantom voters refer to votes by dead people. No evidence was provided to support his conspiracy theories. With over fifty lawsuits filed by Mr. Trump and his allies, none of them was validated or supported by any evidence or the judicial system. Mr. Lindell also made the following false claim about the 2020 election, saying, "It was the most corrupt election in US history, and probably in world history." However, Christopher Krebs, the cybersecurity chief, a lifelong Republican, who was appointed by Mr. Trump, stated that the 2020 election was "the most secure in American history."[57] A few days after he made the statement, Mr. Trump fired him for speaking the truth. The US attorney general, William Barr, stated, "To date, we have not seen fraud on a scale that could have affected a different outcome in the election."[58] A few days later he resigned as the US attorney general. It is obvious, one cannot speak the truth and survive in Mr. Trump's camp.

Mr. Lindell's conspiracy theories became the headline news again when he said he would pay $5 million to any cybersecurity expert who could disprove his data about the 2020 election fraud claims. According to Mr. Lindell, his data revealed that votes transferred from the US to China and were altered and converted from Mr. Trump to Mr. Biden.[59] A cybersecurity

  55. Tanfani, "How Trump's Pied Pipers," para. 3.
  56. Schwartz, "Mike Lindell Says He Spent $25 Million," paras. 2–17.
  57. Sanger and Perlroth, "Trump Fires a Cybersecurity Official," paras. 1–3.
  58. Balsamo, "Barr Says No Wide Election Fraud," para. 1.
  59. Zeidman, "How I Won $5 Million," paras. 2–3.

expert named Robert Zeidman took up the challenge and soon discovered that the data were "nonsensical" and unrelated to the 2020 election. However, Mr. Lindell refused to keep up with his promise, which resulted in an arbitration panel ordering Mr. Lindell to pay Mr. Zeidman $5 million as indicated in his original contract. After reviewing the data, the arbitration panel reached a conclusion that stated Mr. Zeidman "proved the data Lindell LLC provided . . . unequivocally did not reflect November 2020 election data." Oh, it is important to mention that Mr. Zeidman is a Republican who cast his votes for Mr. Trump both in 2016 and 2020. So, this is not a Democrat involved in some kind of "witch hunt" against a Republican.

In February 2021, Dominion Voting Systems filed a $1.3 billion lawsuit against Mr. Lindell due to his false claims concerning the 2020 election results.[60] As a result of his promotion of false conspiracies about the election, retailers removed his products from their shelves, in which he lost $80 million in sales. According to Mr. Lindell, he spent $25 million of his own money to support Mr. Trump's claims about the election fraud, and in the process, he made this statement, "I will spend every dime I have" in fighting for the election results. Indeed, his wish was granted to him. As of October 2023, Mr. Lindell stated, "I'm out of money" as his attorneys sought court permission to withdraw representing him due to unpaid legal fees.[61] It is an unwise and dangerous move to think that there will be no consequences for promoting lies that are destructive to the integrity of our democracy and the lives of the citizens because we are still a country of law and order. Those who support Mr. Trump's lies and corruption need to grab hold of this understanding that "every action must produce an outcome." The intensity of the outcomes depends on the degree of the actions.

Rudy Giuliani is another conspiracy theorist who had a severe financial loss. As a result of promoting unfounded claims about the voting machines switching votes from Mr. Trump to Mr. Biden, Dominion Voting Systems filed a $1.3 billion lawsuit against him, and he is also facing a $2.7 billion lawsuit along with Sidney Powell and Fox News for promoting false claims against Smartmatic, a voting technology company.[62] In addition, in June 2023, he was ordered by US District Judge Beryl Howell to pay more than $89,000 in attorney fees for the two Georgia election workers, Ruby Freeman and Shaye Moss, who were subjects of Mr. Giuliani's 2020 election false claims.[63] Furthermore, a federal judge ruled on August

---

60. Shalin, "MyPillow CEO Hit with $1.3 Billion Lawsuit," para. 1.
61. Wells and Perez, "Mike Lindell Says He's Out of Money," para. 1.
62. Shalin, "MyPillow CEO Hit with $1.3 Billion Lawsuit," para. 1.
63. Gregorian, "Judge Punishes Rudy Giuliani," paras. 1–2.

30, 2023, that Mr. Giuliani defamed former Georgia election worker Ms. Freeman and her daughter, and therefore is liable for damages after he did not produce evidence to support his claims or comply with discovery obligations to validate his conspiracy theories concerning the results of the 2020 election.[64] In Mr. Giuliani's false accusations, he also claimed that the two election workers were passing USB drives "like vials of heroin or cocaine" during ballot-counting operations. However, a review of the video of the scene shows that the rumored "USB drive" was actually a ginger mint. On December 15, 2023, a jury of eight people from Washington, DC, reached a $148 million verdict, ordering Mr. Giuliani to pay Ms. Freeman and her daughter Ms. Moss for defamation.[65] During the four-day trial, Mr. Giuliani vowed that he would testify and said, "When I testify, you'll get the whole story, and it will be definitively clear what I said was true." Guess what, he declined to testify as he promised. It is disturbing that Mr. Trump and his allies keep making false claims that they cannot validate because their supporters buy into their lies without holding them accountable. That is not the way to create a stable and unified society, and it is unbiblical. Prior to the $148 million verdict, he was facing massive unpaid legal fees and debts, and he listed his $6.5 million Manhattan apartment for sale in August 2023, suggesting potential financial difficulties.[66] The fact remains that it is financially debilitating to support Mr. Trump's corruption, and for some, it is too late before they realize that.

Furthermore, Mr. Giuliani did not only experience financial loss in asserting Mr. Trump's lies about the 2020 election results; he was also disbarred from practicing law in New York as of June 24, 2021, by the New York appellate court.[67] It was other lawyers like him, who demonstrated integrity and filed the complaints with the state Supreme Court's Attorney Grievance Committee, accusing him of pushing false conspiracies about the 2020 election results that led to the January 6 riot. The accusation gave rise to his disbarment without a hearing. However, during an interview with Mr. Giuliani, he said, "We do not live in a free state. We live in a state that's controlled by the Democrat Party: Cuomo, de Blasio, and the Democrats. We have a double standard. There's no doubt if I was representing Hillary Clinton, I'd be their hero." The issue is not who you are representing, Mr. Giuliani, but the intentional lies that you promoted that led to the insurrection in the US Capitol on January 6, 2021. You don't have to be a rocket scientist

---

64. Barnes and Concepcion, "Rudy Giuliani Defamed," para. 1.
65. Barnes et al., "Rudy Giuliani Hit with $148M Verdict," para. 1.
66. Polantz et al., "Giuliani Struggling under Massive," paras. 1–2.
67. Feldman, "Rudy Giuliani Suspended from Practicing Law," para. 1.

to understand that, except for a dishonest person. It is very shocking that whenever Mr. Trump and his allies broke the law or engaged in unethical behaviors, they never held themselves accountable for their actions, rather they immediately turned the blame on Democrats. It is a disgraceful response to shift the blame for your actions to another person. The judicial system needs to take a firm position of rendering severe judgment to individuals who engage in such dishonest behavior, including lawyers who intentionally promote lies for the sake of defending their clients. One of the core values of our society is honesty; therefore, our educational and judicial systems have a societal mandate to enforce societal values, to prevent our society from imminent destruction. As long as a person is shifting blame for their actions on another, it suggests that there is no repentance for their actions but they will do the same thing again if the opportunity arises and even worse than the first time.

Steve Bannon, former White House chief strategist for Mr. Trump's administration, received a four-month pending jail sentence on October 21, 2022, for rebelling against a subpoena from the House Committee investigating the January 6 riot at the US Capitol.[68] Mr. Bannon was also fined $6,500 by US District Judge Carl Nichols. In addition, Mr. Bannon accumulated $855,000 in legal fees due to his defiance to comply with the House Committee subpoena and allegation of embezzling some of the funds donated to build a wall on the southern US border.[69] As of February 2023, the firm Davidoff Hutcher and Citron LLP, which represented Mr. Bannon in his criminal cases, filed a lawsuit against him for unpaid legal fees of $480,487. Engaging in criminal behaviors and defending Mr. Trump's corruption is very costly, and it takes criminal-minded individuals to support Mr. Trump's corruption. Honest Republicans do not and will not support Mr. Trump's corruption, and some of them are troubled by the continuous support of Mr. Trump's false election claims by the Republicans. On November 1, 2023, during an MSNBC interview with a House Republican, Ken Buck of Colorado, he suggested that he would not seek reelection. Rep. Buck also explained his reasons for not seeking reelection by saying:

> I always have been disappointed with our inability in Congress to deal with major issues and I'm also disappointed that the Republican party continues to rely on this lie that the 2020 election was stolen and rely on the January 6 narrative and political prisoners from January 6 and other things. If we're going to solve difficult problems, we've got to deal with some very unpleasant

---

68. Whitehurst, "Bannon Gets 4 Months behind Bars," paras. 1–2.
69. Sisak, "Steve Bannon Owes $480K," para. 5.

truths or lies and make sure that we project to the public what the truth is.[70]

Any honest person, regardless of political affiliation will be disappointed by the continued false assertion of a stolen election by Mr. Trump and some GOP lawmakers; it defies common sense and human dignity. Moreover, any honest person would restrain themself from partaking in crooked activities. A wise response when approached to partake in a criminal act is to simply say "No" and walk away. A more reputable approach is to report the matter to the police or appropriate government agency to stop the spread of such crime.

Reporting criminal acts will help to minimize the spread of such crimes, and it will also help to make our society safe. Refusing to partake in criminal acts will protect you and your children and grandchildren from being potential victims of such crimes in the future because the evil acts people do will live after them. It is a universal principle that does not alter, and being in denial does not deter the consequences of a person's actions. Every action must produce a reaction in proportion to the action. Please, do not help the criminals fulfill their corrupt desires unless you are an evildoer.

Association with Mr. Trump does not result in engaging in legal or noncorrupt business activities. It is shocking that anyone would want him to be a president again after knowing about his corrupt relationships. Several former White House staffers do not want Mr. Trump to be president again based on their unpleasant experiences with him, unlike previous presidents. His corrupt endeavors have destroyed many lives. The idea of allowing Mr. Trump to run for another presidential election is very dangerous because the only outcome is Mr. Trump and his allies generating more vicious lies stating, "They have done it again," stealing the election from him. Additional outcomes will be more violence in the country and seditious abuse of our judicial process. Those who support Mr. Trump need to take an honest examination of themselves and the danger they are creating in our society. Senator Mitt Romney (R-Utah) has been honest in acknowledging that Mr. Trump does not have a chance for the 2024 election, and his concern was backed by Senator John Cornyn (R-Texas).[71] A retired Idaho Supreme Court judge, Jim Jones, has echoed the same view.[72]

70. Pengelly, "Republican to Quit House," paras. 2–4.
71. Bolton, "Senator GOP Rallies behind Romney," paras. 1–5.
72. Reed, "Retired GOP Judge Warns," paras. 1–4.

MOBSTER MENTALITY

The MAGA movement is a cult, and its leader Mr. Trump is shameless in his corrupt engagements. To him, it is the end that justifies the means. His actions are unprecedented compared to previous presidents. The purpose of this cult movement is for ingroup benefit, not for the country at large. Therefore, in their perverted perception, there is no America outside their group, and outgroup members are treated as threats and enemies that should be eliminated using whatever means possible, just like what happened on January 6, 2021. The legality of the means of achieving their goals is irrelevant in as much as the goals were accomplished. The end for them is to create an ideal America of White dominance that suppresses the voting power of non-conservative voters. This mobster mentality is evidenced in radical maneuvering in red states redistricting undertakings that are often structured to undermine the voting power of minority groups. Even though they engage in all manner of behaviors that contradict biblical values, they have the Bible in their hands to deceive their followers and unwitting individuals as if their actions are biblical. Another deceptive approach is the use of anti-abortion rhetoric to justify their ungodly practices and condemn others.

THE DANGER OF MOBSTER MENTALITY

If you know someone, perhaps a friend or family member who has been indoctrinated into the MAGA movement and Trumpism, you will notice that their beliefs and occasional response to political-related issues are outside the norm and lack logic. The reason is that the person has been trapped in mobster mentality or is a victim of groupthink, and they lack the ability or freedom to think independently.

Vignette

The danger of mobster mentality is the inability of some to recuse themselves and critically evaluate their group's beliefs and actions, compare them to their moral beliefs, as well as consider the potential consequences of their actions. When people's behavior due to group influence contradicts their attitude, it creates cognitive dissonance.

CANCEL CULTURE

While the Republicans and Evangelical Christians are accusing liberals of cancel culture, they engage in a more radical cancel culture than any group in the United States. But, again, typical of hypocrites, they do not see their sins but others. Cancel culture dominates within the Republican Party and among its members. Mr. Trump uses the concept of cancel culture to intimidate and control the Republican Party. It is evident for an outsider looking inside that the dyadic relationship between Mr. Trump and GOP lawmakers is of unequal power, with one overly intimidated by the other. The United States government is not predicated on traditional authority in which the kings and queens have unbridled authority. It is a rational-legal authority in which everyone is subject to written rules and regulations and guarantees the same constitutional rights and freedom. However, the GOP lawmakers have given Mr. Trump unlimited power to execute his desires at will without accountability. They have also ascribed total power to Mr. Trump and even pledged to perform his corrupt bidding. The relationship between the two is undemocratic; it is a type of relationship common in a third-world autocracy.

The canceling of Representatives Liz Cheney, Adam Kinzinger, and others by the Republican Party because they denounced the lies of President Trump about the stolen election is absurd. Cancel culture has become a common practice within the Republican Party to coerce its members into submission and dishonesty. A major aspect of American cultural values is honesty. Those who spoke the truth are rewarded, and those who lied are punished. However, the present cohort of GOP lawmakers, who are Trump puppets, have perverted this cherished value of our society. If this dangerous trend is not reversed, America will be subjected to a downward spiral of destruction. God cannot endorse or be a part of this type of wickedness or a party that engages in this type of ungodliness. Proverbs 17:15 says, "He who justifies the wicked, and he who condemns the just, both of them alike are an abomination to the Lord." Additionally, the Scripture says, "Also, to punish the righteous is not good, nor to strike princes for their uprightness" (Prov 17:26).

Vignette

It is un-American and, to some extent, inconsistent with the evolutionary adaptation concept that free-will men, who are not under a physical threat, would cowardly submit their God-given, Constitutional guaranteed rights, freedom, and independence to a self-absorbed, self-serving man to rule and control them. And for the dictator's children to rule over their own children. Certainly, your future generations would be ashamed to acknowledge you as a relative because of your cowardice at a time the society needs your bravery.

MR. TRUMP CARES LESS ABOUT OTHER PEOPLE BUT USES THEM TO ADVANCE HIS INTERESTS

Additionally, there is no single piece of evidence to support that Mr. Trump cares for the United States except for himself. People who care for their country will not be promoting disunity and violence in the country. They will endeavor to pay their fair taxes to support the country, but the Trump Organization had implemented crafty means of using the system to avoid paying its fair taxes, and it was found guilty of criminal tax fraud and falsifying business records.[73] Trump Organization was fined $1.6 million, and its chief financial officer Allen H. Weisselberg pleaded guilty and was sentenced to five months in jail. In 2017, after lengthy litigation, federal judge Gonzalo Curiel approved a $25 million settlement of Trump's fraudulent university that defrauded thousands of American students millions of dollars.[74] Part of the allegation against Trump University by the students is that the acclaimed Trump-handpicked instructors for real estate were unqualified and delivered lecture materials that could be found on the internet. Because of the Mexican heritage of Judge Gonzalo Curiel, Mr. Trump cast doubt on his impartiality in the case.[75] That is a faulty and unacceptable accusation; just like in other situations, Mr. Trump accused prosecutors of a witch hunt, but at the same time, he remains in denial of his dubious business practices and behaviors. Trump University was not a licensed university and ceased to exist in 2010. Furthermore, in 2019, President Trump was fined $2 million by New York State Judge Saliann Scarpulla for using funds from his charity organization to advance his business and political interests.[76] Money for kids' cancer treatment was redirected to the Trump foundations. It appears that whatever Mr. Trump touches automatically becomes corrupted. Everything had to be directed for the benefit of Mr. Trump because he could not

---

73. Bromwich et al., "Trump's Company Gets Maximum Punishment," paras. 1–5.
74. Domonoske, "Judge Approves $25 Million Settlement," para. 1.
75. Criss, "Judge Has Finalized $25 Million Settlement," para. 8.
76. Sisak, "Judge Fines Trump $2 Million," para 1.

care less about the welfare of others, except those he could use to advance his ambitions.

Mr. Trump operates on a false consensus that whatever is good for him is good for the nation. He rejects the established legal procedures in our country. He has no respect for the rulings of the Supreme Court and the judges unless the court system is twisted to his benefit. The ruling of all the judges and the Supreme Court that rejected Mr. Trump's false claims about the 2020 election was condemned by Mr. Trump. Again, an indication that he has no regard for the US legal system that advocates equitable justice for all, regardless of one's status. He condemned the Supreme Court for the release of his taxes that he fought for years to hide, and he stated: "The Supreme Court has lost its honor, prestige, and standing, and has become nothing more than a political body, with our Country paying the price."[77] That is insane to make such an ignorant accusation against the US Supreme Court. Three of the justices were appointed by Mr. Trump, and the Supreme Court Justices have an obligation to uphold the US Constitution and render equitable justice to all. It appears if one does not comply with Mr. Trump's corruption, he believes that person is wrong and a criminal instead of himself.

THE NEW NORMAL OF BEING A BOLD AND SHAMELESS CRIMINAL

In the past, when elected or appointed officials were caught in unethical behaviors, corruption, or crime, they often publicly apologized sincerely, with tears in their eyes, to the nation as a whole, and even to their families for their dishonorable behavior. However, Mr. Trump has set a destructive new normal, that is, to turn the table against those who point out his criminal, corrupt, and unethical practices and accuse them of a political witch hunt. No federal or state institutions are off the list of Mr. Trump's accusations of doing their appropriate jobs that are constitutionally endorsed. The US attorneys general, FBI, Supreme Court, federal judges, state judges, state attorneys general, and district attorneys all have been vilified and condemned by Mr. Trump for the same jobs they have been doing for centuries, unlike any other president we have ever had. Even those who did not go along with his lies and corruption are disparaged. Our country may never recover from the damages Mr. Trump has caused if severe actions are not taken by federal and state prosecutors, judges, the FBI, and the Supreme Court, to convey to Mr. Trump and his allies that nobody is above the law in the United States,

77. Vlamis, "Trump Rips the Supreme Court," paras. 1–2.

as implied in our Constitution. We are still a law-abiding nation, and the law is applied on an equal basis to all people. It is dangerous to allow these corrupt minds to normalize criminal behaviors in our country because it will set our country on a path of imminent self-destruction.

Vignette

The success of a society is directly correlated to the depth of its members' unification. Like a family, which is a mini society, the collaborative efforts of all family members ensure stability, unity, equitable justice, peace, and success in accomplishing family goals. When a larger society embraces the same standards, it also experiences the same outcomes. Those who genuinely care for the well-being of America will forgo self-interest and their ingroup interest for the sake of the solidity and efficacy of the larger society. The divisive political concepts often endorsed by the extremists, both left and right groups, are dysfunctional to our society's stability and success.

WHAT ARE THE DRIVING FORCES FOR THE SUPPORT OF MR. TRUMP?

Mr. Trump's records demonstrate that he is morally unfit to be the president of the United States. He lacks integrity, emotional stability, and genuine interest in the unity and well-being of our country, like past presidents. He is driven for self-benefits, not for the benefit of society, and corruption dominates in all his endeavors. Examine all his business activities and his desperate efforts to remain in power after his loss in the 2020 election—all is consummated in corruption. He was the only president in the United States who refused to transfer power after his term was over and crafted corrupt means to overturn the will of the people. The question remains, Why would anyone want such a man to be their president? There are only two possible explanations of why some people are fierce supporters of President Trump; either they have a heart condition for corruption or covert racism. Of course, almost every one of them will most likely deny belonging to either group, which is not an uncommon behavioral pattern of hypocrites—they have a plank across their eyes that they cannot see their own errors. However, as the saying goes, "Birds of a feather flock together," so the fierce supporters of Donald Trump flock around him because he emboldened corruption and racism, which is a major aspect of their behavioral pattern. Corruption and racism are distasteful to individuals with upright hearts and they will not associate themselves with a man who embodies such wickedness, even if the man is a family member. Donald Trump is a litmus test for many from both psychological and spiritual perspectives. He brings the worst out of humanity, especially his close associates. If you were like me, you probably were beside yourself to see the extent people are willing to compromise their integrity, that is, if they have one, to please a man who persuaded them into a debased mindset. These are things you think happen in a movie, not in real life. The tragedy of the whole episode is the cowardliness of elected officials forsaking their sworn oath of office because they do not want to offend Donald Trump. They are afraid of Donald Trump campaigning against them for their reelection. If your fear of Donald Trump paralyzes you from standing up for the truth, it is the more reason you should be voted out of office because we do not want cowards representing us in Congress. America is the land of the brave, not the land of cowards. Regrettably, some preachers have joined the movement by forsaking the preaching of the truth and turning into false preachers and prophets for the sake of partisan politics. As the Scripture says, "An evildoer gives heed to false lips; a liar listens eagerly to a spiteful tongue" (Prov 17:4). Thus, listening to and believing the obvious lies of Donald Trump reveals one's heart conditions, which are falsehoods and corruption.

Furthermore, according to research findings, the motivation for Mr. Trump's support is influenced by outgroup hatred rather than ingroup love.[78] An example of outgroup members will be non-Whites, non-Christians, metropolitan voters, women, etc. Because Mr. Trump embodies racism, it induces high levels of ingroup support, especially for those who harbor outgroup hatred. In addition, the purpose of the big lie about the 2020 election is racism, as stated by *AlterNet*:

> The enthusiasm for the Big Lie among white Evangelicals comes back primarily to one thing: Racism. Scrape away the easily disproven conspiracy theories about voting machines and stolen ballots and what you're left with is the animating belief of the Big Lie, which is that conservative white people are entitled to rule, no matter what. The Big Lie puts a moral gloss on this argument, by recasting the opponents of democracy as the "victims" of a "stolen" election. Actions like trying to throw out the vote total in racially diverse cities in 2020 and rewriting election laws to marginalize voters of color, however, tell the true story.

---

78. Mason et al., "Activating Animus," 1508.

The Big Lie is about preserving white supremacy, even if the cost is ending democracy.[79]

SUMMARY

It is an illusion of the mind to think that Mr. Trump would conserve White supremacy in the US. For one to hold such a view covertly or overtly, it indicates they are deceiving themselves and unwittingly enslaving themselves, their children, and future generations to serve Donald Trump and his family. Mr. Trump is seeking loyalists to enable him to consolidate power and establish an authoritarian type of monarchy for himself and his family, and it does not matter to him which race or group of people pave the way for him to achieve that goal. Moreover, if you carefully examine Mr. Trump's biggest enemies, they are usually his former close allies, those who were very loyal to him in the past, but the first time they refused to carry out his corrupt bidding, he treated them as those who deserved to be eliminated. Guess what, if you are a Trump supporter, you're next! Because he will use you to go after a family member or a friend, who may have disagreed with him or spoken against him, and your refusal to follow through will spell your obliteration. Mr. Trump has no boundaries when it comes to corruption, and he would push his loyalists to do things that are morally unbearable for them. Nobody is safe with a dictator; check the history of dictators, and you will find out that you're doomed just for a slight suspicious thought of your disloyalty. In essence, it is imperative to have an honest desire for clarity of mind to know the truth rather than a twisted mind to please a man or a political party at the detriment of our society's peace and unity.

For those who are racially motivated for political actions, rather than for the benefit and unity of the country, you have inadvertently made your race an idol, which means you have no part in the kingdom of God. Galatians 3:28 says, "There is neither Jew nor Greek, there is neither slave nor free, there is neither male nor female; for you are all one in Christ Jesus." We are all one in Christ, but those who have elevated their race above the word of God have rejected the oneness of believers in Christ Jesus.

---

79. Marcotte, "Evangelicals Are the Backbones," paras. 10–11.

Chapter 12

Remnants Beware

The doctrine of Balaam has dominated among some preachers and churches today, which has led to some Evangelical leaders' apocalyptic rhetoric, to entice their followers to support a man who is the antithesis of what Christ represents in every conceivable standard. The truth of God's word has been complicated to align with partisan politics, to promote a political party and unchristian man as the hope and savior of our country. While they have directed their passion to a man and a political party, they have the Bible in their hand and talk about Jesus, but do not know him nor have a relationship with him. They portray a political party whose practices contradict biblical teachings and a party whose membership includes satanic hate groups, as God's approved party. Blind obedience or compliance with the leaders' postulates has become the norm, and no one dares break the group norms by carefully examining the accuracy of the purported claims and comparing them to biblical teachings. A common noticeable behavioral pattern is the effort of other group members to expand on any proposed misinformation from their group leaders. Their efforts weaken their members to submission of their distortion.

The false promotion and support of a political party as a Christian party opens the door for many fabrications from lying tongues. These lying tongues, agents of Satan, have developed several conniving means to equate Mr. Trump, who is a precursor of the antichrist, with Jesus. It has become a common practice for them to wear hats and display emblems that read "JESUS IS MY SAVIOR, TRUMP IS MY PRESIDENT."[1] Such practice is very dangerous and heresy, and soon, the same group of people who are

---

1. Layne and Ulmer, "How Trump Netted," para. 5.

promoting Mr. Trump as God's anointed will promote him as the savior rather than Jesus. It is shocking how people who call themselves Christians are perverting God's word to embrace falsehoods. Apostle Paul speaking to the Galatian church made the following statements that are still relevant to present-day believers in the United States:

> I marvel that you are turning away so soon from Him who called you in the grace of Christ, to a different gospel, which is not another; but there are some who trouble you and want to pervert the gospel of Christ. But even if we, or an angel from heaven, preach any other gospel to you than what we have preached to you, let him be accursed. As we have said before, so now I say again, if anyone preaches any other gospel to you than what you have received, let him be accursed. For do I now persuade men or God? Or do I seek to please men? For if I still pleased men, I would not be a bondservant of Christ. (Gal 1:6–10)

If you are of upright heart, you too should marvel at how easily some, who called themselves Christians have perverted the gospel and grace of Christ Jesus into partisan politics. There is no fear of God in them to preach a different gospel that contradicts biblical truth.

Some Evangelical preachers have deviated from the preaching of the gospel of the Lord Jesus to preach a political memorandum, and some other preachers have been silent for so long instead of taking action to defend the gospel of the Lord Jesus and set the records straight. It is important to understand that your silence in a critical matter like the misrepresentation of biblical truths is complicity. It is time to break out of your comfort zones and start declaring the truth of God's word, because, as you have seen, the apostates are not relinquishing.

Vignette

> It is heretical to label a man "anointed" by God, especially a man who emerged out of his mother's womb with a lying tongue, whose family members have warned about his corruption, whom former employees desperately advised society to stay away from, who research and editorial data concluded is the most lying and dishonest president ever in the history of the US presidency, a man who attracts hateful and satanic groups, a man whose speech promotes violence and has destroyed thousands of lives within a short period on the political arena, a man whose business practices are shrouded with corruption and who seditiously abused our legal system with numerous lawsuits and

six business bankruptcies, a man who said he has done nothing wrong to ask God for forgiveness, and a man whose life contradicts everything Christ represents.

According to the Scripture, it is the anointing that destroys the yoke (see Isa 10:27). However, the person wrongfully labeled "anointed" has created so much burden, division, hate, and destruction in our country, including destruction within his own ingroup members, as well as outgroup members, unlike any past presidents. How can such a person be anointed by God, since all his behaviors contradict biblical standards? Such anointing came from Satan, who is a liar and a destroyer of God's creation.

UNSUBSTANTIATED CLAIMS BY EVANGELICAL LEADERS ABOUT DONALD TRUMP'S SALVATION

Some Christian Evangelical leaders are quick to present Mr. Trump as a Christian to pressure their followers to support him even though Mr. Trump does not believe he needs a savior since, according to him; he has not done anything wrong to ask for forgiveness of his sins. Mr. Trump's behaviors indicate that he could not be a Christ follower or a saved person according to scriptural standards. Let's examine some key factors associated with believers in the Lord Jesus based on biblical standards and see if Mr. Trump displays any of them.

Asking God's Forgiveness

Below is the comment made by Donald Trump as reported by the *Christian Post*, when he was asked about God's forgiveness; then you decide if his response is consistent with the biblical doctrine about salvation.

> I am not sure if I have ever asked God's forgiveness. I don't bring God into that picture. When I go to church and when I drink my little wine and have my little cracker, I guess that is a form of forgiveness. I do that as often as I can because I feel cleansed. I say let's go on, and let's make it right.[2]

No, Donald Trump, drinking your little wine and eating your little cracker is not a form of forgiveness or salvation. You must admit that you are a sinner, repent of your sins before God, and ask Jesus to come into your life and be your savior. That is how you receive forgiveness and salvation.

2. Nothstine, "I'm Not Sure," para. 2.

In another interview with CNN, Mr. Trump was asked to clarify his previous statement about God's forgiveness, and his response was, "Why do I have to repent or ask for forgiveness if I am not making mistakes? I work hard; I am an honorable person."[3] Really! In the same manner, this man has perverted truth and embraced lies as a way of life for himself; he has convoluted God's approved method of salvation. On a different note, he is right because forgiveness is for those who have sinned, and it is through God's forgiveness that one receives salvation by faith in Christ Jesus. However, those who have not even made a mistake, let alone sin, like Donald Trump, have to depend on their self-righteousness and hard work to save themselves, which is not the biblical standard of salvation. The Scripture says, "For all have sinned and fall short of the glory of God" (Rom 3:23). Perhaps, Donald Trump is excluded from that Scripture because he does not make a mistake and could not possibly see himself sinning to ask for God's forgiveness. The problem here is that Donald Trump's ego could not allow him to humble himself to admit that he is a sinner, a wretched sinner, and ask for God's forgiveness. This is a classic example of the anti-Christ spirit, a prideful spirit when a man can not humble himself to seek God's forgiveness. For Jesus humbled himself, took the form of a bondservant, and made no reputation for himself (see Phil 2:6–9). On the other hand, the devil said, "I will ascend above the heights of clouds; I will be like the Most High" (Isa 14:14). The person who claims he has done no wrong is an imposter and falsely presents himself as the Most High because only God is sinless and, therefore, righteous.

Furthermore, according to *Politico* reporter Nick Gass, Mr. Trump was asked the following question in an interview with Cal Thomas, "You have said you never felt the need to ask for God's forgiveness, and yet repentance for one's sins is a precondition to salvation. I ask you the question Jesus asked of Peter: Who do you say he is?" I will ask you to pay attention to Mr. Trump's response:

> I will be asking for forgiveness, but hopefully, I won't have to be asking for much forgiveness. As you know, I am Presbyterian and Protestant. I've had great relationships and developed even greater relationships with ministers. We have tremendous support from the clergy. I think I will be doing very well during the election with Evangelicals and with Christians.[4]

You noticed how Mr. Trump avoided saying anything about Jesus or referring to him as his Savior but talked about his relationship with ministers,

---

3. Nothstine, "Why Do I Have to Repent?," para. 7.
4. Gass, "I Hope I Don't Have to Ask," paras. 2–3.

perhaps, those who promoted him as their God-sent savior. So, Mr. Thomas went further by asking Mr. Trump again, "Who do you say Jesus is?" Then Mr. Trump said:

> Jesus to me is somebody I can think about for security and confidence. Somebody I can revere in terms of bravery and in terms of courage and, because I consider the Christian religion so important, somebody I can totally rely on in my own mind.[5]

The first and most significant attribute of Jesus to Christians is that he is their Savior. They recognize the cross where Jesus shed his blood for the forgiveness of their sins, but not for Mr. Trump. But he sees Jesus as a brave and courageous person for security and confidence, but not as a Savior. Because someone claims that he is a Christian does not make them a Christian unless they accept Jesus as their Savior, ask God for forgiveness, and walk in the light of Christ. As the Scripture says, "This is the message which we have heard from Him and declare to you, that God is light and in Him is no darkness at all. If we say that we have fellowship with Him, and walk in darkness, we lie and do not practice the truth" (1 John 1:5–6).

Even if one claims to be a Christian but walks in darkness, they lie and do not practice the truth of God's word. You cannot live like a child of the devil and claim to be a Christian; that would be making a mockery of God's word and Christianity. As the Scripture declares, "Whoever does not practice righteousness is not of God" (1 John 3:10).

Furthermore, the Lord Jesus used his teachings to illustrate expected standards of behavior for Christians. Thus, Christ's followers use the teachings of Jesus, as well as the Epistles, as a guide in their daily behaviors, and those who are not of Christ will do the opposite of the Gospels and Epistles. Jesus was also a role model for his followers and taught them how to handle life challenges. However, none of Mr. Trump's behavior is consistent with Jesus' teachings.

Forgiving Others

Forgiving those who offended or sinned against you is a must in Christendom. According to our Lord Jesus, "For if you forgive men their trespasses, your heavenly Father will also forgive you" (Matt 6:14). The significance of forgiveness was emphasized repeatedly in Jesus' teachings. He used the parable of an unforgiving servant to illustrate why we should forgive our debtors (see Matt 18:21–35). Those who have received forgiveness from

---

5. Gass, "I Hope I Don't Have to Ask," paras. 5–6.

their heavenly Father also have an obligation to forgive those who sinned against them. For those who promote Mr. Trump as a Christ follower, my question to you is, Have you ever seen or heard Mr. Trump forgive someone who offended him? Personally, I have not because Mr. Trump believes in tit for tat and does not forgive people who offended him. He does not even forgive those who refuse to promote his lies. Therefore, if someone believes he has not done anything wrong to ask God for forgiveness, like Mr. Trump, he has no incentive to forgive others. Of course, anyone who holds such a view is a deceiver and a liar. As for Christ's followers, forgiveness is central to Christian doctrine and relationship with Christ. Ephesians 4:32 says, "And be kind to one another, tenderhearted, forgiving one another, even as God in Christ forgave you."

Truthfulness

It will be extremely challenging to find a hard-core liar like Mr. Trump. One of the dangerous precedents with Mr. Trump during and after his presidency was the normalization of lies as a way of life for those on the borderline of honesty. He has been described as the most lying president of the United States. During an NBC News interview, a presidential historian, Michael Beschloss, said, "I have never seen a president in American history who has lied so continuously and so outrageously as Donald Trump, period."[6] In essence, if Mr. Trump's mouth is moving, he is lying, and shockingly enough, there are some people whose hearts are conditioned to embrace his lies. A social psychologist professor, in her commentary on the *Washington Post*, stated, "I study liars. I've never seen one like President Trump."[7] In her decades of studying liars and their lies, she thought she had a better understanding of what to expect from liars until she came across President Trump. According to her analysis, Mr. Trump's lies are malicious and numerous compared to other liars. In addition, the *Washington Post* fact checker team uncovered that Mr. Trump engaged in 30,573 false and misleading claims during his presidency.[8]

Many other politicians, including those within his Republican Party, have described him as a pathological liar, such as Ted Cruz and Mitt Romney. Also, during a CNN interview, George Conway, the husband of Kellyanne Conway, who was President Trump's administration senior counsel from 2017 to 2020, said that President Trump is "virtually incapable of telling the

---

6. Timm, "Trump versus the Truth," para. 3.
7. Depaulo, "I Study Liars," para. 1.
8. Kessler et al., "Trump's False or Misleading Claims," para. 2.

truth about anything, even when it's helpful to him. He's a pathological liar."[9] Furthermore, several of Trump's close allies have either pleaded guilty or were convicted of lying conspiracies or false statements by federal prosecutors, such as Roger Stone, Paul Manafort, Michael Cohen, George Papadopoulos, Michael Flynn, Rick Gates, etc. When people associate themselves with a pathological liar like Mr. Trump, they are more likely to be influenced by his lying spirit. Based on Mr. Trump's lying records, he is the closest to the embodiment of a lying evil spirit in the human body, unbeknownst to some Christian Evangelicals who support him. If you carefully and honestly examine his records, you will come to the same understanding.

Scripturally, Jesus described liars like Mr. Trump as children of the devil because they use lies to fulfill the desires of their father, Satan (see John 8:44). There is zero practical evidence to demonstrate that Mr. Trump is a man after God's heart or Christ follower, but a man who represents a child of the devil structured from the mother's womb to destroy America with lying lips and corrupt practices. Proverbs 58:3–4 says, "The wicked are estranged from the womb, they go astray as soon as they are born, speaking lies. Their poison is like the poison of a serpent; they are like the deaf cobra that stops its ear." Mr. Trump has used lies and deceptions all his life to pursue his life goals, such as admission to college and business practices, as some of his family members and close allies have acknowledged his dishonest practices. In the 2020 election that he lost, he resorted to his familiar playbook and used his lying lips to poison the minds of his supporters that the election was stolen from him. Even after some of his supporters and our legal system proved him otherwise, he continued to use his poisonous lying lips as a serpent to divide our country and, at the same time, blocked his ears as a deaf cobra from hearing the truth.

Mr. Trump rejects and condemns people for speaking the truth like the judges and Supreme Court justices, and then upholds liars like himself. Throughout his business practices and presidency, he had relentlessly advocated converting falsehoods into truth and truth into lies. He created a social media he uses to promote his lies and deceptions and called it "Truth Social." In his endeavor with his social media, he subconsciously began to socialize his followers to embrace lies as truth and truth as lies. Mr. Trump's effort to pervert truth is from the demonic realm to displace Christ from the United States, who is the Truth (see John 14:6), and elevate Satan, who is the Liar (see John 8:44). The heartbreaking aspect of this ungodly behavior is that there are some people, like GOP lawmakers and Christian Evangelicals, who embrace Mr. Trump's satanic move to pervert truth as lies. But the

---

9. CNN News Central, "Virtually Incapable," paras. 1–3.

Scripture says, "Lying lips are an abomination to the LORD" (Prov 12:22). Thus, God cannot endorse or approve a man whose life is shrouded with a cloud of lies and deceptions because such behaviors are an abomination before him. "Deceit is in the heart of those who devise evil" (Prov 12:20).

The practices and behaviors of Mr. Trump are surrounded with dishonesties and falsehoods, from business practices to lying to the American people about the danger of COVID-19 and his defeat in the 2020 election, and his purpose is to devise and normalize evil in the United States. Mr. Trump's behaviors can be likened to what happened in heaven when Satan said, "I will ascend above the heights of the clouds; I will be like the Most High" (Isa 14:14). In this scenario, Satan wanted to use corrupt means to pervert God's established standards of authority and power to be like God; therefore, God cast him down from heaven. Astonishingly, a third of the heavenly angels, who were supposed to know the truth, went with the imposter, Satan, who is the father of all lies. In the same manner, Mr. Trump used his toxic lying lips to try to corrupt our Constitution and established standards of electing presidents, and to force himself to be the president of the United States against the will of the people. Shockingly, a substantial number of Christian Evangelicals who were supposed to know the truth went along with Mr. Trump in an attempt to fulfill his demonic missions. However, God is faithful and loves America, and he would not allow the forces of darkness controlling Mr. Trump to succeed in their evil plots. Therefore, God ended his presidency and began to expose him and his evil plots. Proverbs 12:19 says, "The truthful lip shall be established forever, but a lying tongue is but a moment." God could not establish his presidency because of his lying lips and ungodly behaviors. Good will always prevail over evil, truth over lies, and righteousness over unrighteousness.

The fierce support of Christian Evangelicals to Mr. Trump is a mystery, in that, people who are supposed to know the truth have become supporters of one whose life contradicts every scriptural standard for a believer in Christ Jesus. No wonder Jesus, re-emphasizing what Isaiah stated, says, "These people draw to Me with their mouth and honor Me with their lips, but their heart is far from Me. And in vain they worship Me, teaching as doctrines the commandment of men" (Matt 15:8–9). If you carefully pay attention, you will notice that the Evangelical preachers who support Mr. Trump and the Republican Party are more passionate about converting people to the Republican Party than converting them to Christ. They craftily twist Scriptures to conform with their political rhetoric to present the Republican Party as a party approved by God and to persuade people to support Mr. Trump. God forbid, if Mr. Trump ever becomes president again, he will persuade these Evangelical leaders and their false prophets, as we saw in the 2020 election, to preach about Mr. Trump as the awaiting messiah, since according to Mr. Trump, he has never done anything wrong; therefore, he is holy and righteous. The Evangelical preachers who present the Republican Party as God's party will easily present Mr. Trump to their followers as their messiah. Satan is an imposter, always creating a fake portion of God's deeds. The Scripture describes Jesus as a Savior who knew no sin (see 2 Cor 5:21), and Mr. Trump has been laying the groundwork that he had made no mistake and had no reason to ask forgiveness from God, which suggests he knew no sin. If you also listen to his speeches, he often says that everything he does, he is doing for his supporters, when there is no evidence of Mr. Trump making any sacrifice for the benefit of others, but for himself. Such speeches indicate a man elevating himself to the position of a savior, which is an imposter.

Love instead of Hate

Mr. Trump does not hide his hateful expression from people who do not comply with his lies and corruption, and also toward people of color. He labeled the Black Lives Matter protests as "terrorists" and "thugs" while telling a far-right hate group, Proud Boys, to "stand back and stand by."[10] Through his hateful speeches, he made it possible for Asian Americans to be targeted for hate crimes by calling COVID-19 "Chinese virus" and "Kung flu." Moreover, 60 percent of Americans believe that Mr. Trump's presidency promoted division in the United States, and only 12 percent thought he tried to unite our country.[11] The Scripture says, "Whoever hides hatred has lying lips, and whoever spreads slander is a fool" (Prov 10:18). Interestingly, lying lips and hatred are intertwined according to the Scripture, and both are associated with Mr. Trump. Also, 1 John 3:15 says, "Whoever hates his brother is a murderer, and you know that no murderer has eternal life abiding in him." The use of brother and neighbor in the Scriptures does not necessarily mean a blood-related person or one who lives close to you. It also implies other people and fellow citizens. Thus, the practice of hate because of a person's race or national origin is scripturally defined as murder, and such a person will not have eternal life in him. In addition, hate for other people is also hate toward God who created them. The Scripture says:

> If someone says, "I love God," and hates his brother, he is a liar; for he who does not love his brother whom he has seen, how can

10. Ellis, "'Stand Back and Stand By,'" para. 2.
11. Moreno, "Majority Thinks Trump," para 1.

he love God whom he has not seen? And this commandment we have from Him: that he who loves God must love his brother also. (1 John 4:20)

So, all the far-right hate groups like White supremacists, White nationalists, Proud Boys, etc., are all haters of God and murderers; therefore, they have no portion in the kingdom of God. The question then is, Why do some Christian Evangelicals form a coalition with groups that God clearly condemned in the Bible, and deceptively present them as a group approved by God? Furthermore, there are behaviors God hates, and they are an abomination before him, and if you look carefully, you will see that Mr. Trump exhibits all of them. Proverbs 6:16–19 says:

> These six things the LORD hates,
> Yes, seven are an abomination to Him:
> A proud look,
> A lying tongue,
> Hands that shed innocent blood,
> A heart that devises wicked plans,
> Feet that are swift in running to evil,
> A false witness who speaks lies,
> And one who sows discord among brethren.

Mr. Trump has a prideful spirit, which does not allow him to accept the fact that he lost the 2020 election. The spirit of pride that controls him also influences his lying tongue to continue with his baseless claims that the election was stolen from him. The promotion of his lies led to the shedding of innocent blood on January 6, 2021, during the Capitol riot, though he denies any accountability for the insurrection. He devised wicked plans after he lost the election by creating fake electors, calling state election officials to give him fake votes, promoting falsehoods about the election, filing frivolous lawsuits, etc. Mr. Trump's feet are swift in the running to evil; he is drawn to hate groups and those who are willing to execute his corrupt bidding. Donald Trump is both a false witness who speaks lies and drawn to other false witnesses who speak lies, such as false witness of a suitcase of ballots and voting machine obscurities. Mr. Trump is skilled in sowing seeds of discord, as evidenced in his family, supporters, the Republican Party, and the nation at large. This is a man structured from the womb for evil, and there will *never* be anything good for the nation from Mr. Trump but falsehoods, corruption, and destruction.

However, the Lord Jesus has established a new commandment for those who believe in him to love one another. John 13:34–35 says, "A new commandment I give to you, that you love one another; as I have loved you, that you also love one another. By this all will know that you are My disciples if you have love for one another."

The hate groups, including individuals who hate others because of their external characteristics, are not born of God; therefore, they do not know God and cannot love other people, especially those who are different from them. The Scripture says in 1 John 4:7, "Beloved, let us love one another, for love is of God; and everyone who loves is born of God and knows God."

INCORRECT ASSOCIATION OF BIBLICAL CYRUS WITH MR. TRUMP

Some Evangelical preachers have labeled Mr. Trump as modern-day Cyrus in their deceptive effort to persuade other Christians to support and vote for a man who does not recognize God in his life nor care about the things of God.

To label Mr. Trump a modern-day Cyrus because he recognized Jerusalem as the capital of Israel is incorrect and deceptive. The person who should have been labeled modern-day Cyrus was President Harry Truman because what he did for the Israelites coincides with the acts of Cyrus. Let's review what Cyrus did for the Israelites and compare that to what President Truman or President Trump did for the Israelites. Cyrus was an ancient king of Persia (539–530 BC), who allowed the Israelites to return to their homeland and rebuild the temple in Jerusalem. The Jews were invaded and taken into captivity by Babylonian King Nebuchadnezzar because of their idolatry and disobedience to God's commandment (see 2 Kgs 24–25). During their captivity, they were ruled by four different kings: Nebuchadnezzar, Belshazzar, Darius, and Cyrus. To fulfill Isaiah's and Jeremiah's prophecies concerning the return of the Jews (see 2 Chr 36:21–23; Isa 44:28—45:1; Jer 29:10), God inspired Cyrus to issue a decree that allowed the Jews to return to their homeland to rebuild the temple. Ezra 1:1–4 says:

> Now in the first year of Cyrus king of Persia, that the word of the LORD by the mouth of Jeremiah might be fulfilled, the LORD stirred up the spirit of Cyrus king of Persia, so that he made a proclamation throughout all his kingdom, and also put it in writing, saying, Thus says Cyrus king of Persia: All the kingdoms of the earth the LORD God of heaven has given me. And He has commanded me to build Him a house at Jerusalem which is in Judah. Who is among you of all His people? May his God be with him, and let him go up to Jerusalem which is in Judah, and build the house of the LORD God of Israel (He is

> God), which is in Jerusalem. And whoever is left in any place where he dwells, let the men of his place help him with silver and gold, with goods and livestock, besides the freewill offerings for the house of God which is in Jerusalem.

To Compare King Cyrus's actions to President Truman and President Trump, the following factors are considered: First, Cyrus issued a decree that allowed the exiled Jews to return to their country and re-inhabit their homeland, as well as rebuild the temple. On March 14, 1948, President Harry Truman was the first world leader to issue a statement of recognition to acknowledge Israel as an independent state, eleven minutes after its founding.[12] President Truman's action prompted other nations to recognize Israel as a nation, and the exiled Jews around the world eventually began to return and reclaim their homeland. Second, Cyrus requested help from individuals and nations to the Jews in the form of silver, gold, and livestock to enable them to rebuild the temple. In comparison, President Truman's recognition of Israel as a nation was followed by the United States' economic and military assistance to the nation of Israel. But the only thing President Trump did was to recognize Jerusalem as the capital of Israel, which has nothing to do with the return of exiled Jews. So, it is misleading to label Mr. Trump as a modern-day Cyrus. Since 1948, the US has been the strongest ally of the nation of Israel than any other country. Both Democratic and Republican presidents have maintained strong relationships with the nation of Israel.

Furthermore, some have presented Mr. Trump as King Jehu in the Bible. A political preacher in the Sid Roth program promoted Mr. Trump as biblical Jehu in a positive tone and undermined Mr. Trump's corrupt and ungodly behaviors. He did not provide the Bible chapter and verses so that his audience could read for themselves but presented the characters in a manner to justify Mr. Trump's corruption. The degree some Evangelical preachers are willing to compromise truth for political proselytization is shocking. They have shifted from presenting Jesus to the unsaved to presenting partisan politics. Second Kings 9–10 details the story of Jehu. Even though God used Jehu to bring judgment upon the house of King Ahab, Jehu went beyond God's commandment by killing other people he was not commanded to kill, like the slaughtering of the relatives of the king of Judah, Ahaziah.

> And he arose and departed and went to Samaria. On the way, at Beth Eked of the Shepherds, Jehu met with the brothers of Ahaziah king of Judah, and said, "Who are you?" So they answered,

12. Truman Library, "Recognition of Israel," para. 3.

"We are the brothers of Ahaziah; we have come down to greet the sons of the king and the sons of the queen mother." And he said, "Take them alive!" So they took them alive, and killed them at the well of Beth Eked, forty-two men; and he left none of them. (2 Kgs 10:12–14)

In addition, even though Jehu carried out God's commandment, he was controlled by pride and self-ego, and therefore the Scripture says this about him, "But Jehu took no heed to walk in the law of the LORD God of Israel with all his heart; for he did not depart from the sins of Jeroboam, who had made Israel sin" (2 Kgs 10:31).

There are not many positive things to say about Jehu to try to present him in a positive manner so that one can justify promoting Donald Trump as a godly man. One thing is clear, Mr. Trump only cares for his own zeal, not for God or anybody else.

SUMMARY

God's word and commandments are contained in the Holy Bible and the Bible serves as a standard for us to evaluate characters that are godly or ungodly. As God's elect, we should always embrace the truth of God's word at all times, including in situations we might consider to be inconvenient. Displacing God's truth with lies is consequential. The consequences of Adam and Eve believing the devil's lies instead of God's truth brought long-lasting, damaging consequences to mankind. The lies the Christians embrace today could have enduring consequences for future generations. The truth of God's word and the interpretation is at a dangerous crossroads in our country today due to partisan politics. It is time for the remnants in the body of Christ to rise, debunk the lies of partisan politics, and proclaim God's truth.

Conclusion

This book challenges Christian Evangelical leaders to examine their alliance with the Republican Party carefully, which has put them in a compromising position to uphold even the GOP's objectionable policies as biblical truths. Entering into a secret deal with the Republican Party instead of a deal with God is unbiblical and reflects distrust in God's ability to intervene in our country with prayers. On the other hand, this book does not suggest that Christians cannot partake in politics because it is through politics that policies that affect people's lives are enacted. However, the problem is partisan politics that compels one to compromise biblical standards to please their political party, to falsely promote their party's agendas as biblical, and to refuse to condemn ungodly practices within their political party. Christians' participation in politics should be done in truth, in the fear of God, and putting God first, and not a man or their political party. There is always a tendency for some people, after experiencing God's blessing, to forget the source of their blessing, and they begin to compromise their faith and displace God's truths with their religious and political fallacies, as the Pharisees did. It is not surprising for the Scripture to say, "There is none who understands; there is none who seeks after God" (Rom 3:11).

Furthermore, this book confronts the Christian Evangelical leaders who portray themselves as God's representatives, as the Pharisees portrayed themselves during the days of the Lord Jesus; however, their practices contradicted biblical teachings. Jesus frequently confronted the Pharisees, who engaged in double standard lifestyles because they talked about other people's sins while covering their own, and they condemned other people for the same sin they themselves were committing. It is hypocritical to talk about abortion for political purposes and not use the same passion to condemn hatred and discrimination toward marginalized groups in our country, for both acts are murder before God. It is deceptive to claim to be pro-life and then support or remain silent about reckless gun laws enacted by GOP governors and lawmakers that kill about forty thousand Americans every year. It is also hypocritical to call social programs for the poor socialism when your parsonage and ministry receive government programs you labeled socialism. It is two-faced to speak ills about the social programs for the poor while endorsing or being silent about the social programs for the rich. Engaging in the same hypocritical behaviors that were common among the biblical Pharisees, that is, while broadcasting everything the Democrats did wrong, you kept silent about the wrongs of the Republicans, which is ungodly behavior. The biblical approach has always been that judgment should begin within, not outside. According to the Scripture, "Judgment begins at the house of God" (1 Peter 4:17). Thus, if you present the Republican Party as a party endorsed by God, judgment should begin within the party, not the Democrats. If you notice in the Bible, God judged the Israelites when they sinned and was more likely to judge other nations when they mistreated or attacked the Israelites.

Additionally, the New Testament teachings focused on challenging Christians to do right and rebuke those in the body of Christ for biblical violation, not those outside the body of Christ. Thus, I challenge these Christian Evangelical leaders to judge their political party first before judging the Democrats. If the unspeakable evil Donald Trump has done to our country and democracy had been done by a Democratic president, it would have dominated your pulpit preaching every Sunday. But every one of you who is quick to preach socialism and preach against Democratic presidents has been silent and pretended as if the lies, chaos, and betrayal of our democracy by Donald Trump did not happen. Your silence is complicity to Donald Trump's lies and effort to overturn the 2020 election results. If you are not using the same passion you use to preach against socialism to condemn the ungodly deeds of the Republican Party, you are displaying the same characteristics of the Pharisees. Do you think that God exonerates the ungodliness of the Republican Party and their presidents while vilifying the Democrats and their presidents? If you think so, it indicates you do not understand biblical doctrines. But if you do understand biblical doctrines and do not practice them, it is a sin, and you are worse than the people you condemn. The Scripture says, "Therefore, to him who knows to do good and does not do it, to him it is a sin" (Jas 4:17).

The Pharisees also judged others and did not judge themselves. But the Scripture states, "For if we would judge ourselves, we would not be judged" (1 Cor 11:31). So, these modern-day Pharisees must first judge themselves and the evil within their party before judging others.

Yes, affirmatively, God is not a Republican and could not possibly be a Republican or endorse Republican Party agendas for several reasons discussed throughout this book. However, this does not suggest either that he is a Democrat. You may ask then, "Which party does God belong to?" Contrary to popular view among Christian Evangelicals, God does not belong to any political party, and neither does he endorse any party.

Furthermore, it is important to avoid being victimized by groupthink, which often involves relinquishing one's right to think independently. Groupthink can be very dangerous because it forces people to turn off their minds, compromise their integrity, and engage in unbiblical behaviors. However, God never told us to turn off our minds, as he has given us a spirit of power, of love, and of sound mind (see 2 Tim 1:7). The sound mind here indicates an intelligent mind, rational mind, and understanding. We are to be followers of Christ, not men. One of the major issues I observe with Evangelical preachers is that whenever a preacher comes up with a concept, especially politically related issues, others will immediately jump on the bandwagon to start preaching the same thing without any spiritual evaluation to establish the validity of the concept. The drive to conform with most Evangelicals that belong to the Republican Party led to a series of false prophecies during the 2020 presidential election. They desired to hear that Donald Trump would win a second term, so they all prophesied the same thing according to the desires of their hearts. If a true prophet had prophesied otherwise, he would have been demonized, ostracized, stigmatized, and shunned. The rejection of the truth is typical behavior of hypocrites. As it was in the days of Jesus, the Pharisees shunned anyone who disagreed with them or acknowledged Jesus as the Messiah. If Jesus were to come today as it was in the days of the Bible, some of these modern-day Evangelicals who have interjected politics in their preaching would crucify him as they did in the past. They would label him a socialist, a friend of the abortionists and sinners because of his association with them, not because he approves of their lifestyles but because of his love toward them and to save them. They would crucify Jesus because he would not support them in stoning a woman who was caught in the very act of committing an abortion. The fact that Jesus would set her free with the admonition to "sin no more" would suggest to them that Jesus supports abortion. They forgot that Jesus came and died for the sinners, not for the self-proclaimed righteous individuals who have never sinned since childhood.

Jesus would not conform to the self-righteousness and cultural conservatism portrayed by the Republican Party and the modern-day Pharisees, which has nothing to do with biblical teaching. If we were to assume that mid-tribulation is true, guess who will give the antichrist the platform to operate; it would be these modern-day Evangelicals who promote the Republican Party as God's party. Because the antichrist would not come as a Democrat, but as a conservative with deceptive activities and enter into a peace treaty with Israel; thus, the modern-day Pharisees would quickly jump on his bandwagon, proclaiming modern-day Cyrus. If you missed the handwriting on the wall concerning the 2020 presidential election, you would most likely be easily deceived when the antichrist appears, that is, assuming that mid-tribulation prevails. Mr. Trump displays the characteristics of one who represents the precursor of the antichrist. He is not the antichrist but a precursor of the antichrist. Spiritual blindness has kept many from seeing the writing on the wall about Mr. Trump. The last six chapters of this book presented warning signs that were overlooked by Christians who overwhelmingly supported Donald Trump without reservation. Remember what Jesus says, "For false christs and false prophets will rise and show great signs and wonders to deceive, if possible, even the elect" (Matt 24:24).

FINAL VIGNETTE

The transformative power of the word of God has been distorted to conform and align with cultural contours. Truth has been demeaned, while falsehood has been elevated to take the appearance of truth. People's minds are riddled with fables; they can no longer discern the truth or distinguish truth from lies. Evil has multiplied and has been protected and sometimes rewarded, while good has been debased and sometimes punished. The created has been elevated and honored above the Creator. Anarchy has become the order of the day and has taken on a different social meaning, contingent on who is the vigilante and the victim. People are no longer sanctioned for violating the Constitution and breaking laws and orders that have kept our society safe and together but have been elevated as heroes. Justice is no longer neutral or objectively applied to all on an equal basis but has been swayed to favor the privileged while the marginalized suffer. Dehumanization of marginalized groups has been normalized as acceptable behavior, and people are devoid of consciousness; they have become desensitized and lack knowledge of God. Dereliction of duty has been praised; elected and appointed officials are no longer obliging themselves to fulfill their oaths of office. Many march aimlessly toward their destruction, and they take unwitting individuals along with them. No one pauses to ponder about the destructive path they have taken, even with all the warning signs along the pathway indicating that their chosen path leads to destruction. Yet, they continue to march forward aimlessly and unwisely, without the knowledge and fear of God, toward their wit's end. Who can help this generation? Who can deliver them from their chosen destructive path? The preacher, who is supposed to be the light to those in darkness, has not been helpful, for he has chosen to masterfully pervert God's word to conform to his political party agenda. He has abandoned his calling to please a political party rather than God. Indeed, the path to destruction is wide, and many travel that path while the path to life is narrow. Only a few people travel through the narrow path, although there is nothing attractive about the narrow path. The people who travel through the narrow path are intentional with a clear and confident purpose that the path they have chosen is the right path that leads to eternal life, even though there is nothing attractive about the narrow path. But people who travel the wide path do not even know why they are traveling through the wide path, and some think that since many people are traveling through the wide path, it must be the right path. Unconsciously, they collectively forbid themselves from saying anything negative about the wide path they have chosen or embracing any knowledge that will lead them to the truth. To some, the wide path appears enticing, fun, and devoid of God's knowledge. Anything that will espouse the knowledge of God's existence is widely rejected. Thus, the philosophical concepts of existentialism and humanism have become dominant belief systems and the modus operandi. Again, who can deliver this generation from self-destruction? The only hope for this generation and our country is the hope of glory, Jesus Christ, the Son of God and the Savior of the world. Therefore, awake, O mighty men and women, and respond to your calling, the calling of your Savior; for if he is lifted up, he will draw all people unto himself (see John 12:32), not your political party. The preaching of your political party agendas cannot save a single soul or draw men to Christ, and such practice is heresy. Jesus alone is the way, the truth, and the life. No man comes to the Father except through him (John 14:6). Thus, it is not through your political party that people would be saved, but *only* through JESUS. Amen!

Bibliography

Akulich, Maria, and Jerzy Kazmierczyk. "The Socio-Economic Approach to the Study of Main Economic Systems. Socialism and Capitalism." *Management* 22.1 (Sep 2018) 238–50. http://dx.doi.org/10.2478/manment-2018-0017.

Alemany, Jacqueline, et al. "Jan. 6 Committee Refers Trump to Justice Dept. for Criminal Charges." *Washington Post*, Dec 19, 2022. https://www.washingtonpost.com/politics/2022/12/19/trump-referrals-jan-6-committee/.

Alter, Charlotte. "Republicans Are Less Likely Than Democrats to Believe Women Who Make Sexual Assault Accusations: Survey." *Time*, Dec 6, 2017. https://time.com/5049665/republicans-democrats-believe-sexual-assault-accusations-survey/.

Amri, Farnoush. "Explainer: How Fake Electors Tried to Throw Results to Trump." AP News, Feb 21, 2022. https://apnews.com/article/capitol-siege-joe-biden-presidential-elections-election-2020-electoral-college-311f88768b65f7196f52a4757dc162e4.

Ankel, Sophia. "Mary Trump Says Her Uncle, President Trump, Will Spend the Transition Period 'Breaking Stuff' with 'Vengeance.'" *Business Insider*, Nov 8, 2020. https://www.businessinsider.com/mary-trump-president-trump-will-lash-out-during-transition-period-2020-11.

Assets Pearson's School. "The President's Job Description." Accessed December 10, 2021. https://assets.pearsonschool.com/asset_mgr/legacy/200938/section1_job description_26523_1.pdf.

Astor, Maggie. "Trump Is Disqualified from 2024 Ballot, Colorado Court Says in Explosive Ruling." *New York Times*, Dec 19, 2023. https://www.nytimes.com/2023/12/19/us/politics/trump-colorado-ballot-14th-amendment.html.

Azizli, Nicole, et al. "Lies and Crimes: Dark Triad, Misconduct, and High-Stakes Deception." *Personality and Individual Differences* 89 (Jan 2016) 34–39. https://doi.org/10.1016/j.paid.2015.09.034.

Balevic, Katie. "A Christian Group Has Amassed More Than 12,000 Signatures to Oust the Tennessee Republican Leader Who Expelled Two Black Lawmakers." *Business Insider*, Apr 15, 2023. https://www.businessinsider.in/politics/world/news/a-christian-group-has-amassed-more-than-12000-signatures-to-oust-the-tennessee-republican-leader-who-expelled-two-black-lawmakers/articleshow/99523040.cms.

Balsamo, Michael. "Disputing Trump, Barr Says No Widespread Election Fraud." AP News, Dec 1, 2020. https://apnews.com/article/barr-no-widespread-election-fraud-b5809f588690776fcbb1dfc8c6e7308b.

Barnes, Daniel, and Summer Concepcion. "Rudy Giuliani Defamed Former Georgia Election Workers, a Federal Judge Rules." NBC News, Aug 23, 2023. https://www.nbcnews.com/politics/2020-election/judge-rules-rudy-giuliani-defamed-georgia-election-workers-rcna102555.

Barnes, Daniel, et al. "Rudy Giuliani Hit With $148M Verdict for Defaming Two Georgia Election Workers." NBC News, Dec 15, 2023. https://www.msn.com/en-us/news/politics/rudy-giuliani-hit-with-148m-verdict-for-defaming-two-georgia-election-workers/ar-AA1lzwkX?ocid=msedgdhp&pc=HCTS&cvid=643e48bfb49849d8828fdb2171dcf692&ei=45.

Basu, Zachary. "Paul Manafort Sentenced to Total of 7.5 Years in Prison." *Axios*, Mar 13, 2019. https://www.axios.com/2019/03/13/paul-manafort-sentenced-years-prison-russia-mueller-investigation.

Basu, Zachary, and Lauren Meier. "Rick Gates Pleads Guilty to Conspiracy, Lying to Investigators." *Axios*, Feb 23, 2018. https://www.axios.com/2018/02/23/rick-gates-pleads-guilty-to-conspiracy-lying1519407041.

BBC News. "Profile: Nicaraguan President Daniel Ortega: From Revolutionary Leader to Opposition Hate Figure." Jul 19, 2018. https://www.bbc.com/news/world-latin-america-15544315.

———. "Trump Sides with Russia against FBI at Helsinki Summit." Jul 16, 2018. https://www.bbc.com/news/world-europe-44852812.

BerryDunn. "Maricopa County Procurement Evaluation Voting System and Related Equipment." *Maricopa County*, Jul 2021. https://www.maricopa.gov/DocumentCenter/View/70166/Procurement-Evaluation-of-Voting-System-and-Related-Equipment-Report.

Biggs, M. Antonio, et al. "Understanding Why Women Seek Abortions in the US." *BMC Women's Health* 13 (Jul 2013) 1–13. https://bmcwomenshealth.biomedcentral.com/articles/10.1186/1472-6874-13-29.

Billeaud, Jacques, and Michael Kunzelman. "CEO Who Threw Chair inside Capitol on Jan. 6 Gets Jail Time." AP News, Nov 12, 2021. https://apnews.com/article/business-chicago-illinois-capitol-siege-b7b2f67f5d515322855b64faf788e617.

Blinder, Alan S., and Mark W. Watson. "Presidents and the U.S. Economy: An Econometric Exploration." *American Economic Review* 106.4 (Apr 2016) 1015–45 http://dx.doi.org/10.1257/aer.20140913.

Bloom, Laura Begley. "Ranked: The 20 Happiest Countries in the World in 2022." *Forbes*, Mar 18, 2022. https://www.forbes.com/sites/laurabegleybloom/2022/03/18/ranked-the-20-happiest-countries-in-the-world-in-2022/?sh=7e6fe4ea35d5.

Bolton, Alexander. "Senate GOP Rallies behind Romney Call for Winnowing Anti-Trump Field." *Hill*, Jul 28, 2023. https://thehill.com/homenews/senate/4124078-senate-gop-romney-winnowing-anti-trump-field/.

Boschma, Janie. "Mass Shootings in the US: 2022 Could Be the Second-Highest Year." CNN, Nov 23, 2022. https://www.cnn.com/2022/11/23/us/2022-mass-shootings-tracking-second-highest/index.html.

Boyette, Chris, et al. "Guatemalan Boy Died of Flu and a Bacterial Infection while in US Custody, Autopsy Shows." CNN, Apr 2, 2019. https://www.cnn.com/2019/04/02/us/guatemala-felipe-gomez-alonzo-autopsy/index.html.

Bradner, Eric, and Catherine Treyz. "Romney Implores: Bring Down Trump." CNN, Mar 3, 2016. https://www.cnn.com/2016/03/03/politics/mitt-romney-presidential-race-speech/index.html.
Brigham, Bob. "Here's How Jason Miller's Jan. 6 Testimony Documented Trump's Potential Criminal Intent." *Raw Story*, Mar 2, 2022. https://www.rawstory.com/jason-miller-jan-6/.
Britzky, Haley. "George Papadopoulos Ordered to Report to Prison." *Axios*, Nov 25, 2018. https://www.axios.com/2018/11/25/george-papadopoulos-prison-mueller-investigation.
Bromwich, Jonah, et al. "Trump's Company Gets Maximum Punishment for Evading Taxes." *New York Times*, Jan 13, 2023. https://www.nytimes.com/2023/01/13/nyregion/trump-organization-tax-fraud.html.
Brumback, Kate. "Giuliani Concedes He Made Public Comments Falsely Claiming Georgia Election Workers Committed Fraud." AP News, Jul 26, 2023. https://apnews.com/article/giuliani-georgia-election-workers-lawsuit-false-statements-afc64a565ee778c6914a1a69dc756064.
———. "Lawyer Kenneth Chesebro Pleads Guilty over Efforts to Overturn Trump's 2020 Loss in Georgia." AP News, Oct 20, 2023. https://apnews.com/article/chesebro-jury-selection-georgia-election-indictment-2e558eefdffd9c1eaa7ec8c31bf76044.
Brumback, Kate, and Sudhin Thanawala. "Bail Bondsman Charged alongside Trump in Georgia Pleads Guilty, Becoming the First Defendant to Do So." AP News, Sep 29, 2023. https://apnews.com/article/jeffrey-clark-georgia-federal-court-64183e3dc09d1f2e03fc4b4dab1c2bdb.
Bump, Philip. "The Selective Socialism of Donald Trump: Farmers, Yes. Poor Families, No." *Washington Post*, Jul 23, 2019. https://www.washingtonpost.com/politics/2019/07/23/selective-socialism-donald-trump-farmers-yes-poor-families-no/.
Bureau of Labor Statistics. "The Unemployment Situation—January 2023." *Bureau of Labor Statistics*, Feb 3, 2023. https://www.bls.gov/news.release/pdf/empsit.pdf.
Buseck, Craig von. "Prophetic Voices on the Election of Barak Obama." CBN, Nov 13, 2008. https://www1.cbn.com/ChurchWatch/archive/2008/11/13/prophetic-voices-on-the-election-of-barack-obama.
Caldera, Camille. "Fact Check: Biden, Like Trump, Received Multiple Draft Deferments from Vietnam." *USA Today*, Sep 17, 2020. https://www.usatoday.com/story/news/factcheck/2020/09/16/fact-check-biden-received-multiple-draft-deferments-vietnam/5809482002/.
Cameron, Chris. "These Are the People Who Died in Connection with the Capitol Riot." *New York Times*, Oct 13, 2022. https://www.nytimes.com/2022/01/05/us/politics/jan-6-capitol-deaths.html.
Campbell, Jacquelyn, et al. "Risk Factors for Femicide in Abusive Relationships: Results from a Multisite Case Control Study." *American Journal of Public Health*, 93.7 (Jul 2023) 1089–97. http://doi.org/10.2105/AJPH.93.7.1089.
Cappelletti, Joey. "Michigan Charges 16 Fake Electors for Donald Trump with Election Laws and Forgery Felonies." AP News, Jul 18, 2023. https://apnews.com/article/fake-elector-michigan-republican-df7803fca3862be713d9d6d29fb77e81.
Cardoso, Jodi Berger. "Running to Stand Still: Trauma Symptoms, Coping Strategies, and Substance Use Behaviors in Unaccompanied Migrant Youth." *Children*

and Youth Services Review 92 (Sep 2018) 143–52. https://doi.org/10.1016/j.childyouth.2018.04.018.

Carroll, Rebecca. "Margaret Garner." *New York Times*, Accessed May 7, 2021. https://www.nytimes.com/interactive/2019/obituaries/margaret-garner-overlooked.html.

CBS Miami. "Deaths Nearly Triple since 'Stand Your Ground' Enacted." Mar 20, 2012. https://miami.cbslocal.com/2012/03/20/deaths-nearly-triple-since-stand-your-ground-enacted/.

Center for Disease Control and Prevention. "Firearms Violence Prevention." Accessed May 2021. https://www.cdc.gov/violenceprevention/firearms/fastfact.html.

———. "Injury Prevention and Control." Accessed November 23, 2021. https://www.cdc.gov/injury/wisqars/fatal.html.

Cheney, Kyle. "Supreme Court Backs House Effort to Obtain Trump Tax Returns." *Politico*, Nov 22, 2022. https://www.politico.com/news/2022/11/22/supreme-court-backs-house-effort-to-obtain-trump-tax-returns-00070530.

Cheng, Cheng, and Mark Hoekstra. "Does Strengthening Self-Defense Law Deter Crime or Escalate Violence? Evidence from Expansions to Castle Doctrine." *Journal of Human Resources* 48.3 (2013) 821–53. https://www.jstor.org/stable/23799103.

Chosen People Ministries. "U.S. Presidents and Israel: 1948 to Today." Accessed May 7, 2021. https://www.chosenpeople.com/u-s-presidents-israel-1948-today/.

Christina, Greta. "Eight Secular Scientists Who Changed the World: Atheists and Agnostics Have Made Some of Our Most Groundbreaking Discoveries." *Salon*, Aug 21, 2012. https://www.salon.com/2012/08/21/eight_areligious_scientists_who_changed_the_world/.

Ciliberto, Gina, and Stephanie Russell-Kraft. "They Invaded the Capitol Saying 'Jesus Is My Savior. Trump Is My President.'" *Sojourners*, Jan 7, 2021. https://sojo.net/articles/they-invaded-capitol-saying-jesus-my-savior-trump-my-president.

Cillizza, Chris. "Here's Why Fighting the Affordable Care Act Means So Much to Republicans." CNN, Jun 17, 2021. https://www.cnn.com/2021/06/17/politics/affordable-care-act-obamacare-scotus-ruling/index.html.

Clark, Travis. "The Most and Least Trusted News Anchors in the US." *Business Insider*, Nov 13, 2018. https://www.businessinsider.com/most-and-least-trusted-news-anchors-in-us-lester-holt-sean-hannity-2018-11.

Clauw, Michael. "Watchdog Requests IRS Investigate True the Vote for Enriching Key Employees and Directors." Campaign for Accountability, Jun 5, 2023. https://campaignforaccountability.org/watchdog-requests-irs-investigate-true-the-vote-for-enriching-key-employees-and-directors/.

Clement, Kim. "The Middle East: Obama Prophecy by Kim Clement." *Identity Network*, Accessed December 7, 2021. https://www.identitynetwork.net/apps/articles/default.asp?articleid=45106&columnid=.

CNN News Central. "George Conway says President Trump is 'virtually incapable of telling the truth about anything, even when it's helpful to him. He's a pathological liar.'" Twitter (video) Jan 22, 2020. https://twitter.com/NewsCentralCNN/status/1220010768088944641.

Cohen, Susan A. "Abortion and Women of Color: The Bigger Picture." *Guttmacher Institute*, Aug 6, 2008. https://www.guttmacher.org/gpr/2008/08/abortion-and-women-color-bigger-picture.

Bibliography

Concepcion, Summer. "Three Fake Electors Charged in Georgia Election Probe Seek to Move Cases to Federal Court." NBC News, Sep 20, 2023. https://www.nbcnews.com/politics/donald-trump/three-fake-electors-charged-georgia-election-probe-seek-move-cases-fed-rcna107952.

Corn, David. "The Republican Party Is Racist and Soulless. Just Ask This Veteran GOP Strategist." *Mother Jones*, Sep/Oct 2020. https://www.motherjones.com/politics/2020/08/racism-republican-party-stuart-stevens/.

Cox, Jeff. "Jobs Report Shows Increase of 517,000 in January, Crushing Estimates, as Unemployment Rate Hit 53-Lear low." CNBC, Feb 3, 2023. https://www.cnbc.com/2023/02/03/jobs-report-january-2023-.html.

Criss, Doug. "A Judge Has Finalized a $25 Million Settlement for Students Who Claim That They Were Defrauded by Trump University." CNN, Apr 10, 2018. https://www.cnn.com/2018/04/10/politics/trump-university-settlement-finalized-trnd/index.html.

Culliton, Kathleen. "Jenna Ellis Was Told Trump Was 'Not Going to Leave' White House after Losing Election" *Raw Story*, Nov 13, 2023. https://www.rawstory.com/jenna-ellis-donald-trump-not-leaving/.

Daniels, Cheyanne. "Only Three Black Governors Have Ever Been Elected in US History." *Hill*, Nov 23, 2022. https://thehill.com/homenews/state-watch/3747228-only-three-black-governors-have-ever-been-elected-in-us-history/.

Dearman, Eleanor. "Texas Law Enforcement 'Skeptical and Nervous' about Constitutional Carry Bill." *Fort Worth Star-Telegram*, May 12, 2021. https://www.star-telegram.com/news/politics-government/article251298328.html.

Demby, Gene. "How Party and Place Shape Americans' View on Discrimination." NPR, Jul 2, 2017. https://www.npr.org/sections/codeswitch/2017/07/02/535048161/how-party-and-place-shape-americans-views-on-discrimination.

Department of Homeland Security. "Border Security Overview." Accessed May 10, 2021. https://www.dhs.gov/topics/border-security.

———. "The Border Wall System Is Deployed, Effective, and Disrupting Criminals and Smugglers." Accessed May 12, 2021. https://www.dhs.gov/news/2020/10/29/border-wall-system-deployed-effective-and-disrupting-criminals-and-smugglers.

Department of Justice. "Two Sentenced for Assaulting Law Enforcement in Lower West Terrace Tunnel During Jan. 6 Capitol Breach." November 3, 2023. https://www.justice.gov/usao-dc/pr/two-sentenced-assaulting-law-enforcement-lower-west-terrace-tunnel-and-other-charges.

DePaulo, Bella. "I Study Liars. I've Never Seen One Like President Trump." *Washington Post*, Dec 8, 2017. https://www.washingtonpost.com/outlook/i-study-liars-ive-never-seen-one-like-president-trump/2017/12/07/4e529efe-da3f-11e7-a841-2066faf731ef_story.html.

DePaulo, B. M., et al. "Lying in Everyday Life." *Journal of Personality and Social Psychology* 70.5 (1996) 979–95. https://doi.org/10.1037/0022-3514.70.5.979.

Despart, Zach. "Texas Attorney General Ken Paxton Acquitted on All 16 Articles of Impeachment." *Texas Tribune*, Sep 16, 2023. https://www.texastribune.org/2023/09/16/ken-paxton-acquitted-impeachment-texas-attorney-general/.

Despart, Zach, and James Barragan. "Texas AG Ken Paxton Impeached, Suspended from Duties; Will Face Senate Trial." *Texas Tribune*, May 27, 2023. https://www.texastribune.org/2023/05/27/ken-paxton-impeached-texas-attorney-general/.

Dhinakaran, Paul. "Prophecy Update: US Presidential Election 2016—Prophecy by Dr. Paul Dhinakaran." YouTube video, Sep 11, 2015. https://www.youtube.com/watch?v=kRg48VaYQcQ.

Dickson, Caitlin. "Dominion, Fox News Settle Defamation Suit for Stunning $787, Averting Trial." *Yahoo News*, Apr 13, 2023. https://www.aol.com/news/dominion-fox-news-settle-defamation-205038883.html.

Dimock, Michael, and John Gramlich. "How America Changed during Donald Trump's Presidency." *Pew Research Center*, Jan 29, 2021. https://www.pewresearch.org/2021/01/29/how-america-changed-during-donald-trumps-presidency/.

Domonoske, Camila. "Judge Approves $25 Million Settlement of Trump University Lawsuit." NPR, *The Two-Way*, Mar 31, 2017. https://www.npr.org/sections/thetwo-way/2017/03/31/522199535/judge-approves-25-million-settlement-of-trump-university-lawsuit.

Dorman, John L. "DC Metropolitan Police Department Officer Michael Fanone Says 'It's 'Disgraceful'' That Only One GOP Congress Man Appeared at a Capitol Hill Event Commemorating January 6." *Business Insider*, Jan 7, 2023. https://www.businessinsider.in/politics/world/news/former-dc-metropolitan-police-department-officer-michael-fanone-says-its-disgraceful-that-only-one-gop-congressman-appeared-at-a-capitol-hill-event-commemorating-january-6/articleshow/96821150.cms.

Dorn, Sara. "Trump Avoids Definitive Stance on Abortion—But Suggested That DeSantis' 6-Week Ban Is 'Too Harsh.'" *Forbes*, May 15, 2023. https://www.forbes.com/sites/saradorn/2023/05/15/trump-avoids-definitive-stance-on-abortion-but-suggests-desantis-6-week-ban-is-too-harsh/?sh=36fbed706398.

Dreier, Natalie. "Trump Indictment in Georgia: Misty Hampton, Also Known as Emily Misty Hayes, Turns Herself In." *Kiro 7*, Aug 25, 2023. https://www.kiro7.com/news/trending/trump-indictment-georgia-misty-hampton-also-known-emily-misty-hayes-turns-herself/GFI6DY5INBFULMHDWL6AHSCTGA/.

———. "Trump Indictment in Georgia: Trevian Kutti, Kanye West Former Publicist, Surrenders." *Kiro 7*, Aug 25, 2023. https://www.kiro7.com/news/trending/trump-indictment-georgia-trevian-kutti-kanye-wests-former-publicist-surrenders/YP3B7M67QNAONJWGZI7Y4SZD5Y/.

Dumas, Ernest. "Donald Trump's Corrupt Legacy." *Arkansas Times*, Jun 29, 2022. https://arktimes.com/columns/ernest-dumas/2022/06/29/donald-trumps-corrupt-legacy.

Durkee, Alison. "Trump's Ex-Attorney Kenneth Chesebro Takes Plea Deal in Georgia—Averting Trials as Jury Selection Began." *Forbes*, Oct 20, 2023. https://www.forbes.com/sites/alisondurkee/2023/10/20/trumps-ex-attorney-kenneth-chesebros-trial-begins-today---first-to-face-trial-in-georgia-fake-elector-scheme/?sh=6eccee046289.

Duster, Chandelis. "Family of Fallen January 6 Officer Explains Snubbing McConnell and McCarthy: 'This Is an Integrity Issue.'" CNN, Dec 7, 2022. https://www.cnn.com/2022/12/07/politics/brian-sicknick-family-republicans-cnntv/index.html.

Dzhanova, Yelena. "A Texas Lawyer Says He 'Hit Rock Bottom' after Losing His Fiancée, Friends, and Job because of His Participation during the Capitol Riot But Has No Regrets." *Business Insider*, Feb 16, 2022. https://www.businessinsider.com/texas-man-capitol-riot-attendee-lost-friends-fiance-job-2022-2.

Eady, Gregory, et al. "Comparing Trump to the Greatest and the Most Polarizing President in US History." *Brookings*, Mar 20, 2018. https://www.brookings.edu/articles/comparing-trump-to-the-greatest-and-the-most-polarizing-presidents-in-u-s-history/.

Edwards, David. "GOP Rep. Clay Higgins: 'There Is No Such Thing as Gun Violence.'" *Raw Story*. Mar 29, 2023. https://www.rawstory.com/clay-higgins-gun-violence/.

The Educational Fund to Stop Gun Violence. "Domestic Violence and Firearms." Accessed December 10, 2022. https://efsgv.org/learn/type-of-gun-violence/domestic-violence-and-firearms/.

———. "Missouri Gun Deaths: 2019." Accessed November 27, 2021. https://efsgv.org/state/missouri/.

———. "New CDC Data Reveals Persistently High Rates of U.S. Gun Deaths." Assessed December 10, 2022. https://efsgv.org/press/new-2019-cdc-data/.

Eisinger, Jesse, et al. "The Secret IRS Files: Trove of Never-Before-Seen Records Reveal How the Wealthiest Avoid Income Tax." *ProPublica*, Jun 8, 2021. https://www.propublica.org/article/the-secret-irs-files-trove-of-never-before-seen-records-reveal-how-the-wealthiest-avoid-income-tax.

Ellis, Nicquel Terry. "'Stand Back and Stand By': Rhetoric Some Call Racist Has Marked Trump's Entire Presidency." *USA Today*, Oct 13, 2020. https://www.usatoday.com/story/news/politics/elections/2020/10/13/hate-speech-common-theme-trumps-presidency/5873238002/.

Everytown Research & Policy. "The Economic Cost of Gun Violence." February 17, 2021. https://everytownresearch.org/report/the-economic-cost-of-gun-violence/.

———. "Gun Violence in America." Last modified February 13, 2023. https://everytownresearch.org/report/gun-violence-in-america/.

Fahrenthold, David A. "Trump Recorded Having an Extremely Lewd Conversation about Women in 2005." *Washington Post*, Oct 8, 2016. https://www.washingtonpost.com/politics/trump-recorded-having-extremely-lewd-conversation-about-women-in-2005/2016/10/07/3b9ce776-8cb4-11e6-bf8a-3d26847eeed4_story.html.

Farivar, Masood. "Researchers: More Than a Dozen Extremist Groups Took Part in Capitol Riots." *VOA News*, Jan 16, 2021. https://www.voanews.com/a/2020-usa-votes_researchers-more-dozen-extremist-groups-took-part-capitol-riots/6200832.html.

Fausset, Richard. "'It Has to Stop': Georgia Election Official Lashes Trump." *New York Times*, Dec 1, 2020. https://www.nytimes.com/2020/12/01/us/politics/georgia-election-trump.html.

———. "Last Defendant in Trump Election Interference Case in Georgia Is Granted Bond." *New York Times*, Aug 29, 2023. https://www.nytimes.com/2023/08/29/us/trump-election-interference-georgia-harrison-floyd.html.

Fausset, Richard, and Danny Hakim. "Sidney Powell Pleads Guilty in Georgia Trump Case." *New York Times*, Oct 19, 2023. https://www.nytimes.com/2023/10/19/us/sidney-powell-guilty-plea-trump-georgia.html.

Fearnow, Benjamin. "Trump Never Received a Majority Job Approval Rating during His Entire Presidency, 41 Separate Polls Show." *Newsweek*, Nov 1, 2020. https://www.newsweek.com/trump-never-received-majority-job-approval-rating-during-his-entire-presidency-41-separate-polls-1543862.

Federal Bureau of Investigation. "2017 Crime in the United States." Accessed May 17, 2021. https://ucr.fbi.gov/crime-in-the-u.s/2017/crime-in-the-u.s.-2017/topic-pages/tables/expanded-homicide-data-table-6.xls.

Feldman, Ari Ephraim. "Rudy Giuliani Suspended from Practicing Law in New York." *Spectrum News*, Jun 24, 2021. https://ny1.com/nyc/all-boroughs/news/2021/06/24/rudy-giuliani-suspended-from-practicing-law-in-new-york.

Fernandez, Marisa. "All the Trump Associates Convicted or Sentenced in the Mueller Investigation." *Axios*, Feb 20, 2020. https://www.axios.com/2019/11/15/trump-associates-convicted-mueller-investigations.

Floyd, David. "Explaining the Trump Tax Reform Plan." *Investopedia*, Apr 2, 2021. https://www.investopedia.com/taxes/trumps-tax-reform-plan-explained/.

Fouhy, Beth. "Trump: Obama a 'Terrible Student' Not Good Enough for Harvard." *New York News*, Apr 26, 2011. https://www.nbcnewyork.com/news/local/trump-obama-wasnt-good-enough-to-get-into-ivy-schools/1924291/.

Fowler, Stephen. "Trump to Georgia Election Officials: I Just Want to Find 11,780 Votes." *GPD*, Jan 3, 2021. https://www.gpb.org/news/2021/01/03/trump-georgia-election-officials-i-just-want-find-11780-votes.

Frazier, Kierra, "Jan. 6 Sentences Are Piling Up. Here's a Look at Some of the Longest Handed Down." *Politico*, May 31, 2023. https://www.politico.com/news/2023/05/30/january-6-arrest-sentencing-00099158.

Friedman, Matt. "'This Is Horrifying': Top New Jersey Democrats Call on Bob Menedez to Resign after His Second Indictment." *Politico*, Sep 22, 2023. https://www.politico.com/news/2023/09/22/new-jersey-democrats-menendez-indictment-00117693.

Fry, Hannah. "Former La Habra Police Chief Sentenced to More Than 11 Years for Role in Jan. 6 Riot." *Los Angeles Times*, Dec 7, 2023. https://www.latimes.com/california/story/2023-12-07/former-o-c-police-chief-gets-prison-term-for-role-in-jan-6-riot.

Fung, Katherine. "Jenna Ellis Breaks Silence after Pleading Guilty." *Newsweek*, Oct 25, 2023. https://www.newsweek.com/jenna-ellis-breaks-silence-pleading-guilty-1837766.

Gallup. "Pro-Choice or Pro-Life, 2018–2020 Demographic Tables." Accessed July 14, 2021. https://news.gallup.com/poll/244709/pro-choice-pro-life-2018-demographic-tables.aspx.

Gangel, Jamie, et al. "'Play It Down:' Trump Admits to Concealing the True Threat of Coronavirus in New Woodward Book." CNN, Sep 9, 2020. https://www.cnn.com/2020/09/09/politics/bob-woodward-rage-book-trump-coronavirus/index.html.

Gardner, Matthew, and Steve Wamhoff. "55 Corporations Paid $0 in Federal Taxes 2020 Profit. Institute on Taxation and Economic Policy." Institute on Taxation and Economic Policy, Apr 2, 2021. https://itep.org/55-profitable-corporations-zero-corporate-tax/.

Gass, Nick. "Trump: I Hope I Don't Have to Ask 'for Such Forgiveness from God.'" *Politico*, Jun 8, 2016. https://www.politico.com/story/2016/06/trump-forgiveness-god-224068.

Gebeloff, Robert, et al. "Childhood Greatest Danger: The Data on Kids and Gun Violence." *New York Times*, Dec 14, 2022. https://www.nytimes.com/interactive/2022/12/14/magazine/gun-violence-children-data-statistics.html.

Gerstein, Josh, and Kyle Cheney. "Another Trump Lawyer Who Pushed to Overturn 2020 Election Pleads Guilty." *Politico*, Oct 24, 2023. https://www.politico.com/news/2023/10/24/another-trump-lawyer-who-pushed-to-overturn-2020-election-pleads-guilty-00123163.

Gerth, Joseph. "With His 10,000 Lies, President Trump Is the Most Dishonest Politician Ever." *Courier Journal*, May 2, 2019. https://www.courier-journal.com/story/news/local/joseph-gerth/2019/05/02/president-donald-trump-lies-like-no-other-democrat-republican/3649677002/.

Gettys, Travis. "Conservative Cries Bitter Tears after Trump Allies Admit Election Lies: 'It Was All BS.'" *Raw Story*, Jul 27, 2023. https://www.rawstory.com/steve-deace/.

Giddens, A., et al. *Essentials of Sociology*. New York: Norton, 2019.

Giffords. "Annual Scorecard Confirms Gun Laws Save Lives." Mar 31, 2023. https://giffords.org/lawcenter/press-release/2023/03/giffords-annual-scorecard-confirms-gun-laws-save-lives/.

Gilens, Martin, and Benjamin I. Page. "Testing Theories of American Politics: Elites, Interest Groups, and Average Citizens." *Perspectives on Politics* 12.3 (Sep 2014) 564–81. https://doi.org/10.1017/S1537592714001595.

Goldiner, Dave. "Trump Dings Gov. Ron DeSantis over Florida's 'Too Harsh' Abortion Ban, But Won't Say Where He Stands." *New York Daily News*, May 15, 2023. https://www.nydailynews.com/news/politics/us-elections-government/ny-trump-desantis-florida-harsh-abortion-ban-20230515-nx6nzsnqtvbetage75wwladodistory.html.

Gold, Michael, and Grace Ashford. "George Santos Admits to Lying about College and Work History." *New York Times*, Dec 26, 2022. https://www.nytimes.com/2022/12/26/nyregion/george-santos-interview.html.

Goodwin, Jazmin. "Trump's Talk of Martial Law Sends White House Staffers Rushing to the Press." CNN, Dec 20, 2020. https://www.cnn.com/2020/12/20/media/stelter-trump-martial-law/index.html.

Grabenstein, Hannah. "What You Need to Know about Ray Smith III's 2020 Election Charges." PBS, Nov 2, 2023. https://www.pbs.org/newshour/politics/what-you-need-to-know-about-ray-smith-iiis-2020-election-charges.

Gregorian, Dareh. "Judge Punishes Rudy Giuliani for 'Continued and Flagrant Disregard' of Court Orders." NBC News, Oct 13, 2023. https://www.nbcnews.com/politics/politics-news/judge-punishes-rudy-giuliani-flagrant-disregard-court-orders-rcna120412.

Griggs, Taylor. "The Wealth Inequality Gap Is Leading to More Homelessness." *InvisiblePEOPLE*, Jan 7, 2021. https://invisiblepeople.tv/the-wealth-inequality-gap-is-leading-to-more-homelessness/?gclid=EAIaIQobChMI3vC7lfP0_QIV4jizAB2tYgB5EAAYASAAEgKrS_D_BwE.

Grindell, Samantha. "Donald Trump, Who Said He Only Hired the Best People, Was Thoroughly Asked Why So Many Key Players in His Administration Do Not Want Him to Be President Again." *Africa Business Insider*, Jun 20, 2023. https://africa.businessinsider.com/politics/donald-trump-who-said-he-only-hired-the-best-people-was-thoroughly-asked-why-so-many/7zhbddb.amp.

Grinshteyn, Erin, and David Hemenway. "Violent Death Rates in the U.S. Compared to Those of the Other High-Income Countries, 2015. *Preventive Medicine* 123 (Jun 2019) 20–26. https://doi.org/10.1016/j.ypmed.2019.02.026.

Gun Violence Archive. "GVA 10-Year Review." Accessed October 14, 2021. https://www.gunviolencearchive.org/.

———. "Past Summary Ledgers." Accessed January 9, 2023. https://www.gunviolencearchive.org/past-tolls.

Guthrie, Jennifer, and Andrianne Kunkel. "Tell Me Sweet (and Not-So-Sweet) Little Lies: Deception in Romantic Relationships." *Communication Studies* 64.2 (Mar 11, 2013) 141–57. https://doi.org/10.1080/10510974.2012.755637.

Habbach, Hajar, et al. "You Will Never See Your Child Again." *Physicians for Human Rights*, Feb 25, 2020. https://phr.org/our-work/resources/you-will-never-see-your-child-again-the-persistent-psychological-effects-of-family-separation/.

Haberman, Maggie, and Alan Feuer. "Mary Trump's Book Accuses the President of Embracing 'Cheating as a Way of Life.'" *New York Times*, Jul 7, 2020. https://www.nytimes.com/2020/07/07/us/politics/mary-trump-book.html?referringSource=articleShare.

Hartmann, Ray. "Bizarre MAGA Riot Case: QAnon Fan Who Thought He Was Storming the White House Gets Home Confinement but Lives in an RV." *Raw Story*, Jan 14, 2022. https://www.rawstory.com/capitol-rioter-kenneth-kelly/.

Hemel, Daniel. "The Trump Organization Is in Big Trouble." *Atlantic*, Jul 2, 2021. https://www.theatlantic.com/ideas/archive/2021/07/trump-organization-indictment-tax-fraud-trouble/619353/.

Herb, Jeremy. "Trump to DOJ Last December: 'Just Say that the Election Was Corrupt and Leave the Rest to Me.'" CNN, Jul 31, 2021. https://www.cnn.com/2021/07/30/politics/trump-election-justice/index.html.

Herb, Jeremy, et al. "Flynn Pleads Guilty to Lying to FBI, Is Cooperating with Mueller." CNN, Dec 1, 2017. https://www.cnn.com/2017/12/01/politics/michael-flynn-charged/index.html.

Hernandez, Joe. "What We Know about the Deadly Shooting at a Nashville Elementary School." NPR, Mar 28, 2023. https://www.npr.org/2023/03/28/1166482479/nashville-school-shooting-covenant-what-we-know.

Herndon, Joy, et al. "Abortion Surveillance—United States, 1998." *MMWR Surveillance Summaries* 51 (2002) 1–32. https://www.cdc.gov/mmwr/preview/mmwrhtml/ss5103a1.htm.

Holmes, Kristen. "Trump Calls for the Termination of the Constitution in Truth Social Post." CNN, Dec 4, 2022. https://www.cnn.com/2022/12/03/politics/trump-constitution-truth-social/index.html.

Hooghe, Marc, and Ruth Dassonneville. "Explaining the Trump Vote: The Effect of Racist Resentment and Anti-Immigrant Sentiments." *Political Science and Politics* 51.3 (Apr 2018) 528–34. https://doi.org/10.1017/S1049096518000367.

House Committee on the Budget. "Democrats Are the Party of Fiscal Responsibility." Accessed June 14, 2021. https://democrats-budget.house.gov/publications/publication/democrats-are-party-fiscal-responsibility.

Howard, LaQuita. "Racial Gerrymandering and the 2021-2022 Redistricting Process." *League of Women Voters*, Mar 31, 2022. https://www.lwv.org/blog/racial-gerrymandering-and-2021-2022-redistricting-process.

Human Rights Watch. "Nicaragua Events of 2018." Accessed December 21, 2021. World Report 2019: Nicaragua. https://www.hrw.org/world-report/2019/country-chapters/nicaragua.

Huseman, Jessica. "Two Leaders of True the Vote Jailed by Federal Judge for Contempt of Court." *Texas Tribune*, Oct 31, 2022. https://www.texastribune.org/2022/10/31/true-the-vote-leaders-jailed/.

Immigration Equality. "Deferred Action for Childhood Arrivals (DACA)." Last updated September 19, 2023. https://immigrationequality.org/legal/legal-help/other-paths-to-status/deferred-action-for-childhood-arrivals-daca/.

Jacobs, Ben. "Trump Protests over 'Crooked Deal' in Colorado after Cruz Win." *Guardian*, Apr 12, 2016. https://www.theguardian.com/us-news/2016/apr/12/donald-trump-protests-over-crooked-deal-in-colorado-after-ted-cruz-wins.

Jaramillo, Cassandra. "Leaders of Texas-Based Activist Group True the Vote Accused of Using Donations for Personal Gain." *Texas Tribune*, Jun 5, 2023. https://www.texastribune.org/2023/06/05/true-the-vote-complaint/.

Jarrett, Scott, and Rey Valenzuela. "Update on Forensic Audit of Maricopa County's Tabulation Equipment." Maricopa County Elections Department, Feb 23, 2021. https://www.maricopa.gov/DocumentCenter/View/66842/Forensic-Audit-Transmittal-Letter.

Jaschik, Scott. "Trump Threatened Colleges over Any Release of His Grades." *Inside Higher Ed*, Feb 28, 2019. https://www.insidehighered.com/news/2019/02/28/michael-cohen-testifies-trump-threatened-colleges-over-any-release-his-grades.

Jerman, Jenna, et al. "Characteristics of U.S. Abortion Patients in 2014 and Changes since 2008." *Guttmacher Institute*, May 2016. https://www.guttmacher.org/report/characteristics-us-abortion-patients-2014.

Jonason, Peter K., et al. "What a Tangled Web We Weave: The Dark Triad Traits and Deception." *Personality and Individual Differences* 70 (Nov 2014) 117–19. https://doi.org/10.1016/j.paid.2014.06.038.

Joung, Madeleine. "Trump Has Now Had More Cabinet Turnover Than Reagan, Obama, and the Two Bushes." *Time*, Jul 12, 2019. https://time.com/5625699/trump-cabinet-acosta/.

Kaonga, Gerrard. "Donald Trump Prophet Predicts Death of Democrats: 'You Will See Many Die.'" *Newsweek*, Feb 3, 2023. https://www.newsweek.com/donald-trump-prophet-julie-green-democrats-arrest-die-viral-video-1778840.

Karl, Jonathan D. "Inside William Barr's Break Up with Trump." *Atlantic*, Jun 27, 2021. https://www.theatlantic.com/politics/archive/2021/06/william-barrs-trump-administration-attorney-general/619298/.

Karp, Aaron. "Estimating Global Civilian-Held Firearms Numbers." *Small Arms Survey*, Jun 2018. https://www.smallarmssurvey.org/sites/default/files/resources/SAS-BP-Civilian-Firearms-Numbers.pdf.

Keeter, Scott. "How We Know the Drop in Trump's Approval Rating in January Reflected a Real Shift in Public Opinion." *Pew Research Center*, Jan 20, 2021. https://www.pewresearch.org/short-reads/2021/01/20/how-we-know-the-drop-in-trumps-approval-rating-in-january-reflected-a-real-shift-in-public-opinion/.

Keith, Tamara. "Trump Cabinet Turnover Sets Record Going Back 100 Years." NPR, Mar 19, 2018. https://www.npr.org/2018/03/19/594164065/trump-cabinet-turnover-sets-record-going-back-100-years.

———. "White House Staff Turnover Was Already Record-Setting. Then More Advisers Left." NPR, Mar, 7, 2018. https://www.npr.org/2018/03/07/591372397/white-house-staff-turnover-was-already-record-setting-then-more-advisers-left.

Kessler, Glenn, et al. "Trump's False or Misleading Claims Total 30573 over 4 Years." *Washington Post*, Jan 24, 2021. https://www.washingtonpost.com/politics/2021/01/24/trumps-false-or-misleading-claims-total-30573-over-four-years/.

Kortsmit, Katherine, et al. "Abortion Surveillance—United States, 2019." *MMWR Surveillance Summaries* 70.9 (Nov 2021) 1–29. https://www.ncbi.nlm.nih.gov/pmc/articles/PMC8654281/.

Kristian, Bonnie. "What Would Actually Happen If Trump Tried the 'Martial Law' Idea?" *Week*, Dec 23, 2023. https://theweek.com/articles/956872/what-actually-happen-trump-tried-martial-law-idea.

Krogstad, Jens Manuel. "Americans Broadly Support Legal Status for Immigrants Brought to the U.S. Illegally as Children." *Pew Research Center*, Jun 17, 2020. https://www.pewresearch.org/fact-tank/2020/06/17/americans-broadly-support-legal-status-for-immigrants-brought-to-the-u-s-illegally-as-children/.

Kumar, Anita. "Poll: Trump Voters Want to Protect Dreamers." *Politico*, Jun 17, 2020. https://www.politico.com/news/2020/06/17/trump-supporters-dreamers-poll-323432.

Kunzelman, Michael, et al. "Capitol Rioters' Tears, Remorse Don't Spare Them from Jail." *Associate*, Jan 2, 2022. https://apnews.com/article/capitol-siege-rioters-prison-95bdc863812cab48be3d98ada67bd582.

Kurtz, Hilda E. "Trayvon Martin and the Dystopian Turn in U.S. Self-Defense Doctrine." *Antipode* 45.2 (Nov 22, 2012) 248–51. https://doi.org/10.1111/j.1467-8330.2012.01057.x.

Langley, Marty, and Ellie Pasternack. "American Roulette: Murder-Suicide in the United States." *Violence Policy Center*, Oct 2015. https://www.vpc.org/studies/amroul2015.pdf.

Lardner, Richard, and Michelle R. Smith. "Michael Flynn's ReAwaken Roadshow Recruits 'Army of God.'" PBS, *Frontline*, Oct 7, 2022. https://www.pbs.org/wgbh/frontline/article/michael-flynn-reawaken-america-tour/.

Larson, Shannon. "'Our Election Was Not Stolen, and America Has Not Failed': Cheney, Facing an Ousting from Her Post, Continues Criticism of Republicans Who Support Trump." *Boston Globe*, May 11, 2021. https://www.bostonglobe.com/2021/05/11/nation/our-election-was-not-stolen-america-has-not-failed-cheney-facing-an-ousting-her-post-continues-criticism-republicans-who-support-trump/.

Lauria, Maddy, and Matthew Albright. "If Biden Were President, He'd Be in Minority with No Military Service." *USA Today*, Apr 25, 2019. https://www.usatoday.com/story/news/local/2019/04/25/if-biden-were-president-hed-minority-no-military-service/3019445002/.

Layne, Nathan, and Alexandra Ulmer. "How Trump Netted Evangelical Votes in Iowa, with Help from a Young Christian Operative." *Reuters*, Dec 14, 2023. https://www.reuters.com/world/us/how-trump-netted-evangelical-votes-iowa-with-help-young-christian-operative-2023-12-14/.

Lee, David. "Trump Supporters Lose Jobs and Businesses after Participation in Capitol Riot." *Court House News*, Jan 10, 2021. https://www.courthousenews.com/trump-supporters-lose-jobs-and-businesses-after-participation-in-capitol-riot/.

Lee, Morgan. "Trump's Withdrawal from Syria Threatens the Growing Kurdish Church." *Christianity Today*, Oct 16, 2019. https://www.christianitytoday.com/ct/podcasts/quick-to-listen/turkeys-syria-kurd-trump-christians.html.

Legare, Robert, and Scott Macfarlane. "Proud Boys Leader Sentenced in Seditious Conspiracy Case." CBS, Sep 5, 2023. https://www.aol.com/proud-boys-leader-set-sentenced-143210153.html.

Lemon, Jason. "Christian Pastor Claims Prophets Will Call Back Trump for Three Terms." *Newsweek*, Mar 10, 2021. https://www.newsweek.com/christian-pastor-claims-prophets-will-call-back-trump-three-terms-1575199.

Leonhardt, David. "The Democrats Are the Party of Fiscal Responsibility." *New York Times*, Apr 15, 2018. https://www.nytimes.com/2018/04/15/opinion/democrats-fiscal-responsibility.html.

Lima, Cristiano. "Trump Touts Renewed 'Spirit' at State Dept. under Pompeo." *Politico*, May 2, 2018. https://www.politico.com/story/2018/05/02/trump-state-department-mike-pompeo-565612.

Lobel, Thalma. E., and Ilana Levanon. "Self-Esteem, Need for Approval, and Cheating Behavior in Children." *Journal of Educational Psychology* 8.1 (1988) 122–23. https://psycnet.apa.org/doi/10.1037/0022-0663.80.1.122.

Long Hair Care Forum. "Kim Clement Prophetic Word concerning Obama." April 10, 2008. https://longhaircareforum.com/threads/kim-clements-prophetic-word-concerning-obama.220647/.

Long, Heather, and Jeff Stein. "The U.S. Deficit Hit $984 Billion in 2019. Soaring during Trump Era." *Washington Post*, Oct 25, 2019. https://www.washingtonpost.com/business/2019/10/25/us-deficit-hit-billion-marking-nearly-percent-increase-during-trump-era/.

Lord, Debbie. "Trump Indictment in Georgia: Michael Roman Turns Himself In." *Kiro 7*, Aug 25, 2023. https://www.kiro7.com/news/trending/trump-indictment-georgia-michael-roman-turns-himself/XMZJXL7VXVB2JHWPFC7BMGXWNI/.

Luca, Michael, et al. "Handgun Waiting Periods Reduce Gun Deaths." *National Academy of Sciences* 114.46 (Oct 16, 2017) 12162–65. https://doi.org/10.1073/pnas.1619896114.

Lucas, Ryan. "Senate Report Details Trump's Effort to Use DOJ to Overturn Election Results." NPR, Oct 7, 2021. https://www.npr.org/2021/10/07/1044015379/senate-report-details-trumps-efforts-to-use-doj-to-overturn-election-results.

Lupiani, Joyce. "Who Is Cathy Latham? Former Coffee County GOP Chair Accused of Being a 'Fake Elector.'" *Fox 5 Atlanta*, Aug 16, 2023. https://www.fox5atlanta.com/news/cathy-latham-former-coffee-county-gop-chair-accused-of-being-a-fake-elector-for-former-president-trump.

Lu, Yu, and Jeff R. Temple. "Dangerous Weapons or Dangerous People? The Temporal Associations between Violence and Mental Health." *Preventive Medicine* 121 (Apr 2019) 1–6. https://doi.org/10.1016/j.ypmed.2019.01.008.

Lybrand, Holmes, and Hannah Rabinowitz. "ABC News: Mark Meadows Received Immunity to Testify to Special Counsel in Federal Election Subversion Probe." CNN, Oct 24, 2023. https://www.cnn.com/2023/10/24/politics/mark-meadows/index.html.

Mallin, Alexander, et al. "Senate Report Details Russia's Efforts to Meddle in 2016 Election, Ties to Trump Associates." ABC News, Aug 18, 2020. https://abcnews.

go.com/Politics/senate-report-details-russias-efforts-meddle-2016-ties/story?id=72444405.

Mantyla, Kyle. 'There Is a Payback Coming': Christian Nationalist Gather in Oklahoma to Spread the Big Lie." *Right Wing Watch*, Apr 22, 2022. https://www.rightwingwatch.org/post/there-is-a-payback-coming-christian-nationalists-gather-in-oklahoma-to-spread-the-big-lie/.

Marcotte, Amanda. "Evangelicals Are the Backbones of Trump's Big Lie—And It's All about White Supremacy." *AlterNet*, May 3, 2022. https://www.alternet.org/2022/05/trump-big-lie.

Marczak, Trisha. "4 Examples of Corporate Welfare in Action." *Mint News*, Aug 19, 2013. https://www.mintpressnews.com/4-examples-of-corporate-welfare/167149/.

Maricopa County. "Auditing Election Equipment in Maricopa County." January 27, 2021. https://www.maricopa.gov/5681/Elections-Equipment-Audit#Results.

Mark, David. "Ross Elected First Female Governor, Nov. 4, 1924." *Politico*, Nov 2009. https://www.politico.com/story/2009/11/ross-elected-first-female-governor-nov-4-1924-029077.

Markowitz, David. "Who Lied More during Their First 100 Days: Biden, Trump, or Obama?" *Forbes*, Apr 30, 2021. https://www.forbes.com/sites/davidmarkowitz/2021/04/30/who-lied-more-during-their-first-100-days-biden-trump-or-obama/?sh=60bd5e41a89d.

Martin, Jonathan, and Alan Rappeport. "Donald Trump Says John McCain Is No War Hero, Setting Off Another Storm." *New York Times*, Jul 18, 2015. https://www.nytimes.com/2015/07/19/us/politics/trump-belittles-mccains-war-record.html.

Marx, Karl, and Friedrick Engels. *The Communist Manifesto: A 1888 Translation Edition (The Political Philosophy of Karl Marx and Friedrich Engels)*. USA: Amazon, 2021.

Mason, Lilliana, et al. "Activating Animus: The Uniquely Social Roots of Trump Support." *EconPapers* 115.4 (2021) 1508–16. https://econpapers.repec.org/article/cupapsrev/v_3a115_3ay_3a2021_3ai_3a4_3ap_3a1508-1516_5f26.htm.

Maxouris, Christina, and Elizabeth Joseph. "Alex Jones Says 'Form of Psychosis' Made Him Believe Events Like Sandy Hook Massacre Was Staged." *CNN*, Apr 1, 2019. https://www.cnn.com/2019/03/30/us/alex-jones-psychosis-sandy-hook/index.html.

McFadyen, Jennifer. "Weighing the Pros and Cons of U.S.-Mexico Border Barrier." *Thought Co*, Jun 2, 2021. https://www.thoughtco.com/mexico-border-fence-pros-and-cons-1951541.

McIntire Mike, et al. "Trump Paid $1.1 Million during Presidency but Paid $0 in 2020, Report Shows." *New York Times*, Dec 21, 2022. https://www.nytimes.com/2022/12/21/us/politics/trump-taxes-income.html.

Milford, Maureen, and Jonathan Starkey. "Remembering Beau Biden: 'An Outstanding Man.'" *USA Today*, May 31, 2015. https://www.usatoday.com/story/news/local/2015/05/31/remembering-beau-biden-outstanding-man/28284039/.

Miroff, Nick. "A Family Was Separated at the Border and This Distraught Father Took His Own Life." *Washington Post*, Jun 8, 2018. https://www.washingtonpost.com/world/national-security/a-family-was-separated-at-the-border-and-this-distraught-father-took-his-own-life/2018/06/08/24e40b70-6b5d-11e8-9e38-24e693b38637_story.html?noredirect=on.

Moghe, Sonia, and Kara Scannell. "Westchester County District Attorney's Office Investigating Trump Organization Golf Course Property Taxes." *CNN*, Oct

20, 2021. https://www.cnn.com/2021/10/20/politics/trump-organization-westchester-golf-course-investigation/index.html.

Moreno, Edward. "Poll: Majority Thinks Trump Is Making US More Divided." *Hill*, Jun 18, 2020. https://thehill.com/homenews/administration/503437-poll-majority-of-americans-think-trump-is-making-us-more-divided/.

Morse, Ann, et al. "U.S. Supreme Court Ruling on DACA." National Conference of State Legislatures, Jun 18, 2020. https://www.ncsl.org/immigration/us-supreme-court-ruling-on-daca.

Morton, Victor. "MyPillow's Mike Lindell Says He's Broke after Election-Fraud Campaign: 'We've Lost Everything." *Washington Times*, Oct 5, 2023. https://www.washingtontimes.com/news/2023/oct/5/mike-lindell-mypillow-ceo-says-hes-broke-after-ele/.

Muris, Peter, et al. "The Malevolent Side of Human Nature: A Meta-Analysis and Critical Review of the Literature on the Dark Triad (Narcissism, Machiavellianism, and Psychopathy)." *Perspectives on Psychological Science* 12.2 (Mar 27, 2017) 183–204. https://doi.org/10.1177/1745691616666070.

Murse, Tom. "The Biggest Donald Trump Scandals (So Far)." *ThoughtCo*, Jan 19, 2021. https://www.thoughtco.com/trump-scandals-4142784.

———. "Why Donald Trump's Companies Went Bankrupt." *ThoughtCo*, Dec 31, 2020. https://www.thoughtco.com/donald-trump-business-bankruptcies-4152019.

Narea, Nicole. "Romney Just Urged Republicans to Stop Entertaining Trump's Election Lies." *Vox*, Jan 6, 20221. https://www.vox.com/policy-and-politics/2021/1/6/22218093/romney-refutes-trump-election-lies.

National Archives. "Declaration of Independence: A Transcription." Accessed July 2, 2021. https://www.archives.gov/founding-docs/declaration-transcript.

National Association of Evangelicals (NAE). "Evangelical Leaders Own Guns, but Want Stricter Laws." Aug 2017. https://www.nae.org/evangelical-leaders-own-guns-but-want-stricter-laws/.

National Constitution Center Staff. "On This Day, Patrick Henry's Most Famous Quote." Mar 23, 2023. https://constitutioncenter.org/blog/on-this-day-patrick-henrys-most-famous-quote.

Newman, Nic, et al. "Reuters Institute Digital News Report 2021." *Reuter Institute for the Study of Journalism*, 2021. https://reutersinstitute.politics.ox.ac.uk/sites/default/files/2021-06/Digital_News_Report_2021_FINAL.pdf.

Nobles, Ryan, et al. "Tennessee Rep. Burchett Says of School Shootings: 'We're Not Gonna Fix It.'" NBC News, Mar 29, 2023. https://www.nbcnews.com/politics/congress/tennessee-rep-burchett-says-school-shootings-re-not-gonna-fix-rcna77185.

Nothstine, Ray. "Donald Trump: I'm Not Sure If I Ever Asked God's Forgiveness." *Christian Post*, Jul 20, 2015. https://www.christianpost.com/news/donald-trump-im-not-sure-if-i-ever-asked-gods-forgiveness-141706/.

———. "Trump: Why Do I Have to Repent or Ask for Forgiveness If I Am Not Making Mistakes? (Video)." *Christian Post*, Jul 23, 2015. https://www.christianpost.com/news/trump-why-do-i-have-to-repent-or-ask-for-forgiveness-if-i-am-not-making-mistakes-video.html.

Nozicka, Luke, and Kaitlyn Schwers. "2 Dead, at Least 15 Reported Wounded in Shooting outside Kansas City Club, Police Say." *Kansas City Star*, Jan 20, 2020. https://www.kansascity.com/news/local/crime/article239453988.html.

Nussbaum, Matthew. "Trump Publicly Sides with Putin on Election Interference." *Politico*, Jul 16, 2018. https://www.politico.com/story/2018/07/16/trump-russia-putin-summit-722418.

O'Brien, Matthew, et al. "The Fiscal Burden of Illegal Immigration on United States Taxpayers (2017)." *Federation for American Immigration Reform*, 2017. https://www.fairus.org/sites/default/files/2017-09/Fiscal-Burden-of-Illegal-Immigration-2017.pdf.

O'Keefe, Ed. "Rubio Called Trump a Dangerous 'Con Man.' Now He Says Trump Should Be President." *Washington Post*, May 27, 2016. https://www.washingtonpost.com/politics/rubio-called-trump-a-dangerous-con-man-now-he-says-trump-should-be-president/2016/05/27/b837e16c-2410-11e6-aa84-42391ba52c91_story.html.

Orden, Erica, et al. "Michael Cohen Sentenced to Three Years in Prison after Admitting He Covered up Trump's 'Dirty Deeds.'" CNN, Dec 12, 2018. https://www.cnn.com/2018/12/12/politics/michael-cohen-sentencing/index.html.

Ortiz, Rebecca R., and Andrea M. Smith. "A Social Identity Threat Perspective on Why Partisans May Engage in Greater Victim Blaming and Sexual Assault Myth Acceptance in the #MeToo Era." *Violence against Women* 28.5 (Jun 4, 2021) 1302–25. https://doi.org/10.1177/10778012211014554.

Oxford Reference. "Social Justice." Accessed December 14, 2022. https://www.oxfordreference.com/display/10.1093/oi/authority.20110803100515279;jsessionid=ADC7909EA9283049ADD01518E8426E15.

Parks, Miles. "Georgia Election Official: Don't Let Misinformation 'Suppress Your Own Vote.'" NPR, Jan 4, 2021. https://www.npr.org/2021/01/04/953321408/georgia-election-official-dont-let-misinformation-suppress-your-own-vote.

Patterson, Steve. "Two Ways to Be Fooled." *Courageous Christian Father*, Jul 23, 2022. https://www.courageouschristianfather.com/two-ways-to-be-fooled/#axzz8ROM8RpOP.

Paulhus, Delroy L., and Kevin M. Williams. "The Dark Triad of Personality: Narcissism, Machiavellianism and Psychopathy." *Journal of Research in Personality* 36 (Dec 2002) 556–63. https://doi.org/10.1016/S0092-6566(02)00505-6.

Payton, Joseph. "Nurse Loses Job after Admitting of Entering US Capitol Building during Riot." *14 News*, Jan 14, 2021. https://www.14news.com/2021/01/15/ascension-st-vincent-nurse-loses-job-involvement-us-capitol-riots/.

Peacock, Alice. "MAGA Marriage Split: Top Cop Divorces Wife after She Was Caught on Camera with Another Man at US Capitol Riot and Later Arrested." *U.S. Sun*, Mar 21, 2021. https://www.the-sun.com/news/2556224/cop-divorces-wife-maga-capitol-riots-man/.

Pengelly, Martin. "Republican to Quit House Citing Party's Reliance on 'Lie' of Stolen 2020 Election." *Guardian*, Nov 1, 2023. https://www.theguardian.com/us-news/2023/nov/01/ken-buck-republican-quit-house-election-lie.

———. "Trump Pardons Former National Security Advisor Michael Flynn." *Guardian*, Nov 25, 2020. https://www.theguardian.com/us-news/2020/nov/25/donald-trump-pardons-michael-flynn.

Pew Research Center. "Biden Begins Presidency with Positive Ratings; Trump Departs with Lowest-Ever Job Mark." Jan 15, 2021. https://www.pewresearch.org/politics/2021/01/15/biden-begins-presidency-with-positive-ratings-trump-departs-with-lowest-ever-job-mark/.

Bibliography

Phillips, Richard, et al. "Offshore Shell Games 2014." *Digital Ocean Space*, Jun 2014. https://ctj.sfo2.digitaloceanspaces.com/pdf/offshoreshell2014.pdf.

Pickert, Reade. "U.S. Corporate Profits Soar with Margins at Wildest since 1950." *Bloomberg*, Aug 25, 2022. https://www.bloomberg.com/news/articles/2022-08-25/us-corporate-profits-soar-taking-margins-to-widest-since-1950.

Polantz, Katelyn. "Giuliani Struggling under Massive Legal Bill after Defending Trump." CNN, Aug 16, 2023. https://www.cnn.com/2023/08/15/politics/giuliani-money-lawsuits-trump/index.html.

PolitiFact. "Donald Trump." 2021. https://www.politifact.com/personalities/donald-trump/.

Popli, Nik. "These Are the 19 People Charged in the Georgia Election Interference Case." *Time*, Aug 18, 2023. https://time.com/6306031/trump-georgia-indictment-co-conspirators/.

Preza, Elizabeth. "11 Prominent Republicans File Amicus Brief That 'Flies in the Face' of Trump's Trial Delay Demands." *AlterNet*, Aug 14, 2023. https://www.alternet.org/news-politics/trump-republicans-jack-smith/.

Public Religion Research Institute. "Ahead of Anniversary of 1/6 Insurrection, Republicans Remain Entangled in the Big Lie, QAnon, and Temptation toward Political Violence." Jan 4, 2022. https://www.prri.org/spotlight/anniversary-of-jan-6-insurrection/.

———. "The 'Big Lie': Most Republicans Believe the 2020 Election Was Stolen." May 12, 2021. https://www.prri.org/spotlight/the-big-lie-most-republicans-believe-the-2020-election-was-stolen/.

———. "Competing Visions of America: An Evolving Identity or a Culture under Attack? Findings from the 2021 American Value Survey." Nov 1, 2021. https://www.prri.org/research/competing-visions-of-america-an-evolving-identity-or-a-culture-under-attack/.

———. "Survey: Church Attendance, Importance of Religion Declines among Americans Overall, Yet Regular Churchgoers Large Satisfied with Church Experiences." May 16, 2023. https://www.prri.org/press-release/survey-church-attendance-importance-of-religion-declines-among-americans-overall-yet-regular-churchgoers-largely-satisfied-with-church-experiences/.

Queen, Jack, and Jacqueline Thomsen. "Alex Jones Must Pay Sandy Hook Families Nearly $1 Billion For Hoax Claims, Jury Says." *Reuters*, Oct 22, 2022. https://www.reuters.com/legal/jury-begins-third-day-deliberations-alex-jones-sandy-hook-defamation-trial-2022-10-12/.

Quinnipiac University National Poll. "Trump Is Dividing the Country, U.S. Voters Say 2-1, Quinnipiac University National Poll Finds; Most Trust Media More Than President." Aug 23, 2017. https://poll.qu.edu/Poll-Release-Legacy?releaseid=2482.

———. "U.S. Voters Dislike Trump Almost 2-1, Quinnipiac University National Poll Finds; Media Is Important to Democracy, 65% of Voters Say." Aug 14, 2018. https://poll.qu.edu/Poll-Release-Legacy?releaseid=2561.

Ramsey, Ross. "UT/TT Poll: Majority of Texans Oppose Permitless Carry, Would Ban Police Chokeholds and Taxpayer-Funded Lobby." *Texas Tribune*, May 3, 2021. https://www.texastribune.org/2021/05/03/texas-voters-legislature-poll/.

Reed, Brad. "'Deal with the Devil': Evangelical Pastor Testifies about Bargain Christian Conservatives Made with GOP." *Raw Story*, Dec 8, 2022. https://www.rawstory.com/robert-schenck-testimony-video/.

———. "Retired GOP Judge Warns 'Lemming' Republicans Are Running towards 'Huge Election Losses.'" *Raw Story*, Jul 24, 2023. https://www.rawstory.com/trump-2024-2662330647/.

———. "'We Shelter the Ignorant, the Racist': Adam Kinzinger Delivers Scathing Obituary for GOP in a Farewell Speech." *Raw Story*, Dec 15, 2022. https://www.rawstory.com/adam-kinzinger-farewell-speech/.

Reilly, Katie. "Former Trump Lawyer Michael Cohen Sentenced to 3 Years in Prison." *Time*, Dec 12, 2018. https://time.com/5477719/michael-cohen-sentenced-prison/.

Relman, Eliza. "Republican Rep. Dan Crenshaw Is Heckled at a Fundraiser for Insisting the 2020 Election Was 'Absolutely Not' Stolen from Trump." *Business Insider*, Aug 12, 2021. https://www.businessinsider.com/video-republican-rep-dan-crenshaw-heckled-saying-election-wasnt-stolen-2021-8.

Remnick, David. "Are We Sleepwalking into Dictatorship?" *New Yorker*, Dec 10, 2023. https://www.newyorker.com/magazine/2023/12/18/are-we-sleepwalking-into-dictatorship.

Reuter, Dominick, and Andy Kiersz. "Companies Are Pocketing Their Fattest Profits in More Than 70 Years, Even as They Complain about Inflation." *Business Insider*, Dec 2, 2021. https://www.businessinsider.com/companies-pocket-largest-profits-in-70-years-amid-inflation-complaints-2021-12.

Rogers, Tim. "The Unraveling of Nicaragua." *Atlantic*, Jun 6, 2018. https://www.theatlantic.com/international/archive/2018/06/nicaragua-ortega-protests/562094/.

Romo, Vanessa. "Judge Orders Trump Administration to Restore DACA as It Existed under Obama." NPR, Dec 4, 2020. https://www.npr.org/2020/12/04/943355234/judge-orders-trump-administration-to-restore-daca-as-it-existed-under-obama.

Ross, Martha. "Before Lori Loughlin, Did Trump Cheat in College Admissions?" *Mercury News*, Jul 8, 2020. https://www.mercurynews.com/2020/07/07/before-lori-loughlin-did-donald-trump-cheat-in-college-admissions/.

Russert, Tim. "Trump in 1999: 'I Am Very Pro-Choice.'" YouTube video, Oct 24, 1999. https://www.youtube.com/watch?v=-d4s1S520n4.

Safe Home. "Gun Sales in the U.S.—2021 Second Highest Year for Gun Sales since 2000." Accessed February 16, 2022. https://www.safehome.org/data/firearms-guns-statistics/.

Samuels, Brett. "Trump Calls Barr 'a Disappointment in Every Sense of the Word.'" *Hill*, Jun 7, 2021. https://thehill.com/homenews/campaign/560478-trump-calls-barr-a-disappointment-in-every-sense-of-the-word.

Samuels, Brett, and Rebecca Beitsch. "Giuliani Hits New Low with Georgia Indictment." *Hill*, Sep 2, 2023. https://thehill.com/regulation/court-battles/4180673-giuliani-hits-new-low-with-georgia-indictment/.

Sanchez, Ray. "A 7-Year-Old Guatemalan Girl Who Died in Border Patrol Custody Is Identified." CNN, Dec 14, 2018. https://www.cnn.com/2018/12/14/us/guatemalan-girl-death-ice/index.html.

Sanchez, Carolina. "Timeline of Texas Mass Shootings over the Years." *Fox 26 Houston*, May 25, 2022. https://www.fox26houston.com/news/texas-mass-shootings.

Sangal, Aditi, et al. "Trump DOJ Official Jeffrey Clark Surrenders at Fulton County Jail." CNN, Aug 25, 2023. https://www.cnn.com/politics/live-news/georgia-trump-indictment-surrender-08-25-23/h_bdf613445c361d24735e71c5c5244208.

Bibliography

Sanger, David E., and Nicole Periroth. "Trump Fires a Cybersecurity Official Who Called the Election 'the Most Secure in American History.'" *New York Times*, Dec 8, 2020. https://www.nytimes.com/2020/11/18/us/politics/trump-fires-a-cybersecurity-official-who-called-the-election-the-most-secure-in-american-history.html.

Scannell, Kara. "Former CFO of Trump Organization Pleads Guilty for His Role in Tax Fraud Scheme and Agrees to Testify against Company." CNN, Aug 18, 2022. https://www.cnn.com/2022/08/18/politics/allen-weisselberg-pleads-guilty/index.html.

Scannell, Kara, and Lauren del Valle. "Allen Weisselberg, Former Trump Org. CFO, Sentenced to 5 Months in Jail." CNN, Jan 10, 2023. https://www.cnn.com/2023/01/10/politics/allen-weisselberg-sentencing-trump-organization/index.html.

Schaefer, Richard T. *Sociology: A Brief Introduction*. New York: McGraw Hill Education, 2019.

Schaeffer, Katherine. "Share of Americans Who Favor Stricter Gun Control Laws Has Increased Since 2017." *Pew Research Center*, Oct 16, 2019. https://www.pewresearch.org/fact-tank/2019/10/16/share-of-americans-who-favor-stricter-gun-laws-has-increased-since-2017/.

Schifrin, Nick, and Layla Quran. "How Daniel Ortega Demolished Democracy in Nicaragua." PBS, Nov 5, 2021. https://www.pbs.org/newshour/show/how-daniel-ortega-demolished-democracy-in-nicaragua.

Schonfeld, Zach. "Here Are All the GOP Legal Challenges to Arizona's Election Results." *Hill*, Dec 15, 2022. https://thehill.com/homenews/campaign/3774934-here-are-all-the-gop-legal-challenges-to-arizonas-election-results/.

———. "Trump Found Liable for Sexual Battery, Defamation in E. Jean Carroll Trial." *Hill*, May 9, 2023. https://thehill.com/regulation/court-battles/3994107-trump-sexual-battery-defamation-e-jean-carroll-trial/.

Schwartz, Brian. "MyPillow CEO Mike Lindell Says He Spent $25 Million to Push False Pro-Trump Election Claims: 'I Will Spend Whatever It Takes.'" CNBC, Dec 16, 2021. https://www.cnbc.com/2021/12/16/mypillow-ceo-mike-lindell-spent-25-million-to-push-false-pro-trump-election-claims.html.

Scott, J. M. "Miriam 'Ma' Ferguson, Texas' First Woman Governor, Was Born on This Day in 1875." *San Antonio Express-News*, Jun 13, 2016. https://www.mysanantonio.com/news/local/history-culture/article/birthday-Ma-Ferguson-Texas-first-woman-governor-8102790.php.

Security.org Staff. "Gun Country: Where in the U.S. Are Guns Most Popular?" Accessed May 11, 2021. https://www.security.org/resources/gun-ownership-statistics/.

Shabad, Rebecca, et al. "Republicans Launched an Investigation into the Jan, 6 Committee That Examined the Riot." NBC News, Mar 8, 2023. https://www.nbcnews.com/politics/congress/republicans-launch-investigation-jan-6-committee-examined-riot-rcna74017.

Shalin, Dan. "MyPillow CEO Hit with $1.3 Billion Lawsuit over Election Claims." *Patch*, Feb 22, 2021. https://patch.com/minnesota/across-mn/mypillow-ceo-hit-1-3-billion-lawsuit-over-election-claims.

Shamsian, Jacob, and Sonam Sheth. "Trump and His Allies Filed More Than 40 Lawsuits Challenging the 2020 Election Results. All of Them Failed." *Business Insider*, Feb

22, 2021. https://www.businessinsider.com/trump-campaign-lawsuits-election-results-2020-11.

Shivaram, Deepa. "The House Jan. 6 Committee Releases Its Final Report on the Capitol Attack." NPR, Dec 22, 2022. https://www.npr.org/2022/12/21/1144489935/january-6-committee-full-report-release.

Sisak, Michael R. "Judge Fines Trump $2 Million for Misusing Charity Foundation." AP News, Nov 18, 2019. https://apnews.com/article/campaigns-donald-trump-us-news-ap-top-news-lawsuits-7b8d0f5ce9cb4cadad948c2c414afd57.

———. "Lawsuit: Steve Bannon Owes $480K for Unpaid Legal Bills." AP News, Feb 22, 2023. https://apnews.com/article/steve-bannon-politics-legal-proceedings-mexico-donald-trump-d60063acff77bc846a4ff4faa0cd8aac.

Slisco, Aila. "Thousands of Christians Call to Expel Pastor Indicted with Trump." *Newsweek*, Aug 21, 2023. https://www.newsweek.com/thousands-christians-call-expel-pastor-indicted-trump-1821448.

Small Arms Analytic. "U.S. Firearms Sales December 2020: Sales Increases Slowing Down, Year's Total Sales Clock in at 23 Million Units." Jan 5, 2021. http://smallarmsanalytics.com/v1/pr/2021-01-05.pdf.

Smith, David, and Sabrina Siddique. "Trump Claims 'Cheating' Is Only Way He Can Lose Pennsylvania." *Guardian*, Aug 13, 2016. https://www.theguardian.com/us-news/2016/aug/13/donald-trump-claims-cheating-is-only-way-he-can-lose-pennsylvania.

Spies, Mike, and Ashley Balcerzak. "The NRA Place Big Bets on the 2016 Election and Won Almost All of Them." *Trace*, Nov 9, 2016. https://www.thetrace.org/2016/11/nra-big-bets-election-2016-results/.

Stern, Gabe. "Nevada Grand Jury Indicts Six Republicans Who Falsely Certified That Trump Won the State in 2020." AP News, Dec 6, 2023. https://apnews.com/article/fake-electors-nevada-indictment-ba84be72465e635dbaadc312a9632fc8.

Stieb, Matt, and Margaret Hartmann. "Here's Every Single Lie Told by George Santos." *New York Magazine*, May 10, 2023. https://nymag.com/intelligencer/article/guide-george-santos-lies.html.

Sunday, Nwafor. "U.S. Election: Trump's Defeat Confirms Apostle Johnson Suleman Prophecy." *Vanguard*, Nov 7, 2020. https://www.vanguardngr.com/2020/11/u-s-election-trumps-defeat-confirms-apostle-johnson-sulemans-prophecy/.

Svajlenka, Nicole Prchal. "A Demographic Profile of DACA Recipients on the Frontlines of the Coronavirus Response." *Center for American Progress*, Apr 6, 2020. https://www.americanprogress.org/issues/immigration/news/2020/04/06/482708/demographic-profile-daca-recipients-frontlines-coronavirus-response/.

Swartz, David. "Ron Sider and Evangelicals for McGovern." *Patheos*, Sep 21, 2022. https://www.patheos.com/blogs/anxiousbench/2022/09/ron-sider-and-evangelicals-for-mcgovern/.

Szep, Jason, and Linda So. "Kanye West Publicist Pressed Georgia Election Worker to Confess to Bogus Fraud Charges." *Reuters*, Dec 23, 2021. https://www.reuters.com/business/media-telecom/kanye-west-publicist-pressed-georgia-election-worker-confess-bogus-fraud-charges-2021-12-10/.

Tabachnick, Cara. "What Do 'Stand Your Ground' Laws Allow For—Which States Have Them." CBS News, Apr 19, 2023. https://www.cbsnews.com/news/ralph-yarl-shooting-andrew-lester-stand-your-ground-laws/.

Bibliography

Tanfani, Joseph, et al. "How Trump's Pied Pipers Rallied a Faithful Mob to the Capitol." *Reuters*, Jan 11, 2021. https://www.reuters.com/article/us-usa-trump-protest-organizers-insight/how-trumps-pied-pipers-rallied-a-faithful-mob-to-the-capitol-idUSKBN29G2UP.

Taylor, Matt. "Fox News Reaches $757.5 Million Settlement in Dominion's Defamation Lawsuit." *Politico*, Apr 18, 2023. https://www.politico.com/news/2023/04/18/fox-news-reaches-settlement-with-dominion-in-defamation-lawsuit-00092621.

Texas Capital. "How Many Guns Are in Texas?" May 18, 2022. https://www.texascapital.org/how-many-guns/.

Texas Council of Family Violence. "2020 Honoring Texas Victims." Accessed February 11, 2024. https://tcfv.org/wp-content/uploads/tcfv_htv_summary_facts_2020.pdf.

Timm, Jane C. "Trump versus the Truth: The Most Outrageous Falsehoods of His Presidency." NBC News, Dec 31, 2020. https://www.nbcnews.com/politics/donald-trump/trump-versus-truth-most-outrageous-falsehoods-his-presidency-n1252580.

Truman Library. "Recognition of Israel." Accessed December 17, 2024. https://www.trumanlibrary.gov/education/presidential-inquiries/recognition-israel.

Tucker, Emma. "Gun-Loving Texas, Where Most Households Own a Firearm, Has Become an Epicenter of Mass Shootings." CNN, May 17, 2023. https://www.cnn.com/2023/05/17/us/texas-gun-ownership-mass-shootings/index.html.

U.S. Citizenship and Immigration Services. "Consideration for Deferred Action for Childhood Arrivals (DACA)." Accessed July 12, 2021. https://www.uscis.gov/humanitarian/consideration-of-deferred-action-for-childhood-arrivals-daca.

———. "Count of Active DACA Recipients by Month of Current DACA Expiration." December 31, 2020. https://www.uscis.gov/sites/default/files/document/reports/Active_DACA_Recipients_December_31_2020.pdf.

U.S. Customs and Border Protection. "On a Typical Day in Fiscal Year 2018, CBP . . . " Last updated May 11, 2022. https://www.cbp.gov/newsroom/stats/typical-day-fy2018.

U.S. Department of Commerce. "News: Unemployment Is at Its Lowest Level in 54 Years." Feb 3, 2023. https://www.commerce.gov/news/blog/2023/02/news-unemployment-its-lowest-level-54-years.

Valania, Jonathan. "Fact-Checking All the Mysteries Surrounding Donald Trump and Penn." *PhillyMag*. Sep 14, 2019. https://www.phillymag.com/news/2019/09/14/donald-trump-at-wharton-university-of-pennsylvania/.

Valle, Sabrina. "Exxon Smashes Western Oil Majors' Profits with $56 Billion in 2022." *Reuters*, Jan 31, 2023. https://www.reuters.com/business/energy/exxon-smashes-western-oil-majors-earnings-record-with-59-billion-profit-2023-01-31/.

Vertuno, Jim, and Jake Bleiberg. "Why Texas' GOP-Controlled House Wants to Impeach Republican Attorney General Ken Paxton." AP News, May 26, 2023. https://apnews.com/article/texas-attorney-general-paxton-impeachment-explainer-15f1495D045dce8d838f9937d76d48ed.

Villarreal, Daniel. "Pastor Robin Bullock Says It's a Sin to Recognize Joe Biden as President." *Newsweek*, May 3, 2021. https://www.newsweek.com/pastor-robin-bullock-says-its-sin-recognize-joe-biden-president-1588361.

Villeneuve, Marina. "Report: Trump Commission Did Not Find Widespread Voter Fraud." AP News, Aug 3, 2018. https://apnews.com/article/f5f6a73b2af546ee97816bb35e82c18d.

Vlamis, Kelsey. "Trump Rips the Supreme Court as 'Nothing More Than a Political Body' after They Ruled against Him, Even Though He Appointed 3 Justices of the Conservative Majority." *Business Insider*, Nov 23, 2022. https://www.businessinsider.com/trump-rips-supreme-court-political-body-after-ruling-against-him-2022-11.

Wainscott, Kent. "Paul Ryan Says Former President Donald Trump Lost the 2020 Election." *WISN*, Aug 30, 2021. https://www.wisn.com/article/paul-ryan-says-former-president-donald-trump-lost-the-2020-election/37436025#.

Webster, Daniel, et al. "Effects of the Repeal of Missouri Handgun Purchaser Licensing Law on Homicides." *Journal of Urban Health* 91.2 (Mar 7, 2014) 293–302. https://doi.org/10.1007%2Fs11524-014-9865-8.

Weisman, Jonathan, and Reid J. Epstein. "G.O.P. Declares Jan. 6 Attack 'Legitimate Political Discourse.'" *New York Times*, Feb 4, 2021. https://www.nytimes.com/2022/02/04/us/politics/republicans-jan-6-cheney-censure.html.

Welker, Bryce. "Donald Trump Settlement and Lawsuits—History of Legal Affairs." *CRUSH the LSAT*, Oct 15, 2021. https://crushthelsatexam.com/deep-dive-donald-trumps-long-history-of-lawsuits/.

Wells, Zoe, and Kate Perez. "MyPillow CEO Mike Lindell Says He's Out of Money, Can't Pay Lawyers in Defamation Case." *USA Today*, Oct 12, 2023. https://www.msn.com/en-us/money/news/mypillow-ceo-mike-lindell-says-he-s-out-of-money-can-t-pay-lawyers-in-defamation-case/ar-AA1i3lA6?ocid=msedgntp&cvid=5bbe48ca574d458d95cff1a9dc0786fd&ei=33.

Welna, David. "GOP's History of Resistance to Social Welfare Programs." NPR, Oct 7, 2013. https://www.npr.org/2013/10/07/230023627/gops-history-of-resistance-to-social-welfare-programs.

Wertheimer, Fred, and Norman Eisen. "Trump Illegally Asked Russia to Help Him Win in 2016. He Shouldn't Get Away with It." *USA Today*, Jan 2, 2019. https://www.usatoday.com/story/opinion/2019/01/02/trump-broke-law-russia-clinton-emails-hold-him-accountable-column/2449564002/.

Whitehurst, Lindsay. "Bannon Gets 4 Months behind Bars for Defying 1/6 Subpoena." AP News, Oct 21, 2022. https://apnews.com/article/capitol-siege-steve-bannon-congress-donald-trump-sentencing-36d412eba9e1609a030859852378ae3d.

Wickert, David. "Raffensperger Disputes Fraud Claims, Welcomes Ballot Review." *Atlanta Journal-Constitution*, May 27, 2021. https://www.ajc.com/politics/election/raffensperger-disputes-fraud-claims-welcomes-ballot-review/2LCSWPDMLVAGPM45Q5FP2XWDE4/.

Wikipedia. "List of Mass Shootings in the United States in 2020." Accessed August 2, 2021. https://en.wikipedia.org/wiki/List_of_mass_shootings_in_the_United_States_in_2020.

———. "Stand-Your-Ground Law." Accessed January 8, 2024. https://en.wikipedia.org/wiki/Stand-your-ground_law.

Wiley, Ella. "Why Race Matters in Redistricting: Protecting Black Power and Preserving Democracy." Legal Defense Fund, Sep 27, 2022. https://www.naacpldf.org/redistricting-racism/.

Wolf, Elizabeth, and Raja Razek. "Democrats in Retaliation over Gun Control Protest on 'Sad Day for Democracy.'" CNN, Apr 7, 2023. https://www.cnn.com/2023/04/07/us/tennessee-democrat-house-representatives-expelled-friday/index.html.

Wolf, Zachary B. "States with the Most Gun Violence Share One Trait." CNN Politics, May 26, 2022. https://www.cnn.com/2022/05/26/politics/gun-violence-data-what-matters/index.html.

———. "Trump's Ukraine Scandal: Who Is Who?" CNN, Sep 28, 2019. https://www.cnn.com/2019/09/28/politics/trump-ukraine-scandal-people/index.html.

Wong, Scott, et al. "Jan. 6 Committee Report Details the Scope of Trump's Pressure Campaign to Overturn the Election." *Yahoo News*, Dec 23, 2022. https://news.yahoo.com/jan-6-committee-unveils-final-050406097.html.

Woodruff, Chase. "'Unprecedented' Threat: Trump 14th Amendment Trial in Colorado Comes to a Close." *Raw Story*, Nov 16, 2023. https://www.rawstory.com/trump-colorado-2666285897/.

Woolley, John T. "The 2022 Midterm Elections: What the Historical Data Suggest." The American Presidency Project, Aug 30, 2022. https://www.presidency.ucsb.edu/analyses/the-2022-midterm-elections-what-the-historical-data-suggest.

Wright, David, et al. "Cruz Unloads with Epic Takedown of 'Pathological Liar,' 'Narcissist' Donald Trump." CNN, May 3, 2016. https://www.cnn.com/2016/05/03/politics/donald-trump-rafael-cruz-indiana/index.html.

Yousif, Nadine. "Trump Organization Fined $1.6 Million for Tax Fraud." BBC, Jan 13, 2023. https://www.bbc.com/news/world-us-canada-64257735.

Zeidman, Bob. "How I Won $5 Million from MyPillow Guy and Saved Democracy." *Politico*, May 26, 20232. https://www.politico.com/news/magazine/2023/05/26/my-pillow-mike-lindell-investigation-00097903.

Zorthian, Julian, et al. "50 Women Who Made American Political History." *Time*, Mar 8, 2017. https://time.com/4551817/50-women-political-history/.

Index

abortion
    anti-abortion, 14, 38–40, 42–43, 50, 97–98, 140, 185, 214
    antiabortionist, 50, 185
    Molech worship, 47–48
    personal analysis, 48
    political punch bag, xi, 107, 111
    pro-choice, 38–39, 185
    pro-life, xi, 38–39, 42–43, 46–47, 85, 185, 234
    rates of abortion in the US, 44–45, 47
    reasons for abortion, 45–46
    Roe v. Wade, x, 44–45
    under Democratic presidents, 44–45
    under Republican presidents, 44–45
Abram, 100
Abraham, 19, 26, 100–101
Affordable Care Act (ACA), 13
African Americans, 55, 72
agape love, 23
Ahab, 130–32, 232
Ahaziah, 232–33
Ahijah, 141–42
Alabama, 72
Alaska, 83, 95
Albany, 156
allies, 116, 118, 122, 144, 148–50, 153, 156–58, 160, 162, 177–79, 183, 186, 188–89, 191–93, 204, 209, 211–13, 217
Alonzo, Felipe Gomez, 109
AlterNet, 219

America, 47, 68–69, 101, 139, 178, 180, 185–86, 197, 214–15, 218–19, 227–28
American Indians and Alaska Natives, 55
amoral, 123–124, 163, 188
anoint, 70, 139, 141
anointed, xii, 35, 70, 101, 128, 139, 141–43, 222–23
antichrist, 33, 185–86, 221, 236–37
    precursor 186, 221, 237
apocalyptic warning, 10, 193, 195
apostates, xii, 222
Apostle Paul, 22–23, 79, 148, 188, 222
Arizona, 67, 159, 177, 191
Arkansas, 72
Arkansas Times, 163
Asian Americans, 55, 229
asylum, 110
Atlanta Journal-Constitution, 160
authoritarian, 4, 184, 193, 220
autocracy, 180, 192–93, 215

Babylon, 150
Baier, Bret, 119
Balaam, 133–34
    doctrine, xii, 32, 134, 145, 152, 222
Balak, 133–34
Bannon, Steve, 212
Barr, Bill, 119–20, 144, 158–59, 209
Barrett, Amy Coney, 150
Batavia, New York, 147
Beschloss, Michael, 226
Bible
    verses to help the poor, 34–36

Index

Biden, Beau, 169
Biden, Hunter, 117, 177
Biden, Joe, 17, 58, 117, 132–33, 139, 144, 148–50, 155, 158, 161–62, 164–65, 169, 177, 191, 203–4, 206–7
   economy, 17
big lies, 154, 187
Black Lives Matter, 229
Black Voices, 206
Boaz, 8
Bolton, John, 119
Border Patrol agents, 110–11
Border wall, 110–11
   drug smuggling, 110
   human trafficking, 110
bourgeoisie, 4, 12
Brennan, John, 117
Buck, Ken, 212
Burns, Mark, 115
Bush, George H.W. (father), 16, 44, 184,
Bush, George W. (son), 44, 137, 167, 184
business grants, 6
bystander, 44

Caesar, 29
California, 201
cancel culture, 32, 215
capitalism, xi, 3–9, 11–12, 22, 33
   biblical example, 9
Capito, Shelley Moore, 38
Capitol riot, 70, 75–76, 187, 189–90, 199–200, 230
Carroll, E. Jean, 59
Carter, Jimmy, 186
Casey, Bob, 38
Castle doctrine, 82
Catholic Church, 185
census, 72
Centers for Disease Control and Prevention (CDC), 45, 82
Certified Public Accounting Firm, 159
Chamorro, Violeta, 182
charity, 61
charity organization, 216
Cheeley, Robert, 205

Cheney, Liz, 63, 76, 161, 181, 183, 215
Chesebro, Kenneth, 204
Chicago, Illinois, 199, 205
China, 4, 65, 71, 120, 196, 209
Christendom, 225
Christian evangelicals, 14–15, 27, 44–45, 48, 108, 115–17, 121, 127, 133, 140, 143, 154, 169, 177, 184, 187, 192–93, 227–28, 230,
Christian Nationalism, 205
Christianity, 42, 50, 208, 225
Christians, x, xii, 29, 31, 47–48, 50–51, 77, 79, 95–96, 98, 122, 126, 132, 137, 143, 152, 154, 169, 174, 181, 192–93, 215, 219, 222, 224–25, 231, 233–35, 237
Church, 9 11, 19, 21, 28, 30–31, 40, 51–52, 77–78, 89, 98, 122, 145, 151–52, 183, 185, 196, 205, 221–23, 231
Church of Sardis, 52
Citigroup, 60
civic, 50, 91, 102, 190
Civil Liberties, 183
civilization, 197
Clark, Clay, 147
Clark, Jeffrey, 163
classified documents, 190
Clement, Kim, 137–38
Clinton, Bill, 45
Clinton, Hillary, 55, 155, 203, 211
CNBC, 209
CNN, 124, 169, 224
Coats, Dan, 120
Coffee County, Georgia, 207
Cohen, Michael, 167, 201–2, 215, 227,
Cold War, 116
Collins, Susan, 38
Colorado, 156, 190, 212
Colorado caucuses, 156
Colorado Supreme Court, 190
commandment, 7, 20–23, 27, 34, 68, 74, 77–78, 107, 139, 141, 143, 152, 172, 228, 230–33
communism, 4–9
   biblical example, 9
Communist Manifesto, 4
community service, 199, 203–4, 207

confirmation bias, 69
Congress, 16–17, 43–44, 58, 60, 69, 87, 124, 149, 168, 190, 195, 201, 203, 208, 212, 219
Congress and National Archives, 208
Congressional Democrats, 13, 110
Congressional Republicans, 13, 84–85, 87, 89–91, 96, 106–9, 163, 180
Connecticut, 89
conservative media, 50, 63–65, 163
conservatives, 6, 44, 50, 63–65, 107, 117, 163, 185, 219, 237
conspiracy theories, 65, 156, 162, 177, 203–5, 209, 211, 219
Constitution, 67, 123, 157, 161, 182–83, 190, 192–94, 217–18, 228, 237
Conway, George, 226
Conway, Kellyanne, 226
Cornyn, John, 213
Coronavirus Aid, Relief, & Economic Security (CARES), 10
corporate
    bailout, 7
    business subsidies, 7
    profit, 17
    tax, 14
    welfare, 10
corruption, x, 8, 61–62, 91, 95, 120, 122–23, 125–26, 144, 157, 163, 173–74, 179–80, 185, 187–89, 191–95, 197, 208–12, 217–20, 222, 229–30, 232
Courier-Journal, 118
Covenant School in Nashville, TN, 93
COVID-19, 118, 228–29
    vaccines, 19
Crenshaw, Dan, 162
criminal immunity, 61
Cruz, Ted, 123, 156, 226
Cuba, 4
cult mentality, 75, 192
Cuomo, Andrew, 58, 211
Curiel, Gonzalo, 216
cybersecurity, 158, 209
Cybersecurity and Infrastructure Security Agency (CISA), 158

Cyrus, 115, 179, 231–32, 237

Daily Pennsylvanian, 167
Dallas, Texas, 139
Daniels, Stormy, 118
Dark Triad traits, 171
David, 8, 70, 139–42, 144
Davidoff Hutcher & Citron LLP, 212
Daystar, ix
Deace, Steve, 203
deception, 15, 32, 76, 142, 147, 152, 172, 174, 194
Declaration of Independence, 54
Deferred Action for Childhood Arrival (DACA), 105–9, 111, See also Dreamers
DeFreytag, Kyle, 75
dehumanization 44, 47, 49, 69, 73, 94
Delaware Army National Guard, 169
delusion, ix, 148
democracy
    assault, 157
    efficacy, 90, 197
    national identity, 90, 180
    threat, 125
Democrats
    abortion, 38–40, 43, 48, 98
    DACA, 107–109
    economy, 16–17,
    equitable justice, 25
    immigration, 100
    gerrymandering, 72
    love and help toward marginalized groups, 25, 27
    opportunities for political advancement, 55
    reducing the federal deficit, 16
    social justice, 53, 55
    social programs, 37
Denmark, 4
Department of Homeland Security, 106
Department of Justice, 165, 181, 200
dereliction of duty, 124, 237
DeSantis, Ron, 185
dictator, 178, 180–81–82, 184–86, 193, 195, 220
disability insurance, 7
discrimination, 69, 71, 78, 234

disenfranchisement, 16, 47, 73, 78
dishonest, ix, xii, 12, 60, 64, 72, 117–18, 124, 150, 162, 164–65, 167, 170–71, 177, 195–96, 204, 209, 211–12, 222, 227
dishonest scales, 72, 150
diversity, 42, 68
divorce, 23
domestic violence, 57, 85
Dominion Voting Systems, 64, 160, 203, 210
Dreamers, 106–10
dysfunctional, 218

Eastman, John, 203
Economic systems
  capitalism, xi, 4–9, 12, 22, 33
  communism, 4–9
  socialism, xi, 3–11, 18–19, 21, 23, 25–26, 30–33, 37, 43, 46, 70, 76, 103, 126, 151, 235
economically disadvantaged, 17
Edison, Thomas, 33
Electoral College, 204
El Paso sector, 111
Ellis, Jenna, 179, 207
endorsement, 44, 64, 172, 174
Engels, Friedrich, 4
equitable justice, 25, 44, 47, 55, 57–58, 63, 67, 71, 73, 77–79, 189, 191, 217–18
Ethiopian, 4
Exxon Mobile, 11

Faithful Americans, 205
fake electors, 191, 203–6, 208, 230
false prophecies, 127–33, 135–6, 147–49, 151, 178, 236
false prophets, xiii, 77, 127–33, 150–51, 154, 173, 185, 195, 228, 237
  biblical examples, 130–31
Falwell, Jerry, ix
farm subsidies, 6
Faustian bargain, x, 11, 84
Federal Bureau of Investigation (FBI), 65, 72, 87, 116, 126, 181, 189, 202–3, 217
Federal deficits, 16

Federal Emergency Management Agency (FEMA), 7
federal government, 6, 11, 20
Ferguson, Miriam, 56
Ferguson, James, 63
financial loss, 61, 198, 209–11
Finland, 4
firearms homicides, 82, 92–4
First Baptist Church in Sutherland Springs, 89
Florida, 39, 83, 87, 199, 209
Floyd, Harrison, 206–7
Flynn, Michael, 147, 163, 202, 227
food stamps, 7
Ford, Aaron, 208
Ford, Christine Blasey, 58
Fox News, 63–64, 119, 181, 188, 194, 210
  promotion of falsehoods, 210
  lawsuits settlement with Dominion, 64
free lunch program, 7
Freeman, Ruby, 201, 205–7, 210–11
Frisco, Texas, 199
Fulton County, 203, 205–8
  District Attorney Fani Willis, 203, 207–8
  Indictments, 203–7

Gabbard, Tulsi, 38
Garner, Margaret, 46
Gass, Nick, 224
Georgia, 160, 162, 164, 177, 191, 200, 203–7, 210–11
  election workers, 200, 204–5, 210–11
  fake electors, 191, 203–6, 208, 230
Georgia racketeering, 204, 206–7
gerrymandering, 72
Giuliani, Rudy, 200, 203, 207, 210–11
  disbarred, 211
  lawsuits, 210–11
Goldman Sachs, 60
  black governors, 56
  female governors, 56
GPS locator, 199
Graham, Franklin, ix
Graham, Jack, ix

Index

grant for churches and non-profit organizations, 7
Grasso, Ella T, 56
greatest commandment, 23
Griswold, Jena, 190
Gross Domestic Product (GDP), 16
groupthink, xii, 214
guns
    accessibility and homicide, 85–86, 88
    argument that guns do not kill people, 92
    biblical perspectives on guns, 95
    death rates for children in the US, 81–82
    death rates for women in the US, 82
    death rates in the US, 43, 82
    domestic violence, 85
    financial cost, 82
    laws and mass shooting, 87–89, 93
    NRA financial support to GOP campaign, 90
    number of mass shootings in the US, 87–88
    permitless law, 88
    public opinion on stricter gun laws, 86
    recommendations to reduce gun violence, 94–95
    repeal background check, 84–85
    Second Amendment, 91
    stand your ground, 82–84, 95, 98

Hagee, John, xi
Hall, Scott Graham, 206
Hampton, Misty, 207
Hannity, Sean, 63, 181
happiest countries, 4
Harris, Kamala, 56
Harvard Law School, 166
Hashida, Gunther, 75
hate groups, 40–42, 44, 48, 50, 66, 70, 184, 187, 192, 221, 230–31
    Proud Boys, 184, 194, 200, 229–30
    QAnon, 70, 184
    Oath Keepers, 70, 184, 194, 200
    militiamen, 70
    White supremacists, 41, 70, 230
Helsinki, Finland, 116–17
Henry, Patrick, 124
heresy, 187, 221, 238
high-capacity ammunition magazines, 86, 92, 95
Hill, Anita, 58
Hispanics, 55
holier-than-thou, 39, 138
Holt, Lester, 63
Holy Spirit, 47, 77, 128–29, 132, 136, 139, 154, 192
homeless, 132
House Bill (H.B.) 1927, 88
House Committee, 178, 188–90, 212
House Judiciary Committee, x
House Select Committee, 165, 200
House Ways and Means Committee, 168
Houston, Texas, 65
Howell, Beryl, 210
human trafficking, 110
hush money, 201
hypocrites, xi, 11, 29, 33, 39–41, 69, 107, 146, 151, 166, 215, 218

Iceland, 4
Idaho, 213
Illinois, 76, 205
immigration, 14, 100–101, 105, 108–11, 118–19
    biblical origin of immigration, 100
    DACA, 107–9, 111
    God's justice for immigrants, 102–5
    zero tolerance, 109–10, 119, 184
immoral, ix–x, 25, 59, 62, 68, 91, 94, 116, 122, 150, 161, 188, 195
immunity, 135, 143, 204
impeachment, 61–63, 118, 165
incandescent light bulb, 33
Industrial Revolution, 4
inflation, 11–12, 17, 149, 169
influenza infection, 109
injustice, 143, 176, 57, 59, 65–66, 71
Iowa caucus, 156
Israel, 8, 30, 48, 59, 71, 101, 104, 115, 127, 131, 133–34, 139–43, 150, 185, 232–33, 237

Jackson County, 84
James, Letitia, 58

Jehoshaphat, 130–31
Jehu, 232–33
Jericho, 24–25
Jeroboam, 141–43, 233
Jerusalem, 24–25, 30, 115, 141–42, 185, 231–32
Jesse, 8, 70
Jesus, 95, 223–25
Jews, 7, 30, 54, 101, 108, 115, 174, 231–32
Johnson, Jeremiah, 133
Jonathan, 144,
Jones, Jim, 213
Judah, 22, 77, 130, 141, 232

Kansas City, 84
Karl Max, 4, 33
Kavanaugh, Brett, 58, 60
Kelly, Kenneth, 199
Kemp, Brian, 203
Kentucky, 199
Kierkegaard, Søren, 153
Kim Jong-Un, 182, 186
Kinzinger, Adam, 69, 76, 215
Krebs, Christopher, 158, 209
Kutti, Trevian, 206–7

Latham, Cathay, 205
Latin America, 184
Lazarus, 25–26
Lee, Stephen Cliffgard, 205
Levite, 9, 24–25, 35
Liars, xii, 23, 41–42, 65–66, 68–69, 74, 159, 161, 163, 167, 171–72, 188, 191, 223, 226–27
  biblical views of lies, 171–72
  lying tongue, 222, 228, 230
  psychological analysis, 171
  psychological liar, 119, 123, 196, 200, 226–27
Liberation theology, 77–78
Liebengood, Howard S., 75
Lindell, Mike, 209–210
litmus test, 24, 219
lives tumbledown, 199, 208
Locke, Gary, 56
Louisiana, 72
Lutheran Church, 205

Machiavellianism, 171
mammon, 28, 77–78, 131, 145, 150, 155
Manafort, Paul, 116, 202, 227
Manchin, Joe, 38
Manhattan apartment, 211
Manhattan Criminal Court, 169
Maquin, Jakelin Caal, 109
marginalization, x
marginalized groups, 8, 14, 16, 20, 27, 42, 46–47, 54, 66, 76–77, 103–4, 140, 234, 237
Maricopa County, 159–60
Marjory Stoneman Douglas High School, 87
Martin, Trayvon, 83
mass shootings, 85, 87–89, 93
Mattis, James, 120
McCain, John, 116, 170, 184
McFadden, Trevor N., 201
Meadows, Mark, 204
Medicaid, 7
Medicare, 7
Meet the Press, 38
Menendez, Bob, 60
Merchan, Juan, 169
mercy, 24–26, 28, 54–55, 79, 108, 143, 175
Messiah, xii, 27, 138, 140, 174, 229
Micaiah, 130–32
Michal, 140, 144
Michigan, 191, 208
Michigan State Attorney General, 208
Midian, 133–34
Miller, Jason, 200, 203
Milwaukee's WISN TV, 161
minority groups, 25, 41, 45–47, 55–56, 67, 72–73, 77–78, 214
Miriam, 41
Missouri, 84
Moab, 8, 133
mobster, 184, 214
  danger of mobster mentality, 214
  mentality, 214
  new normal, 217
modern-day Pharisees, xi–xii, 18–19, 27–28, 146, 151, 235–37
Molech worship, 47–48

monarchy, 123, 179–80, 187, 193–94, 220
Moore, Roy, 58
Moore, Wes, 56
moral authority, 13, 158
moral reasoning, 68, 77
Mortgage deduction, 7
Moscow, 116
Moses, 34, 41, 101
Moss, Shaye, 201, 205, 210–11
MSNBC, 212
Mueller investigation, 118, 159
Munoz, Marco Antonio, 109–10
Murkowski, Lisa, 38
Murphy, Phil, 60
MyPillow, 209
myths about welfare programs, 16

narcissism, 171
Nashville, Tennessee, 93
National Association of Evangelicals, ix
National Rifle Association (NRA), 74, 83, 87–90, 94, 96–97
  donations to GOP campaigns, 90
Native Americans, 47, 71, 100, 102
NBC, 63
Nehemiah, 22
Nessel, Dana, 208
Netherlands, 4
Nevada, 84, 177, 191, 208
New Mexico, 191
New Testament, 98, 235
New York, 33, 58, 147, 168–69, 211
New York appellate court, 211
New York Times, 164, 168, 168
Newsmax, 163
Newsweek, 147
Nicaragua, 182–84
Nichols, Carl, 212
Nixon, Richard, ix
North Korea, 186
Northwestern University, 90
Norway, 4

Obama, Barack, 13, 45, 55, 105
  immigration 105–9, 111
Obamacare, 13
obedience, 20–21, 30, 108, 221

Ockenga, Harold, ix
Oral Robert University, 154
Ortega, Daniel, 182–86, 193

Papadopoulos, George, 202, 227
parables
  good Samaritan, 24–25, 79
  Pharisee and a tax collector, 40
  rich man and Lazarus, 25–26
  talents, 9
  unforgiving servant, 225
Parkland, Florida, 87
parsonages, 11–12
partisan politics, xii, 23, 28, 31, 39, 49, 53, 57, 77, 129, 144–46, 150–51, 173, 176, 193, 219, 221–22, 232–34
Patrick, Deval, 56
Pelosi, Nancy, 55
permitless, 88
permit-to-purchase (PTP), 84
Pence, Mike, 119, 144, 191, 193, 203, 207
Peter, 96, 98, 224
Pew Research Center, 86, 109
Phantom voters, 209
Pharisees, xi–xi, 10, 18–19, 23, 27–29, 40, 50, 69, 77, 138, 140, 146, 149, 151, 174–76, 234–37
Philistines, 137, 140
philosopher, 153
political advancement, 55
political preacher (poli-preacher), xi, 149–50, 154, 165
political proselytization, 176, 232
political punch bag, xi, 107, 111
political witch hunt, 59, 190–91, 217
politics, 27, 31, 77, 100, 108, 146, 150, 151, 154–55, 234
PolitiFact
Pompeo, Mike, 119, 167
post-modern society, 25, 95
posttraumatic stress disorder (PTSD), 109–10
poverty, 4, 10, 14–15, 25–26, 43
  structural problem, 15–16, 46
Powell, Sidney, 203, 210
Presbyterian, 224
presidential historian, 226

priests, 22, 25, 77, 140, 142, 144
Princeton University, 16, 90
Pro V&V, 159–60
pro-choice, 38–39
proletariat, 4, 12
pro-life, 185, 234
Prophecies in presidential elections
    Biden's presidency, 139
    Obama's presidency, 137
    Trump's presidency, 139
prophecy
    false prophecies of the 2020 election, 127, 129, 132–33
    God's providence in presidential election, 136
proselytization, 176, 232
Protestant, 3, 40
Proud Boys, 184, 194, 200, 229–30
pseudo-love, 23
psychological liar, 119, 123, 196, 200, 226–27
psychopathy, 171
public defender, 7
public school, 7, 87
Putin, Vladimir, 116–17, 182, 186, 194

QAnon, 70, 184
quid pro quo, 117
Quinnipiac University National Poll, 121–22

race, 8, 27, 42–44, 46, 49, 68–69, 71–74, 78, 108, 140, 176, 188–89, 229
    idol, 220
racial and ethnic groups, 67, 71–72
racial injustice, 46–47
racism, 44, 49, 51, 68–71, 73–74, 78, 218–19
Racketeer Influenced and Corrupt Organizations Act (RICO) Act, 205–7
Raffensperger, Brad, 160, 162, 164, 191, 203
Ramoth Gilead, 130–31
rational-legal authority, 215
Reagan, Ronald, 184, 186
ReAwaken American, 147

redistricting, 72, 214
remnants, xii, 233
repeal of background checks,
Republicans
    abortion, xi, 14, 38–39, 43–45
    Dreamers, 107–8
    equitable justice, 44, 57–58, 67, 189, 191
    Faustian deal, x, 11, 84
    gerrymandering, 72
    hate groups, 40–41, 48, 50, 66, 70, 221
    immigration, 107
    opposition to welfare programs for the poor, 13–15
    social justice, 14
    social programs, 99, 108, 235
Revolutionary War for American Independence, 124
Riggleman, Denver, 63
right-wing extremists, xii, 191
Robb Elementary School shooting, 89
Robertson, Pat, ix, 129, 144
Roe vs. Wade, x, 44–45
Roman Catholic, 40
Roman, Michael, 206
Romney, Mitt, 124, 161, 184, 213
Rosen, Jeffrey A, 162
Ross, Nellie Tayloe, 56
Rubio, Marco, 123
Russert, Tim, 38
Russia, 59, 182, 186, 194–96, 201–202
    meddling with the 2016 election, 116
Ruth, 8
Ryan, Paul, 116, 161

sacrifice, 28, 48, 170, 229
Samaritan, 24–25, 79
Samson, 137
sanctimonious, 28, 39, 138
San Diego border, 110–11
Sandy Hook Elementary School shooting, 66, 89
Saul, 137, 139–40, 142, 144, 148
Scarpulla, Saliann, 216
Scavino, Dan, 179
Schenck, Robert, x
Schumer, Chuck, 117

Scripture
    verses to help the poor, 34–37
Second Amendment, 43, 66, 90–91
Section 3 of the 14th Amendment, 190
seditious conspiracy, 200
Senate Intelligence Committee, 116
Sessions, Jeff, 106
sexual assault, 57–61
Shafer, David, 205
shoot first laws, 82
Sicknick, Brian D., 75
Simpson, Alan, 63
SLI Compliance, 159–160
Smartmatic, 210
Smith, Jack, 189
Smith, Jeffrey, 75
Smith, Ray, 204
social class, 42–43, 49, 68, 71, 140
social justice, 8–9, 47, 57, 71, 73–74, 78–79, 140
social media, 65, 199, 227,
social norms, 71–72, 175
social programs and biblical verses, 34–35
    biblical examples, 20–23
    examples 6–7
    opposition to social programs, 14–15
    originated with God, 18, 32–33
Social Security, 6, 13
social stratification, 4
socialist countries, 4
Solomon, 141
South Carolina, 72
Special Counsel's Office, 202
Stand-your-ground laws, 82–83, 95
Sterling, Gabriel, 160, 164
Stevens, Stuart, 70
stewardship, 9
Still, Shawn, 205
stimulus checks, 7
Stone, Roger, 203, 227
stratification, 9, 44
streptococcal sepsis, 109
subliminal message, xi, 145
suicide, 75, 86, 109
suicide ideation, 109

Suleman, Johnson, 139
Supreme Court, 157, 194
    accusation of sexual assaults, 58
    cases, 67–68
    decline to strike down Obama care, 13
    Justices nominated by GOP presidents
    immigration, 106
    Roe v. Wade case, 45
    ruling in the Roe v. Wade case, 44
    Trump's tax records, 168
Sweden, 4
Switzerland, 4
systemic racism, 40–41, 46, 48

Tabernacle, 30
Tax Cuts and Job Act (TCJA), 14
tax exemptions
    churches, (501(c)(3), 7, 11, 19
    pastor's house (parsonage), 7, 11–12, 19, 33, 235
tax reform, 14, 43
Temple, 115, 140, 231–232
Temporary Assistance for Needy Families (TANF), 7
Tennessee, 78, 93
Tennessee House GOP, 67–68
Texas, 63, 66, 72, 83, 88
    First Baptist Church in Sutherland Springs, 89
    gun ownership, 83, 89, 92
    mass shootings, 89
    permitless law, 88
    Robb Elementary School, 89
Texas A&M University, 83
Texas House Republican impeachment, 61–62
Texas Senate Committee, 62
Texas Tribune, 62
theologian, 153
Thomas, Cal, 224
Thomas, Clarence, 58
Thompson, Bennie, 165
Tillerson, Rex, 120
tithes, 20, 30
tithes and offering, 30–31
Trinity Broadcasting Network (TBN), ix

True the Vote, 65
Truman, Harry, 231–232
Trump, Donald
 abuse of legal system, 156–57, 165, 213
 bankruptcies, 166, 170, 223
 business practices, 216, 227–28
 COVID-19, 118
 dictatorship and monarchy aspirations, 181–82, 185, 187, 193
 disregards the court's rulings, 217, 227
 divisive, 121
 election of 2016 and, 122–23
 election of 2020 and, 156, 158
 evangelical' false claims of salvation, 115, 223–25
 facts about the 2020 election, 158–59
 false claims about academic records, 166–68
 false conspiracies about elections, 155–56
 forgiveness of sins, 223
 fraudulent efforts to overturn 2020 election results, 162–63
 GOP lawmakers' views, 123
 hush money, 201
 impeachments, 118, 123, 125
 incorrect association with Cyrus, 179–80, 231–32, 237
 incorrect association with David, 144
 lawsuit threats against alma mater, 167–68
 legal battles, 165–66, 168
 MAGA movement, 180, 194, 199, 202, 214
 Mueller investigation, 118
 never achieved popular votes, 122
 never reached an approval rate of 50 percent, 121
 popular vote loss, 122, 155
 post-election lawsuits, 156
 pro-choice, 38–39, 185
 quid pro quo, 117, 193
 reasons for support, 185, 219–20
 refusal to ask God for forgiveness, 115, 223–25
 Russia, 116
 SAT, 166–67
 sexual assaults, 59
 threat to democracy, 125, 157, 181, 187
 ties with evangelical Christians, 154
 ties with hate groups, 229
 unchristian behavioral patterns, 223–31
 Ukraine scandal, 117–18
 zero tolerance immigration policy, 109
Trump, Mary, 178
Trump, Maryanne, 122, 168
Trump Organization, 168–69, 202, 216
Trump University, 124, 216
Trumpism, 70, 214
Turing, Alan, 34

Ukraine, 117–18
unbiblical, x, 62, 94, 97, 116, 126, 149, 211, 234
underprivileged, 20
unemployment, 17
unholy alliance, x, 13
University of Pennsylvania, 166–67
University of Texas Medical Branch, 85
USB drives, 211
US Customs and Border Protection, 111
US government, 70, 75–76, 90, 164, 187, 190
US Justice Department, 180
US-Mexico border, 109–10, 119
Utah, 213
Uvalde, Texas, 89

Vietnam, 169
voter data and ballot-counting equipment, 207
Voting System Testing Laboratories, 159

Walsh, Joe, 63
Washington, DC, 200, 211

Washington Post, 226
Watergate scandal, ix
Weisselberg, Allen, 168, 202
welfare programs
  corporate, 10–11
Wharton Business School, 166–67
White House, 119–20, 163, 178–79, 85, 189, 202, 204, 212–13
White House staffers, 117, 213
White supremacists, 41, 70, 230
WikiLeaks, 203
Wilder, Lawrence Douglas, 56
William, Pauley, 201

Willis, Fani, 203, 207–8
Wisconsin, 161, 177, 191
Wolf, Chad, 106
Women, Infants, and Children (WIC), 7
Wyoming, 56, 76, 161

xenophobia, 102

YouTube, 87

Zelensky, Volodymyr, 117
zero-tolerance, 109–10, 119, 184

www.ingramcontent.com/pod-product-compliance
Lightning Source LLC
Chambersburg PA
CBHW050841230426
43667CB00012B/2094